First World War
and Army of Occupation
War Diary
France, Belgium and Germany

52 DIVISION
Headquarters, Branches and Services
Adjutant and Quarter-Master General
1 April 1918 - 31 May 1919

WO95/2890/1

The Naval & Military Press Ltd
www.nmarchive.com
Published in association with The National Archives

Published by

The Naval & Military Press Ltd

Unit 10 Ridgewood Industrial Park,

Uckfield, East Sussex,

TN22 5QE England

Tel: +44 (0) 1825 749494

www.naval-military-press.com

www.nmarchive.com

This diary has been reprinted in facsimile from the original. Any imperfections are inevitably reproduced and the quality may fall short of modern type and cartographic standards.

© **Crown Copyright**
Images reproduced by permission of The National Archives, London, England, 2015.

Contents

Document type	Place/Title	Date From	Date To
Heading	WO95/2890/1 Adjutant & Quartermaster General		
Heading	52nd Division 'A' & 'Q' Branch Apr 1918-May 1919		
Heading	Division Came From Egypt: Disembarked Marseilles 17.4.18		
War Diary	Jaffa	01/04/1918	01/04/1918
War Diary	Surafend	02/04/1918	02/04/1918
War Diary	Kantara	03/04/1918	11/04/1918
War Diary	At Sea	12/04/1918	17/04/1918
War Diary	Marseilles	17/04/1918	20/04/1918
War Diary	Rue	21/04/1918	27/04/1918
War Diary	Aire	28/04/1918	30/04/1918
Miscellaneous	52nd Division Administrative Instructions No.13	31/03/1918	31/03/1918
Miscellaneous	52nd Division Administrative Instructions No.14	31/03/1918	31/03/1918
Miscellaneous	52nd Division Administrative Instructions No.15	01/04/1918	01/04/1918
Miscellaneous	52nd Division Administrative Instructions No.13 A	01/04/1918	01/04/1918
Miscellaneous	52nd Division Administrative Instructions No.16		
Miscellaneous	52nd Division Administrative Instructions No.17		
Miscellaneous	52nd Division Administrative Instructions No. K.1.	05/04/1918	05/04/1918
Miscellaneous	52nd (Lowland) Division Administrative Instructions No.K.2	03/04/1918	03/04/1918
Miscellaneous	52nd (Lowland) Division Administrative Instructions No.K.3	04/04/1918	04/04/1918
Miscellaneous	52nd (Lowland) Division Administrative Instructions No.K.4	04/04/1918	04/04/1918
Miscellaneous	52nd (Lowland) Division Administrative Instructions No.K.5	05/04/1918	05/04/1918
Miscellaneous	52nd (Lowland) Division Administrative Instructions No.K.6	06/04/1918	06/04/1918
Miscellaneous	52nd (Lowland) Division Administrative Instructions No.K.7	07/04/1918	07/04/1918
Miscellaneous	Inspector, Palestine L. Of C	01/04/1918	01/04/1918
Miscellaneous	Inspector, Palestine L. Of C	02/04/1918	02/04/1918
Miscellaneous	Inspector, Palestine L. Of C	04/04/1918	04/04/1918
Miscellaneous	Inspector, Palestine L. Of C	05/04/1918	05/04/1918
Miscellaneous	Embarkation State Of 52nd Division	11/04/1918	11/04/1918
Miscellaneous	52nd (Lowland) Division Administrative Instruction No. AF.1	24/04/1918	24/04/1918
Miscellaneous	Time Table		
Miscellaneous	52nd (Lowland) Division Administrative Instruction No. AF.2	26/04/1918	26/04/1918
Miscellaneous	Time Table		
War Diary	Aire	01/05/1918	06/05/1918
War Diary	ACQ	07/05/1918	31/05/1918
Miscellaneous	52nd (Lowland) Division Administrative Instruction No.AF.3	04/05/1918	04/05/1918
Miscellaneous	Time Table For Entrainment		
Miscellaneous	52nd (Lowland) Division Administrative Instruction No.1	07/05/1918	07/05/1918
Miscellaneous	52nd (Lowland) Division Administrative Instruction No.AF.4.	08/05/1918	08/05/1918

Miscellaneous	A Branch 52nd (Lowland) Division	10/05/1918	10/05/1918
Miscellaneous	Appendix		
Miscellaneous	Appendix IV A Branch 52 Divisions	11/05/1918	11/05/1918
Miscellaneous	C.R.A. 155th Bde. Appendix V	11/05/1918	11/05/1918
Miscellaneous	52nd (Lowland) Division Administrative Circular Memorandum No.2	12/05/1918	12/05/1918
Miscellaneous	52nd (Lowland) Division Administrative Instruction No.AF 5	13/05/1918	13/05/1918
Miscellaneous	52nd (Lowland) Division Administrative Instruction No.AF 6	15/05/1918	15/05/1918
Miscellaneous	52nd (Lowland) Division Administrative Instruction No.7	16/05/1918	16/05/1918
Miscellaneous	52nd (Lowland) Division Administrative Circular Memorandum No.5	17/05/1918	17/05/1918
Miscellaneous	52nd (Lowland) Division Administrative Circular Memorandum No.4	18/05/1918	18/05/1918
Miscellaneous	Dripping	20/05/1918	20/05/1918
Miscellaneous	52nd (Lowland) Division Administrative Instruction No.AF.8	22/05/1918	22/05/1918
Miscellaneous	52nd (Lowland) Division Administrative Circular Memorandum No.5	23/05/1918	23/05/1918
Miscellaneous	52nd (Lowland) Division Administrative Circular Memorandum No.7	24/05/1918	24/05/1918
Miscellaneous	Appendix List Of Water Points In 52nd Divisional Area And Responsibility For Picqueting Them.		
Miscellaneous	A Returns	24/05/1918	24/05/1918
Miscellaneous	List of Returns To Be Rendered To "A" March 52nd (Lowland) Division		
Miscellaneous	52nd (Lowland) Division Administrative Instructions No.AF.9	25/05/1918	25/05/1918
Miscellaneous	Appendix "A" 52nd (Lowland) Division		
Miscellaneous	52nd (Lowland) Division Administrative Circular Memorandum No.8	27/05/1918	27/05/1918
Heading	War Diary A Branch 52nd (Lowland) Division Volume XXXVI 1-30th June 1918		
War Diary	Acq	01/06/1918	30/06/1918
Miscellaneous	Appointments		
Miscellaneous	Strength Of Division		
Miscellaneous	52nd (Lowland) Division	29/06/1918	29/06/1918
Miscellaneous	Details Of Officers "Taken On" Or "Struck Off" Strength		
Miscellaneous	52nd (Lowland) Division-Infantry Brigades Abstract Of Strength Return-Column 'B' Week Ending 29/6/18	29/06/1918	29/06/1918
Miscellaneous	52nd (Lowland) Division Administrative Instructions No.AF.11	01/06/1918	01/06/1918
Miscellaneous	52nd (Lowland) Division "A" Summary No.1	01/06/1918	01/06/1918
Miscellaneous	A Form Messages And Signals.		
Miscellaneous	52nd (Lowland) Division Addendum To Administrative Instruction No.A.F.10	06/06/1918	06/06/1918
Miscellaneous	52nd (Lowland) Division Administrative Circular Memorandum No.9	05/06/1918	05/06/1918
Miscellaneous	52nd (Lowland) Division "A" Summary No.2	08/06/1918	08/06/1918
Miscellaneous	52nd (Lowland) Division Administrative Circular Memorandum No.9	09/06/1918	09/06/1918
Miscellaneous	52nd (Lowland) Division Administrative Instruction No.AF.12.	09/06/1918	09/06/1918

Miscellaneous	52nd (Lowland) Division Administrative Instruction No.AF.13.	10/06/1918	10/06/1918
Miscellaneous	52nd (Lowland) Division Administrative Circular Memorandum No.13	12/06/1918	12/06/1918
Miscellaneous	Establishment Of 52nd Divisional Pack Transport Corps		
Miscellaneous	52nd (Lowland) Division Administrative Circular Memorandum No.14	13/06/1918	13/06/1918
Miscellaneous	52nd (Lowland) Division Administrative Circular Memorandum No.15	13/06/1918	13/06/1918
Miscellaneous	R.A. 155th Inf. Bde. 17th North'd Fus. App XII	15/06/1918	15/06/1918
Miscellaneous	Ordinary Leave Allotment-Schedule "A"		
Miscellaneous	52nd (Lowland) Division Administrative Circular Memorandum No.16	15/06/1918	15/06/1918
Miscellaneous	R.A. 155th Bde. D.A.D.V.S. Camp Commdt. App XIV	17/06/1918	17/06/1918
Miscellaneous	Ordinary Leave Allotment-Schedule "A"		
Miscellaneous	52nd (Lowland) Division Administrative Instructions No.14	17/06/1918	17/06/1918
Miscellaneous	52nd (Lowland) Division Administrative Circular Memorandum No.17	17/06/1918	17/06/1918
Miscellaneous	52nd (Lowland) Division Administrative Circular Memorandum No.18	17/06/1918	17/06/1918
Miscellaneous	52nd (Lowland) Division Administrative Circular Memorandum No.10	20/06/1918	20/06/1918
Miscellaneous	52nd (Lowland) Division Administrative Circular Memorandum No.19	20/06/1918	20/06/1918
Miscellaneous	52nd (Lowland) Division "A" Summary No.3	20/06/1918	20/06/1918
Miscellaneous	52nd (Lowland) Division Administrative Circular Memorandum No.20	22/06/1918	22/06/1918
Miscellaneous	52nd (Lowland) Division Administrative Circular Memorandum No.21	23/06/1918	23/06/1918
Miscellaneous	52nd (Lowland) Division Administrative Instruction No.15	24/06/1918	24/06/1918
Miscellaneous	52nd (Lowland) Division Administrative Circular Memorandum No.21.	26/06/1918	26/06/1918
Miscellaneous	Orders To Be Hung Up In Every Cookhouse		
Miscellaneous	52nd (Lowland) Division Administrative Instruction No.16	26/06/1918	26/06/1918
Miscellaneous	52nd (Lowland) Division Corrigendium to Administrative Instruction No.16	27/06/1918	27/06/1918
Miscellaneous	52nd (Lowland) Division Administrative Instruction No.17	27/06/1918	27/06/1918
War Diary	Acq	01/07/1918	22/07/1918
Heading	HQ A & Q 52d Vol 4 July 1918		
Miscellaneous	On His Majesty's Service.		
Heading	War Diary "A" Branch 52nd (Lowland) Division 1st To 31st July 1918 Volume XXXVII		
War Diary	Acq	23/07/1918	23/07/1918
War Diary	Pernes	23/07/1918	31/07/1918
Miscellaneous	Strength Of Division	27/07/1918	27/07/1918
Miscellaneous	52nd (Lowland) Division	27/07/1918	27/07/1918
Miscellaneous	Details Of Officers "Taken On" Or "Struck Off" Strength		
Miscellaneous	52nd (Lowland) Division-Infantry Brigade Abstract Of Strength-Column 'B'	27/07/1918	27/07/1918
Miscellaneous	Daily Location Report No.20	30/06/1918	30/06/1918

Miscellaneous	52nd (Lowland) Division Administrative Instruction No.AF.18	03/07/1918	03/07/1918
Miscellaneous	52nd (Lowland) Division Administrative Instruction No.AF.19	05/07/1918	05/07/1918
Miscellaneous	52nd (Lowland) Division Administrative Circular Memorandum No.22	06/07/1918	06/07/1918
Miscellaneous	52nd (Lowland) Division Administrative Instruction No.A.F.20	13/07/1918	13/07/1918
Miscellaneous	52nd (Lowland) Division Administrative Instruction No.A.F.21.	14/07/1918	14/07/1918
Miscellaneous	52nd (Lowland) Division Administrative Instruction No.A.F.22.	19/07/1918	19/07/1918
Miscellaneous	52nd (Lowland) Division Administrative Instruction No.A.F.22	19/07/1918	19/07/1918
Miscellaneous	52nd (Lowland) Division Administrative Instructions No.A.F.23	20/07/1918	20/07/1918
Miscellaneous	52nd (Lowland) Division Administrative Instructions No.A.F.24	20/07/1918	20/07/1918
Miscellaneous	52nd (Lowland) Division Administrative Instructions No.A.F.25	20/07/1918	20/07/1918
Miscellaneous	A Form Messages And Signals.		
Miscellaneous	52nd (Lowland) Division Administrative Instruction No.A.F.26	21/07/1918	21/07/1918
Miscellaneous	52nd (Lowland) Division Administrative Instruction No.A.F.27	22/07/1918	22/07/1918
Miscellaneous	52nd (Lowland) Division Administrative Instruction No.A.F.28	29/07/1918	29/07/1918
Miscellaneous	52nd (Lowland) Division Administrative Instruction No.A.F.29	30/07/1918	30/07/1918
Miscellaneous	52nd (Lowland) Division Administrative Instruction No.A.F.30	30/07/1918	30/07/1918
Heading	52nd (Lowland) Division War Diary For August Volume XXXIX		
War Diary	Pernes	01/08/1918	01/08/1918
War Diary	Maroeuil	02/08/1918	16/08/1918
War Diary	Villers Chatel	17/08/1918	22/08/1918
War Diary	Bretencourt	23/08/1918	23/08/1918
War Diary	Blaireville	24/08/1918	31/08/1918
Miscellaneous	52nd (Lowland) Division "A" And "Q"	31/08/1918	31/08/1918
Miscellaneous	52nd (Lowland) Division Administrative Instruction No.AF.31	10/08/1918	10/08/1918
Miscellaneous	Table "A"		
Miscellaneous	Table "B"		
Miscellaneous	52nd (Lowland) Division Administrative Circular Memorandum No.23	11/08/1918	11/08/1918
Miscellaneous	52nd (Lowland) Division Administrative Circular Memorandum No.24	13/08/1918	13/08/1918
Miscellaneous	52nd (Lowland) Division Administrative Instruction No.AF.32	15/08/1918	15/08/1918
Miscellaneous	Location List		
Miscellaneous	52nd (Lowland) Division Administrative Circular Memorandum No.25	15/08/1918	15/08/1918
Miscellaneous	52nd (Lowland) Division Administrative Instruction No.AF.33	17/08/1918	17/08/1918
Miscellaneous	52nd (Lowland) Division Amendment To Administrative Instruction No.AF.33	18/08/1918	18/08/1918

Miscellaneous	52nd (Lowland) Division Administrative Circular Memorandum No.26	19/08/1918	19/08/1918
Miscellaneous	Divisional Dumps		
Miscellaneous	52nd (Lowland) Division Administrative Arrangements In Connection With Current Operations No.AF.34	22/08/1918	22/08/1918
Miscellaneous	Administrative Arrangements		
Miscellaneous	Water Supply Location		
Miscellaneous	52nd (Lowland) Division Addendum To Administrative Instruction No.AF.35	31/08/1918	31/08/1918
Heading	52nd (Lowland) Division "A" & "Q" Branch War Diary From 1st September 1918 To 30th September 1918 Volume XI		
War Diary	St Leger	01/09/1918	13/09/1918
War Diary	Queant	14/09/1918	30/09/1918
Miscellaneous	Strength Of Division		
Miscellaneous	52nd (Lowland) Division Abstract Column "B"	28/09/1918	28/09/1918
Miscellaneous	52nd (Lowland) Division Strength Return	28/09/1918	28/09/1918
Miscellaneous	52nd (Lowland) Division Administrative Instruction No.A.F.37	04/09/1918	04/09/1918
Miscellaneous	52nd (Lowland) Division Administrative Instruction No.A.F.38	06/09/1918	06/09/1918
Miscellaneous	52nd (Lowland) Division Administrative Instruction No.A.F.39	13/09/1918	13/09/1918
Miscellaneous	A Form Messages And Signals.		
Miscellaneous	52nd (Lowland) Division Administrative Instruction No.A.F.40	14/09/1918	14/09/1918
Miscellaneous	52nd (Lowland) Division Location List		
Miscellaneous	52nd (Lowland) Division Addendum To Administrative Instructions No.AF.41	25/09/1918	25/09/1918
Miscellaneous	52nd (Lowland) Division Appendix "A" To Administrative Instruction No.AF.41	26/09/1918	26/09/1918
Miscellaneous	52nd (Lowland) Division Administrative Instructions No.AF.41	24/09/1918	24/09/1918
Heading	52nd (Lowland) Division "A" And "Q" Branch War Diary For October 1918 Volume XLI		
War Diary	Graincourt	01/10/1918	06/10/1918
War Diary	Vaulx-Vraucourt	06/10/1918	06/10/1918
War Diary	Lecauroy	07/10/1918	20/10/1918
War Diary	Heninlietard	21/10/1918	21/10/1918
War Diary	Ch. Maison Blanche (Q20.c)	22/10/1918	23/10/1918
War Diary	Flines	24/10/1918	28/10/1918
War Diary	Sameon	29/10/1918	31/10/1918
Miscellaneous	52nd (Lowland) Division Administrative Instructions No.AF.42	01/10/1918	01/10/1918
Miscellaneous	52nd (Lowland) Division Administrative Instructions No.AF.43	03/10/1918	03/10/1918
Miscellaneous	52nd (Lowland) Division Administrative Instructions No.AF.44	06/10/1918	06/10/1918
Miscellaneous	52nd (Lowland) Division Administrative Instructions No.AF.45	06/10/1918	06/10/1918
Miscellaneous	Entraining Table		
Miscellaneous	B Entraining Station-Fremicourt		
Miscellaneous	Transport And Mounted Personnel March Table		
Miscellaneous	52nd (Lowland) Division Administrative Instructions No.AF 46	18/10/1918	18/10/1918

Type	Description	Date From	Date To
Miscellaneous	52nd (Lowland) Division Administrative Instructions No.AF 47	19/10/1918	19/10/1918
Miscellaneous	Location List For Night October 20/21st		
Miscellaneous	52nd (Lowland) Division Administrative Instructions No.A.F 48	20/10/1918	20/10/1918
Miscellaneous	52nd (Lowland) Division Administrative Instructions No.A.F 50	27/10/1918	27/10/1918
Miscellaneous	52nd (Lowland) Division Strength Return	26/10/1918	26/10/1918
Miscellaneous	52nd (Lowland) Division Abstract Column "B"	26/10/1918	26/10/1918
Miscellaneous	Strength Of Division	26/10/1918	26/10/1918
Heading	52nd (Lowland) Division "A" And "Q" War Diary November 1918 Vol XLII		
War Diary	Sameon	01/11/1918	08/11/1918
War Diary	Mont De Peruwelz	09/11/1918	09/11/1918
War Diary	Sirault	10/11/1918	17/11/1918
War Diary	Chateau De La Bruyere Nimy	18/11/1918	30/11/1918
Miscellaneous	Strength Of Division	29/12/1918	29/12/1918
Miscellaneous	52nd (Lowland) Division Strength Return	30/11/1918	30/11/1918
Miscellaneous	52nd (Lowland) Division Abstract Column "B"	30/11/1918	30/11/1918
Miscellaneous	Headquarters 52nd (Lowland) Division "A" & "Q" Summary No.1	02/11/1918	02/11/1918
Miscellaneous	52nd (Lowland) Division Administrative Circular Memorandum No.35	02/11/1918	02/11/1918
Miscellaneous	Routine Orders By Major General F.J. Marshall CMG. DSO. Commanding 52nd (Lowland)	02/11/1918	02/11/1918
Miscellaneous	Headquarters 52nd (Lowland) Division "A" & "Q" Summary No.2	04/11/1918	04/11/1918
Map	Provisional Traffic Circuits		
Miscellaneous	Headquarters 52nd (Lowland) Division "A" & "Q" Summary No.3	05/11/1918	05/11/1918
Miscellaneous	Headquarters 52nd (Lowland) Division "A" & "Q" Summary No.4	07/11/1918	07/11/1918
Miscellaneous	Headquarters 52nd (Lowland) Division "A" & "Q" Summary No.5	13/11/1918	13/11/1918
Miscellaneous	52nd (Lowland) Division Administrative Instructions No.A.F.51	14/11/1918	14/11/1918
Miscellaneous	Camp Comdt. 155th Brigade. D.A.D.V.S. 17th Northd Fus. Appendix X	15/11/1918	15/11/1918
Miscellaneous	Headquarters 52nd (Lowland) Division "A" & "Q" Summary No.6	16/11/1918	16/11/1918
Miscellaneous	Headquarters 52nd (Lowland) Division "A" & "Q" Summary No.7	17/11/1918	17/11/1918
Miscellaneous	Headquarters 52nd (Lowland) Division "A" & "Q" Summary No.8	20/11/1918	20/11/1918
Miscellaneous	Headquarters 52nd (Lowland) Division "A" & "Q" Summary No.9	23/11/1918	23/11/1918
Miscellaneous	Headquarters 52nd (Lowland) Division "A" & "Q" Summary No.10	25/11/1918	25/11/1918
Miscellaneous	Headquarters 52nd (Lowland) Division "A" & "Q" Summary No.11	26/11/1918	26/11/1918
Miscellaneous	Headquarters 52nd (Lowland) Division "A" & "Q" Summary No.12	27/11/1918	27/11/1918
Miscellaneous	Headquarters 52nd (Lowland) Division "A" & "Q" Summary No.13	29/11/1918	29/11/1918
Heading	52nd (Lowland) Division "A" & "Q" Branch For December 1918 Volume XLIII		

War Diary	Chateau De La Bruyere Nimy	01/12/1918	15/12/1918
War Diary	Nimy	16/12/1918	31/12/1918
Miscellaneous	Strength Of Division	28/12/1918	28/12/1918
Miscellaneous	52nd (Lowland) Division Strength Return	28/12/1918	28/12/1918
Miscellaneous	52nd (Lowland) Division Abstract Column "B"	28/12/1918	28/12/1918
Miscellaneous	Headquarters 52nd (Lowland) Division "A" & "Q" Summary No.14	02/12/1918	02/12/1918
Miscellaneous	Headquarters 52nd (Lowland) Division "A" & "Q" Summary No.15	03/12/1918	03/12/1918
Miscellaneous	Headquarters 52nd (Lowland) Division "A" & "Q" Summary No.16	07/12/1918	07/12/1918
Miscellaneous	52nd (Lowland) Division Administrative Instructions No.A.F.52	08/12/1918	08/12/1918
Miscellaneous	Appendix "A". Details of personnel for staff of Corps Concentration Camp to be found by units of 52nd Division.		
Miscellaneous	Duty Order Initials And Name		
Miscellaneous	Duties Of A Conducting Officer		
Miscellaneous	Headquarters 52nd (Lowland) Division "A" & "Q" Summary No.17	09/12/1918	09/12/1918
Miscellaneous	Headquarters 52nd (Lowland) Division "A" & "Q" Summary No.18	13/12/1918	13/12/1918
Miscellaneous	Headquarters 52nd (Lowland) Division "A" & "Q" Summary No.19	16/12/1918	16/12/1918
Miscellaneous	Headquarters 52nd (Lowland) Division "A" & "Q" Summary No.20	18/12/1918	18/12/1918
Miscellaneous	Headquarters 52nd (Lowland) Division "A" & "Q" Summary No.21	22/12/1918	22/12/1918
Miscellaneous	Headquarters 52nd (Lowland) Division "A" & "Q" Summary No.22	26/12/1918	26/12/1918
Miscellaneous	Headquarters 52nd (Lowland) Division "A" & "Q" Summary No.23	30/12/1918	30/12/1918
Heading	52nd (Lowland) Division "A" & "Q" Branch For January 1919 Volume XLIV		
War Diary	Nimy	01/01/1919	31/01/1919
Miscellaneous	Strength Of Division	31/01/1919	31/01/1919
Miscellaneous	Strength Return	01/02/1919	01/02/1919
Miscellaneous	Changes In Nominal Rolls Of Officers		
Miscellaneous	52nd (Lowland) Division Abstract Column "B"	01/02/1919	01/02/1919
Miscellaneous	Headquarters 52nd (Lowland) Division "A" & "Q" Summary No.24	03/01/1918	03/01/1918
Miscellaneous	Headquarters 52nd (Lowland) Division "A" & "Q" Summary No.25	08/01/1919	08/01/1919
Miscellaneous	Headquarters 52nd (Lowland) Division "A" & "Q" Summary No.26	09/01/1919	09/01/1919
Miscellaneous	52nd (Lowland) Division Administrative Circular Memorandum No.39	13/01/1919	13/01/1919
Miscellaneous	Headquarters 52nd (Lowland) Division "A" & "Q" Summary No.27	13/01/1919	13/01/1919
Miscellaneous	Headquarters 52nd (Lowland) Division Administrative Circular Memorandum No.40	15/01/1919	15/01/1919
Miscellaneous	Headquarters 52nd (Lowland) Division "A" & "Q" Summary No.28	15/01/1919	15/01/1919
Miscellaneous	Headquarters 52nd (Lowland) Division "A" & "Q" Summary No.29	18/01/1919	18/01/1919
Miscellaneous	Leave Trains		

Type	Description	Date From	Date To
Miscellaneous	52nd (Lowland) Division Numbers On Parade At Divisional Ceremonial Parade	18/01/1919	18/01/1919
Miscellaneous	Headquarters 52nd (Lowland) Division "A" & "Q" Summary No.30	24/01/1919	24/01/1919
Miscellaneous	Headquarters, XXIInd Corps "A"	23/01/1919	23/01/1919
Miscellaneous	Headquarters, XXIInd Corps "A" Demobilisation	17/01/1919	17/01/1919
War Diary	Nimy	01/02/1919	28/02/1919
Miscellaneous	52nd (Lowland)		
Miscellaneous	Strength Of Division	01/03/1919	01/03/1919
Miscellaneous	Headquarters 52nd (Lowland) Division "A" & "Q" Summary No.31	02/02/1919	02/02/1919
Miscellaneous	Headquarters 52nd (Lowland) Division "A" & "Q" Summary No.32	07/02/1919	07/02/1919
Miscellaneous	Headquarters 52nd (Lowland) Division "A" & "Q" Summary No.33	10/02/1919	10/02/1919
Miscellaneous	52nd (Lowland) Division Administrative Circular Memorandum No.41	03/02/1919	03/02/1919
Miscellaneous	Notice		
Heading	War Diary March 1919 Vol 12		
War Diary	Nimy	01/03/1919	24/03/1919
War Diary	Soignies	25/03/1919	31/03/1919
Miscellaneous	Strength Return	29/03/1919	29/03/1919
Miscellaneous	Changes In Nominal Rolls Of Officers		
Miscellaneous	Strength Of Division	28/03/1919	28/03/1919
Heading	52nd (Lowland) Division "A" And "Q" Branch May 1919		
War Diary	Soignies	01/05/1919	31/05/1919
Miscellaneous	Strength Of Division	31/05/1919	31/05/1919
Miscellaneous	52nd (Lowland) Division Cadres Strength Return	31/05/1919	31/05/1919
Miscellaneous	Changes In Nominal Roll Of Officers	31/05/1919	31/05/1919

WO 95/2890/11

Adjutant & Quartermaster General

52ND DIVISION

'A' & 'Q' BRANCH

APR 1918-MAY 1919

Division came from EGYPT:Disembarked MARSEILLES 17.4.18

A. & Q.

52nd DIVISION

APRIL 1918.

WAR DIARY or INTELLIGENCE SUMMARY

Army Form C. 2118.

Vol. XXXIV April 1st-30th 1918

A Branch 52nd (Lowland) Divn.

Place	Date	Hour	Summary of Events and Information	Remarks and references to Appendices
JAFFA	1.		Move of Division to SURAFEND proceeding on lines laid down in administration Instructions issued on March 30/31st. A/A.I.A. Alarm Inst. 11,12,13,14,15,16 & 17. 7th Indian Divn. took over command of Coastal Sector. Gen Order No 101 issued. Events as move to France. Signal Coy. handed Electric light equipment to 7th (Ind.) Divison. Advanced DHQ. moved to Kantara.	WIIA
SURAFEND	2.			
KANTARA	3.		380? and DEGING embarked on H.M.S. "MANITOU" for Marseilles to arrange for disembarkation of Division. 4/2 Coy RE also on board. Together with HQ RA — 56th FA Bde +DAC, 1 Section H.M.T. "Kingstonian" which was loaded at some time took on board the 4/13 Coy RE, 9th FA Bde 133/134 TM Bty & 1st Line SAC. The whole Artillery were taken from → Egypt to The Survequil battling, an exchange having affected (by order DHQ) with the 7th (Indian) Division who retained in the Coastal Sector, the Artillery previously with this Divn.	

Army Form C. 2118.

Page 2

WAR DIARY
or
INTELLIGENCE SUMMARY.
(Erase heading not required.)

Vol. XXXIV
April 1918.
A Branch 52(Lowl)Divn

Instructions regarding War Diaries and Intelligence Summaries are contained in F. S. Regs., Part II. and the Staff Manual respectively. Title pages will be prepared in manuscript.

Place	Date	Hour	Summary of Events and Information	Remarks and references to Appendices
KANTARA	4 4/8		H.M.T? Kingstonian & Manitou sailed for Alexandria. The men of the Division from SURAFEND to ALEXANDRIA via LUDD & KANTARA proceeded as laid down in administrative Instruction K157 attached to this Diary as Appendix I.5 VII & A.C. instruction MK VIII. All animals and transport were left at LUDD except for the Artillery which took all its guns & the RE (Signals) Coy which took their technical vehicles (1 Air Signal Coy + 1 R.E. Coy see App. VIII.)	App. VII MK VIII
	10/		All troops on board convoys as shown in app. I XI. Convoy sailed 157 Thy/Rgt, 217 Coy/RSC, 219 do, Divnl Employment Coy, Divnl Cyclist Coy.	App IX
	11/		This day M.T.T. Kingstonian was torpedoed. She was somewhere to the east of Sardinia. Casualties 2 killed 4 wounded. All equipment on board was lost to units. It may be noted	

Army Form C. 2118
page 3

WAR DIARY
or
INTELLIGENCE SUMMARY
(Erase heading not required.)

Vol XXIV
April 1918
A Branch 52nd (Low.) Divn.

Place	Date	Hour	Summary of Events and Information	Remarks and references to Appendices
AT SEA.	12.		52nd Divn Arty + 2 Coys RE arrived MARSAILLES - Remainder Divn at Sea	
	13.		HQ Ra, 56 Bde RA A.C. entrained for ABBEVILLE district - Remainder Divn at Sea	
	14.		9 Bde Ra & 413 Coy RE — do —	
	17.		Ra & 413 Coy RE arrived NOYELLE & were billeted in SAILLY-LE-SEC. Ra & 413 Coy RE in SAILLY BRAY district. Refitment commenced at once area. 413 Coy RE	
MARSEILLES	18/20		Remainder Divn arrived MARSEILLES. Divn moving by train to ABBEVILLE area	
	21		DHQ opened at RUE. Divn became part of Reserve Army. Refitting commenced	
RUE	22		Divn concentrated in RUE area extending to district round ST VALERIE - Requipping	
	23		Warning order received from Reserve Army Jn. on Bde to move to First Army on 25th inst. and remainder of Divn on 28th	
	24		Admin Instruct A.F.I. nature of 1st Bde Appx I	MM Appx I

1875 Wt. W593/826 1,000,000 4/15 J.B.C. & A. A.D.S.S./Forms/C. 2118.

Army Form C. 2118.

WAR DIARY
or
INTELLIGENCE SUMMARY.

VI XXXIV

April 1918   A Blanch 52 (Lowland) Division

Place	Date	Hour	Summary of Events and Information	Remarks and references to Appendices
RUE	24		Warning orders received for Artillery Brigades to be ready to strong arm	
	25		4.R.S.F. + H.Q.R.A. proceeded to Scarlet Three (4 cours) at notice	
	26		Orders received to move to reinforcement Division (i.e. the 1st Div ready to move) to First Army area, to commence 28 & following days.	
			Rue + Nouvelle, estaires, AIRE & Berguette. Strategic trains 15/15	aff IX
			+ H.Q.R.A. to rendez Norcon obtain instruction A.2 on 14th	aff X
27			Advance D.H.Q. opened Rue St. Omer - AIRE	
			Div Artillery marched from South Thiennes & Auxi le Chateau	
			D.H.Q. closed AIRE.	
AIRE	28			
			Orders received for H.Q.R.A. to move by rail to AIRE district	
	30		Orders issued to J.Hewst Brit. Regt (P) and 410th & 412th Bde Orde to move to THIENNES for dropping with these on the line under 5-Division.	
			Division continued refitting & training —	
			Div Artillery moved by First Army to remain in CRECQUY	
			Weather has been cold and now showing of Dun to snow	

Army Form C. 2118.

A Branch
52 (Lowland) Division
April 1/30th 1918

WAR DIARY
or
INTELLIGENCE SUMMARY.
(Erase heading not required.)

Infantry Brigades.

Available Fighting Strength a/s 27/4/18

	Officers	OR
155 Bde	131	3422
156 L/Bde	158	3336
157 "	160	3769
5th R.I. Rif.	29	833
52nd M.G. Bn	43	748
TOTAL	521	12108

SECRET.   Copy No _____

52nd Division Administrative Instructions No.13.

31st March, 1918.

1. The 156th Infantry Brigade, less 412th Field Company, R.E., will be prepared to commence entrainment at LUDD Railway Station by 0800 on the morning of April 3rd.
   Train timings will be communicated immediately received in this office.

2. 48 hours rations will be drawn on April 2nd for consumption on April 3rd and 4th, preserved meat being drawn in lieu of fresh meat.

3. On April 1st 156th Brigade Group will transport all baggage and equipment and stores, which cannot be carried when vehicles have been withdrawn, to LUDD Railway Station.
   D.A.Q.M.G., 52nd Division will point out sites for stacking these stores, etc.
   <u>They will be stacked by units and under a guard.</u>

4. Subsequent to removing baggage, etc. all equipment special to the E.E.F., as detailed in list issued by D.A.D.O.S., will be returned to A.O.D. Depot LUDD; this will include one blanket per man and bivouac sheets.
   Subsequent to returning these articles and on the same day, all units of the Group will draw one waterproof sheet per man and one Box Respirator from A.O.D. Depot LUDD.

5. On April 2nd all vehicles will be returned to a temporary A.O.D. Receiving Depot established in SURAFEND Camp, with the exception of technical vehicles.
   Subsequent to return of vehicles, harness will be handed in to the same Depot.
   Animals will finally be led with head rope, head collar and nose bag to Field Remount Section, LUDD, and handed over.

6. A.S.C. vehicles, harness and animals will not be dealt with as in para. 5, but will be returned to Advanced Horse Transport Depot LUDD with all Egyptian Native Drivers.
   Ambulance Wagons, however, will be returned to A.O.D. Receiving Depot SURAFEND.

7. Fanatis will all be handed over to O.C. "D" Company, C.T.C., who will arrange to return them to A.O.D. LUDD after the troops have left.

8. Transport to move cooking utensils and any officers kits to LUDD Station on day of entrainment may be obtained from O.C. "D" Company, C.T.C. - only a minimum number of camels will be provided.

9. Loading parties will be detailed for each troop train from the troops entraining previous to arrival at the Station.
   These loading parties will not be changed until embarkation is completed.
   They should be of such a size as to warrant the most rapid handling of baggage, etc. possible.
   Trains will be cleared of troops and baggage within 30 minutes of arrival at Station of detrainment.

P.T.O.

10. A representative of the Brigade Staff will travel in the first train carrying troops of the Group and report to D.A.A.G. 52nd Division at the Railway Station on arrival at KANTARA for orders.

D.A.A.G. will arrange with Headquarters, KANTARA Sub-Section for transport from KANTARA EAST to KANTARA WEST.

11. Base kits will be collected from Base Depot at KANTARA and proceed with Units from KANTARA WEST.

D.A.A.G. will telegraph weights of these kits by units to DAGLOCK, CAIRO, so that accommodation may be provided on train from KANTARA WEST.

Separate orders have been issued concerning base kits of Machine Gun Companies.

12. The Brigade Group will probably entrain from KANTARA WEST during night, April 4th/5th.

If train timings have not been issued for the journey from KANTARA WEST before the Group entrains at LUDD they will be obtained from D.A.A.G. 52nd Division at KANTARA.

13. A representative of the Brigade Staff will proceed to ALEXANDRIA on April 4th and report to E.S.O. to ascertain arrangements for embarkation and inform troops on arrival.

List and description of returns to be rendered will be forwarded later.

ACKNOWLEDGE.

Issued at 1500

W A Thornton
Lieut.Colonel.
A.A. & Q.M.G. 52nd (Lowland) Division.

Copy No.		
1	A.D.C. for G.O.C.	
2	"G".	
3	155th Infantry Brigade.	
4	156th Infantry Brigade.	
5	157th Infantry Brigade.	
6	C.R.A.	
7	C.R.E.	
8	O.C. Signal Coy.	
9	Divisional Train.	
10	D.A.D.O.S.	
11	A.D.M.S.	
12	A.D.V.S.	
13	A.P.M.	
14	Acting/Town Major, SAROHA.	
15 & 16	XXIst Corps.	
17	File.	
18 & 19	Diary.	
20	S.S.O.	
21	W.S.O.	
22	O.C., D. Company C.T.C.	

A Diary April 1918
Ap I a.

SECRET.   Copy No. 17

52nd Division Administrative Instructions No.14.

31st March, 1918.

Move of 157th Infantry Brigade to SARONA and thence to LUDD District.

1. **CAMP.** The 157th Infantry Brigade will occupy a bivouac area in SARONA on night 2nd/3rd April and the site will be pointed out by the Acting Town Major.
    On the evening of the 3rd April the Brigade will march and occupy the camp area indicated on the map issued with this office No.A.5960 dated 27/3/18 on arrival at SURAFEND Camp.

2. **TENTS.** Tents will be taken over from the Brigade of the 7th Indian Division relieving 157th Infantry Brigade.
    These tents will be taken over on the Camping Ground at SURAFEND at 1800 on the 2nd April.

3. **TRANSPORT.** (a) 219th Company A.S.C., 52nd Divisional Train, will provide transport for the move of the 157th Infantry Brigade.
    Both units Baggage and Supply wagons will be made available for the transport of the Brigade baggage.
    Train wagons will report for loading at 0800 on the 3rd April to units.
    The Train will march under the orders of O.C. Divisional Train behind the Brigade - the remaining portion of the 52nd Divisional Train will also accompany this party.
    G.O.C. 157th Infantry Brigade will arrange to transport as much heavy baggage to SARONA as possible before leaving the line, also the unhorsed vehicles.
    (b) The allotment of camels and loads will be as laid down in this office Q.3421/15 dated 13/3/18.
    (c) All fanatis surplus to those that can be carried will be handed over to O.C. "D" Company, C.T.C.; by 1000 on the 3rd April.
    O.C. "D" Company, C.T.C. will arrange to transport these to SURAFEND.
    (d) C.R.A. will provide 16 teams of 4 and 9 pairs of wheelers to draw the unhorsed vehicles of Battalions.
    These will report to Headquarters 157th Infantry Brigade on the afternoon of the 3rd April at SARONA at an hour to be arranged between G.O.C. 157th Infantry Brigade and C.R.A.
    On the 4th April the teams will be returned to their units, but before returning it should be ascertained whether the 7th Indian Division require their assistance to draw to SARONA the 4 Cookers and Water Carts of the British Battalion in the relieving Brigade.
    O.C. Units to which these teams are attached will arrange for the rations of both men and animals for consumption on the day after arrival at SURAFEND.
    Cookers and Water Carts will proceed empty.
    (e) One blanket and Bivouac Sheet will be carried on the man.

4. **SUPPLIES.** Supplies for consumption on the 3rd April will be drawn on the morning of that day from SARONA Dump in the usual manner.
    Supplies for consumption on 4th April will be drawn from Supply Dump at SURAFEND Camp.

P.T.O.

(2)

5. **WATER.** Water both for animals and men drinking at SULAFEND will be obtained from the water area of the camp. A time table has been completed and will be communicated to the Brigade on arrival by the Divisional Water Officer.

6. **DETAIL.** G.O.C. 157th Infantry Brigade will arrange to attach Acting/Town Major SAROMA and his staff to a unit during the move. The A/Town Major will relinquish his appointment at 1800 on 3rd April.

ACKNOWLEDGE.

[signature]

Lieut. Colonel.
A.A. & Q.M.G. 52nd (Lowland) Division.

Issued at 1800.

Copy No.
```
         1   A.D.C. for G.O.C.
         2   "G"
         3   155th Infantry Brigade.
         4   156th Infantry Brigade.
         5   157th Infantry Brigade.
         6   C.R.A.
         7   C.R.E.
         8   O.C. Signal Coy.
         9   O.C. Divisional Train.
        10   D.A.D.C.S.
        11   A.D.M.S.
        12   A.D.V.S.
        13   A.P.M.
        14   A/Town Major, SAROMA.
   15 &  16   XXIst Corps.
        17   File.
   18 &  19   Diary.
        20   S.S.O.
        21   W.S.O.
        22   D. Coy. C.T.C.
        23   7th Division.
```

A Diary April 1918

app 1 A.

SECRET.
Copy No. 19

52nd Division Administrative Instructions No. 15.

1st April, 1918.

Move of 52nd Divisional Headquarters and Divisional Signal Company to SURAFEND.

1. **MOVE.** Headquarters 52nd Division and Signal Company attached, Headquarters Royal Engineers and Headquarters Divisional Train will proceed to SURAFEND by day on 2nd instant.

2. **CAMP.** On the evening of the 2nd instant the Headquarters and Signal Company will occupy the camp area as indicated on the map issued with this office No.A.5960 dated 27/3/18, a copy of which is attached for the information of O.C. Signal Company.

3. **BILLETS.** All billets at present occupied will be handed over to Jewish Committee, the usual certificates being obtained and transmitted to these Headquarters.

4. **TENTS.** All tents which are surplus to the requirements already arranged for, will be handed to Town Major SAROHA by 1200 on 2nd instant.
   Tents will be available at SURAFEND as laid down in this office No.Q.3683 dated 19/3/18 for Mobile Scale and arranged by Camp Commandant.

5. **TRANSPORT.** (a) All first and second line wheeled transport will be available for this move, with the addition of 5 Motor Lorries for Divisional Headquarters, and camels as allotted in this office No.Q.3421/15 dated 13/3/18.
   (b) All fanatis surplus to those which can be carried to be handed to O.C. "D" Company, C.T.C. by 1200 on 2nd instant. O.C. "D" Company, C.T.C. will arrange to carry these under orders already issued.
   (c) One blanket and bivouac sheet will be carried on the man, or on transport with second blanket if accommodation available.
   (d) Train wagons will report for loading at 0600 on 2nd instant and will march with first line transport to SURAFEND, thereafter being returned to Train Headquarters at SURAFEND.
   The Motor Lorries will report to Camp Commandant at 0900 on 2nd instant.
   Transport to move officers kits to LUDD Station on day of entrainment may be obtained from O.C. "D" Company, C.T.C. - only a minimum number of camels will be provided.

6. **HANDING OVER.** The Electric Lighting Set at present on charge to Signal Company will be handed over to 7th Indian Division complete with transport and personnel, further instructions will be issued later.

7. **STORES & TECHNICAL VEHICLES.** On April 3rd, all baggage, equipment and stores, which cannot be carried when vehicles have been withdrawn, will be transported to LUDD Railway Station, where they will be stacked by formations under a guard.
   Subsequent to removing baggage etc. all equipment special to the E.E.F., as detailed in list issued by D.A.D.O.S., will be returned to A.O.D. LUDD; this will include one blanket per man and bivouac sheets.

P.T.O.

(2)

7. **STORES & TECHNICAL VEHICLES** contd. Subsequent to returning these articles and on the same day will be drawn one waterproof sheet and Box Respirator per man from A.O.D. Depot LUDD.

8. **ANIMALS, HARNESS & VEHICLES.** On April 4th all vehicles and harness, less technical vehicles, will be returned to a temporary A.O.D. Receiving Depot established in SURAFEND Camp. Animals will then be led with head rope, head collar and nose bag to Field Remounts LUDD and handed over, with the exception of those of the A.S.C. whose animals, harness and vehicles will be returned to Advanced Horse Transport Depot LUDD.

9. **M.T. VEHICLES.** All motor vehicles will be returned to Advanced Mechanical Transport Depot LUDD, on day of entrainment.

10. **BASE KITS.** Base kits will be collected from Base Depots at KANTARA and proceed with formations from KANTARA WEST.

11. **WATER.** Water both for animals and men drinking at SURAFEND will be obtained from the water area of the camp. A time table has been completed and may be obtained after arrival on application to Divisional Water Officer.

12. **SUPPLIES.** Supplies for consumption on the 2nd instant will be carried on the man, those for consumption on 3rd instant will be drawn at SURAFEND on the morning of that day.

13. **NOTE.** Attention is directed to Administrative Instructions No.11 dated 30th March, 1918.

ACKNOWLEDGE.

[signature]

Lieut.Colonel.
A.A. & Q.M.G. 52nd (Lowland) Division.

Issued at 1500.

Copies to
Copies No
Copy No.
1 A.D.C. for G.O.C.
2 "G"
3 155th Infantry Brigade.
4 156th Infantry Brigade.
5 157th Infantry Brigade.
6 G.R.A.
7 C.R.E.
8 O.C. Signal Company.
9 O.C. Divisional Train.
10 D.A.D.O.S.
11 A.D.M.S.
12 A.D.V.S.
13 A.P.M.
14 A/Town Major SARONA.
15/16 XXIst Corps.
17 File.
18/19 Diary.
20 S.S.O.
21 W.S.O.
22 O.C. D. Company, C.T.C.
23 7th Division.
24 Camp Commandant.
25 Billeting Officer.

A Diary April 1918

App I. A.

SECRET.   Copy No. _____

52nd Division Administrative Instructions No. 13 A.

1st April, 1918.

1. 155th Brigade Group, less 413th Field Company, R.E., but including 211th Machine Gun Company, Divisional Sanitary and Mobile Veterinary Sections, will be prepared to commence entrainment by 0700 on April 4th.
   Train timings will be communicated immediately received in this office.

2. 48 hours rations will be drawn on April 3rd for consumption on April 4th and 5th.

3. On April 2nd, 155th Brigade Group will transport all baggage and equipment and stores, which cannot be carried when vehicles have been withdrawn, to LUDD Railway Station.
   A site for stacking these stores has already been pointed out by D.A.Q.M.G.
   They will be stacked by units and under a guard.

4. Subsequent to removing baggage, etc. all equipment special to the E.E.F. as detailed in list issued by D.A.D.O.S., and also all tents in use at SURAFEND Camp, will be returned to A.O.D. Depot LUDD; this will include one blanket per man and bivouac sheets.
   Subsequent to returning these articles and on the same day all units of the group will draw one waterproof sheet per man and one Box Respirator from A.O.D. Depot LUDD.

5. On April 3rd all vehicles will be returned to a temporary A.O.D. Receiving Depot, established in SURAFEND Camp.
   Subsequent to the return of vehicles harness will be handed in to the same Depot.
   Animals will finally be led with head rope, head collar and nose bag to Field Remount Section LUDD and handed over.

6. A.S.C. vehicles, harness and animals will not be dealt with as in para 5, but will be returned to Advanced Horse Transport Depot LUDD with all Egyptian Native Drivers.
   Ambulance wagons and harness will be returned to A.O.D. SURAFEND Camp and animals to Remount Depot. The Egyptian Native Drivers only returning to the Advanced Horse Transport Depot.

7. Fanatis will be handed over to O.C. "D" Company, C.T.C. who will arrange to return them to A.O.D. LUDD after the troops have left.

8. Transport to move cooking utensils and any officers kits to LUDD Station on day of entrainment may be obtained from O.C. "D" Company, C.T.C. - only the minimum number of camels will be provided.

9. Loading parties will be detailed for each troop train from the troops entraining previous to arrival at the Station.
   These loading parties will be under two officers and will not be changed until embarkation is completed. They should be of such a size as to warrant the most rapid handling of baggage, etc. possible.
   Trains will be cleared of troops and baggage within 30 minutes of arrival at Station of detrainment.

P.T.O.

(2)

10. A representative of the Brigade Staff will travel in the first train carrying troops of the Group and report to D.A.A.G. 52nd Division at the railway Station on arrival at KANTARA for orders.
    D.A.A.G. will arrange with Headquarters KANTARA Sub-Section for transport from KANTARA EAST to KANTARA WEST.

11. Base kits will be collected from Base Depot at KANTARA and proceed with Units from KANTARA WEST.
    D.A.A.G. 52nd Division will telegraph weights of these kits by units to DAGLOCK CAIRO, so that accommodation may be provided on train from KANTARA WEST.
    Separate orders have been issued concerning Base Kits of Machine Gun Companies.

12. The Brigade Group will probably entrain from KANTARA WEST during the night April 5th/6th.
    If train timings have not been issued for the journey from KANTARA WEST before the Group entrains at LUDD, they will be obtained from D.A.A.G. 52nd Division at KANTARA.

13. A representative of the Brigade Staff will proceed to ALEXANDRIA on April 4th and report to E.S.O. to ascertain arrangements for embarkation and inform troops on arrival.
    Instructions concerning returns to be rendered on embarkation will be forwarded later. It should be clearly understood that O.C. Ship is responsible for the compilation and rendering of these returns to the E.S.O.

14. G.O.C. 155th Infantry Brigade will ensure the transmission of these orders to O.C. Sanitary Section, O.C. Mobile Veterinary Section and O.C. 211th Machine Gun Company, and also subsequent orders regarding train timings.

ACKNOWLEDGE.

H A Thornton

Lieut Colonel.

Issued at 1230.   A.A. & Q.M.G. 52nd (Lowland) Division.

Copy No.			
1	A.D.C. for G.O.C.	13	A.P.M.
2	"G"	14	Acting Town Major SARONA
3	155th Infantry Brigade.	15/16	XXIst Corps
4	156th Infantry Brigade.	17	File.
5	157th Infantry Brigade.	18/19	Diary.
6	C.R.A.	20	S.S.O.
7	C.R.E.	21	W.S.O.
8	O.C. Signal Coy.	22	O.C. D Company, C.T.C.
9	Divisional Train.	23	C.O.O. LUDD.
10	D.A.D.M.S.	24	Communications, RAMLEH.
11	A.D.M.S.	25	D.Q.M.G. G.H.Q.
12	A.D.V.S.	26	O.C. 211th M.G. Coy.

SECRET.   Copy No. ....

52nd Division Administrative Instructions No. 13.

1. 157th Brigade Group, with the addition of Divisional Headquarters, H.Q. R.E., H.Q. Divisional Train, 217th Company A.S.C., Divisional Signal Company, will be prepared to commence entrainment by 0700 on April, 6th.
    Train times will be communicated immediately received in this Office.

2. 48 hours rations will be drawn on April 5th for consumption on April 6th and 7th; preserved meat being drawn in lieu of fresh meat.

3. On April 4th, 157th Brigade Group will transport all baggage and equipment and stores which cannot be carried when vehicles have been withdrawn to LUDD Railway Station. A site for stacking these stores has already been pointed out by D.A.Q.M.G.
    They will be stacked by Units and under a guard.

4. Subsequent to removing baggage, etc., all equipment special to the E.E.F., as detailed in list issued by D.A.D.O.S. (This special equipment will include latrine equipment, bivouac sheets and one blanket per man) will be returned to LUDD depot. Subsequent to returning these articles and on the same day all Units of the Group will draw one waterproof sheet per man and one box respirator from A.O.D. LUDD.
    All tents in use at SURAFEND Camp will also be returned to LUDD Depot.

5. On April 3rd all vehicles will be returned to a temporary A.O.D. Receiving Depot established in SURAFEND Camp subsequent to the return of vehicles, harness will be handed into the same depot.
    Animals will finally be led with head rope, head collar and nose bag to Field Remount Section, LUDD and handed over.
    It should be clearly understood that the A.O.D. Receiving Depot at LUDD can only accept vehicles, harness and bivouac sheets - all other stores will be returned to A.O.D. Depot LUDD.
    S.A.A. of surplus Lewis Gun Magazines will be returned to Ammunition Depot, LUDD.

6. A.S.C. vehicles, harness and animals of H.Q., Divnl. Train, 217th and 219th Coys. A.S.C. will not be dealt with as in para. 5, but will be returned to Advanced Horse Transport Depot, LUDD, with all Egyptian Native Drivers.
    Ambulance wagons and harness will be returned to A.O.D. SURAFEND Camp, and animals to Remount Depot.
    The Egyptian Native Drivers only return to the Advanced Horse Transport Depot.

7. Funatis will be handed over to O.C., D Company C.T.C. who will arrange to return them to A.O.D., LUDD, after the troops have left.

8. Transport to move cooking utensils and any officers kits to LUDD Station on day of entrainment may be obtained from O.C., D Company C.T.C., only the minimum number of camels will be provided.

                                                                  P/T/O.

9. Loading parties will be detailed for each troop train from the troops entraining previous to arrival at the station.
   The loading parties will be under two officers and will not be changed until embarkation is completed. They should be of such a size as to warrant the most rapid handling of baggage, etc., possible.
   Trains will be cleared of troops and baggage within 30 minutes of arrival at Station of detrainment.

10. A representative of the Brigade Staff will travel in the first train carrying troops of the Group and report to D.A.A.G. 52nd Division at the Railway Station on arrival at KANTARA for orders.
    D.A.A.G. will arrange with Headquarters, KANTARA SUB-SECTION for transport from KANTARA EAST to KANTARA WEST.

11. Base kits will be collected from Base Depot, KANTARA and proceed with Units from KANTARA WEST. D.A.A.G. 52nd Division will telegraph weights of these kits by Units to DAGLOCK, CAIRO, so that accommodation may be provided on train from KANTARA WEST.
    Separate orders have been issued concerning Base kits of Machine Gun Companies.

12. The Brigade Group will probably entrain from KANTARA WEST during the night 7th/8th.
    If train timings have not been issued before the journey from KANTARA WEST before the Group entrain at LUDD they will be obtained from D.A.A.G. 52nd Division at KANTARA.

13. A representative of the Brigade Staff will proceed to ALEXANDRIA on April 7th and report E.S.O. to ascertain arrangements for embarkation and inform troops on arrival.
    Instructions concerning returns to be rendered on embarkation have been issued. It should be clearly understood that O.C. Ship is responsible for the compilation and rendering of returns to E.S.O.

14. G.O.C., 157th Infantry Brigade GROUP will be responsible for the transmission of these orders and subsequent orders regarding train timings to all units of his group and attached troops with the exception of H.Q., R.E., H.Q., Divisional Train, Headquarters Division, Divisional Signal Coy. who will receive orders direct from this office.

ACKNOWLEDGE.

W A Shoulton

Lieut. Colonel.
A.A. & Q.M.G., 52nd (Lowland) Division.

Issued at 1530.

Copy No.				
1	A.D.C. to G.O.C.		16	Camp Commandant.
2	"G"		17	File.
3	155th Infantry Brigade.		18)	Diary
4	156th Infantry Brigade.		19)	
5	157th Infantry Brigade.		20	O.C., Cyclist Coy.
6	C.R.E.		21	O.C., 211th M.G. Coy
7	O.C. Signal Coy.		22	D.Q.M.G., G.H.Q.
8	O.C., Divisional Train.		23	Communication, RAMLEH
9	D.A.D.C.S.		24	O.C.O., LUDD.
10	A.D.M.S.			
11	A.D.V.S.			
12	A.P.M.			
13	S.S.O.			
14	W.S.O.			
15	D. Coy. O.T.C.			

A Diary April 1918
Add I.A.

SECRET.   Copy No. 7

52nd Division Administrative Instructions No. 17.

1. The 5th Battalion, The Royal Irish Regiment (Pioneer), 52nd Divisional Cyclist Coy. and the Divisional Troops Supply Details will be prepared to commence entrainment by 2200 on April 6th. The whole under the command of the Officer Commanding, The 5th Battalion, The Royal Irish Regiment (Pioneer) who will be responsible for the transmission of any subsequent orders.
    Train timings will be communicated immediately received in this office.

2. 48 hours rations will be drawn on April 6th for consumption on April 7th/8th, preserved meat will be drawn in lieu of fresh meat.

3. On April 4th all baggage and equipment not being returned to Ordnance, and for which transport will not be available on day of entrainment will be transported to LUDD Station and stacked by units under a guard. The site for this will be pointed out by a representative of the Divisional Staff.

4. Subsequent to removing baggage, etc., all equipment special to the E.E.F. (a list of which will be given as soon as the necessary information is received; this will include latrine equipment, tents, bivouac sheets and one blanket per man) will be returned to LUDD Ordnance Depot.
    Subsequent to the returning of these articles and on the same day units will draw one water-proof sheet and one box respirator per man from A.O.D., LUDD.

5. On April 6th all vehicles and harness will be returned to a temporary A.O.D. Receiving Depot established in SURAFEND Camp near Divisional Headquarters.
    Animals will then be led with head-rope, head-collar and nose-bag to Field Remount Section, LUDD, and handed over.
    All Egyptian Native Drivers will be returned to the Advanced Horse Transport Depot, LUDD.
    It should be clearly understood that the A.O.D. Receiving Depot, SURAFEND Camp will only accept vehicles, harness and bivouac sheets, all other stores will be returned to A.O.D. Depot, LUDD.
    All bulk or loose S.A.A. surplus to 120 rounds carried on the man will be returned to the Ammunition Dump, LUDD. Before returning surplus all Lewis Gun Magazines should be filled.

6. All fanatis will be handed to O.C., 'D' Coy. C.T.C. who will arrange to return them to A.O.D., LUDD, after the troops have left.

7. Transport to move cooking utensils and officers kits to LUDD Station on day of entrainment may be obtained from O.C., 'D' Coy. C.T.C.; only the minimum of camels will be provided.

8. Loading parties under an officer will be detailed by each Unit previous to arrival at Station, these will not be changed until embarkation is completed. They should be of such a size as to warrant the most rapid handling of baggage, etc., possible.
    Trains will be cleared of troops and baggage within 30 minutes of arrival at Station of detrainment.

P.T.O.

9.   A representative from the 5th Battalion, The Royal Irish Regiment, (Pioneers) will travel in the first train of the 157th Brigade Group at 0851 on the 6th instant, he will report on arrival at Kantara to D.A.A.G., 52nd Division at Railway Station.

    D.A.A.G. will arrange with Headquarters, KANTARA SUB-SECTION for transport from KANTARA EAST to KANTARA WEST.

10.   Base kits will be collected from Base Depot, KANTARA, by the advanced parties concerned and proceed with Unit from KANTARA WEST.   D.A.A.G., 52nd Division will telegraph weights of these kits by units to DAGLOOK, CAIRO, so that accommodation may be provided on train from KANTARA WEST.

11.   The Units will probably entrain from KANTARA WEST during night 7th/8th.

    If train timings have not been issued for the journey from KANTARA WEST before Units entrain at LUDD they will be obtained from D.A.A.G., 52nd Division at KANTARA.

12.   A representative of the 5th Battalion, The Royal Irish Regiment (Pioneers) will proceed to ALEXANDRIA on April 7th and report E.S.O. to ascertain arrangements for embarkation and inform Units on arrival.

    Instructions concerning returns required on embarkation have already been issued. It should be clearly understood that O.C. Ship is responsible for the compilation and rendering of returns to E.S.O.

ACKNOWLEDGE.

C.G.Maude
Lieut. Colonel.

Issued at 1800.   A.A. & Q.M.G., 52nd (Lowland) Division.

Copy No. 1   "G"
        2   157th Infantry Brigade.
        3   O.C., Train.
        4   D.A.D.O.S.
        5   A.P.M.
        6   S.S.O.
        7   W.S.O.
        8   O.C. "D" Coy C.T.C.
        9   O.C., 5th Royal Irish Regiment (Pioneer)
       10   O.C. 52nd Divnl. Cyclist Coy.
       11   C.O.O., LUDD.
       12   D.Q.M.G., G.H.Q.
       13   Communications, RAMLEH.
       14   D.A.A.G., 52nd Division.
       15   File.
       16)   Diary.
       17)

SECRET.   52nd (LOWLAND) DIVISION.   Copy No.....

April 1918
App I

ADMINISTRATIVE INSTRUCTIONS No. K.1.

1. The passage of 52nd Division through KANTARA will be carried out as follows :-
   156 Bde

2. On arrival, troops will at once detrain and march off to the Base Depot for which they have been detailed.
   A guide of one officer and one N.C.O. from No.1 Base Depot will meet each party at KANTARA EAST Station. The officer will guide the main body and the N.C.O. the baggage party (see para.4).

3. The baggage party already detailed will unload the baggage and stack it at a place which will be pointed out by an officer representing the Division who will meet each train.

4. A guard will be left in charge of baggage of each unit, remainder of the baggage party will proceed to Base Depot camp and rejoin their unit guided by the N.C.O. mentioned in para.2.

5. Baggage will be moved from KANTARA EAST to KANTARA WEST commencing at 0830.
   A loading party of 2 officers, 4 N.C.O.s and 100 men will be provided by No.1 Base Depot at KANTARA EAST and a discharging party of a similar number at KANTARA WEST, where baggage will be handed over to the Advanced Baggage Party. The guard left with the baggage at KANTARA EAST will accompany it to KANTARA WEST. The Base kits will be moved to KANTARA WEST on previous evening.
   All these kits will be stacked in special Dumps according to trains at KANTARA WEST Station and will be under the charge of the Advanced Baggage Parties.

6. Units will leave their Base Depots for KANTARA WEST at the following hours

1st train.	4th Royal Scots.	1800.	5th train.	156th B.H.Q.	
2nd train.	7th Royal Scots.	2000.		156 M.G. Coy.	
3rd train.	7th Scottish Rifles	2145.		156 L.T.M.Bty.	
4th train.	8th Scottish Rifles			1/1st L. F. A.	0100.
		23/1		220th Coy. A.S.C.	
				156th Supp. Sect.	

7. Officers in charge units will report arrival at KANTARA WEST to the officer in command of their train.

8. The Base Depots have arranged to provide tea for troops, details will be advised on arrival there. Units will hand to Quartermaster, Base Depots, the tea, milk and sugar required.

9. Advanced Baggage Parties will rejoin units at KANTARA WEST Station.

10. O.C. trains will make their own arrangements for the loading of the baggage on to the train.

5/4/18.
D.A.A.G. 52nd (Lowland) Division.
Captain.

Copies No. 1. 4th Royal Scots.   8. 1/1st L. F. A.
          2. 7th Royal Scots.   9. 220th Coy. A.S.C.
          3. 7th Scottish Rifles.   10. 156th Brigade Supply Section.
          4. 8th Scottish Rifles.   11. No.1 Infantry Base Depot.
          5. 156th Brigade H.Q.   12. No.2 Infantry Base Depot.
          6. 156th M.G. Company.   13. R.A.M.C. Depot.
          7. 156th L.T.M. Battery.   14. B.H.T. Depot.
                                     15. File.

NOTE. Whilst at KANTARA each unit will send a representative to Ordnance Depot, KANTARA.

SECRET.   April 1918   app II   Copy No.....

52nd (LOWLAND) DIVISION.

ADMINISTRATIVE INSTRUCTIONS NO. K.2.

1. The baggage of 156th Infantry Brigade will be moved to KANTARA WEST under following arrangements :-

2. The following Base kits will be taken with units. -
   (a) Kits of all officers known to be proceeding with unit.
       Kits of officers who are in hospital or are, for any reason, not with unit will be kept at Base Depot.
       Any officers joining at last minute will draw their own kits.
   (b) Kits of all Other Ranks except those known as NOT proceeding.

3. Lorries will report at Base Depots at 1730 to-day as follows to move Base kits.
   - No.1 Base Depot............6.7
   - R.A.M.C. Base Depot........1.
   - B. H. T. D..................1.

4. These lorries will be loaded by the Advanced Baggage Parties who will accompany the baggage to KANTARA WEST Station and unload it there. They will remain for the night as Baggage Guard.

5. An officer representing the Division will be waiting the arrival of these lorries at KANTARA WEST and will point out the sites for the various dumps.

6. The baggage accompanying units will be transported from KANTARA EAST to KANTARA WEST by Motor Lorries during 4th instant.
   This baggage will be loaded and discharged by party of 2 officers, 4 N.C.O.s and 100 men provided by No.1 Base Depot.
   O.C. Advanced Party will take charge of this baggage at KANTARA WEST and will do all in his power to assist in the quick discharge of Lorries.

7. Advanced Baggage Parties will draw rations from the Base Depot for 4th instant.

8. On arrival of Main Body at KANTARA WEST Advanced Baggage Parties will report to O.C. Units and rejoin.

3/4/18.

D.A.A.G. 52nd (Lowland) Division.
Captain.

Copy No. 1. 156th Infantry Brigade.
     2. O.C. Advanced Baggage Party. 156 Bde.
     3. No.1 Base Depot.
     4. 220th Company A.S.C.
     5. 1/1st L. F. A.
     6. R.A.M.C. Depot.
     7. B.H.T. Depot.
     8. File.

S.E.C.R.E.T. *April 1918 a'Diary apx IV* Copy No...

52nd (LOWLAND) DIVISION.

ADMINISTRATIVE INSTRUCTIONS No. K.5.

1. The baggage of the 155th Infantry Brigade will be moved to KANTARA WEST under following arrangements :-

2. The undernoted Base Kits will be taken with units -

   (a) Kits of all officers known to be proceeding with unit.
   Kits of officers who are in hospital or are, for any reason, not with unit will be kept at Base Depot.
   Any officers joining at last minute will draw their own kits.

   (b) Kits of all O.R. except those known as NOT proceeding.

3. Lorries will report at Base Depots at 1730 to-day as follows to move Base Kits :-

   No. 1 Base Depot............ 7.
   R.A.M.C. Base Depot........ 1.

4. These lorries will be loaded by the Advanced Baggage Parties who will accompany the baggage to KANTARA WEST Station and unload it there.
   They will remain for the night as Baggage Guard.

5. An officer representing the Division will be waiting the arrival of these lorries at KANTARA WEST and will point out the sites for the various dumps.

6. The baggage accompanying units will be transported from KANTARA EAST to KANTARA WEST by motor lorries during 5th instant.
   This baggage will be loaded and discharged by party of 2 officers 4 N.C.O.s and 100 men provided by No.1 Base Depot.
   O.C. Advanced Party will take charge of this baggage at KANTARA WEST and will do all in his power to assist in the quick discharge of Lorries

7. Advanced Baggage Parties will draw rations from the Base Depot for 5th instant.

8. On arrival of Main body at KANTARA WEST Advanced Baggage Parties will report to O.C. Units and rejoin.

Captain.

4/4/18.   D.A.A.G. 52nd (Lowland) Division.

Copy No.1 155th Infantry Brigade.
     2 O.C. Advanced Baggage Party 155th Brigade.
     3 No.1 Base Depot.
     4 R.A.M.C. Depot.
     5 File.
     6. *17/OLF A*
     7. *52nd San Oct*
     8. *Not Yet Sent*

S E C R E T.   *April 1918 A Diary Ap IV*   Copy No... 12

52nd (LOWLAND) DIVISION.

ADMINISTRATIVE INSTRUCTIONS No. K.4.

1. The passage of the 155th Brigade through KANTARA will be carried out as follows :- *arrival Kantara East*

2. On arrival, troops will at once detrain and march off to the Base Depot for which they have been detailed.
   A guide of one officer, and one N.C.O. from No.1 Base Depot will meet each party at KANTARA EAST Station. The officer will guide the main body and the N.C.O. the baggage party (see para.4).

3. *Baggage* The baggage party already detailed will unload the baggage and stack it at a place which will be pointed out by an officer representing the Division who will meet each train.

4. A guard will be left in charge of baggage of each unit, remainder of the baggage party will proceed to Base Depot camp and rejoin their unit guided by the N.C.O. mentioned in para.2.

5. Baggage will be moved from KANTARA EAST to KANTARA WEST commencing at 0530.
   A loading party of 2 officers, 4 N.C.O.s and 100 men will be provided at KANTARA EAST and a discharging party of a similar number at KANTARA WEST by No.1 Base Depot. Baggage will be handed over to the Advanced Baggage Party at KANTARA WEST. The guard left with the baggage at KANTARA EAST will accompany it to KANTARA WEST. The Base Kits will be moved to KANTARA WEST on previous evening.
   All these Kits will be stacked in special dumps according to trains at KANTARA WEST Station and will be under the charge of the Advanced Baggage Parties. *departure K.W.*

6. Units will leave their Base Depots for KANTARA WEST at the following hours on 5th inst.

   1st train. 5th R.S.F.   1800.   5th train. H.Q. 155th Inf. Bde. 2
   2nd train. 4th K.O.S.B. 2000.   155 L.T.M. Bty.   2
   3rd train. 4th R.S.F.   2145.   156 M.G. Company.   1
   4th train. 5th K.O.S.B. ~~2215~~   1/3rd L. F. A.
                            2315   218th Coy. A.S.C.   0100
                                                   155th Bde. Supply Sec.   6th
                                                   211th M. G. Company.   2
                                                   Mob. Vet. Sect.
                                                   Sanitary Section.

7. Officers in charge units will report arrival at KANTARA WEST to the officer in command of their train.

8. *Base Depot* The Base Depots have arranged to provide tea for troops, details will be advised on arrival there. Units will hand to Quartermaster, Base Depots, the tea, milk and sugar required.

9. Advanced Baggage Parties will rejoin units at KANTARA WEST Station.

10. Officers commanding trains will make their own arrangements for the loading of the baggage *& vehicles* on to the train.

11. A nominal roll of officers proceeding with unit will be handed to O.C. No.1 Base Depot.

12. Whilst at KANTARA each unit will send a representative to Ordnance Depot, KANTARA.

                                                              Captain.
4/4/18.   D.A.A.G. 52nd (Lowland) Division.

Copy No. 1   5th R. S. F.
        2   4th K. O. S. B.
        3   4th R. S. F.
        4   5th K. O. S. B.
        5   155th Brigade Headquarters.
        6   155th L.T.M. Battery.
        7   155th M. G. Company.
        8   1/3rd L. F. A.
        9   218th Company, A.S.C.
        10   155th Brigade Supply Section.
        11   211th M.G. Company.
        12   Mobile Veterinary Section.
        13   Sanitary Section.
        14   No.1 Infantry Base Depot.
        15   No.2 Infantry Base Depot.
        16   R.A.M.C. Records.
        17   B.M.I. Depot.
        18   File.

April 1918. *A. Diary* *att ?*

B.E.F.R.I.   Copy No....

52nd (LOWLAND) DIVISION.

ADMINISTRATIVE INSTRUCTIONS No. H.Q.

1. The baggage of the 157th Infantry Brigade will be moved to KANTARA WEST under the following arrangements :-

2. The undernoted Base kits will be taken with units :-

   (a) Kits of all officers known to be proceeding with unit.
       Kits of officers who are in hospital or are, for any reason, not with unit will be kept at Base Depot.
       Any officers joining at last minute will draw their own kits.

   (b) Kits of all O.R. except those known as NOT proceeding.

3. (i) The Base kits of the following units will be moved from No.1 Base Depot to KANTARA WEST at 1830 on 6th instant.

   157th Inf. Brigade H.Q.
   5th H.L.I.
   6th H.L.I.
   7th H.L.I.
   5th A. & S.H.

   (ii) The Base kits of the following Divisional units will be moved at the same time. -

   Divisional Headquarters.
   H.Q. R.E.
   Divl. Signal Company.
   HQ Divnl Train

   (iii) The Base kits of the following units will NOT be moved on 6th inst. - they will probably be moved on 7th instant.

   157th L.T.M. Battery.   *157th M.G. Coy.*
   410th Field Company, R.E.   *217th Coy ASC*
   1/2nd Low. Field Ambce.   *219th Coy ASC*

   Further instructions regarding the kits of these units will be issued later.

4. To enable the moves detailed in para.3 (a) and (b) to be carried out Motor lorries will report at Base Depot at 1830 on 6th inst. as follows :-

   No.1 Inf. Base Depot............ 8.
   R.A.M.C. Base Depot............. 1.
   General Base Depot.............. 1.

5. These lorries will be loaded by the Advanced Baggage Parties who will accompany the baggage to KANTARA WEST Station and unload it there. They will remain for the night as Baggage Guard.

6. An officer representing the Division will be awaiting the arrival of these lorries at KANTARA WEST and will point out the sites for the various dumps.

7. The baggage accompanying units will be transported from KANTARA EAST to KANTARA WEST by motor lorries during 7th instant.
   This baggage will be loaded and discharged by parties of 2 officers 4 N.C.O.s and 100 men provided by No.1 Base Depot.
   O.C. Advanced Party will take charge of this baggage at KANTARA WEST and will do all in his power to assist in the quick discharge of lorries.

8. Advanced Baggage Parties will draw rations from the Base Depot for 7th instant.

9. On arrival of main body at KANTARA WEST Advanced Baggage Parties will report to O.C. Units and rejoin.

                                                                    Captain.
6/4/18.   D.A.A.G. 52nd (Lowland) Division.

Copy No.1 187th Inf. Brigade.
     2 O.C. Advanced Baggage Party 187th Brigade.
     3 R.Q. R.E.
     4 Divl. Signal Coy.
     5 1/2nd L. F. A.
     6 430th Field Coy. R.E.
     7 No.1 Inf. Base Depot.
     8 No.2 Inf. Base Depot.
     9 R.A.M.C. Depot.
    10 D.B.D.
    11 File.

SECRET.   Copy No....

52nd (LOWLAND) DIVISION.

ADMINISTRATIVE INSTRUCTIONS No. K.6.

1. The passage of the 157th Brigade through KANTARA will be carried out as follows :-

ARRIVAL KANTARA EAST.

2. On arrival, troops will at once detrain and march off to the Base Depot for which they have been detailed.
A guide of 1 officer and 1 N.C.O. from No.1 Base Depot will meet each party at KANTARA EAST Station. The officer will guide the main body and the N.C.O. the baggage party. (see para.4)

BAGGAGE.

3. The baggage party already detailed will unload the baggage and stack it at a place which will be pointed out by an officer representing the Division who will meet each train.

4. A guard will be left in charge of baggage of each unit, remainder of the baggage party will proceed to Base Depot camp and rejoin their unit guided by the N.C.O. mentioned in para.2.

5. Baggage will be moved from KANTARA EAST to KANTARA WEST commencing at 0530, by motor lorries.
No.1 Base Depot will detail a loading party of 2 officers 4 N.C.O.s and 100 men at KANTARA EAST and a discharging party of a similar number at KANTARA WEST. The guard left with the baggage at KANTARA EAST will accompany it to KANTARA WEST where it will be handed over to the Advanced Baggage Party. The Base Kits will be moved to KANTARA WEST on previous evening.
All these kits will be stacked in special dumps according to trains at KANTARA WEST Station and will be under the charge of the Advanced Baggage Parties.

VEHICLES.

6. O.C. 410th Field Company Detachment will draw 6 Pontoon Wagons and 3 Trestle Wagons from Ordnance on the afternoon of the 6th inst.
It has been arranged with Station Transport Officer, KANTARA, to supply the necessary animals to draw these vehicles from Ordnance Depot to KANTARA WEST Military Station, where the vehicles will be parked at a site already pointed out and left there under a guard.

7. Station Transport Officer, KANTARA, will supply the animals necessary to draw the vehicles of Divisional Signal Company and the 410th Field Company R.E., from KANTARA EAST to KANTARA WEST. These animals will report at KANTARA EAST at 1300 on 7th instant.
On arrival at KANTARA WEST Station the vehicles will be parked along side the Pontoon Wagons.

BASE DEPOT.

8. The Base Depots have arranged to provide tea for the troops, details will be advised on arrival there. Units will hand to Quartermaster, Base Depots, the tea, milk and sugar required.

9. A nominal roll of officers proceeding with unit will be handed to O.C. No.1 Base Depot.

10. Whilst at KANTARA each Unit will send a representative to Ordnance Depot, KANTARA.

P.T.O.

DEPARTURE² KANTARA WEST.

11.   Units will leave their Base Depots for KANTARA WEST at following hours on 7th and 8th inst.

No. 1 Train.	5th H.L.I.	1800	7th
No. 2 Train.	7th H.L.I.	2000	"
No. 3 Train.	157th Bde. H.Q.		
	6th H.L.I.	2145	"
No. 4 Train.	5th A. & S.H.	2315	"
No. 5 Train.	Divl. Headquarters.		
	Divl. Signal Coy.		
	H.Q. R.E.		
	H.Q. Divl. Train.		
	A.P.M.	0100	8th
	D.A.D.O.S.		
	410th Field Coy. R.E. (party of 1 off. 30 O.R. in charge of vehicles).		
No. 6 Train.	5th R.I. Regt. (Pioneers).		
	410th Field Coy. R.E. (less party in charge of vehicles).	1800	8th.
No. 7 Train.	157th M.G. Company.		
	157th L.T.M. Battery.		
	1/2nd Low. Field Amboc.		
	217th Company A.S.C.	2000	8th
	219th Company A.S.C.		
	157th Brigade Supply Sect.		
	Divl. Cyclist Coy.		

12.   52nd Division Cyclist Company will arrive at KANTARA at 1735 on the 7th inst. and the 5th R.I. Regt. (Pioneers) at 1830 on same day.
       The Base kits of these units will be moved at 1000 on 8th inst. Further instructions regarding this will be issued later.

13.   Officers in charge of units will report arrival at KANTARA WEST to the officer in command of their train.

14.   Advanced Baggage Parties will rejoin units at KANTARA WEST Station.

15.   Officers commanding trains will make their own arrangements for the loading of the baggage and vehicles on to the train.

16.   Trains will depart from KANTARA WEST Military Station, best route being across South Bridge then to the left along the Canal Bank for about 200 yards, avoiding main KANTARA Station.

GENERAL.

17.   As far as the Reinforcements at his disposal make it possible O.C. No.1 Base Depot will reinforce units up to

Establishment

6/4/18.

P. Mulloch
Captain.
D.A.A.G. 52nd (Lowland) Division.

Copy No.1 5th H.L.I.	10. A.P.M.	19. 5th R.I. Regt.
2 6th H.L.I.	11 D.A.D.O.S.	20. No.1 Base Depot.
3 7th H.L.I.	12 157th M.G.Co.	21. No. 2 " "
4 5th A & S.H.	13 157th L.T.M.B.	22. R.A.M.C.
5 157th B.H.Q.	14 1/2nd L.F.A.	23 B.H.T.D.
6 C.C. D.H.Q.	15 217th Coy. A.S.C.	24 G. B. D.
7 Div. Sig. Co.	16 219th Coy. A.S.C.	25 410th Fd.Coy.
8 H.Q. R.E.	17 157th Supp. Sec.	26 " " "
9 Divl. Train.	18. Div. Cyclist Coy.	27 File.

April 1918   A. Diary app VII

SECRET.   Copy. No...

52nd (LOWLAND) DIVISION.

ADMINISTRATIVE INSTRUCTIONS NO. K.7.

1.   The arrangements to move the baggage of the following units to KANTARA WEST Station will be as under -

    410th Field Company, R.E.
    1/2nd Lowland Field Ambulance.
    52nd Division Cyclist Company.
    5th R.I. Regt. (Pioneers).

2.   The baggage left by the units on evening of 7th inst. at KANTARA EAST will be loaded on Motor Lorries commencing at 0530 on 8th inst. and taken to KANTARA WEST. The guard left in charge of the baggage will accompany it.

   This baggage will be loaded and discharged by parties of 2 officers, 4 N.C.O.s and 100 men provided by No.1 Base Depot.

3.   The undernoted Base Kits will be taken with units -

   (a) Kits of all officers known to be proceeding with units.
       Kits of officers who are in hospital or are, for any reason, not with unit will be kept at Base Depot.
       Any officers joining at last minute will draw their own kits.

   (b) Kits of all Other Ranks except those known as NOT proceeding.

4.   The Base Kits will be moved to KANTARA WEST commencing at 1000 on 8th instant and to enable this to be done lorries as under will report at the Base Depots at the above hours. -

    No.1 Base Depot.   1.
    No.2 Base Depot.   1.
    R.A.M.C. Depot.   1.
    G. B. Depot.   1.

   The above kits will be loaded by the Advanced Baggage Parties who will accompany the baggage to KANTARA WEST Station and unload it there.

   This baggage will be placed in the same dump as the baggage referred to in para.2 and the O.C. Advanced Baggage Party will take charge of his units baggage dump.

5.   On arrival of Main Body at KANTARA WEST Advanced Baggage Parties will report to O.C. Units and rejoin.

                                                sgd J. Mulloch
                                                          Captain.
7/4/18.   D.A.A.G. 52nd (Lowland) Division.

Copy No. 1   410th Field Company R.E.
        2   1/2nd Lowland Field Ambce.
        3   52nd Division Cyclist Coy.
        4   5th R.I. Regt. (Pioneers).
        5   No.1 Base Depot.
        6   No.2 Base Depot.
        7   R.A.M.C. Base Depot.
        8   G.B.D.
        9   File.

April 1918
a Diary
app VIII

SECRET.   CHQ.11692/2.

INSPECTOR, PALESTINE L. of C.
G.O.C., ALEXANDRIA DISTRICT.
----

1.   The embarkation of the 52nd Division will be continued at Alexandria on the morning of 5th April.

2.   The Units of the 156th Infantry Brigade Group arriving at Kantara East on the 4th instant will re-entrain at Kantara West on the night of April 4th/5th in the same order, i.e.-

			Off.	O.R.
1st Train	834/701	1/4th Royal Scots	22	759
2nd "	836A/703	1/7th Royal Scots	23	794
3rd "	840/707	1/7th Scottish Rifles	26	750
4th "	800/711	1/8th Scottish Rifles	26	770
5th "	804A/713A	156th Inf. Bde. H.Q.	5	95
		156th Bde. M.G.C.	10	214
		156th Lt. T.M.Batty.	3	74
		1/1st Lowland Fld. Amb.	7	230
		220th Coy. A.S.C.	2	45
		156th Bde. Supply Sec.	1	5

Train timings are as follow :-

No.	Ready to load Ar. 4th.	Depart. 4th	Arr. Gabbary Quays. April 5th.
834/701	1900	2050	0540
836A/703	2100	2230	0645
840/707	2245	2400	0845
800/711	0015 ..5th.	0150 ..5th.	1045
804A/713A	0205 .. "	0345 .. "	1310

Each Unit will be thus given upwards of twelve hours at Kantara; consequently the train timings must be closely adhered to.
Each of the trains will accommodate the Unit or Units mentioned, plus any reinforcements or details who may be ordered to join them at Kantara, up to Establishment (Personnel) Strength.

3.   Embarkation will take place immediately on arrival at Gabbary, but, in the unlikely event of sufficient ships not being berthed, it may be necessary to divert the last two trains to Sidi Bishr where their personnel would be encamped. Should this necessity arise, E.S.O. Alexandria will give the earliest possible intimation to H.Q., Alexandria District and this office, and will issue orders for the subsequent move from Sidi Bishr to the Quays for embarkation.

4.   E.S.O., Alexandria, will issue orders regarding allotments of troops to vessels, care being exercised to prevent, as far as possible, the splitting of Units, but the personnel of the Brigade Field Ambulance must be distributed among the ships carrying the Brigade Group.

5.   Rations will be issued on board from and including the Dinner meal on date of embarkation. Such additional rations as are necessary will therefore be issued at Kantara.

(Contd.)

6. Three copies of Special Embarkation Return and three copies of Nominal Roll of troops embarking will be required by the Embarkation Staff Officer. A supply of the former has been issued to H.Q., Kantara Area, for distribution to the Units as they pass through.

7. Eight copies of this order have been issued to H.Q., Kantara Area, for transmission to the D.A.A.G., 52nd Division, and to H.Q. and Units of the 156th Infantry Brigade Group on their arrival at Kantara.

[signature]
Lieut.-Colonel,
A.Q.M.G.,
for D.Q.M.G.

2nd Echelon, G.H.Q.
1st April, 1918.

Copies to :- A.M.S.; G.S.; G.S., I; D.A.G.; D.Q.M.G.(2); M.G.R.A.; D.A.S.; E.-in-C; D.M.S.; P.C.; D.A.G., 3rd Echelon; D.S.T.; D.R.T.; D.O.S.; D.O.S., Base; D.V.S.; D.R.; D.A.D.A.P.S.; P.M.T.O.; C.P.

H.Q., Force-in-Egypt.
H.Q., 52nd Division.

H.Q., Kantara Area.
A.D.R.T., Cairo.

D.A.D.R.T., Cairo.
D.A.D.R.T., Alexandria.
E.S.O., Alexandria.(2).
D.M.T.O., Alexandria.
R.T.O., Kantara.

	Off.	O.R.
1/7th Scottish Rifles	39	981
1/8th Scottish Rifles	38	972

[signed] Mainwaring
Lieut.-Colonel,
A.Q.M.G.,
for D.Q.M.G.

2nd Echelon, G.H.Q.,
2nd April, 1918.

Copies to :- A.M.S.; G.S.; D.A.G.; G.S.,I; D.Q.M.G.(2); M.G.R.A.; D.A.S.; E.-in-C; D.M.S.; P.C.; D.A.G.,3rd Echelon; D.S.T.; D.R.T.; D.O.S.; D.O.S.,Base; D.V.S.; D.R.; D.A.D.A.P.S.; P.N.T.O.; C.P.

H.Q., Force-in-Egypt.
H.Q., 52nd Division.
H.Q., Kantara Area.
A.D.R.T., Cairo.
D.N.T.O., Cairo.
R.T.O., Kantara.
D.A.D.R.T., Cairo.
D.A.D.R.T., Alexandria.
E.S.O., Alexandria.
D.N.T.O., Alexandria.

P.S. - Reference paras. 2 and 9 above.

The following further information as to strengths on leaving Kantara have been received :-

	Off.	O.R.
220th Coy. A.S.C.	3	65
156th Bde. Supply Sect.	1	9
218th Coy. A.S.C.	3	65
155th Bde. Supply Sect.	1	9

Similar details for the remainder of the Units will be published as soon as received.

SECRET. CMQ 11692/3.

INSPECTOR, PALESTINE L. of C.
G.O.C., ALEXANDRIA DISTRICT.
----

   1. The embarkation of the 52nd Division will be continued at Alexandria on the morning of 6th April.

   2. The Units of the 155th Infantry Brigade Group arriving at Kantara East on the 5th instant will re-entrain at Kantara West on the night of April 5th/6th in the same order, except that the Headquarters, 155th Infantry Brigade, and 155th L.T.M. Battery will leave on the last train, i.e. :-

			Off.	O.R.
1st Train ... 834/701	...	1/5th R. Scots Fusrs ..	(34 (37	783(a) 917(b)
2nd Train ... 836A/703	...	1/4th K.O.S.B. ...	(29 (34	807(a) 963(b)
3rd Train ... 840/707	...	1/4th R. Scots Fusrs...	(25 (35	719(a) 855(b)
4th Train ... 800/711	...	1/5th K.O.S.B. ...	(28 (36	742(a) 963(b)
5th Train ... 804A/713A	...	H.Q., 155th Inf. Bde...	6	98(a)
		155th L.T.M. Battery...	3	75(a)
		155th M.G.C.	8	210(a)
		1/3 Lowland Fld. Amb...	7	228(a)
		218th Coy. A.S.C. ...	2	46(a)
		155th Bde. Supply Sect.	1	7(a)
		211th M.G.C.	10	195(a)
		Mobile Veterinary Sect.	1	30(a)
		Sanitary Section ...	1	27(a)

Note :-

   Strengths at (a) denote those shewn in advice from H.Q., 52nd Division.

   "   " (b) denote those to which, I am informed by D.A.G.,3rd Echelon, the Units will probably be made up while passing through Kantara.

   For these Units, no new strength has been notified.

(Contd.)

- 2 -

Train timings are as follow :-

No.		leave	Ready to load 5th.	Depart 5th.	Arr. Gabbary Quays 6th	
1 RSF 834/701	...	1800	1900	2050	0540	1845/1930
4 KOSB 836A/703	...	2000	2100	2230	0645	2045/2130
4 RSF 840/707	...	2145	2245	2400	0845	2230/2315
1 KOSB 800/711	...	2315	0015 .. 6th.	0150 ..6th.	1045	2400/0030
+ 4th Coy 804A/713A	...	0150	0205 .. "	0345.. "	1310	0130/0200
Sunday						until told times

Each Unit will thus be given upwards of twelve hours at Kantara; consequently the train timings must be closely adhered to.

Each of the trains will accommodate the Unit or Units mentioned at Establishment (Personnel) Strength.

3. Embarkation will take place immediately on arrival at Gabbary, but, in the event of sufficient ships not being berthed, it may be necessary to divert some trains to Sidi Bishr where their personnel would be encamped. Should this necessity arise, E.S.O. Alexandria will give the earliest possible intimation to H.Q., Alexandria Dist. and this office, and will issue orders for the subsequent move from Sidi Bishr to the Quays for embarkation.

4. E.S.O., Alexandria, will issue orders regarding allotments of troops to vessels, care being exercised to prevent, as far as possible, the splitting of Units, but the personnel of the Brigade Field Ambulance must be distributed among the ships carrying the Brigade Group.

5. Rations will be issued on board from and including the Dinner meal on date of embarkation. Such additional rations as are necessary will therefore be issued at Kantara.

6. Three copies of Special Embarkation Return and three copies of Nominal Roll of troops embarking will be required by the Embarkation Staff Officer. A supply of the former has been issued to H.Q., Kantara Area, for distribution to the Units as they pass through.

7. Twelve copies of this order have been issued to H.Q., Kantara Area, for transmission to the D.A.A.G., 52nd Division.

8. The following corrections should be made to the train timings in my CMQ 11692/2 of 1st April :-

No.800/711,.. time depart should read 0150.

No.804A/703A. should read 804A/713A.

9. The strengths of the Infantry Battalions mentioned in my CMQ 11692/2 of 1st April will probably be made up by D.A.G., 3rd Echelon to -

	Off.	O.R.
1/4th Royal Scots	30	891
1/7th Royal Scots	33	980

(Contd.)

	Off.	O.R.
1/7th Scottish Rifles	39	981
1/8th Scottish Rifles	38	872

R. Mainwaring

2nd Echelon, G.H.Q.,
2nd April, 1918.

Lieut.-Colonel,
A.Q.M.G.,
for D.Q.M.G.

Copies to :- A.M.S.; G.S.; D.A.G.; G.S.,I; D.Q.M.G.(2); M.G.R.A.;
D.A.S.; E.-in-C; D.M.S.; P.C.; D.A.G.,3rd Echelon; D.S.T.;
D.R.T.; D.O.S.; D.O.S.,Base; D.V.S.; D.R.; D.A.D.A.P.S.; P.N.T.O.;
C.P.

H.Q., Force-in-Egypt.
H.Q., 52nd Division.
H.Q., Kantara Area.
A.D.R.T., Cairo.
D.N.T.O., Cairo.
R.T.O., Kantara.

D.A.D.R.T., Cairo.
D.A.D.R.T., Alexandria.
E.S.O., Alexandria.
D.N.T.O., Alexandria.

P.S. - Reference paras. 2 and 9 above.

The following further information as to strengths on leaving Kantara have been received :-

	Off.	O.R.
220th Coy. A.S.C.	3	65
156th Bde. Supply Sect.	1	9
218th Coy. A.S.C.	3	65
155th Bde. Supply Sect.	1	9

Similar details for the remainder of the Units will be published as soon as received.

SECRET.   CMQ 11692/4.

INSPECTOR, PALESTINE L. of C.

G.O.C., ALEXANDRIA DISTRICT.
----

1.   The embarkation of the 52nd Division will be continued at Alexandria on the morning of the 8th April.

2.   The Units of the 157th Brigade Group and Divisional Troops, (except as stated below) arriving at Kantara East on the 7th inst., will re-entrain at Kantara West on the night of April 7th/8th in the same order, i.e. :-

				Off.	O.R.
1st Train	..	834/701	... 1/5th H.L.I.	33	870 (a)
				38	1009 (b)
2nd "	..	836A/703	... 1/7th H.L.I.	36	858 (a)
				42	976 (b)
3rd "	..	840/707	... H.Q., 157th Inf.Bde.	7	108
			... 1/6th H.L.I.	24	710 (a)
				41	909 (b)
4th "	..	800/711	... 1/5th A. & S.H.	36	918 (a)
				36	964 (b)
5th "	..	804A/713A	... H.Q., R.E.	3	14
			... Divnl. Signal Coy.	4	185
			(with one 4-Wh. and 16 2-Wh. Vehicles).		
			... Divnl. H.Q.	27	244
			... H.Q., Divnl. Train.	4	13
			... A.P.M.	2	32
			... D.A.D.O.S.	1	16
			... 410th Fld. Coy. R.E.	1	30
			in charge of 18 2-Wh. Vehicles, six Pontoon Wagons, and 3 Trestle Wagons, (without Pontoons or Trestles).		

NOTE :-
    Strenghts at (a) denote those shewn in advice from Inspector, P. L. of C.

    "   " (b) denote those to which, I am informed by D.A.G., 3rd Echelon, the units will probably be made up, while passing through Kantara.

(P.T.O.

Train timings are as follow :-

No.	Ready to load. 7th.	Depart 7th.	Arr. Gabbary Quays, 8th.
834/701	1900	2050	0540
836A/703	2100	2230	0645
840/707	2245	2400	0845
800/711	0015 .. 8th.	0150 .. 8th.	1045
804A/713A	0205 .. "	0345 .. "	1310

Each Unit will thus be given upwards of twelve hours at Kantara; consequently the train timings must be closely adhered to.

Each of the first four trains will accommodate the Unit or Units mentioned at Establishment (personnel) Strength. The fifth will have sufficient Flat Trucks attached for the Vehicles.

3. The Units, as under, arriving at Kantara East on the 6th Train, and the remaining personnel of the 410th Field Coy. R.E. on the 5th Train, from LUDD, will remain at Kantara for about 24 hours. Orders for their move to Alexandria will be issued in due course.

	Off.	O.R.
410th Fld. Coy. R.E.	6	186
157th M.G.C.	9	212
157th L.T.M. Battery	4	83
1/2nd Lowland Fld. Amb.	6	248
217th Coy. A.S.C.	5	128
219th Coy. A.S.C.	2	54

4. Embarkation will take place immediately on arrival at Gabbary, but, in the event of sufficient ships not being berthed, it may be necessary to divert some trains to Sidi Bishr where their personnel would be encamped. Should this necessity arise, E.S.O. Alexandria will give the earliest possible intimation to H.Q., Alexandria Dist. and this office, and will issue orders for the subsequent move from Sidi Bishr to the Quays for embarkation.

5. E.S.O., Alexandria, will issue orders regarding allotment of troops to vessels, care being exercised to prevent, as far as possible, the splitting of Units.

It will be necessary to embark on the vessels to carry the above troops a suitable proportion of the 1/2nd Lowland Brigade Field Ambulance, which unit will arrive at Gabbary on the morning of the 9th.

6. Rations will be issued on board from and including the Dinner meal on date of embarkation. Such additional rations as are necessary will therefore be issued at Kantara.

7. Three copies of Special Embarkation Return and three copies of Nominal Rolls of troops embarking will be required by the Embarkation Staff Officer. A supply of the former has been issued to H.Q., Kantara Area, for distribution to the Units as they pass through.

(Contd.)

8. Twelve copies of this order have been issued to H.Q., Kantara Area, for transmission to the D.A.A.G., 52nd Division.

9. With reference to P.S. of CMQ 11692/3 of 2nd April, the strengths of the "remainder of the Units" are not expected to vary to any appreciable extent.

10. With reference to my telegram CMQT 7476 of 2nd April, adding 39 Other Ranks and 21 Motor Ambulances of the three Brigade Field Ambulances to the allotment of ships in my CMQ 11692/1 of 31st March, it has been found impossible to load these Vehicles in the vessels mentioned. The Ambulances and the 39 men will (if possible) be embarked in one or more of the other vessels to carry the Division.

11. The attention of all Units is drawn to the necessity for strict accuracy in train states rendered to the R.T.O., Kantara West, on entrainment, as ship-room will be calculated thereon. It will not be possible to embark any personnel in addition to the numbers sh shewn.

R. Mainwaring
Lieut.-Colonel,
A.Q.M.G.,
for D.Q.M.G.

2nd Echelon, G.H.Q.
4th April, 1918.

Copies to :- A.M.S.; G.S.; G.S.,I; D.A.G.; D.Q.M.G.(2); M.G.R.A.; D.A.S.; E.-in-C; D.M.S.; P.C.; D.A.G., 3rd Echelon; D.S.T.; D.R.T.; D.O.S.; D.O.S.,Base; D.V.S.; D.R.; D.A.P.S.; D.A.D.A.P.S.; P.N.T.O.(2); C.P.

H.Q., Force-in-Egypt.
H.Q., 52nd Division.
H.Q., Kantara Area.
A.D.R.T., Cairo.

D.A.D.R.T., Cairo.
D.A.D.R.T., Alexandria.
E.S.O., Alexandria.
D.N.T.O., Alexandria.

D.N.T.O., Cairo.
R.T.O., Kantara.

HW

SECRET.

CMQ 11692/5.

INSPECTOR, PALESTINE L. of C.

G.O.C., ALEXANDRIA DISTRICT.
----

1. The Embarkation of the 52nd Division will be continued at Alexandria on the morning of 9th April. After that date no further vessels will be immediately available.

2. The Units mentioned in para. 3 of my CMQ 11692/4 of 4th instant together with the 5th (Pioneer) Battalion Royal Irish Regiment, and the 52nd Divisional Cyclist Co. arriving at Kantara East on the 7th instant, will re-entrain at Kantara West on the night of the 8th/9th in the following order :-

			Off.	O.R.
1st Train ... 834/701	...	5th (Pioneer) Batt. R. Irish Regt.	21	810
	...*	410th Fld. Coy. R.E.	5	165
2nd Train ... 836A/703	...	157th M.G.C.	10	176
	...	157th L.T.M. Battery	4	83
	...	1/2nd Lowland Fld. Amb.	7	248
	...	Divnl. Cyclist Co.	10	226
	...	217 Co. A.S.C. (including Supply Details).	10	170
	...	219 Co. A.S.C. (including Supply Details).	4	74

The above strengths (except A.S.C.) may be increased slightly. There will be ample train accommodation.

* Advance Party of 1 Officer, 21 Other Ranks, and 1 Officer and 30 Other Ranks in charge of Vehicles will have left for Alexandria, and are not included.

Train timings are as follow :-

No.	Ready to load 8th.	Depart 8th.	Arr. Gabbary Quays. 9th.
834/701 ...	1900 ...	2050 ...	0540
836A/703 ...	2100 ...	2230 ...	0645

3. Embarkation will take place immediately on arrival at Gabbary in the order of priority shewn in para. 2. Provided the vessels detailed are berthed, there will be accommodation for the bulk of the personnel mentioned above. Any surplus will be encamped at Alexandria.

In the event, however, of sufficient ships not being berthed, it will be necessary to divert these trains to Sidi Bishr where their

(P.T.O.

their/ -2-

~~personnel will be encamped;~~ in this case, orders will be issued from this office.

4. E.S.O., Alexandria, will issue orders regarding the allotment of troops to vessels, care being exercised to prevent, as far as possible, the splitting of units, except as regards the 1/2nd Lowland Brigade Field Ambulance, mentioned in para.5 of my CMQ 11692/4 of 4th instant.

5. Rations will be issued on board from and including the Dinner Meal on date of embarkation. Such additional rations as are necessary will therefore be issued at Kantara.

6. Three copies of Special Embarkation Return and three copies of Nominal Rolls of troops embarking will be required by the Embarkation Staff Officer. A supply of the former has been issued to H.Q., Kantara Area, for distribution to the Units as they pass through.

7. Eight copies of this order have been issued to H.Q., Kantara Area, for transmission to the D.A.A.G., 52nd Division.

8. The attention of all Units is drawn to the necessity for strict accuracy in train states rendered to the R.T.O., Kantara West, on entrainment, as ship-room will be calculated thereon. It will not be possible to embark any personnel in addition to the numbers so shewn.

9. 600 R.A.M.C. Personnel, now at Alexandria under orders to return to France, will be embarked on the vessels to carry the 52nd Division.

10. The 3rd Echelon Records Section, 52nd Division, (now at Alexandria) consisting of 1 Officer and 19 Other Ranks, will be embarked next after the 410th Field Co. R.E.

11. The Pontoons, Trestles, and Equipment of the 3 Field Companies, which are to be drawn at Alexandria by an Advance Party detailed for the purpose, will be embarked.

12. Orders have now been issued in respect of the embarkation of all Units of the 52nd Division for overseas, with the exception of the Area Employment Coy.,(embarkation strength - 2 Officers and 230 Other Ranks) and the Base Reinforcements. O.C., Kantara Area, will shew the strength of the latter in his daily return of personnel awaiting passage.

R. Mainwaring.
Lieut.-Colonel,
A.Q.M.G.,
for D.Q.M.G.

2nd Echelon, G.H.Q.,
5th April, 1918.

Copies to :- A.M.S.; G.S.; G.S.,I; D.A.G.; D.Q.M.G.(2); M.G.R.A.; D.A.S.; E.-in-C.; D.M.S.; P.C.; D.A.G.,3rd Echelon; D.S.T.; D.R.T.; D.O.S.; D.O.S.,Base; D.V.S.; D.R.; D.A.P.S.; D.A.D.A.P.S.; P.N.T.O(2); C.P.
H.Q., Force-in-Egypt.   D.A.D.R.T., Cairo.
H.Q., 52nd Division.   D.A.D.R.T., Alexandria.
H.Q., Kantara Area.   E.S.O., Alexandria.
A.D.R.T., Cairo.   D.N.T.O., Alexandria.
            D.N.T.O., Cairo.
            R.T.O., Kantara.

HW

a Diary April 1918 Apt **XLIX**

EMBARKATION STATE of 52nd DIVISION

UNIT	LEASOWE CASTLE		CANBERRA		MALWA		KAISAR I HIND		CALEDONIA		OMRAH		INDARRA		TOTAL UNIT	
	Offrs	O.Rs	Offrs	O.Rs	Offrs	O.Rs	Offrs	O.Rs	Ofrs	O.Rs	Ofrs	O.Rs	Ofrs	O.Rs	Ofrs	O.Rs
1/5th R.S.F.					35	851									35	85
1/4th K.O.S.B.					37	932									37	93
1/3rd Low. Fld. Amb.					3	115	5	119							8	23
155th M.G. Coy.					10	184									10	18
155th L.T.M. Battery.					4	79									4	7
218th Coy. A.S.C.					3	52									3	5
211th M.G. Coy.					10	171									10	17
155th Bde. Supply Sect.					1	6									1	
1/1st Mob. Vet. Sect.					2	29									2	2
Sanitary Section.						26										2
1/4th R.S.F.							35	820							35	8
1/5th K.O.S.B.							34	860							34	86
155th Inf. Bde. H.Q.							5	80							5	8
R.E. Sig. Sect. attd. H.Q.							1	27							1	
R.E. Pos. Sect. attd. H.Q.								3								
3rd Hussars.								1								
1/5th A. A S.H.							39	1001							39	100
Various Units attd. -do-							1	27							1	
1/7th Royal Scots.	38	901													38	90
1/7th S. Rifles.	36	870													36	87
156th Bde. H.Q.	8	75													8	7
R.E. Sig. Sect. attd. H.Q.	1	24													1	
156th Bde. Supply Sect	1	5													1	
220th Coy. A.S.C.	2	51													2	
1/1st Low. Fld. Amb.	3	64	5	166											8	23
1/4th Royal Scots.	39	821													39	82
52nd D.H.Q.	3	5													3	
156th L.T.M. Bty.			3	75											3	7
156th M.G. Coy.			11	216											11	21
1/8th S. Rifles.			37	843											37	84
1/5th H.L.I.									40	1010					40	101
410th Fld Coy R.E.									2	52	3	128	2	51	7	23
1/2nd Low. Fld. Amb.									3	119	2	93	2	29	7	2
412th Fld. Coy. R.E.											6	213			6	21
157th M.G. Coy.									4	77	2	33	5	118	11	2
1/6th H.L.I.									38	862					38	86
5th Pnr. R.I. Regt.									33	882					33	88
1/7th H.L.I.													45	940	45	94
Military Police													2	51	2	3
H.Q., Staff.													13	143	13	14
H.Q., R.E.													3	14	3	1
D.A.D.O.S.													1	18	1	1
218th Coy. D.T.													2	21	2	2
220th Coy. B.T.													1	16	1	1
H.Q., Divnl. Train.													4	29	4	
Divnl. Sig. Coy. R.E.													6	192	6	19
H.Q., 157th Bde.													8	73	8	7

ALSO embarked on "INDARRA" 6 Pontoons, 6 Weldon Trestles, 9 4Whd. Veh. 8 2Whd. Veh. for 410th Field Coy. R.E.
1 -do- 16 -do- for Divnl. Sig. Coy. R.E.

The following are at present at SIDE BISHR. To be despatched later.

	Officers.	O.Rs.
157th Bde. L.T.M. Battery.	4	83
52nd Divnl. Cyclists Coy.	10	222
217th Coy. A.S.C.	5	165
219th Coy. A.S.C.	5	77
R.A.M.C. for Bde Field Ambs.		39 and 21 Motor Ambulances.

(Sd) J. NEWTON BROWN.
Lieut. Colonel.
April 11th 1918.

A Diary April 1918
App X

SECRET.

COPY No. 118

52nd (Lowland) DIVISION.

Administrative Instruction No. AF. 1.

issued with reference to Divisional Wire No. G.A. of 24/4/18.

Map Reference
ABBEVILLE 1/100000
Sheet 14.

24th April, 1918.

1. MOVE.

(a) 156th Infantry Brigade complete and No. 220th Coy. A.S.C. Divisional Train will move by Rail to First Army tomorrow 25th instant.

Entraining Station — RUE.
Detraining Station — WIZERNES (not shown on above quoted map)

Time table for units entraining is attached.

(b) In conjunction with above 1 Section of 52nd Divisional M.T. Coy. will move tomorrow by road to destination to be notified later.

2. ENTRAINING OFFICER.

156th Infantry Brigade will furnish an Entraining Officer to report to R.T.O., RUE, at 6 a.m., 25th instant.

3. DETRAINING OFFICER.

156th Infantry Brigade will detail an officer to act as Detraining Officer on arrival at WIZERNES.

4. ARRIVAL AT ENTRAINING STATION.

(a) The vehicles and baggage of each train load will be at the entraining Station 3 hours before the train is timed to leave.
(b) A loading party of 1 officer and 60 O.R. will be detailed for each train and will arrive at the Entraining Station at the same time as the vehicles, etc.
(c) The Unit concerned will be at the Station 1 hour before each train is timed to leave.

5. DETRAINING STATION.

Units will move from Detraining Station under orders to be issued by First Army.

6. BILLETING PARTIES.

Billeting Parties for all Units including the Train Company will proceed by the first train taking bicycles with them.

7. WATER CARTS.

All water carts will move full.

8. SUPPLIES.

The following supplies will accompany units :-
Rations for 25th instant — With Units.
Rations for 26th instant — On Train vehicles.
Rations for 27th instant — On M.T. Lorries.

P.T.O.

- 2 -

9. AMMUNITION.

(a) 1st Line and M.T. Echelons will move with full Establishment of S.A.A.
(b) Grenades, stokes morter shells, Very's Lights, etc., will be drawn on arrival at destination.

10. POLICE.

A.P.M. will detail sufficient police to regulate traffic in the vicinity of RUE STATION during entrainment.

11. KITS, STORES, ETC.

The baggage wagons of the Train Company will proceed to Units on the afternoon of the 24th instant and will be ready loaded by the evening of the 24th. These wagons will entrain with the remainder of the 220th Coy. A.S.C. in No. 6 Train.

Five Lorries to be detailed by O.C., 52nd M.T. Coy. will report to Headquarters, 156th Infantry Brigade at 6.30 a.m. to take second blanket and L.T.M. Battery Stores, etc., to RUE Station.

12. STATES.

A movement order showing the number of personnel, the vehicles and the animals proceeding by each train will be handed by Units to the R.T.O. on arrival at RUE Station.

13. ACKNOWLEDGE.

Copies issued at 4 hrs to

```
No.  1.   A.D.C. for D.O.C.
     2.   'G'
3 to 8.   156th Infantry Brigade.
     9.   Divisional Train.
    10.   52nd Divnl. M.T. Coy.
    11.   D.A.D.O.S.
    12.   A.D.M.S.
    13.   D.A.D.V.S.
    14.   A.P.M.
    15.   O.C., Signals.
    16.   Reserve Army 'Q'
    17.   File.
    18.)
    19.)  Diary.
    20.   S.S.O.
    21.   A.D.R.T., ABBEVILLE.
    22.   R.T.O., RUE.
    23.   D.A. & Q.M.G., First Army.
```

(Ghaude)
Lieut. Colonel.
A.A. & Q.M.G.,
52nd (Lowland) Division.

TIME TABLE.

No. 1 Train departs 8.44 a.m. 25th instant. Brigade H.Qrs. 1 Coy., 1 Cooker and team of 4th Royal Scots. Brigade Signal Sect. L.T.M. Battery. Postal Section. Supply Sect, and following details of A.S.C. transport (220th Coy. A.S.C.) 1 Officer, 20 O.R. 10 4Whld. Vehicles and teams, 5 Cycles.

No. 2 Train. departs 11.34 a.m. -do- 4th Royal Scots less 1 Coy., 1 Cooker and team.

No. 3 Train. departs 2.24 p.m. -do- 7th Royal Scots less 1 Coy., 1 Cooker and team.

No. 4 Train. departs 5.4 p.m. -do- 7th S. Rifles less 1 Coy., 1 Cooker and team.

No. 5 Train. departs 8.34 p.m. -do- 8th S. Rifles less 1 Coy., 1 Cooker and team.

No. 6 Train. departs 12.14 a.m. 26th instant 1 Coy. 7th S. Rifles. 1 Coy. 7th R. Scots. 1 Coy. 8th S. Rifles. with Cookers and teams in each case. Remainder of A.S.C. Coy. and transport.

A.Diary April 1918
app^x XI

SECRET.　　　　　　　　　　　　　　　　　　　　　　　　Copy No. 18.

52nd (Lowland) DIVISION.

Administrative Instruction No. A. 2.

26th APRIL, 1918

1. **MOVE.**
    (a) 52nd Division, less 156th Infantry Brigade, 1/4th Battn. Royal Scots Fusiliers, Machine Gun Battalion and Divisional Artillery, will move by rail on April, 28th, in accordance with attached Time Table on transfer from Reserve to First Army.
    On arrival in new area the Division will come under orders of XIth Corps.
    (b) 52nd Divisional M.T. Coy. will move by road to XI th Corps Area on 28th instant, under orders of O.C.

2. **ENTRAINING OFFICERS.**
    Entraining Officers will be detailed as under to report to R.T.O's concerned three hours before the first trains are due to leave. They will travel on the last trains leaving their respective entraining stations :-

    1 Officer detailed by 155th Infantry Brigade at RUE STATION.
    1 Officer detailed by 157th Infantry Brigade　　NOYELLES STATION.

3. **DETRAINING OFFICERS.**
    155th and 157th Infantry Brigades will detail detraining officers to assist the R.T.O's at their detraining Stations. These officers will remain at their respective Stations until all Units of the Division have arrived.

4. **BILLETING PARTIES.**
    (a) Billeting parties will proceed by lorry to the new area on the 27th instant in accordance with attached programme.
    (b) A proportion of cycles to be taken in the 155th and 157th Infantry Brigade lorries to enable billeting parties to send guides to the detraining Station on the 28th instant.
    (c) In the new area Field Companies and Field Ambulances will be billeted in Brigade Areas as under :-

    410th Field Coy. R.E. and 1/3rd Lowland Field Ambulance
    　　　　　　　　　　　with 155th Infantry Brigade.
    411th Field Coy. R.E. and 1/1st Lowland Field Ambulance
    　　　　　　　　　　　with 156th Infantry Brigade.
    415th Field Coy. R.E. and 1/2nd Lowland Field Ambulance
    　　　　　　　　　　　with 157th Infantry Brigade.

    (d) 1 Officer and 5 Other Ranks will be sufficient billeting party for a battalion for the purposes of this move owing to limited lorry accommodation - other Units in proportion.

5. **LOADING PARTIES.**
    155th and 157th Infantry Brigade will each detail a loading party of 1 Officer and 100 Other Ranks to report at their respective Entraining Stations 3 hours before the first trains are timed to start. These parties should be found from the Units on the last trains so that loading work may be continuous.

6. **ARRIVAL AT ENTRAINING STATIONS.**
    (a) All transport and animals will arrive at the Entraining Station 3 hours before their train leaves.
    (b) Personnel to entrain will arrive one hour before the train leaves.

　　　　　　　　　　　　　　　　　　　　　　　　　　　P.T.O.

(2)

7. **TRANSPORT.**
   (a) Baggage wagons of the Train will join Units on the afternoon of the 27th instant.
   (b) Baggage and Supply vehicles of the Train will entrain with the Units to which they are affiliated. One man per Train vehicle will be detailed by Units to act as baggage guard or supply loader. On arrival in new area these men will remain attached to the Train till further orders.

8. **SUPPLIES.**
   (a) Railhead up to 28th inclusive, RUE, from 29th instant a new Railhead will be allotted in First Army Area.
   (b) On entrainment 28th instant Supply Situation will be as follows :-
   Rations for 28th instant with Units.
   Rations for 29th instant on Supply Vehicles of Train.
   Rations for 30th instant drawn from Railhead by M.T.

9. **M.T. Company.**
   After drawing from Railhead on 28th instant, 52nd Divisional M.T. Coy., will proceed to new Area under orders of O.C.

10. **WATER CARTS.**
    All Water Carts will entrain full.

11. **LORRIES.**
    (a) Signal lorries will proceed to new Area under orders of O.C., 52nd Divisional M.T. Coy.,
    (b) Lorries as under will be detailed by O.C., 52nd Divisional M.T. Coy. for conveyance of second blankets and extra kits to entraining Stations :-
    To report to D.H.Q., RUE, at 9 a.m., 28th inst. 1 Lorry.
    To report to 155th Bde. H.Q. PONTHOILE at 9 a.m. 2 Lorries.
    To report to 157th Bde. H.Q. St. VALERY at 9 a.m. 2 Lorries.
    On completion of duty these lorries will rejoin 52nd Divisional M.T. Coy.

12. **TRAFFIC CONTROL.**
    A.P.M., will arrange for traffic control round RUE and NOYELLES Stations during entrainment.

13. **MEDICAL.**
    A.D.M.S., will arrange for a Medical Officer and Ambulance to be on duty at each Station during entrainment.

14. **STATES.**
    A movement order showing the number of personnel, vehicles and animals proceeding by each Train will be handed by Units to the R.T.O. on arrival at entraining Station.

15. **AMMUNITION.**
    (a) Units will entrain with full establishment of S.A.A.
    (b) Grenades, Stokes Mortar Shells, Very Lights etc., will be drawn on arrival in First Army Area.

16. **CLAIMS.**
    Great care is to be taken that the usual billeting certificates are completed and that no claim for damages or private hirings remain unsettled in the present area occupied by 52nd Division.

17. **TRAIN TIMINGS.**
    Train Timings will be notified as soon as received.

18. **ACKNOWLEDGE.**

C.G. Maude
Lieut. Colonel.
A.A. & Q.M.G., 52nd (Lowland)
DIVISION.

TIMETABLE (for Billeting party)

Unit.	No. of lorries allotted.	Starting place and time of lorries.	Route.	Destination.
155th Inf. Brigade. Pioneer Battalion. Divnl. Train. 1st and 3rd Lowland Field Ambulance. 410th/155th Field Coy. R.E.	2	Headquarters, 155th Infantry Brigade. 9 a.m.	HESDIN - BEAUMETZ LES AIRE - ESTREE BLANCHE.	Area Commandants Office, AIRE.
Divisional Headquarters. Signal Coy., T.A. Headquarters, R.A.	1	Divisional H.Qrs. 9.30 a.m.	-do-	-do-
157th Inf. Brigade. 410th Field Coy. R.E. 2nd Lowland Field Amb.	2	H.Qrs. 157th Infantry Brigade. 9 a.m.	-do-	-do-

Copies issued at 8.a.m.

No. 1.   A.D.C. for G.O.C.
    2.   "G"
    3.   155th Infantry Brigade.
    4.   156th Infantry Brigade.
    5.   157th Infantry Brigade.
    6.   52nd Divnl. Train.
    7.   S.S.O.
    8.   A.D.M.S.
    9.   D.A.D.V.S.
   10.   C.R.A.
   11.   C.R.E.
   12.   O.C., Signal Coy.
   13.   A.P.M.
   14.   D.A.D.O.S.
   15.   Camp Commandant.
   16.   52nd M.T. Company.
   17.   File.
18 & 19 Diary.
   20   Reserve Army, "Q"
   21   XIst Corps.
   22   A.D.R.T., ABBEVILLE.
   23   5th R.I. (Pioneer) Regt.
   24   52nd Machine Gun Battn.
   25   W.S.O.

P.T.O.

WAR DIARY
INTELLIGENCE SUMMARY.

Army Form C. 2118.

V.I. XXXV.
1/31 May 1918
Abrunel 1-2 (Unleat) Braam

Place	Date	Hour	Summary of Events and Information	Remarks and references to Appendices
AIRE	May 1		5th Royal Irish Regt. moved to THIENNES along with 410 & 412 Coys RE	
	3		12 M.G. Bn. left NIEURIN to move to AIRE district by rail	
	4		4th K.S.L.I. left NOVRON & BYRNE disentrained	
	5		(return location) R.A.F. 3 moved with ref. to our order A=702 (App I) App I.
			reg. move to VIII Corps area	
			410 & 412 Coys RE. moved from THIENNES to AIRE	
	6		5th Royal Irish Regt. (18) returned to AIRE	
			157 & 17 M.G. Batty. moved down at AIRE. A new App below Airemot App	
			here by rail to XVIII Corps area commences - Transport by road	
	7		157 - Infy Bde took over part of the 2E CHAUDIERE Sector Canadian Corps. App IV
			relieving 4th Canadian Division (Very Rapid)	
	8		153 Inf. Bde relieved 1st at Divn of XVII Corps in WILLERVAL Sector in	
			ref. to 157 Bde.	
	9		strong Instructions A.E.G. source of elements of our own Corps. App VI
			realisation of line & move of Divn. to XVIII Corps, an & another	
	10		Brig. Gen. Kincaid Inman O.C. moved Coke temporary command Div.	
			Divn. Allocated to Corps artillery arm. Patrol attaining 1 inf. App III.	App III
	7		Divn. Con. Divry R.C.T. 145 Steamboats recent (App II)	App II

Army Form C. 2118.

WAR DIARY
or
INTELLIGENCE SUMMARY.
(Erase heading not required.)

A Branch
52 (Lowland) Division
Vol - XXXV
May 1918
p. 2

Place	Date	Hour	Summary of Events and Information	Remarks and references to Appendices
A.C.Q.	11.		Enc. held by Divn. extended. Circular memo A.68 re: order of Staff weekdays inspn. to Divn. (A.F.1)	Appx. IV
			— do — O.178 arrival of transport in hours (All issued c/No issued) (Appx. 2)	Appx. I.
	12.		Admin. Circ. memo A.2 issued. re: Baths	Appx. VI
	13.		Admin. Instruction A.F.5 issued re: Burials	Appx. VII
	15.		125th Infantry Bde. Admin. Instruction A.F.6 issued re: Lunch battalion	Appx. VIII
	16.		do — 7 issued of Gen. Bean	Appx. IX
	17.		Orders to carry issued Brms & answer to Lt Cukan (By waggon) to carry the Picts slightly detained, released Lt Bir 20.5.17 Admin. Circ. memo 103 of Relief issued	Appx. X
	18.		do — 4 of R.M.L.I. Reinforcement convoys Armored Entrenching — Mg 790's issued from Depot Circ. ref: Bathing issued	Appx. XI
	20.			No. XII

Army Form C. 2118.

WAR DIARY
or
INTELLIGENCE SUMMARY.
(Erase heading not required.)

Vol XXV
4 Branch
52 Division
May 1918

Place	Date	Hour	Summary of Events and Information	Remarks and references to Appendices
a.d	21		Base depôts in no place. Supply — "M" Importh Bne after Calais	
	22		R.H. & R.F.A – R.F.A – 9 – A.S.C. R.E & R.A m.c Admin Instruction a F-8 — Havre Rouen	XIII, XIV XV, XVI — XVI app III, app III app VI, app IX app VI — XI
	23		Admin Circ memo ff — course of Instruction do — 1.6 — — scouting	
	24		do 1.7 — — Water Supply	
			memo A 44/28 course with Rein ff.Return Copy to Batteries — { app XVIII, app XVII attached	app XVIII, app XVII
	25		Admin Instruction a/29 issued ref Storyken hits 1st Bn Warwick 157 Regt	app XVIII
	27		Admin Cir memo R-8 issued ref movements of Btns & Coys	app XIX, app XX

Army Form C. 2118.

WAR DIARY
or
INTELLIGENCE SUMMARY.
(Erase heading not required.)

Vol XXXV p 4
A France
52nd (Lowland) Division
May 1918

Place	Date	Hour	Summary of Events and Information	Remarks and references to Appendices
Acd.	27		The following events were during the month & later one whatever.	
			On 11th Schaefer clubs was renewed to 40th	
			4th Reinforcements were sent & return 2nd Fusiliers	
			12 — Two Cohorts of Scots to receive an entire reinforcements as boys	
			Notes Mentioned	
			15th — 2 rifles & discharged to act upon turbulence of boys in Town & from us to & 6 & 7, 60%. Rifles are now found from Trenches near something to elevate the exercises of the stew.	
			18th — Owing to shortage of Water in particular of our old encampment near 200 bollow laths at funds as to lye	
			21st — The Middless Lewis to be within 100 yds of position	
	31		Lewis Guns with ack-ack however been increased to 32 per Bn Div — the ack-ack took from Bde has 12 making 396 from Div & the morn and 48 additional of ack-ack defence	

Army Form C. 2118.

WAR DIARY
or
INTELLIGENCE SUMMARY.
(Erase heading not required.)

VOL XXXV
1st May 1918
Appendix 5 — Summary

Place	Date	Hour	Summary of Events and Information	Remarks and references to Appendices
			Infantry Brigades	App 5
			Available Infantry Strength as 16/4/18	
			Officers OR	
			155 Brigade 113 2839	
			156 Brigade 119 2890	
			157 Brigade 119 3029	
			TOTAL 351 — 8458	
			Casualties for Month of May.	
			Killed Wounded Missing Sick	
			Off OR Off OR Off OR Off OR	
			155 Bde 0 9 1 27 0 0 4 — 271
			156 Bde 1 8 6 39 2 1 4 — 214
			157 Bde 4 2 48 3 P — 251
			TOTAL 2 — 21 8 — 114 5 13 — 736	
			Reinforcements.	
			Officers OR	
			155 Bde 18 446	
			156 Bde 15 409	
			157 Bde 12 256	
			45 1111	

Appendix I
52 (Lowland) Division
A Branch

SECRET.
Copy No........

52nd (Lowland) DIVISION.

Administrative Instruction No. AF. 3.

Issued with reference to 52nd Divisional Order No. 102.

4th MAY, 1918.

1. **MOVES.**
   52nd Division (less Artillery) will be transferred on May 5th, 6th, 7th and 8th from XIth Corps to XVIIIth Corps, and will move as follows:-
   (a) Dismounted personnel by tactical trains in accordance with attached Time Table. For purposes of entrainment on the 8th instant, the units in Train No. 3 will form part of 157th Infantry Brigade Group.
   (b) All horse transport and riding animals by march route in accordance with March Table issued with 52nd Divisional Order No. 102.
   (c) 52nd M.T. Coy, A.S.C. will proceed under special instructions to be issued to O.C.

2. **ENTRAINING AND DETRAINING OFFICERS.**
   155th, 156th and 157th Infantry Brigades will each detail an entraining officer and a detraining officer to report to the R.T.Os. (a) of the entraining stations 2 hours before the first train leaves (b) of the detraining stations on arrival of first train.
   The entraining officers will travel on the last train of the day leaving the entraining station.
   The detraining officer will remain on duty till after the arrival at the detraining station of the last train of his group.

3. **ENTRAINING AND DETRAINING.**
   (a) G.Os.C., Infantry Brigade Groups will be responsible for the order of entrainment of their Units, and their arrival at entrainment stations.
   (b) The last unit on each train should arrive at the entraining station not less than one hour before the train is due to start.
   (c) On arrival at detraining stations units will be met by guides from billeting parties and led to billeting areas.

4. **LOADING PARTIES.**
   (a) Each Infantry Brigade will detail a loading party of 1 Officer and 50 other ranks from an unit on the last train to report at the entraining station two hours before the first train is due to start.
   These parties will remain on duty till the last train of the day is loaded.
   They will be responsible for loading baggage and stores brought to the entraining station by lorry. The lorry loads should be put on the trains before any personnel starts entraining.
   (b) Unloading parties will similarly be detailed at detraining stations.
   Each Infantry Brigade will detail a party from the first train to unload all trains of that particular Brigade Group.

5. **SPARE KITS, BLANKETS, ETC.**
   (a) As much kit as possible will be sent on the day preceding entrainment in the baggage wagons of the train.

(2)

(b) Minimum officers kits, 2nd blankets, a proportion of cooking utensils, and of medical equipment and one or two bicycles per unit can be taken in the tactical trains. Lorries to take these and one days extra rations for personnel to entraining stations will be provided as below (para. 8).

6. **SUPPLIES.**
(a) Railhead up to May 6th inclusive AIRE.
   from May 7th inclusive St. ELOI.
(b) Transport of Brigade Groups moving by road on 5th, 6th and 7th instant will take two days rations for men and animals with them.
(c) Personnel of Brigade Groups proceeding by tactical trains will entrain with rations for the day following entrainment, in addition to the current days rations.
(d) All detached parties proceeding by lorry, etc., will take two days rations with them.
(e) Rations for 156th Infantry Brigade Group will be drawn on the 7th instant from R.S.O., AIRE, as a detail issue.
S.S.O. will arrange details direct with R.S.O.

7. **BILLETING PARTIES.**
(a) The billeting parties of all units of the Division will proceed direct to new area in lorries on the 5th instant, and will be responsible for meeting units on arrival at detraining stations in the usual way.
(b) 2 lorries for conveyance of these parties will start from the bandstand, Grande Place, AIRE, at 11 a.m. on the 5th instant.
(c) As the accommodation in the new area is almost entirely in huts, the following billeting parties will be sufficient :-
(1) Per Infantry Brigade ... ... 1 officer
(2) Per Infantry, Pioneer and Machine
    Gun Battalion... ... . 1 Officer. 3 O.R.
(3) Per smaller unit ... . 1 officer. 1 O.R.
One bicycle a man should be taken.

8. **LORRIES.**
C.O., 52nd Divn. M.T. Coy. will detail lorries as follows in connection with the move :-
(a) One lorry to accompany the march of each Brigade Group Transport. This lorry will be under the orders of the senior officer of the Brigade Group, and will deal with breakdowns, stragglers, etc. No men will however be allowed to ride on the lorry without written permission from an officer.
(b) Lorries as in 7(b) above to convey billeting parties to new area.
(c) Two lorries to report to A.P.M. at 10 a.m., 5th instant, to take traffic control personnel to new area.
(d) 10 lorries to report to Camp Commandant, 52nd Divnl. Headquarters, on the morning of the 5th instant to convey a portion of Divisional Headquarters direct to the new area.
(e) Lorries as under for conveying kits, blankets, etc., to entraining stations:-
On 6th instant - 2 lorries to H.Q., 157th Infantry Brigade,
    LA LACQUE Camp at 6 a.m.
    1 lorry to H.Q., Machine Gun Battalion,
    QUIESTEDE at 6 a.m.
    1 lorry to H.Q., Pioneer Battalion, THIENNE
    Station at 6 a.m.

On 7th instant - 2 lorries to H.Q., 155th Infantry Brigade,
    WITTES at 6 a.m.

On 8th instant - 2 lorries to H.Q., 156th Infantry Brigade,
    LINETZ at 6 a.m.

9. **AMMUNITION.**
Full establishment of S.A.A. will be taken on H.T. and

10. **AREA STORES.**
All area stores which may have been drawn in present area will be handed in to Sub Area Commandants, who will give receipts for them.

11. **TENTS.**
(a) All tents and shelters not forming part of authorised Unit equipment will be handed in before departure to O.C., XIth Corps. Troops at the French Barracks close to the Church at AIRE. If possible units will do this by means of 1st Line Transport; otherwise direct application for required transport may be made to O.C., Divisional Train.
(b) Tents in the 5th Division Area occupied by the Pioneer Battalion and 2 Field Coys. R.E. will be returned to the same place on the morning of the 6th instant by means of transport to be provided by O.C., Divisional Train.

12. **STATES.**
A movement order showing the number of personnel proceeding by each train will be handed by units to the R.T.O., on arrival at the entraining stations.

13. **VETERINARY.**
The Mobile Veterinary Section will march on 6th instant with transport of 155th Infantry Brigade Group.

14. **ACKNOWLEDGE.**

C.G.Maude
Lieut. Colonel.
A.A. & Q.M.G., 52nd (Lowland) DIVISION.

Issued at .5 A.M...

Copy to :-
No.			No.	
1	A.D.C. for G.O.C.		17	French Mission.
2	"G"		18	First Army 'Q'
3	155th Infantry Brigade.		19)	XIth Corps 'Q'
4	156th -do-		20)	
5	157th -do-		21)	Canadian Corps 'Q'
6	52nd Divnl. Train.		22)	
7	S.S.O.		23)	XVIIth Corps 'Q'
8	A.D.M.S.		24)	
9	D.A.D.V.S.		25 and 26	4th Canadian Divn.
10	C.R.A.		27	5th Division 'Q'.
11	C.R.E.		28)	D.A.Q.M.G., 52nd Divn.
12	O.C., Signal Coy.			attd. 4th Canadian Divn.
13	A.P.M.		29	R.T.O., AIRE.
14	D.A.D.O.S.		30	R.S.O., AIRE
15	Camp Commandant.		31	R.T.O., ACQ.
16	52nd M.T. Coy.		32	R.T.O., MAROEUIL.
			33	File.
		34 and 35	War Diary.	
			36	5th R.I.Regt.(P)
			37	52nd M.G. Battalion.
			38	W.S.O.

TIME TABLE FOR ENTRAINMENT.

Train No.	Time of departure	Date.	UNIT.	Entrain.	Detrain.
1.		May 5th	157th Infantry Brigade Group.	AIRE	MAROEUIL
2.		May 6th	157th Infantry Brigade Group.	AIRE	MAROEUIL
3.		May 6th	Divnl. H.Q. H.Q.R.E. M.G. Bn. Pioneer Bn. Divnl.Sig.Coy. } counting as part of 157th Infantry Brigade Group.	AIRE	ACQ.
4.		May 7th	155th Infantry Brigade Group.	AIRE	MAROEUIL
5.		May 7th	155th Infantry Brigade Group.	AIRE	MAROEUIL
6.		May 8th	156th Infantry Brigade Group.	AIRE	ACQ.
7.		May 8th	156th Infantry Brigade Group.	AIRE	ACQ.

The journey should take approximately 4 hours.

Appendix 1A
"A" Branch
52 (Lowland) Division

52nd (LOWLAND) DIVISION.

ADMINISTRATIVE CIRCULAR MEMORANDUM No. 1.

7th May, 1918.

TRANSPORT.

During a recent inspection of transport on the march the G.O.C. noticed the following points, which require the immediate attention of all concerned.

1. FITTING OF HARNESS.
Harness, particularly in unit 1st Line Transport, has been very badly fitted. Breechings especially were in many cases far too loose.

2. SALUTING.
Saluting by drivers is very bad. The regulation salute with the whip by the lead drivers must be given smartly and correctly. Men on the driving seat will salute as follows:-
(a) If driving on the seat of a G.S. wagon, etc. the soldier will bring his whip to a perpendicular position, with the right hand resting on the thigh, and turn his head smartly towards an officer when passing him.
(b) A soldier riding on a vehicle will turn his head smartly towards an officer when passing him. Folding the arms is not part of the regulation salute.

3. RIDING ON LOADED VEHICLES.
On no account are men other than the driver (in vehicles with a double driving seat, the driver and one other) to ride on loaded wagons, without the written permission of an officer.

4. BRAKESMEN:
One man to manipulate the brake will invariably march in rear of every vehicle fitted only with a rear brake. Each brakesman must be able to work the brake quickly and intelligently, i.e. At the inspection in question many brakes were too stiff to work properly, and vehicles were observed going up a steep hill with the brakes full on.

5. COOKERS:
The chimneys of cookers will normally be down on the march. They will only be raised when cooking is actually in progress.

6. WHIPS and SPURS:
Some units were deficient of whips and spurs for their drivers. Indents to make good deficiencies will be sent in at once to D.A.D.T.O.S.

7. TURNOUT of MEN:
The general turn out of drivers was indifferent. Their association with horses is no excuse for grime. Many men were deficient of cap badges. Great-coats when worn will be properly buttoned up and the collars only turned up during inclement weather. The collar will not be turned half up and half down.

8. VEHICLES:
Vehicles and harness want a great deal of attention. The harness will be carefully dubbined, all metal work will be polished, and vehicles will be kept scrupulously clean.
A new divisional sign to be painted on all vehicles will shortly be approved, and instructions for painting will be issued to all concerned.

P.T.O.

9. SPARE ANIMALS:
Spare animals are not to be continuously ridden on the line of march, and never without the sanction of an officer.
As an exceptional case a man may be permitted to ride a spare animal during a portion of a march, but normally the spare animals will be led in the same way as pack animals.

10. PERSONNEL with TRANSPORT:
Any N.C.Os. or men other than brakesmen, marching with Transport will do so in a formed body immediately behind the transport of their Unit. They will not be allowed to straggle up and down the column.

11. INSPECTION of TRANSPORT:
Transport officers of all units will invariably inspect all vehicles before marching off.

The G.O.C. is determined that the transport of the 52nd Division will shortly be the best in FRANCE, and as a first step in this direction he wishes all O.C. units and Transport Officers to give the points enumerated above their immediate and careful attention.

C J Maude

Lieut. Colonel,
A.A. & Q.M.G., 52nd (Lowland) DIVISION.

Appendix II
'A' Branch
52nd (Lowland) Division

SECRET.   Copy No........

52nd (Lowland) DIVISION.

ADMINISTRATIVE INSTRUCTION No. AP. 4.

8th May, 1918.

Full administrative instructions and information regarding the area now occupied by 52nd Division will be issued shortly.

The following brief notes are for the guidance of all concerned until more ample instructions can be issued.

1. **SUPPLIES.**
   (a) Arrive at RAILHEAD (St. ELOI) daily by 'Pack Train' from the BASE.
   (b) Thence (i) for all units EAST of St. ELOI by Light Railway in bulk to Divisional Refilling point LA TARGETTE.
   (ii) for units at or WEST of St. ELOI to a supplementary refilling point at St. ELOI.
   (c) From b(i) to unit 1st Line Transport, where the supplies for Battalions, etc., in trenches are cut up, cooked, sand-bagged and sent up to the front line by Light Railway wherever possible (application for L.R. transport forward from NEUVILLE St. VAAST direct to Tramways ZIVVY).
   From b(ii) by 1st Line Transport to Units.

2. **AMMUNITION. (ARTILLERY)**
   The Main Divisional Ammunition Refilling point will be at LA TARGETTE.
   O.R.A. will arrange to take over and control this R.P. forthwith. Ammunition will be forwarded whenever possible by light Railway, and Staff Captain R.A. will get into touch with XVIIIth Corps Light Railway Officer (CAMBLAIN L'ABBE) and "TRAMWAYS" ZIVVY (A.10.a.)

3. **TRENCH MUNITIONS.**
   Main Divisional Dump. "HOOPERS" A.7.d.8.5.
   (a) This dump contains S.A.A., grenades, rockets, Stokes Mortar Ammunition, etc.
   (b) Brigade Dumps can be refilled from HOOPERS dump by Light Railway, indents for requirements being sent to D.A.Q.M.G., 52nd Division.
   (c) Brigades in the line will report forthwith the location and contents of their Brigade dumps.

4. **LIGHT RAILWAYS.**
   1. The Divisional area is served by a well organised system of Light Railways (60 c.m.).
   2. Exact details and a map will be issued later.
   3. The G.O.C. wishes the fullest possible use made of the Light Railway to the exclusion of M.T. and H.T. Brigades, etc., will make themselves fully acquainted with the Light Railway system in the Divisional Area.
   4. Application for Light Railway transport may be made direct by Brigades and other units or departments as follows :-
   (a) For transport from St. ELOI to NEUVILLE St. VAAST area application to XVIIIth Corps Light Railway Officer, who is on the telephone.
   (b) For transport forward of "ZIVVY" Station application to Traffic Officer ("TRAMWAYS") ZIVVY, who is also on the telephone.

P.T.O.

- 2 -

5. ORDNANCE.
   Stores for forward units will be sent up in bulk by Light Railway to LA TARGETTE Refilling point, whence units will draw.

6. ACKNOWLEDGE.

(signature)
Lieut. Colonel.
A.A. & Q.M.G., 52nd (Lowland) DIVISION.

Issued at

Copy to:-

    No. 1 A.D.C. for G.O.C.
        2 "G"
        3 155th Brigade.
        4 156th Brigade.
        5 157th Brigade.
        6 C.R.A.
        7 C.R.E.
        8 C.C., Signals.
        9 A.D.M.S.
       10 D.A.D.V.S.
       11 O.C., Divisional Train.
       12 D.A.D.O.S.
       13 A.P.M.
       14 Camp Commandant.
       15 1/5th Bn. R.I. Regt. (Pioneers)
       16 52nd M.G. Bn.
       17 52nd M.T. Coy. A.S.C.
       18 S.S.O.
       19 File.
       20) War Diary.
       21)
       22 W.S.O.
       23 Divisional Salvage Officer.

Appendix III
A Branch
52nd (Lowland) Division
B.L. 2/63.

C.R.A.	157th Brigade.	O.C., Divnl. Train.	M.G. Bn.
C.R.E.	A.D.M.S.	O.C., Signal Coy.	
155th Brigade.	D.A.D.V.S.	O.C., 5th R.I. Regt (P)	
156th Brigade.	D.A.D.O.S.	Camp Commandant.	

-------- * ---------

1. As a special concession a small daily allotment of leave for special cases has been made to 52nd Division.
   It is to be distinctly understood that leave is not generally open form the B.E.F. and all ranks should be warned before proceeding on leave not to talk whilst on the journey or at home in such a way as to create this impression, so as to avoid creating disappointment amongst the relatives of men in other formations.

2. (a) This leave will commence tomorrow, May 11th, and will be for 14 days, leave to count from day of embarkation.
   (b) The daily allotment to units is shown on attached Appendix.
   (c) Vacancies for officers will be in porportion to men.
   (d) The G.O.C. wishes preference given to men, who have been absent from England longest, and to really urgent cases of "private affairs".

3. The granting of this leave must not reduce the strength of sections in the front line below that of 1 leader and 6 men.

4. The personnel selected to proceed on leave should be drawn from the 10% personnel left out of action.

5. Should it be necessary in cases of an especially urgent nature to grant leave to an individual in the front line, he must first of all be replaced from the 10% personnel left out of action.

6. All warrants will be clearly marked "SPECIAL LEAVE" and the Corps authority quoted on each. These warrants will be sent to units from this office.

7. (a) Personnel proceeding on this leave should report to the R.T.O., MONT St. ELOI Station by 12 noon daily for conveyance by empty supply trains.
   (b) They will bring rations with them for the current day and the day following entrainment.
   (c) They will be paid at the entraining station by the Divisional Railhead Disbursing Officer (Captain Sir R.G.W. GRIERSON, Bart., 1/5th Bn. K.O.S.B.).
   (d) An officer, to be detailed till further notice by 155th Infantry Brigade, will be placed in charge of all leave parties from the Division and will be responsible for them till they embark on the leave boat.

8. Special attention of all ranks proceeding on leave is to be drawn to the various G.R.Os. on the subject published in "Extracts from G.R.Os., Parts I and II, A.Gs. and Q.M.Gs. Branch" (see index). It must be impressed on all men that neglect to observe these orders will inevitably lead to the return of the individual concerned to his unit, and possibly the cancellation of this special allotment of leave to the Division.

Headquarters.
10/5/18.

Lieut. Colonel.
A.A. & Q.M.G., 52nd (Lowland) Division.

APPENDIX.

1. The following is the allocation of leave. The numbers shown below may proceed daily.

2. Until Warrant Books are available Divisional Headquarters will issue Warrants specially marked to be completed by Units.

3. Formations and Units shown below must wire daily by 1800 the number of these warrants used for embarkation following day.
Wires should state numbers only and be in reply to BL 3/13.

4. Any warrants not used one day will be used following day, but those used for any one day must not exceed numbers shown below.

ALLOCATION.

Divisional Artillery 10

Divisional Engineers
including Signal Coy. 6

155th Infantry Brigade 18

156th Infantry Brigade 18

157th Infantry Brigade 18

Machine Gun. Battn. 4

5th R.I. (P) Rgt. 3

A.D.M.S. 4

Divnl. Train 2

Divisional Troops 2
                                   ──
                                   85
                                   ══

(Signed)
Lieut. Colonel,
A.A. & Q.M.G., 52nd (Lowland) Division.

Appendix IV
A Branch
52 Division

Headquarters,
C.R.A.   155th Inf. Bde.   D.A.D.V.S.   D.A.D.O.S.   A 68.
C.R.E.   156th Inf. Bde.   Div. Train.   Camp Commdt.
Sig. Coy.   157th Inf. Bde.   52nd M.G. Battn. "G"
A.D.M.S.   5th R.I.(P) Regt. A.P.M.

==

The G.O.C. has approved the following distinguishing marks for Infantry of the Division in accordance with Section XXII, "Training and Employment of Divisions, 1918" (S.S. 135)

(A) Colours.

 155th Infantry Brigade .... BLUE.
 156th Infantry Brigade .... RED.
 157th Infantry Brigade .... YELLOW.
 52nd Machine Gun Battalion .... PURPLE.
 5th Royal Irish (P) Regiment .... GREEN.

These colours to be used,
(i) For the distinguishing marks given in (B) below.
(ii) For painting the Divisional sign on vehicles.
(iii) For painting devices on the steel helmet.

Separate instructions on the painting of vehicles will be issued by O.C., 52nd Divisional Train who is in possession of the approved sign.

(B) DISTINGUISHING MARKS:
(a) Bands of coloured material (as above) approximately 1" wide worn round the right sleeve of the S.D. jacket below the elbow (in the case of officers with rank badges and service chevrons, on their sleeve immediately above the latter).

Senior Battalion in each Brigade .... one band.
Second Senior Battalion in each Brigade .... two bands.
Third Senior Battalion in each Brigade .... three bands.
Fourth Senior Battalion in each Brigade .... four bands.
Machine Gun Battalion and Pioneer Battalion .... one band.

(b) Light Trench Mortar Batteries will wear one broad band approximately 2" wide of their Brigade colours.

Indents for the material and paint required to be submitted to D.A.D.O.S. forthwith.

Headquarters.
11th May, 1918.

C.J. Mandell
Lieut. Colonel.
A.A. & Q.M.G., 52nd (Lowland) DIVISION.

Appendix V
A Branch
52 Division

C.R.A.	C.R.E.	O.C., Signals.	O.C., 5th R.I.R.(P).
155th Bde.	A.D.M.S.	O.C., Divnl. Train.	D.A.D.O.S.
156th Bde.	D.A.D.V.S.	O.C., Divnl. M.T. Coy.	Camp Commdt.
157th Bde.	A.P.M.	O.C., Divnl. M.G. Bn.	

----

1. It must be clearly understood that 1st Line and Train baggage vehicles will be the only means available, during Mobile operations for carrying stores and baggage.

2. During any such period the lorries of the Divnl. M.T. Coy. would be fully engaged in their normal duties of carrying ammunition and supplies between railhead and Divisional Refilling Points, and would not be available to assist units with their extra kit., blankets etc.

3. During movements under peace conditions from one area to another, such as this Division has done since landing in France, it is usually possible to supply a few lorries to carry extra kits to or from entraining stations, but it must be realised that these are either:-
   (a) Ammunition lorries of the Divnl. M.T. Coy. whose loads have been dumped, or
   (b) Lorries borrowed from outside the Division.
   Neither of these sources would be available during active operations.

4. The G.O.C. wishes all Unit Commanders to give attention to the subject of reduction of stores and kits to strictly Mobile Scale. Orders for the withdrawal of second blankets and horserugs will be issued later. Surplus Officers Kits will be sent to railhead and handed over to M.F.O.

5. With reference to para (1) above it must be understood that the overloading of baggage wagons will not be countenanced. Overloading will only result, during long marches, in the vehicles concerned breaking down and the probable loss of their entire contents.

Lieut. Colonel,
A.A. & Q.M.G., 52nd (Lowland) DIVISION.

11th May, 1918.

Copy to "G".

Appendix VI
A Branch
52nd Division

52nd (LOWLAND) DIVISION.

ADMINISTRATIVE CIRCULAR MEMORANDUM NO. 2.

12th May, 1918.

B A T H S.

1. Baths are now ready for use at the following places:-

PLACE.	SPRAYS.	CAPACITY.
(a) NEUVILLE St. VAAST.	12 Sprays	150 men per hour.
(b) BERTONVAL FARM.	17 Sprays	200 men per hour.
(c) St. ELOI.	11 Sprays	100 men per hour.

2. Application for their use will be sent direct to Officer i/c. Baths, 52nd Division, whose headquarters are at BERTONVAL FARM. Whenever possible 48 hours notice should be given.

3. Bathing parties of over 30 will be accompanied by an Officer. Men will bring their own towels and, for the present, their own soap.

4. Clean underclothing is not ready for immediate issue, but it is hoped to remedy this shortly.

Lieut.Colonel,
A. & Q.M.G., 52nd (Lowland) DIVISION.

12/5/18.

SECRET.

Appendix VII
A Branch
Copy No........
52nd Division

52nd (Lowland) DIVISION.

ADMINISTRATIVE INSTRUCTION No. AF 5.

13th MAY, 1919.

BURIAL ARRANGEMENTS.

1. The arrangements for the collecting and burying of the dead in the Area are as follows:-

2. Two Collecting Stations, marked by boards, have been established at
   (a) Junction of Light Railway and embankment - FERBUS VINY line - map location, FOOT HILL, 1/20,000, T.19.B.8.4.
   (b) Junction of MERSEY and NORRISON Valley and Brown Trench - map location, FOOT HILL 1/20,000, B.2.B.2.8.

3. The Unit is responsible for taking the bodies to the Collecting Stations named in para. 2, bodies are removed from there in early morning and late evening by the Burial Party.

4. The following are the Cemeteries in the Area. THELUS will normally be used except under exceptional circumstances.

   THELUS MILITARY CEMETERY. (C.B. 8)   31.b.A. 5.c.8.5.
   AUX RIETZ MILITARY CEMETERY.   51.b.A. 8.c.5.9.

5. Units will immediately inform Divisional Burial Officer, AUX RIETZ, when any bodies are being sent to the above Collecting Stations.

6. ACKNOWLEDGE.

                                        C.Hand
                                        Lieut. Colonel.
            A.A. & Q.M.G., 52nd (Lowland) DIVISION.

Issued at ....

Copy No. 1 A.C. for G.O.C.   23 ARM CO DT. THELUS.
        2   "G"   24) War Diary.
        3   155th Inf. Brigade.   25)
        4   156th Inf. Brigade.   26 File.
        5   157th Inf. Brigade.
        6   S.O.R.E., 52nd Division.
        7   C.R.E., 52nd Division.
        8   O.C., Signal Coy.
        9   A.D.M.S.
        10 D.A.D.V.S.
        11 O.C., Divisional Train.
        12 D.A.D.O.S.
        13 A.P.M.
        14 Camp Commandant.
        15 5th R.I. (P) Regt.
        16 52nd M.G. Battalion.
        17 52nd M.T. Coy.
        18 S.S.O., 52nd Division.
        19 Div. Burial Officer.
        20 Div. Water & Baths Officer.
        21 Div. Salvage Officer.
        22 D.R.D.O.

SECRET.   Copy No.........

Appendix VIII
A Branch
52 Division

52nd (Lowland) DIVISION.

ADMINISTRATIVE INSTRUCTION No. AF. 6.

15th May, 1918.

NOTES ON TRENCH WARFARE.

1. **RATIONS.**
    It is essential that whenever possible men in trenches should get at least one hot meal a day, and all units in front line will take immediate steps to provide this in future.

2. **COOKING.**
    (a) Where it is impossible to cook with ordinary fuel in the front or support trenches, Solidified Alcohol ("Tommy's Cooker") will be used. These cookers may be obtained through Brigade Supply Officers, but as their issue is limited they must be used as economically as possible, and nowhere where other forms of cooking can be done.
    (b) Wherever the nature of the ground and the approaches permit, two Travelling Kitchens (cookers) per battalion should be got up as far forward as possible in the trench area. These can be brought up by night and kept permanently in suitable emplacements e.g. in the shelter of a ruin, embankment, sunk road or specially dug emplacement.

3. **SOYERS STOVES.**
    Soyers stoves are being obtained at the rate of one per Company in the trenches.
    These will be sent up to ZIVVY DUMP as soon as they arrive, and Brigades will arrange for them to be conveyed forward to the vicinity of Company Headquarters, where they will be erected in suitable emplacements. They are to be used to provide hot water and hot drinks for the men.

4. **QUARTERMASTERS.**
    It is essential that Quartermasters should visit Battalion Headquarters every night to enquire whether the rations are reaching the men satisfactorily - similarly, Company Quartermaster Sergeants must go up to Company Headquarters each night with the rations.

5. **RUM.**
    (a) Until further notice a rum issue 3 times a week is sanctioned.
    In addition Brigades will hold a Reserve of one complete issue, which may be issued at the discretion of Brigadiers in case of emergency.
    (b) Rum will always be issued to the men and drunk by them in the present of an officer.

6. **WATER.**
    (a) Brigades will report any difficulties in the water situation at once, with suggestions for overcoming these.
    (b) Extra petrol tins may be drawn on application to Divisional Headquarters "Q". Where petrol tins are used and the carry is a long one, units should be in possession of two echelons of tins - one echelon full in the trenches, the other at the nearest water source, waiting to be brought up with the rations, or whenever the tins in front want renewing.
    (c) The YUKON PACK is very useful for carrying petrol tins full of water. Brigades will report whether they require any of these contrivances and if so how many (N.B. one man can carry 4 tins in a Yukon Pack).
    (d) Wherever it is desired to do so, one water cart a battalion may be taken up and emplaced in the trench area in the same way as cookers.

7. **CARE OF FEET.**
    All men should take off their boots and socks for a short period every 24 hours. This is easily organised by allowing a few

/men

men at a time to go to the Company 'dry dug-out'.

When the weather is cold or wet, socks should be changed at the same time, and men should hand rub each othersfeet.

8. DRYING ROOMS.

Each Company, if possible, should have a special dug-out told off as a 'Drying room'.

One man should be in charge, and one or more braziers and a few strands of wire, to hang wet clothing on, will ensure at least a proportion of wet garments being dried.

9. BATHS.

The Baths at NEUVILLE ST. VAAST (this office Administrative Circular Memorandum No. 2 of 12/5/18) are always at the services of any men who can be spared from the line.

10. ACKNOWLEDGE.

Issued at 4 p.m.   (Sd). C.G. MAUDE, Lieut. Col.
A.A. & Q.M.G., 52nd (Lowland) DIVISION.

SECRET.

Appendix IX

Copy No.
A Branch
52 Division

52nd (Lowland) Division.

ADMINISTRATIVE INSTRUCTION No. 7.

16th MAY, 1918.

With reference to G.R. 25/1/35 of 15/5/18.

1. No rations will be sent up to Battalions on the evening immediately preceding the Gas Discharge, as the Light Railway forward of ZIVVY will be earmarked for special traffic, and it is undesirable to send up abnormal transport (Horse Transport) that night.

2. The extra days rations now held by units will accordingly be consumed during the 24 hours following the Gas attack.

3. Should the attack be postponed, however, rations will be sent up from transport lines as usual, until the night of attack, and the extra days rations will be kept for the following day following the attack.

4. ACKNOWLEDGE.

Issued at 7 a.m.   (Sgd) C.G. MAUDE, Lieut. Colonel.

A.A. & Q.M.G., 52nd (Lowland) DIVISION.

Copy to :- 1 A.D.C. for G.O.C.
        2 "G"
        3 156th Inf. Brigade.
        4 157th Inf. Brigade.
        5 C. R. A.
        6 C. R. E.
        7 52nd Division M.G. Battn.
        8 S.S.O.
        9 File.
      10)
      11) War Diary.

52nd (Lowland) DIVISION.

Appendix X.
A Branch
52nd (Lowland) Division

ADMINISTRATIVE CIRCULAR MEMORANDUM No. 3.

17th MAY, 1918.

SALVAGE.

1. Captain C.G. DALY, 1/6th Battn. Highland Light Infantry (T.F.) has been appointed Divisional Salvage Officer. His Headquarters are at AUX RIETZ near Hoopers Dump. He will exercise a general supervision over all salvage operations in the Area, and will make every endeavour to increase the amount of salvage sent back by the Division.

2. Brigades in front line will be responsible for salving forward of Brigade Headquarters, and will form dumps at convenient points in their areas in consultation with the Divisional Salvage Officer. From these the Divisional Salvage Officer will collect the salved articles and arrange to convey them to the Divisional Salvage Dump.

3. All other units will be responsible for salvage in their immediate vicinity, and will forward it to the Divisional Salvage Dump.

4. The importance of salvage must be impressed on all units. It should be a point of honour for every party or individual coming back from the trenches to bring some articles of salvage with them — if only a few old tins.

5. O.C., Salvage Company will keep a strict account of all salvage taken over from Brigades and other units. These amounts will be published monthly in D.R.Os. and the G.O.C. will consider granting extra leave vacancies to those formations or units, who produce the best results.

6. Owing to the present shortage of paper it is most important to salve as much waste paper as possible.
Units will collect all wastepaper in sacks or sand-bags and forward it to the Divisional Salvage Officer. Papers marked "SECRET" or "CONFIDENTIAL", when no longer required, will not be included but will be burned.

7. Solder from old tins (bully beef, etc.) is badly wanted at the Base, so as to reduce the demands on Home authorities.
All old tins will be collected by units and sent to one of the following area commandants:—
    NEUVILLE St. VAAST,
    BERTONVAL FARM,
    MONT St. ELOY,
    VILLERS AU BOIS,
who run special kilns for melting solder.
The Divisional Salvage Officer will arrange to collect all solder from the above Area Commandants and send it in to Corps Salvage Officer. The amount obtained from each Division will be published monthly in Corps Orders.
The plan of one of these solder incinerators is being sent to Divisional Salvage Officer who will erect one at his salvage dump to deal with any excess of tins which he may from time to time find in his own dump.

Lieut. Colonel.
A.A. & Q.M.G., 52nd (Lowland) DIVISION.

17/5/18.

Appendix XI
A Branch
52nd (Lowland) Division

52nd (Lowland) DIVISION.

ADMINISTRATIVE CIRCULAR MEMORANDUM No. 4.

18th MAY, 1918.

BILLET IMPROVEMENTS.

1. The G.O.C. wishes no efforts to be spared to make the hut camps and billets occupied by units out of the trenches as comfortable as possible. He is convinced that every endeavour to house men under the best possible conditions will be amply repaid by the response, which is always forthcoming, when the men see that their welfare is being looked after, and by a corresponding improvement in discipline and morale.

2. With this end in view he wishes attention given to the following points; many others will doubtless occur to O.C., Units.
    (a) Cleanliness of huts and their surroundings. The fact that huts have in some cases been taken over in a dirty condition, is no reason why they should remain so.
    (b) Super-cleanliness of all cook-houses. Cooks should be the cleanest men in the Unit, not, as so frequently happens, the dirtiest. The canvas clothing allowed by regulation for troops should be obtained from D.A.D.O.S. at once, and in addition it is hoped to provide shortly washable aprons, which can be worn over the canvas suits.
    The rules for cook-houses circulated to Units by this Office on 15th instant, will be hung up in a conspicuous place and will be closely adhered to.
    (c) Each hut will have a refuse bin, clearly marked as such, in its immediate vicinity. These will be used for all rubbish from cigarette ends to old tins, and will be regularly cleared under Unit arrangements.
    (d) Provision of wire beds, or, where they already exist, their maintenance in good repair. Material to be obtained from C.R.E.
    (e) Provision of Officers and Sergeants' Messes, and dining rooms for the men. Endeavours are being made to obtain extra huts for the latter, where accommodation is crowded.
    Tables and forms for these messes, etc., will be made from material drawn from C.R.E.
    (f) Provision of Unit dry and wet canteens, and if possible recreation rooms. A unit wet canteen is much more easily supervised and is much better for the men than some of the squalid Estaminets which abound in this part of the World.
    (g) A liberal use of whitewash to smarten camps up generally.
    Whitewashed stones to be used to delimit camps, etc. Whitewash to be demanded through Supply Officers concerned.

3. The above list may be roughly divided into two headings :-
    (a) Billet Sanitation.
    (b) Billet Improvements.
    (a) Billet sanitation must be carried out by units themselves.
    (b) Billet Improvement is best carried out by parties working continuously under central control, until all improvements have been effected. Brigades under present conditions change too often to allow of continuous work, and consequently it has been decided to form a Divisional Billet Improvement Party: which will work under an officer to be detailed by C.R.E., until the required standard is reached.
    As soon as preliminary reconnaissance have been made by C.R.E., this party will be formed, and units will be asked to send men to join it at the rate of 2 or 3 carpenters or joiners per Battalion. It will be in the interests of all if the best men can be sent.

Lieut. Colonel.
A.A. & Q.M.G., 52nd (Lowland) DIVISION.

Appendix XII
A Branch
52 Division

DRIPPING.

All dripping should be returned by Units to B.S.O. on MONDAYS and THURSDAYS at Brigade Refilling Points. The dripping must be so packed that there is no chance of leakage, otherwise R.S.O. cannot accept it. This packing entails a certain amount of trouble for the Unit, the best method is to take a biscuit tin, cut the edges square, and turn them over so as to make a slight overlap. Then fill the tin and block the opening with a square of wood so cut as to wedge firmly into the top of the tin and prevent any leakage. The tin should be marked with paint showing number of Army to which the Division belongs and the name of the Unit.

B.S.Os. will keep a careful record of the reputed weights of each tin sent, and will return all dripping to S.O., M.T. Company at Railhead on TUESDAYS and FRIDAYS before 1200. A representative of the B.S.O. will hand over the dripping to the S.O., M.T. Company, who in turn hands it over to the R.S.O. who weighs it in the presence of S.O., M.T. Company, and forwards vouchers on the E.C. Canteen to S.S.O. for the money value of the dripping returned (A separate voucher for each unit). The S.S.O. will keep a record of these transactions and forward the vouchers above mentioned to the various Units.

The value of the dripping is 3½d per lb.

C.R.A.	157th Brigade.	Divnl. Train.	M.T.Coy.
C.R.E.	A.D.M.S.	S.S.O.	A.S.C.
155th Brigade.	D.A.D.V.S.	Signal Coy.	5th R.I.Regt.
156th Brigade.	Camp Commandant.	M.G. Battalion.	(P)

For information and necessary action.

E.F. Malton-Barrett

Headquarters.
20th May, 1918.
D.A.Q.M.G., 52nd (Lowland) DIVISION.
Major.

SECRET.
Appendix XIII
A Branch
52d Division
Copy No. 12

52nd (Lowland) DIVISION.

ADMINISTRATIVE INSTRUCTION No. AF. 8.

Reference 52nd Divisional Order No. 106 dated 21/5/18.

22nd MAY, 1918.

1. Refilling points commencing 25th instant will be as follows :-

   155th Brigade.   LEADLEY SIDING.   A.2.c.5.9.

   157th Brigade.   BLACKPOOL SIDING   A.7.d.4.8.
   (less one Battalion
   HANSON CAMP).

   One Battalion in   LEADLEY SIDING.   A.2.c.5.9.
   HANSON CAMP.

2. 157th Infantry Brigade should hand over 1 days rations which are being retained in the trenches for a special purpose. They should draw rations from present R.P. for consumption 25th on the afternoon of the 24th and on the morning of the 25th those for consumption 26th from the new R.P.

   155th Brigade should draw rations as usual on the 24th and take them up to the trenches that evening.

3. Reference paragraph 4 of above mentioned order, Soyers Stoves, Hot food containers and petrol tins are to be considered trench stores.
   Numbers of above mentioned stores taken over should be reported to this office not later than 24 hours after completion of relief.

4. 20 Lorries will report to 155th Infantry Brigade Headquarters at 7 p.m., 24th instant to take troops forward, these will be used on return journey by 157th Infantry Brigade. The lorries will continue working till the relief is completed.

5. Acknowledge.

                                                Lieut. Colonel.
                            A.A. & Q.M.G., 52nd (Lowland) DIVISION.

Issued at 7 P.M.

   Copy No. 1   A.D.C. for G.O.C.   7 M.G. Battalion.
          2   "G"   8 A.D.M.S.
          3   "A" and "Q"   9 D.A.D.V.S.
          4   155th Infantry Brigade.   10 Divnl. Train.
          5   157th Infantry Brigade.   11 S.S.O.
          6   C.R.E.   12) War Diary.
                                          13)
                                          14 File.

Appendix XIV
A Branch
52 (Lowland) Division

52nd (Lowland) DIVISION.

ADMINISTRATIVE CIRCULAR MEMORANDUM No. 5.

23rd MAY, 1918.

THE 1918 CHRISTMAS CARD.

1. The G.O.C. would like designs for a Divisional Christmas Card sent in by July 1st., as the process of getting the approved design censored and subsequently reproduced in large numbers is a lengthy one.

2. Please ask all competitors to produce their designs by the above date, and have them sent to Divisional Headquarters.

3. The G.O.C. has decided to offer a prize of £5 for the design which is finally selected.

C.Branch

Lieut. Colonel,
A.A. & Q.M.G., 52nd (Lowland) DIVISION.

LOCATION.	NATURE OF SUPPLY.	Formation or Unit responsible for picquoting

AUX RIETZ - GOODMAN (West of ARRAS - BETHUNE ROAD).

A.1.d.5.5.	294' Horse Troughs. (disconnected)	DIVISIONAL TRAIN.
A.2.c.2.3.	96' -do-	
A.8.c.2.6.	24' Horse Troughs.	
A.8.c.1.2.	400 gall. Tank. 3 - 2" S.P. 1 W.D.F.	
A.8.c.3.3.	16' Horse Troughs.	
A.8.c.2.3.	1600 gall. tank for Railway.	A.D.M.S.
A.8.c.4.4.	200 gall. tank.	
A.8.c.5.7.	24' Horse Troughs.	
A.8.c.1.9.	243' Horse Troughs.	

ECOIVRES - AUX RIETZ.

A.7.b.1.6.	72' Horse Troughs.	A.D.M.S.
A.7.b.1.4.	2" S.P.	

Appendix XVI
A Branch
52° Division

52nd (Lowland) DIVISION.
ADMINISTRATIVE CIRCULAR MEMORANDUM No. 7.
WATER SUPPLY.

1. **GENERAL.**

   (a) Piped systems of water supply have been developed over the greater part of the Divisional Area to meet all requirements for drinking, cooking and horse watering, and must not be used for any other purpose..

   (b) It must be realised that this piped supply is by no means inexhaustable and particular care is to be taken to impress on all ranks the necessity for economy of water from pipe lines. Disciplinary action is to be taken against any individual found wasting or improperly using these water sources.

   (c) A complete list of watering points in the Divisional Area is given in attached Appendix.

2. **MAINTENANCE.**

   The system of maintenance is as follows :-

   (a) Pipe lines in the Forward Area (East of a line running along the BETHUNE-ARRAS Road) are maintained by permanent Corps patrols on each System, with certain exceptions named below.

   (b) Pipe lines in the Rear Area (West of the above line) are patrolled by area patrols provided by Corps, and repaired by the 3rd Canadian Army Troop Coy., Headquarters, F.8.a.2.3. (Sheet 51C).

   (c) The following details of maintenance are given for information -

   ### FORWARD AREA.

   (i) AUX RIETZ, GOODMAN and ZIVY SYSTEMS.
   Pumps operated by 350th E. & M. Coy. R.E.
   Piped system maintained by XVIIIth Corps.
   Maintenance party of a Labour Coy. reports daily to the 3rd Canadian Army Troops Coy. MONT ST. ELOY, F.8.a.2.3.

   (ii) ECOIVRES SYSTEM.
   Pumps operated by 350th E. & M. Coy. R.E.
   Pipe system West of ARRAS-LENS Road maintained by XVIIIth Corps.
   Pipe system East of ARRAS-LENS Road maintained by 52nd DIVISION.
   Maintenance party of a Labour Coy. reports daily to the 3rd Canadian Army Troop Coy., F.8.a.2.3.

   (iii) VIMY BREWERY (T.19.d.9.5.) FOSSE 1 & LA CHAUDIERE SYSTEM (S.24.b.5.8.)
   Pumps operated by 3rd Canadian A.T. Coy.
   Systems maintained by Corps maintenance party billeted at LA CHAUDIERE, (S.18.c.8.2.)

   (iv) MONT FORET SYSTEM (T.16.c.9.3.)
   Operated and maintained by the 52nd DIVISION.

   (v) WILLERVAL TANKS (B.9.b.9.1.)
   Maintained by XVII th Corps.
   In case of any breakage of the mains, application for repair should be made to the maintenance patrol for the system concerned.
   In case of the breakdown of the Pumping Stations, notify C.R.E., who will communicate with 350th E. & M. Coy. R.E. at GOUY-SERVINS. W.5.b.7.6.

   ### REAR AREA.

   (vi) No. 3 PATROL AT VILLERS AU BOIS, No. 16 BILLET, X.19.a.8.3.
   Patrolling - VILLERS AU BOIS.
   LE PENDU.

P.T.O.

(vii) **No. 6 PATROL AT BOIS DES ALLEUX.**
Patrolling - ECOIVRES SYSTEM.

Should any prolonged enemy artillery activity develop, it is considered that no attempt should be made to maintain many of the Forward Mains, but that each forward plant should be operated as a local supply only. These forward plants are well protected with cover.

3. **WELLS.**

The following wells exist in Forward Area and C.R.E. is taking steps to improve the water supply from as many of them as possible so as to supplement the pipe supplies in case of breakdown.

RIGHT BRIGADE.

LOCATION. B.9.b.4.3.   B.3.d.8.2.
           B.3.d.4.1.   B.3.d.5.1.
           B.3.d.4.9.   B.3.d.5.2.
           B.1.d.95.20.   B.3.a.92.40.
           A.12.b.2.3.   B.1.b.5.5.

LEFT BRIGADE.

LOCATION. T.13.b.5.3.   T.13.b.6.8.
           S.30.a.7.7.   S.18.c.9.3.
           T.19.b.4.4.   S.24.d.9.4.
           T.19.b.2.6.   T.22.a.5.5.
           T.25.a.7.7.   T.25.a.2.5.

4. **ORGANISATION.**

The whole system, i.e. Mains, Horse Water Points, Reservoirs, etc., is patrolled by the XVIIIth Corps Water Patrols.
The Divisional Water Supply Officer, working under the Corps Water Supply Officer, has charge of all Water Points. He supervises the delivery of water and keeps a record of the consumption at each point (i.e. the number of carts filled and the number of horses watered) through the patrols and picquets.

5. **PICQUETS.**

(A) A picquet of one man will be found by formations and units over each water point or group of water points in accordance with attached Appendix.

(B) These picquets will be on duty from 6 a.m. to 9 p.m. daily, and will be responsible to the Corps patrols for the performance of the following duties :-

(I) **HORSE WATER POINTS.**

(a) The care and prevention of damage to all tanks, troughs, valves, fittings, etc., at the points.
(b) The keeping clean of all tanks, troughs, standings, approaches, drains, etc. and execution of all possible repairs, to any part of the enclosure, standing and approaches between watering periods.
(c) The control of   valves, which should be operated by the picquet.
(d) The prevention of wastage of water and wilful misuse of fixtures, e.g.
       The dipping of any water from storage tanks.
       The dipping of dixies into horse troughs.
       Washing in horse troughs.
       Bathing in horse troughs.

(e) The/

(e) The keeping of a record of the number of horse waterings per day.
(f) The prompt reporting of any irregularity on the part of Units using the water points either to the W.S.O. or to the Corps Water patrol concerned.
(g) The control of the entrance and exit of the enclosure, so as to ensure that -

All drivers dismount outside the enclosure.
All horses are led in through the "IN" entrance and along the troughing as far as possible.
All bits are removed from the horses mouths before watering - ordinarily bits should be removed before the horses are led into the enclosure.
All disorderly conduct - shouting or exciting of animals - is prevented, and no bunching at the entrance or exit is allowed.
When points are in much use, the watering time for each lot shall not be longer than five minutes.

(II) <u>WATER CART OR DRINKING WATER POINTS.</u>

(a) The general care and prevention of damage to all fixtures.
(b) The cleanliness of all tanks and of the point and its surroundings generally; also to carrying out of all possible repairs to any fixtures, roadways, approaches, drains, etc.
(c) To see that all water drawn is chlorinated in accordance with instructions.
(d) The prevention of wastage of water and wilful misuse, e.g.
The filling of water bottles from cart filling hose.
The drinking direct out of taps or hose.
The dipping of water from any tanks.
(e) The keeping of a record of the number of carts filled at the point.

(C) All picquets will be in possession of their duties in writing, and be well acquainted with them.

6. <u>GENERAL.</u>

No additions to the water supply system will be made without authority.

24th MAY, 1918.

Lieut. Colonel.
A.A. & Q.M.G., 52nd (Lowland) DIVISION.

APPENDIX.

LIST OF WATER POINTS IN 52nd DIVISIONAL AREA AND RESPONSIBILITY
FOR PICQUETING THEM.

LOCATION.	NATURE OF SUPPLY.	Formation or unit responsible for picqueting.
MONT FORET SYSTEM.		
T.15.b.7.6.	3 - 400 gall. Tanks - Taps.	
T.16.c.6.8.	3 - 400 gall. Tanks - Taps.	
T.16.c.8.3.	1 - 400 gall. Tank. - Taps.	LEFT
T.16.c.9.2.	2 - 400 gall. Tanks. - Taps.	BRIGADE.
T.16.d.2.7.	3 - 400 gall. Tanks - Taps.	
T.16.b.9.1.	3 - 400 gall. Tanks - Taps.	
GIVENCHY MAIN.		
S.12.b.9.6.	1 - W.B.F. (12 taps)	
S.12.b.8.6.	2 - 400 gall. Tanks - 6 Taps.	
T.8.a.0.0.	1 - 200 gall. Tank - Taps.	LEFT
T.8.a.7.8.	4 - 200 gall. Tanks - Taps.	BRIGADE.
T.8.d.5.6.	4 - 200 gall. Tanks - Taps.	
VIMY.		
S.18.c.9.3.	2 - 400 gall. Tanks (not in use) Taps - 2" S.P.)	LEFT
S.24.b.2.9.	2 - 200 gall. Tanks - Taps.	BRIGADE.
T.20.c.3.1.	2 - 400 gall. Tanks - Taps.	
GOODMAN MAIN.		
S.27.d.7.5.	1 - 100 gall. Tank.	
	1 - 400 gall. Tank.	
S.27.d.6.5.	2 - 50 gall. Tanks.	
	1 - 400 gall. Tank - Taps.	LEFT
S.28.c.5.4.	2 - 50 gall. Tanks.	BRIGADE.
	1 - 400 gall. Tank - Taps.	
S.28.d.3.5.	2 - 400 gall. Tanks - Taps.	
A.2.c.4.9.	144' Horse Troughs.	
A.2.c.3.9.	1 - 1600 gall. Tank.	
	6 - 400 gall. Tanks.	
	1 - 400 gall. chlor. Tank.	
	1 W.B.F., 6 S.P's.	RIGHT
A.2.a.9.1.	114' Horse Troughs.	BRIGADE.
	4 - 400 gall. Tanks (not in use)	
A.2.d.7.5.	1 - 3200 gall. Tank.	
	2 - 100 gall. Tanks.	
	3 - S.P's. for Ablution Shed.	
A.3.a.3.3.	2 - 400 gall. Tanks.	
A.5.b.6.8.	1 - 400 gall. Tank., 1 W.B.F.	
ZIVY MAIN.		
A.9.a.0.6.	1 - 3200 gall. Tank.	
	4 - 100 gall. Tank.	
	2 - S.P's at Ablution Tables.	
A.9.c.9.4.	114' Horse Troughs (not in use).	
A.9.d.5.8.	92' Horse Troughs (not in use).	RIGHT
A.10.a.4.6.	1 - 200 gall. Tank - Taps (disconnected)	BRIGADE.
A.10.a.6.7.	2 - 100 gall. Tanks. W.B.F., 2 S.P's.	
A.11.c.7.8.	6 - 400 gall. Tanks.	
	2 - 250 gall. chlor. Tanks.	
	1 - W.B.F., 3 S.P's.	

P.T.O.

- 2 -

LOCATION.	NATURE OF SUPPLY.	Formation or Unit responsible for picqueting
ZIVY MAIN (continued)		
A.11.b.5.8.	1 - 250 gall. Chlor. Tank. 1 - W.B.F., 1 S.P.	RIGHT
A.6.c.6.4.	1 - 400 gall. Tank.	BRIGADE.
AUX RIETZ - GOODMAN (West of ARRAS-BETHUNE Road).		
A.8.a.1.5.	35' Horse Troughs.	
A.8.a.3.6.	24' -do-	BRIGADE IN
A.8.a.3.8.	2 - 2" S.P's.	RESERVE.
A.8.b.0.5.	40' Horse Troughs.	
ECOIVRES - AUX RIETZ.		
F.3.a.8.2.	Chlor. Set and . W.B.F.	
F.8.b.3.1.	28' Horse Troughs.	
F.9.c.5.9.	1600 gall. tank (light Railway)	
F.2.a.2.8.	400 gall. tank. - taps.	
F.2.c.1.4.	400 gall. tank. - taps.	
F.4.d.1.2.	127' Horse Troughs.	
F.4.d.2.1.	2" S.P.	
F.10.b.2.7.	271' Horse Troughs.	
F.9.c.9.1.	72' -do-	
F.9.c.8.4.	Chlor. Set.	BRIGADE IN
F.9.c.95.55.	72' Horse Troughs.	RESERVE.
F.9.d.4.3.	2" S.P.	
F.10.d.1.4.	9000 gall. Tank.	
F.10.d.1.8.	72' Horse Troughs.	
F.11.b.1.2.	16' -do-	
F.11.b.6.3.	12' -do-	
F.12.a.1.4.	12' -do-	
F.12.a.2.1.	2 - 200 gall. Tanks. 2 - 2" S.P's.	
F.12.a.6.2.	46' Horse Troughs.	
F.12.a. 4.6.	1" Tap.	
F.12.a.3.6.	1" Tap.	
F.12.a.6.9.	1" Tap.	
A.7.d.7.6.	2 - 8000 gall. Tanks.	
A.7.d.9.2.	240' Horse Troughs (not in use)	
CARENCY.		
X.21.a.2.8.	24' Horse Troughs.	ROYAL
X.21.a.6.6.	2" S.P. - W.B.F.	ARTILLERY.
X.21.a.7.7.	80' Horse Troughs.	
ECOIVRES - AUXRIETZ.		
X.25.c.4.1.	192' Horse Troughs (disconnected)	
W.30.d.8.1.	50' -do-	ROYAL
E.6.b.8.8.	2" S.P. for Railway.	ARTILLERY.
F.7.b.3.9.	192' Horse Troughs.	
F.1.d.3.2.	Chlor. Set and 2 - 2" S.P's.	
VILLERS AU BOIS.		
X.19.d.1.9.	450 gall. Tank. Bath House.	ROYAL
W.24.b.10.0.	1 - 400 gall. Tank. 1 S.P.	ARTILLERY.
HILL 131 - ARRAS - BETHUNE ROAD.		
X.30.d.10.7.	210' Horse Troughs (not in use)	
F.6.a.1.1.	150' -do-	
S.19.d.5.4.	1" Tap.	DIVISIONAL
S.25.c.9.1.	150' Horse Troughs.	TRAIN.
S.26.c.5.6.	2 - 400 gall. Tanks.	
A.2.a.2.2.	90' Horse Troughs.	

Appendix XVII
A Branch
52 Division

No. A444/28.

Hdqtrs.,
R.A.   155th Inf. Bde.   D.A.D.V.S.   A.P.M.
R.E.   156th Inf. Bde.   Dvnl. Train.   Camp Comdt.
Sig. Coy.   157th Inf. Bde.   52nd M.G.Bn.   Dvn. Emp. Coy.
A.D.M.S.   5th R.I.Regt. (P).   D.A.D.O.S.

"A" RETURNS.

1. Attached is a List of the Returns required by "A" Branch. Attention is drawn to the following points:-

2. All Reinforcements of Brigades in the line will be sent to the Training Camps and it is suggested that arrangements be made by Brigades by which Return No. 2 is rendered direct to Divisional Headquarters by O.C., Training Camp.

3. Return No. 10 is not required from Units who render Return No. 8.

4. The Court Martial Officer will be allotted to Brigades for Courts Martial on Fridays, according to the applications received under Return No. 13.

5. The time allowed for compiling Returns at Divisional Headquarters is sufficient to do this if Returns are rendered correctly and by the hour stated. If a Return is complete except for one or two figures, it will simplify matters if it is forwarded to reach here up to time, the figures required to complete being sent by wire.

6. Nil Returns will be forwarded in all cases.

[signature]
Major,

D.H.Q.,
24/5/18.

D.A.A.G., 52nd (Lowland) DIVISION.

P. T. O.

LIST OF RETURNS TO BE RENDERED TO "A" BRANCH, 52nd (LOWLAND) DIVISION.

Serial No.	DESCRIPTION OF RETURN.	B.- WHO RENDERED.	Made up to.	B.H.Q.	Due Dwn.H.Qrs.
DAILY.					
1.	Casualties.	All Formations.	12 noon.		3 p.m.
2.	Reinforcements received.	All Formations.	12 noon.		3 p.m.
3.	Prisoners of War captured.	Inf. Bdes., M.G. & Pioneer Bns.	4 p.m.		4-30 p.m.
4.	Leave. (Numbers embarking following day.)	All Formations.			3 p.m.
WEEKLY.					
8.	Fighting Strength. (Increases and Decreases in Officers by names attached.)	Inf. Bdes., M.G. & Pioneer Bns.	12 noon, SATURDAYS.		9 a.m., SATURDAYS.
9.	Other Ranks struck off strength during week (if exceeding 20 per Unit.)	All Formations.	12 noon, SATURDAYS.		5 p.m., SATURDAYS.
10.	List of corrections to Nominal Roll of Officers.	All Formations.	12 noon, SATURDAYS.		3 p.m., SATURDAYS.
11.	Divisional Artillery Officers, showing increase or decrease.	Divnl. Artillery.	3 p.m., FRIDAYS.		9 p.m., FRIDAYS.
12.	Army Form B.213.	All Formations.			12 noon, SUNDAYS.
13.	Application for Court Martial Officer.	Inf. Bdes., and R.A.	12 noon, FRIDAYS.		9 a.m., THURSDAYS.
14.	Candidates for Temporary Commissions in Artillery and Infantry. (Nominal Rolls.)	All Formations.			12 noon, SATURDAYS.
MONTHLY.					
18.	Number of O.R.s without leave.	All Formations.	28th.		30th.
19.	Commissions permanent, Regular Army, R.A., Infantry and A.S.C. (A.F. B.15a.)	Inf. Bdes, R.A., and A.S.C.			12th.
20.	War Diary.	All Formations.			3rd.
21.	Recommendations for Command and Advancement on the Staff, in acc. with S.S.327. (A.F.W.3725.)	All Formations.			16th.
QUARTERLY.					
24.	Do. (As in No. 21.)	All Formations.			} 15th Jan, Apr, Jly. & Octr.
25.	Complete Nominal Roll of all Officers.	All Formations.			

Headquarters, 52nd (Lowland Division, 24/5/18.

Period.	Return.	Pro-forma No.	By whom rendered.	Made up to.	Due at Divl. H.Q.
Daily.	Gun Ammunition Return.		Div. Arty.	Noon.	Addressed to Corps reptd Divn. as soon after as possible.
Weekly.	Guns, Howitzers and their carriages captured.		Bdes.,R.A.,R.E., Pioneers, M.G.Bn.	Saturday.	6 p.m.) and wd
"	Machine Guns, Trench Mortars and war material captured.		—do—	Saturday.	6 p.m.) Saturday. until capture guns o have b
"	Claims for captured gun, etc.		—do—		ovacua
"	Location of Units.	D.	All Units.	When despatch ed to Base. possible after despatch
" ×	List of Units other than Divl.Units rationed showing locations.		Divl. Train.	Noon Sunday.	Noon Saturday.
"	Gun Ammunition.			Noon Sunday.	Noon Saturday.
"	S.A. Ammn. Grenades, Rockets, etc.	E.	Div. Arty.	Noon Sunday.	Addressed to Corps reptd Divn. 3 p.m.Sunday.
"	Requirements of Solidified Alcohol.	F.	Bdes.,R.A.,R.E. Pioneers, M.G.Bn.	Noon Sunday.	Noon Saturday.
"	Requirements of coal.		Divl. Train.	7 days ending Saturday.	9 a.m. Friday.
Fortnightly.	Transport Return. Remount Demand.		Divl. Train.	7 days ending Thursday.	10 a.m. Wednesday.
Monthly.	Claims paid by Div.Claims officer.	G.	All Units.	Saturday.	9 a.m. Saturday.
		H.	All units.	15th & last a.m. 15th & last	
"	Articles salved during month.		Divl.Claims Offr.	day of month. Last day f	day of month.
"Secret".	Return of Reserve Supplies.	I.	Divl.Salvage Offr. Divl.Train, Bdes. O.C.Hoopers Pump.	month.	9 a.m. 1st each month.
×	Hutting.		All Units.	—do—	—do—
				—do—	—do—
				—do—	—do—

× This cancels Location List called for in O.2.u 9/4/18

Appendix XVIII
A Branch
52nd Division

Copy No. ___

SECRET.

52nd (Lowland) DIVISION.

ADMINISTRATIVE INSTRUCTIONS No. AF 9.

25th MAY, 1918.

STRAGGLERS POSTS.

1. The personnel at present manning the Stragglers Posts, detailed in Appendix "A", will be relieved on 26th instant, as follows. They will in future be found by the parties detailed below.

2. Each Brigade will furnish 1 Sergeant, 2 N.C.Os. and 9 men, who will be permanently attached to A.P.M. They will report to A.P.M. at Traffic Control Post LES TILLEULS Cross-roads (close to Canadian Monument) at 1100 on 26th instant, rationed for 27th instant.

3. 155th Brigade will detail an officer to be in charge of 1st Line Stragglers Posts. He will be detached from all Battalion duties for this purpose.

4. Captain R. HUTCHISON, 1/7th Battn. Scottish Rifles, will be in charge of the Battle Stragglers Collecting Station at LES TILLEULS cross-roads. The Brigade in Reserve will detail 1 N.C.O. and 5 men to report to Captain HUTCHISON at this Station when the order to man it is received.

5. Captain M. MORRISON, 1/5th Battn. A. & S.H., will be in charge of the Prisoners of War Compound at AUX RIETZ corner. The Brigade in Reserve will detail 1 N.C.O. and 12 men to report to Captain MORRISON at the Compound when the order to man it is received.

6. The 156th Brigade will detail 1 Sergeant, 2 N.C.Os. and 9 men to man the 2nd Line Stragglers Posts. These parties must know their Posts but will not man them until orders to do so are received.

7. The Divisional Band will man the 3rd Line Stragglers Posts. They must know their posts, but will not man them until definite orders to do so are received.

8. The men mentioned in paras. 4, 5, 6 and 7 must be detailed and must know their way to their Posts by day and night. The A.P.M. will be informed of the Unit providing them, their billets and their names.

9. The Permanent Party detailed in para. 2 will be the only party which will permanently man their Posts.

10. ACKNOWLEDGE.

E. L. Moulton-Barrett
for D.A.A.G., 52nd (Lowland) DIVISION. Major.

Issued at 1 p.m.

Copy No. 1.	A.D.C. for G.O.C.	38.	5th R.I. Rgt. (P)
2.	"G"	39.	D.A.D.O.S.
3.	"Q"	40 to 44	A.D.M.S.
4 to 9.	155th Inf. Brigade.	45	A.D.V.S.
10 to 15	156th Inf. Brigade.	46	O.C. Div. Train.
16 to 21	157th Inf. Brigade.	47	S.S.O.
22 to 27	C.R.A.	48	Camp Commdt.
28 to 31	C.R.E.	49 to 60	A.P.M.
32	O.C. Sig. Coy.	61	XVIII Corps.
33 to 37	O.C. M.G. Battn.	62 & 63	Diary.
		64	File.

APPENDIX "A".
LIST OF BATTLE STRAGGLER POSTS, COLLECTING STATIONS, etc., PRESENTLY MANNED BY DIVISION.
52nd (LOWLAND) DIVISION.
(Ref. Map: LAROUIL. 1:20,000.)

No. and DESCRIPTION OF POST, etc.	MAP LOCATION.	Offrs.	Sgts.	Cpls.	Men.	REMARKS.
(1). PERMANENTLY MANNED.						
No. 1	S.11.d.4.2.	-	-	1	3	
" 2	S.18.c.9.2.	-	-	1	3	
" 3	S.24.b.4.5.	-	-	1	3	
" 4 1st Line Battle Stragglers Posts.	T.19.c.2.5.	1	-	1	3	
" 5	T.25.a.5.9.	-	-	1	3	
" 6	B. 1.b.3.3.	-	-	1	3	
" 7	B. 7.d.5.5.	-	-	1	3	
(b). Forward Battle Stragglers Collecting Station.	A.11.b.1.8.	2*	1	-	5	*Includes 1 Medical Officer. (b).Rear Battle Stragglers Collecting Station, F.10.b.1.1., will be manned by this party in event of withdrawal.
(c). Prisoners of War Cage.	A. 3.c.5.7.	1	1	-	5	
(2). SUPPLIED BY BRIGADE IN RESERVE.						
(a). Forward Battle Stragglers Collecting Station.	A.11.b.1.8.	-	-	1	5	
(b). Prisoners of War Cage.	A. 8.c.5.7.	-	-	1	12	
(3). SUPPLIED BY 155th BRIGADE.						
No. 1	A. 2.c.5.9.	1	-	1	3	
" 2 2nd Line Battle Stragglers Posts.	A. 8.a.4.7.	-	1	-	3	
" 3	A. 8.c.5.8.	-	1	-	5	
(4). SUPPLIED BY DVAL. H.Q.						
No. 1	A.25.a.5.5.	-	-	1	3	
" 2	F. 2.d.5.9.	-	-	1	3	
" 3 3rd Line Battle Stragglers Posts.	F. 9.a.0.8.	-	1	-	3	
" 4	F. 9.a.4.4.	-	1	-	3	
" 5	F.15.a.0.5.	-	-	1	3	

Appendix XIX
A Branch
52 Division

52nd (Lowland) DIVISION.

ADMINISTRATIVE CIRCULAR MEMORANDUM No. 8.

MOVEMENTS BY BUS OR LORRY.

As it may happen that the whole or part of the Division may be called upon to move at short notice by bus or lorry, the following points are circulated for the information and compliance of all concerned :-

1. **LOADS.**

    Maximum loads in full marching order are :-

    Bus............ 25 men.) one vehicle in every 10
    Lorry......... 25 men.) should, if possible, travel
    Seated Lorry.. 20 men.) empty, as a spare.

2. **MOVE.**

    The move is to be carried out in the same manner as a move by rail. The O.C. Unit or Formation will be in the position of O.C., Troops, and the senior A.S.C. Officer of the convoy will be in the position of the Technical Railway Staff.

3. **RESPONSIBILITIES.**

    (A) Responsibilities of O.C. Unit or Formation are
    (a) To have his men at the place selected for embussing at the correct time.
    (b) To see that the embussing and debussing is carried out expeditiously, and that the number of officers and men in any one vehicle is neither smaller nor greater than the O.C. Omnibus Company directs.
    (c) To see that officers are distributed among the vehicles forming the convoy, and that vehicles are not reserved for officers only.
    (d) To maintain discipline during the move.

    (B) Responsibilities of the A.S.C. officer i/c Busses or Lorries are :-
    (a) To ensure that the bus (or lorry) unit is at the embussing point selected.
    (b) To exercise control of the vehicles, including regulating the pace, stoppage for repairs, if necessary, and division of the convoy into convenient sections.

4. **EMBUSSING AND DEBUSSING.**

    The following points will be observed :-
    (a) Troops for embussing will be distributed along the roadside as follows :-
    FOR SEATED LORRIES. - Six groups (of 20 men each) per 80 yards of road space.
    FOR 3 TON LORRIES AND OMNIBUSES. - Six groups (of 25 men each) per 80 yards of road space.
    (b) Embussing will begin from the front of each Section of the convoy, unless the embussing point is of sufficient length to fill all vehicles of a section simultaneously.
    (c) The points for embussing and debussing will, if possible, be selected on a loop road, which will, for the time, be considered as a railway siding, and closed to all other traffic.
    If this is not possible, care must be taken to have the men drawn up on the right hand side of the road, when embussing, to avoid interference with other traffic.
    (d) The intervals of time at which the various groups to be convoyed are to reach embussing points will be carefully

/arranged

arranged between the representative of the formation or unit and the A.S.C. officer concerned.

(e) A Staff Officer of the Brigade or a responsible officer from each Battalion will invariably be present to superintend both embussing and debussing.

(f) As soon as the signal to debus is given, all troops will immediately get out and clear off the road to the right. As soon as the troops are clear, the whole bus column will move off. When the bus column has cleared the road the troops will fall in on it. Troops will not fall in or move on the road until the bus column has moved off. O.C. Bus Column will detail a motor cyclist to report to all O.C. Battalions, etc. as soon as the last vehicle has moved off.

5. BAGGAGE.

Baggage will not be taken on the bus column with the exception of a certain number of 'camp kettles', if a halt for tea is to be made en route. Advance parties, officers kits and cooking apparatus will, whenever possible be sent on ahead to the new destination in other lorries.

6. GUIDES.

Careful arrangements must be made for guides from the debussing point to billets or camps, not only for actual units but for parties of stragglers.

25th MAY, 1918.

Lieut. Colonel,
A.A. & Q.M.G., 52nd (Lowland) DIVISION.

17

Vol 3

War Diary
A Branch
52nd (Lowland) Division

Volume XXXVI

1 – 30th June. 1918

WAR DIARY or INTELLIGENCE SUMMARY

Army Form C. 2118.

Vol XXXVI 1/30 June 1918

a Brouck (Sokolwski)/Brown

Place	Date	Hour	Summary of Events and Information	Remarks and references to Appendices
Ac Q			JUNE 1918	
	1		Accumulator instruction A.C.I. attached (april & may 3rd)	app I app II
	3		A summary of rumours received 157th Bde returned 156th Bde in right sector	
	5		CPs proceed to reconn car for CPR	
	6		Addendum issued to admin Instruction No A 710 at reverse from admin Instruction 107 issued of reinforcements	app III app IV
	7		CPs report that CPs is there a box car	app V
	8		A's summary 8 & 2 issued	
	9		Div ammunu. [illegible] other were to Sr & O.C. went admin Gen. 107 issued at Bar Carlton went P. 120— admin Instruction A.T.R.12 ref move 155th Bde reinforcements 156th Bde to Sect 157th Bde CPs requested to issue Box Car (original comm) to Signals	app VI app VII
	11/ 2/10		[struck out] admin instruction A 713. at redistribution of Artillery Ammunition	app VIII
	11.		15-5 A.P.M. released by [illegible]	

WAR DIARY
INTELLIGENCE SUMMARY

Army Form C. 2118.

52 (New) Division VI XX II 13 June 1918 a Ismalia

Place	Date	Hour	Summary of Events and Information	Remarks and references to Appendices
ACD	12		Morning distribution of Clean Clothes to be held in line to cover effects by Mustard Gas arrange. Each Bn + Cy HQ in the line 4 suits each, " Support 8 " " Reserve 6/73 ref Peek Transport moved Admin Instruction 6/73 ref Peek Transport moved	A/F IV
	13		4 Instructions + 4 reinforcements + 4 Gun Flumettes trailers + G admin aid a.c. + not Practices of HD in camp now HD on the line in [Question] places admin Circular 36/15 of Div Question Course now	A/F V A/F VI A/F VII
	14		100 Vickers Parts received - 48 Lewis Rifle + 6 belts (Hotwens Pt auslees) 7 own allotment B/2/84 recipt — 38 admin air.9 Reinforcement sent 8 Bicycles to Bn not available circulars (9 HA)	A/F VIII A/F IX
	15		Admin Circ 16 ref Sanitation course	
	17		Cable advice that in answer to [?] pricing Gas in a response these authorities must be consulted so + additional Premier to repeat. S-Cleft Button received last wk at Div Dept was Brigadier S.A.J.	

WAR DIARY or INTELLIGENCE SUMMARY

Army Form C. 2118.

XXXVI

JUNE 1918   A Branch 52 (Ln) Dn   p 2

Place	Date	Hour	Summary of Events and Information	Remarks and references to Appendices
ACD	17		ictinity received statistics / blanket forms of proa	XXXIV
			Rear Hours Bh 2/83 issued showing 60 - Rining's Range to 97	
			Admin Circ R 077 of Dn. Chief of Staff Difficiencies	XV/45
			Admin Instruct R 0.14 ref relief in 19th of 157th Bde by 151st Bde issued	XVI/45
			Admin Circ R 078 ref Div Ammunition Shops issued	XVII/45
	18		Cyfa begged reductions of Bicycles of following Dien supply	
			Div9 Hors from 9 to 5	
			Bd 9 Am - 33 18 } No reduction	
			" " Cy " - 33 65 } selection to 24	
			BG R.F.A. - 7 5 } 24 sigs/M cyclorderlies	
			151st Bde retained 157 Bde in light	previously zero
				No reduction
	20		Addendum issued to Admin Circ R 70 ref acceptations	XVIII/45
			Admin Circ R 79 issued ref Recreations against P 40	XIX/45
			Cyfa advised that no complete unit of armoured lorries can at present	
			be an nonproclearies	Loco RS to usually round of 1400 wy M

Army Form C. 2118.

WAR DIARY
or
INTELLIGENCE SUMMARY.
(Erase heading not required.)

JUNE 1918   VI XXXVI A.D.M.S. (?) (12(E.A.) Div

Place	Date	Hour	Summary of Events and Information	Remarks and references to Appendices
Aff	20		A. Summary R.O.3 issued	9/H xx
	21		Admin Circ? R.O.20 issue of glasses y [illegible] inhabitant	9/H xxI
			96 Rifle grenade dischargers issued. 8 to each Bn	
	22		Admin Circ? R.O.21 issue of Iron	9/H xxII
	23		Admin Instr? R.O.75 issue of Reserve Rations	9/H xxIII
	24			
	25		30 DLOR vans received for Divn	
	26		Admin Circ? R.121 issue of Gdn? Horses	9/H xxIV
			Admin Instr? R.O.76 issue of [illegible] here of 55 K of B, 8th S R	9/H xxV
			5 # of PH & 34 Divn (originally about to move to 30 Divn)	
	27		Admin Instr? R.76 (corrigendum) issued	9/H xxVI
			Admin Instr? R.77 issued re Relief of 156 Bde by 157 Bde in 28—	9/H xxVII
	29		Cabs informed that issue of Water Cart & [illegible] not [illegible]	9/H xxVIII
			[illegible] team in consequence	
			157 Bde relieved 156 Bde in Left Sector	

Instructions regarding War Diaries and Intelligence Summaries are contained in F. S. Regs., Part II. and the Staff Manual respectively. Title pages will be prepared in manuscript.

WAR DIARY
or
INTELLIGENCE SUMMARY.
(*Erase heading not required.*)

Army Form C. 2118.

Vol XXXV

JUNE 1918 — A Branch 52 (Lowland) Divn — 105

Place	Date	Hour	Summary of Events and Information	Remarks and references to Appendices
ACQ	29		authority asked for issue of 2 ~~extra stretchers~~ to each Bde & to DAC owing to scattered nature of Bttys	
			Rum not to be issued on order of Corps Cmdr only, on recommendation of DDMS except for men in trenches & Arty in Action (G.R.O. 4?49 - A.R.O. 5?76)	
			17th Northd Fusiliers (N.E.Rly P.) to be equipped as Pioneers & to be this Div P. Bn.	
	30		1/5th Bn K.O.S.B., 1/8th Bn Scottish Rifles & 1/5th Bn A & S H left the Divn for the 34th Divn. These Bns had served with the Divn, the first two since mobilisation the third since April 1915. This is first loss to Divn reducing Bdes to strength of 3 Bns each.	
			Suggested that 40 suits of Dungarees be issued to each D.T.M.O. in order to save clothing of personnel in trench mortar pits.	

(A7092). Wt. W12839/M1293. 750,000. 1/17. D. D. & L., Ltd. Forms/C.2118/14.

Army Form C. 2118.

Vol LXXXVI

1st June
Aubigny
St Vaast
Page 6

WAR DIARY
or
INTELLIGENCE SUMMARY.
(Erase heading not required.)

Instructions regarding War Diaries and Intelligence Summaries are contained in F. S. Regs., Part II. and the Staff Manual respectively. Title pages will be prepared in manuscript.

Place	Date	Hour	Summary of Events and Information	Remarks and references to Appendices
			June 1918	
			Appointments —	
			Capt. T. A. Hill M.C. Wounds 1st Bn. to the Staff as Staff Captain 15th Infantry Brigade dated 27/5/18	
			Brigadier General T. Forbes-Robertson to Command 15th Infantry Brigade dated 19/6/18.	

VOLUME XXXVI.

WAR DIARY
or
INTELLIGENCE SUMMARY.

(Erase heading not required.)

1/30th JUNE, 1918. Army Form C. 2118.

"A" BRANCH, 52nd (Lowland) DIVISION.

page. 7

Summary of Events and Information

STRENGTH OF DIVISION.
WEEK ENDING - 29/7/18.

	Offrs.	Other Ranks.
Divisional Troops.	42	705
Divnl. Artillery.	95	2108
Divnl. Engineers.	35	880
155th Infantry Brigade.	125	2403
156th --do--	135	2606
157th --do--	127	2732
52nd Machine Gun Battalion.	44	934
17th Bn. Northumberland Fus.	35	861
R. A. M. C.	21	705
TOTAL.	659	13934

INFANTRY BRIGADES - REINFORCEMENTS
RECEIVED FOR MONTH OF JUNE.

Week ending.	Offrs.	O. R.
9/6/18.	8	181
16/6/18.	5	325
23/6/18.	2	189
30/6/18.	12	516
TOTAL.	25	1211

CASUALTIES - INFANTRY BRIGADES.

	Killed.		Wounded.		Missing.		Sick.	
Week ending.	Offrs.	O.R.	Offrs.	O.R.	Offrs.	O.R.	Offrs.	O.R.
9/6/18.	---	10	---	46	---	1	8	387
16/6/18.	---	8	1	24	---	---	25	503
23/6/18.	---	1	1	38	---	---	22	732
30/6/18.	---	---	---	14	---	---	10	237
TOTAL.	---	19	1	122	---	1	65	1859

First Army Pro Forma No. 3.

52nd (Lowland) DIVISION.

Strength Return made up to 12 noon Saturday, 29th June, 1918.

UNIT.	A. Strength Return excluding attached.		B. Not present with the unit and not at the disposal of C.O. (included in Column A).		A. minus B. Available Fighting Strength (including personnel of Battalion Transport and Quartermaster's Stores).	
	Officers.	O.R.	Officers.	O.R.	Officers.	O.R.
155th Inf. Brigade.						
1/4th Bn. R.S.F.	41	729	23	180	18	549
1/5th Bn. R.S.F.	41	868	15	169	26	699
1/4th Bn. K.O.S.B.	43	806	16	175	27	631
TOTAL.	125	2403	54	524	71	1879
156th Inf. Brigade.						
1/4th Bn. R. Scots.	45	865	13	158	32	707
1/7th Bn. R. Scots.	44	870	16	157	28	713
1/7th Bn. S. Rifles.	46	871	15	166	31	705
TOTAL.	135	2606	44	481	91	2125
157th Inf. Brigade.						
1/5th Bn. H.L.I.	44	958	12	148	32	810
1/6th Bn. H.L.I.	43	890	15	139	28	751
1/7th Bn. H.L.I.	40	884	13	158	27	726
TOTAL.	127	2732	40	445	87	2287
17th Bn. Northumberland Fus. (N.E.R.P.)	35	861	9	22	26	839
GRAND TOTAL.	422	8602	147	1472	275	7130
52nd Machine Gun Battalion.	44	934	6	70	38	864
TOTALS						

First Army Pro Forma No. 3—*continued.*

DETAILS OF OFFICERS "TAKEN ON" OR "STRUCK OFF" STRENGTH.

UNIT.	Rank.	Name.	Initials.	Remarks.

'A' BRANCH.
WAR DIARY.
52nd DIVISION.

APPENDIX

52nd (Lowland) DIVISION - INFANTRY BRIGADES.

ABSTRACT OF STRENGTH RETURN. - COLUMN 'B'. WEEK ENDING 29/6/18.

UNIT.	Courses.		Sick.		Leave.		Pioneers.		Bde. Employ.		Divnl. Employ.		Extra Regtl. employ.		TOTAL.	
	O.	O.R.	O.	O.R.	O.	O.R.	O.	O.R.	O.	O.R.	O.	O.R.	O.	O.R.	O.	O.R.
1/4th Bn. R.S.F.	3	26	1	38	5	46		6	2	27	1	29		8	23	180
1/5th Bn. R.S.F.	3	21	6	10	3	52	1	29	2	26	1	26	1	5	15	169
1/4th Bn. K.O.S.B.	4	41	8	11	3	51		31		21		20			16	175
	10	88	25	59	11	149	1	66	4	74	2	75	1	13	54	524
1/4th Bn. R. Scots.	4	23	4	22	2	52		23	1	16	2	20		2	13	158
1/7th Bn. -do-	5	16	2	8	3	64	1	25	3	17	2	25		2	16	157
1/7th Bn. S. Rifles	6	32	3	22	2	52	1	22	2	22	1	16			15	166
	15	71	9	52	7	168	2	70	6	55	5	61		4	44	481
1/5th Bn. H.L.I.	3	22	3	16	2	53	1	23	2	17	1	15		2	12	148
1/6th Bn. H.L.I.	4	22	1	12	5	45		21	3	15	2	21		3	15	139
1/7th Bn. H.L.I.	3	23	2	27	3	49	1	18	2	23	2	15		3	13	158
	10	67	6	55	10	147	2	62	7	55	5	51		8	40	445
GRAND TOTAL.	35	226	40	166	28	464	5	198	17	184	12	187	1	25	138	1450

A Branch Diary June 1918

SECRET.   COPY No. 12

52nd (Lowland) DIVISION.

ADMINISTRATIVE INSTRUCTION No. AF. 11.

with reference to 52nd Divisional Order No. 108.

1st JUNE, 1918.

1. **REFILLING POINTS.**

   From 3rd June inclusive as follows :-

   157th Infantry Brigade.   LEADLEY SIDING A.2.c.5.9.

   156th Infantry Brigade.   BLACKPOOL SIDING. A.7.d.4.8.

2. **LORRIES.**

   18 Lorries will report to Reserve Brigade Headquarters, St. ELOY at 9 a.m. June 2nd, and will be available for taking troops up to NEUVILLE ST. VAAST Area, and bringing back troops to Reserve Area, until relief is complete.

3. **BILLET IMPROVEMENTS.**

   156th Infantry Brigade will take over and continue the billet improvement work now being undertaken by 157th Infantry Brigade.

4. **DISCIPLINE.**

   The same restrictions as are now in force for 157th Infantry Brigade as regards men not leaving the Divisional Area, particularly with reference to ECOIVRES and other villages in 51st Divisional Area (i.e. all area South of an E. and W. line through Cross Roads F.14.b.10.6.) will hold good for 156th Infantry Brigade. This includes finding picquets in relief of those now found by 157th Infantry Brigade.

   Trouble has been caused in the past by men disregarding these orders on the first day of arrival in ST. ELOY area, and then pleading ignorance of the orders with reference to bounds. G.O.C., 156th Infantry Brigade will take most careful steps to ensure that all ranks under his command are made acquainted with these orders immediately they arrive in billets, and before they are dismissed from parade. No excuse will be accepted in the cases of men found out of bounds; any such offences are to be severely punished, and the leave of the offenders stopped.

5. **ACKNOWLEDGE.**

                                                    C.H.Mandl
                                                    Lieut. Colonel.
                                A.A. & Q.M.G., 52nd (Lowland) DIVISION.

Issued at..........

   Copy No. 1   A.D.C. for G.O.C.   8   D.A.D.V.S.
           2   "G"   9   Divnl. Train.
           3   155th Infantry Brigade.   10   S.S.O.
           4   157th Infantry Brigade.   11) War Diary.
           5   C.R.E.   12)
           6   52nd M.G. Battalion.   13   File.
           7   A.D.M.S.

A Branch Diary, June 1918
App II

52nd (Lowland) DIVISION.

"A" SUMMARY. No. 1. — 1st JUNE, 1918.

1. REINFORCEMENTS.
(a) Reinforcements are directed straight to Units except for the two Infantry Brigades in the line, whose reinforcements are sent to the Detail Camps at Villers Aux Bois and Rispin.
(b) The report of arrival of reinforcements should be rendered to Divisional Headquarters by O.C. these Camps for all Units of the Brigades occupying them, a copy being sent to Brigades.
(c) All officer reinforcements will be repeated by name.
(d) Brigades will also render to Divisional Headquarters returns of any reinforcements who may report direct to units, but care must be taken to avoid duplication, i.e. that those once reported from Detail Camps are not again reported from Units.
(e) The term "Reinforcement" includes all who are rejoining after having been struck off the strength of their Unit. Officers returning from Hospital who have never left this Country and who consequently have never been struck off strength, are not reinforcements. Similarly men who have not been 7 days in the Divisional Ambulances, including the Divisional Rest Camp, are still on strength and are not reinforcements.

2. DISCIPLINE:
Charge Reports. Attention is drawn to G.R.O. No. 2548 which lays down that if a charge submitted by an A.P.M. has been dismissed by the accused's C.O., the latter should state when returning the charge report, in what respects the evidence of the M.P. has been found not to substantiate the charge.

3. COURTS MARTIAL:
(a) The insertion of lengthy and detailed charges on page 2 of A.F. A 3, which was insisted on in EGYPT, is not the practice here. Skeleton charges only are required, such as :-
(1) "When on active service, Drunkenness."
(2) "When on active service, Sleeping at his Post."
(3) "When on active service, Striking his Superior Officer."
The charge must clearly indicate the type of offence, the instance must on course be fully proved in Court.
(b) Great care must be exercised in framing additional charges in cases where Drunkenness is one of the offences.
M.M.L. page 22, para. 31, should be studied in all cases where a second charge is added to one of Drunkenness.

4. BURIAL.
The following instructions regarding transport, etc., of bodies for burial are issued for information.
(a) Mortuaries have been placed at,
(i) Peggy Dump. T.19.b.8.4.
(ii) Morrison or Mersey Dump. B.2.b.2.6.
These mortuaries are marked as such and bodies must be placed on the actual plot marked. If this is not done there is a possibility of the burial party failing to locate them.
(b) The Mortuaries are visited every evening and bodies are removed by empty ration trains.
(c) Bodies should be properly tied up in blankets, not in ground sheets, they should in every case have securely attached a slip of paper giving regimental number, rank, name, unit and cause of death.
(d) A wire should be sent to Divisional Burial Officer informing him when bodies are being sent to the dumps.

P.T.O.

5. RETURNS.
   (a) Strength Returns. (Infantry Units.)
   Units will continue to pay special attention to Column "B" of the Weekly Strength Return. Herewith are a supply of abstracts which will be used with the return. In particular the details entered in columns for those in Brigade and Divisional Employment should be closely scrutinised. To assist in this a complete list of those in Divisional Employment is at present being compiled.
   (b) A.F. B 213.
   Copies of the statistical sheet of A.F. B 213 is required from all units, that is copy of the sheets showing the Strength and the Reinforcement Demands.
   This reinforcement demand must be carefully compiled showing personnel required to complete. This is not at present done by all Units.
   (c) General.
   The following alterations will be made on List of "A" Returns issued on 24/5/18.

   Already notified.
   (i)   No. 4 is cancelled.
   (ii) Add No. 15. Return of personnel of the Division Missing and estimated to be Prisoners of War: To be rendered by all formations; made up to 0800 Sunday; due Divisional Headquarters 1800 Sundays.
   Additional.
   (iii) Return No. 13. (Application for Court Martial Officer) must reach Divisional Headquarters on Wednesday.

                                            Lieut. Colonel.
                            A.A. & Q.M.G., 52nd (Lowland) DIVISION.

"A" Form.
MESSAGES AND SIGNALS.

Army Form C. 2121.
(In pads of 100.)

TO	WELV	WEJO	ADMS	WEVO
	WEKU	G	APM	
	WEQU	WEBO	SSO WEJO	

Sender's Number.	Day of Month.	In reply to Number.	AAA
Q 824	6		

Reference	addendum	to	AF 10
of	todays	date	further
2	cases	of	PM
and	it	cases	biscuits
authorised	to	be	held
by	WEVO	aaa	Acknowledge

From Place: PEQO

(1a) 07 Moulton Rew

SECRET. Copy No....12....

52nd (Lowland) Division.

ADDENDUM to ADMINISTRATIVE INSTRUCTION No. A.F.10.

6th June, 1918.

1. The 52nd Machine Gun Battalion are authorised to keep on hand -

    15 cases of P.M.
    29 cases of Biscuits.

        or

    720 rations of P.M.
    725 rations of Biscuits.

2. The positions in which these rations are placed will be reported to this office and the co-ordinates will then be reported to all concerned so that they will not be duplicated in returns.

3. The Machine Gun Battalion is responsible for the safeguarding and inspection of these rations.

4. This re-organisation should be carried out forthwith.

5. ACKNOWLEDGE.

Issued at....6..p.m....

                    E. F. Moulton-Barrett Major
                    for Lieut.Colonel.
                  A.A. & Q.M.G. 52nd (Lowland) DIVISI

Copy to - No.1. 155th Brigade.   7. A.D.M.S.
          2. 156th Brigade.   8. A.P.M.
          3. 157th Brigade.   9. S.S.O.
          4. Divl. Train.   10. 52nd M.G. Battn.
          5. "G"   11. File.
          6. C.R.E.   12.) War Diary.
                              13.)

"A" Branch War Diary June 1918
App IV

52nd. (Lowland) DIVISION.

ADMINISTRATIVE CIRCULAR MEMORANDUM No. 9.

5th JUNE, 1918.

FIELD PUNISHMENT.

1. A Divisional Field Punishment Compound has been established at AUX RIETZ Caves. (Army Map B, A.S.C...C.)

2. From 10th. inst. inclusive all units of the Division, with the exception of those in the Trenches, will send their Field Punishment prisoners to this Compound. Field punishment prisoners of units in the line will be with their units.

3. This Compound will be frequently inspected by the A.P.M., who will ensure that the regulations for Field Punishment prisoners laid down in S.S.414, page 30, Sec. 3 (Regulations for the use of the Provost Marshal's Branch) are strictly adhered to.

4. The Staff for the Field Punishment Compound will be found as follows:
   The permanent Staff of the F.P.Compound will be detailed by Brigades in accordance with instructions from this Office. Strength will be as follows:
      1 Sergt., 1 Corpl., 2 L/Corpls., 6 men.
   These N.C.O's. and men will have some provost experience and are to be strict disciplinarians.
   The Brigade in Reserve will detail a Guard of the undermentioned strength to report to N.C.O. i/c Compound at 9 a.m. daily.
      1 Sergt., 1 L/Corpl., 6 men.

5. These field punishment prisoners will work for 8 hours daily at tasks to be allotted by O.C., 17th Northumberland Fusiliers.

6. All prisoners sent to the Compound will arrive there between the hours of 2 and 4 p.m. They will bring full equipment and unexpended portion of rations for day of admission, and also rations for day following that of admission.

7. A receipt will be obtained by the N.C.O. i/c of the escort from the N.C.O. i/c of the Field Punishment Compound for all Prisoners admitted.

8. The following documents will accompany each prisoner sent to the Compound:
      Medical Officer's certificate.
      Form Transfer "B".
      Pro forma (as shown on reverse).

   These proformas will be retained by the N.C.O. i/c of the Compound, who will keep them in a special file ready for production to an inspecting officer.

C.Y.Mander
Lieut. Colonel,

A.A. & Q.M.G., 52nd (Lowland) DIVISION.

52nd (Lowland) DIVISION.

"A" SUMMARY. No. 2.   8th JUNE, 1918.

1. **RETURNS.**
   (a) No. 12, A.F. B.213. Where possible the nature of the casualty should be stated on A.F. B.213 i.e. whether caused by bullet, shell, gas, etc.
   The particulars showing those proceeding on leave and date, and those returning from leave should be shown on A.F. B.213.
   (b) No. 18, Number of O.R. without leave. In rendering this monthly leave return, approximately correct figures showing the numbers without leave for 35 and 36 months should always be added for G.O.C's information.

2. **ARMY FORMS.**
   Every effort should be made to secure for use the printed forms issued by Stationery Office. In some cases typewritten forms have been returned as not acceptable.
   A.F. W.3723. Care must be taken to leave space for the remarks of the G.O.C., Division, in the bottom right hand corner of the form, in the column for "Remarks of Reporting Officer". The space on left hand "Higher Commander's Remarks" is reserved for Corps Commander's remarks.
   A.F. W.3436. This form is forwarded by O.C., Special Hospital, to be completed and returned by O.C., Unit. It is used in cases where a report is required regarding an Officer or man who without visible wound becomes non-effective from physical conditions claimed or presumed to have originated from effects of British or Enemy weapons in action. This form should be returned direct to the Special Hospital (see note 4 on Form), except in cases where in the opinion of the O.C. unit the circumstances are such as to render further enquiry desirable. In the latter case papers should be returned to Army Headquarters.

3. **F.G.C.M.**
   In intricate cases on which Courts Martial Officer is to act as a member of the Court, a copy of the Summary of Evidence should be forwarded to him direct so as to reach him if possible 24 hours before the trial.

4. **PRISONERS.**
   Attention is drawn to extracts from G.R.O's. (A.G.Branch), Part I, pages 92 and 94, G.R.O's. 1292, 1300 and 1807. In all cases where prisoners are committed to prison, 24 hours notice should be given to A.P.M. If this notice is not given, R.T.O. may be unable to arrange escort and the escort from the unit will then have to take prisoner to Base.

5. **SOLDIERS ACCUSED OF DRUNKENNESS.**
   Attention is drawn to D.R.O. No. 11 of 1918 which is repeated for information.
   "Whenever possible medical evidence should be obtained in the case of a soldier accused of drunkenness. Attention is however called to K.R. 478 which lays down that a soldier suspected of being drunk is not to be put through drill or tested for the purpose of ascertaining his condition."

6. **TRAFFIC CONTROL.**
   When traffic control personnel become casualties A.P.M. will inform the unit concerned direct and will at same time apply for a replacement.

7. /-   P. T. O.

(2).

7. F.P. COMPOUND.
Casualties amongst permanent staff at F.P. Compound will be reported and replacements asked for in a similar manner as above.

8. WAR SAVINGS CERTIFICATES.
Every effort should be made to assist in the sale of War Savings Certificates. On application being made to him the D.A.D.P.S. will arrange for men to be present to explain at a Coy. "Pay" the principal advantages of those Certificates and to sell them.

9. REINFORCEMENTS.
The following letter from A.G., G.H.Q. (No. A.G./67 (P) of 31/5/18) is circulated for information :-
"HEADQUARTERS,
"ALL ARMIES.

"In order that the best use may be made of our available "resources, it is regretted that it will be necessary to depart from "the procedure hitherto in force under which N.C.O's. and men of "British Infantry rejoined their Battalions on discharge from hospitals "or convalescent depots in France.

"As far as possible this will be carried out, but it is of "primary importance that the strength of Battalions should be "maintained at the same level, so casuals will be posted to the "Battalion of their own regiment in which they are most required.

"The necessity for this step has been exemplified during the "recent operations, and certain battalions which had been brought up "to establishment continued to increase in strength owing to the return "of casuals whilst others of the same regiment remained very weak.
"G.H.Q.,   "(Sgd.) J. BENNETT STEUART, M.G.,
"31/5/18.   for Adjutant General."

10. ADDRESSES.
Correspondence from home should be addressed so as to show unit to which soldiers belong and no more, i.e. Pte. J. SWORDS, 410th Field Coy., R.E., B.E.F. Brigades and Divisions must not be mentioned except in cases of letters addressed to Brigade and Divisional Headquarters, when the Headquarters will appear alone, i.e. Pte. J. SNOOKS, H.Q., 52nd Division, B.E.F. From a test made recently 25% of letters sent to this Division were incorrectly addressed.

For information G.R.O. No. 3454 - "Addresses - Censorship Orders, paras 15 and 16", dated 24/2/18, is republished.

"Numerous cases of particulars of the Brigade, Divisions, and "higher formations being given as part of the addresses of units "continue to come to notice, and the addresses on incoming correspond-"ence show that the above orders are constantly disregarded. All ranks "are again reminded that such particulars, besides being contrary to "orders, in that they furnish information to the enemy in the event of "communications so addressed falling into his hands, do not facilitate, "but rather retard, the delivery of correspondence. It is the duty of "all who have given forbidden matter as part of their address to ensure "that the unnecessary details are omitted by their correspondents in "future."

Lieut.Colonel,
A.A. & Q.M.G., 52nd (Lowland) DIVISION.

52nd (Lowland) DIVISION.

ADMINISTRATIVE CIRCULAR MEMORANDUM No. 9.

9th JUNE, 1918.

1. A Divisional Wet Canteen will open at FRASER CAMP, MONT ST. ELOY, at 5.30 p.m., 9th June, 1918.

2. Beer, Coffee and Cigarettes will be on sale, and it is hoped to include other beverages, teetotal and otherwise, as stocks become available.

3. After the 9th instant the Canteen will be open nightly -
HOURS ... ... 5.30 p.m. - 8.30 p.m.
as long as stocks of beer, etc. are procurable.

4. Reserve Brigade will provide one Sergeant nightly for duty at the Canteen. This N.C.O. will be responsible that order is maintained, and that the Canteen closes at the right hour.

Lieut. Colonel.
A.A. & Q.M.G., 52nd (Lowland) DIVISION.

SECRET.   Copy No...11...

52nd (Lowland) DIVISION.

ADMINISTRATIVE INSTRUCTION No. AF.12.

With reference to 52nd Divisional Order No. 108.

9th June, 1918.

1. **REFILLING POINTS.**

   From 11th June inclusive as follows :-

   156th Infantry Brigade.   LEADLEY SIDING A.2.c.5.9.

   155th Infantry Brigade.   BLACKPOOL SIDING. A.7.d.4.8.

2. **LORRIES.**

   10 lorries will report at FRASER CAMP, MONT ST. ELOY, at 9 a.m. on June 11th and a further 10 at 12 noon at the same place.
   These will be available for taking troops to NEUVILLE ST. VAAST Area, and bringing back troops to Reserve Area, until relief is complete.

3. **BILLET IMPROVEMENT.**
   155th Infantry Brigade will take over and continue the billet improvement work now being undertaken by 156th Infantry Brigade.

4. **DISCIPLINE.**

   The same restrictions as are now in force for 156th Infantry Brigade as regards men not leaving the Divisional Area, particularly with reference to ECOIVRES and other villages in 51st Divisional Area (i.e. all area south of an E. and W. line through Cross Roads F.14.b.10.6.) will hold good for 155th Infantry Brigade. This includes finding picquets in relief of those now found by 156th Infantry Brigade.

   Trouble has been caused in the past by men disregarding these orders on the first day of arrival in ST. ELOY area, and then pleading ignorance of the orders with reference to bounds. G.O.C. 155th Infantry Brigade will take most careful steps to ensure that all ranks under his command are made acquainted with these orders immediately they arrive in billets, and before they are dismissed from parade. No excuse will be accepted in the cases of men found out of bounds; any such offences are to be severely punished, and the leave of the offenders stopped.

5. **ACKNOWLEDGE.**

                                                   Lieut. Colonel.
                                        A.A. & Q.M.G. 52nd (Lowland)DIVISION

Issued at 7.0 a.m.

Copy No.1	A.D.C. for G.O.C.	8	D.A.D.V.S.
2	"G"	9	Divisional Train.
3	155th Infantry Brigade.	10	S.S.O.
4	156th Infantry Brigade.	11)	
5	C.R.E.	12)	War Diary.
6	52nd M.G. Battalion.	13	File.
7	A.D.M.S.		

SECRET.   Copy No. 15

52nd (Lowland) DIVISION.

ADMINISTRATIVE INSTRUCTION No. AF.13.

10th JUNE, 1918.

1. Owing to the overcrowding in the St. ELOI Camps, the following redistribution of accommodation will take effect on relief of 155th Brigade by 157th Brigade, and return of former to Reserve Area:

"A" Battalion will be quartered in LE PENDU Camp instead of DURHAM - LANCASTER.

"B" Battalion in FRAZER Camp will take over as additional accommodation the sleeping and dining huts of LANCASTER Camp.

"C" Battalion in OTTAWA Camp will take over 2 sleeping huts of FRAZER Camp.

2. The Divisional Wet Canteen may be used between the hours of 12 noon and 2 p.m. as a dining hut for the Battalion in FRAZER Camp. O.C. this Battalion will be responsible that the Canteen is properly cleaned up after the midday meal. No beer can be sold from the canteen at this hour.

3. Dining huts are being erected in OTTAWA and Le PENDU Camps as soon as possible.

4. The Le PENDU estaminets are again placed in bounds, but O.C. the Battalion at this Camp will be responsible for seeing that this privilege is not abused. Men going to these estaminets will wear belts and otherwise fulfil the conditions laid down for men proceeding beyond their Battalion billeting area.

5. The Transport of "A" Battalion can either remain in its present site at St. ELOI or move to Le PENDU.

6. Acknowledge.

Lieut. Colonel,

A.A. & Q.M.G., 52nd (Lowland) DIVISION.

```
Copy No. 1 A.D.C. for G.O.C.        9  D.A.D.O.S.
         2. "G"                    10  A.P.M.
         3 155th Infantry Brigade. 11  Divnl. Train.
         4 156th Infantry Brigade. 12  Area Comdt., St.ELOI.
         5 157th Infantry Brigade. 13  Canteen Officer, 52nd Divn.
         6 C.R.A.                  14)
         7 C.R.E.                  15) War Diary.
         8 A.D.M.S.                16  File.
```

SECRET.   App IX   A Branch
52 Division

52nd (Lowland) DIVISION.

ADMINISTRATIVE CIRCULAR MEMORANDUM No. 13.

1.   PACK TRANSPORT.

1. In order to prepare for any occasion on which it may be necessary for the Division to use Pack Transport owing to hostile shell fire or the nature of the terrain forbidding the use of wheels, it has been decided to earmark the establishment of a Divisional Pack Transport Corps and to hold a practise mobilization of this unit.

2. The establishment of this unit will be as shown in the attached Appendix. The Commanding Officer will be an A.S.C. officer appointed by O.C., Train, and the mobilization will take place under his orders.

3. The Pack Transport Corps will be mobilized on Friday, June 14th, 1918, for the following purposes :-

(a) A parade of the whole Corps at 1130 in the field opposite DALY's Camp, on the St. ELOI-LA TARGETTE road.
(b) To send up the rations, etc., of the two brigades in front line on the evening of the 14th June.
(c) To allow every Officer, N.C.O. and Man, who will form part of the Pack Corps in an emergency, to know his role.

4. All Officers, N.C.Os. and men of the establishment will by the 21st June reconnoitre all the available routes which might have to be used in an emergency forward over the VIMY ridge, as far as the H.Q. of Battalions in the line.

5. The following extra pack saddles may be drawn from D.A.D.O.S. prior to the parade mentioned in 3 (a) above.
Those pack saddles must be returned by 6 p.m. on the 15th instant.

Each Infantry Brigade Pack Company .... 30.

12th JUNE, 1918.   Lieut. Colonel.
A.A. & Q.M.G., 52nd (Lowland) DIVISION.

ESTABLISHMENT OF 52nd DIVISIONAL PACK TRANSPORT CORPS.

Headquarters, Divisional Pack Transport Corps.

	Officers	O. Ranks	Horses	Cycles	
O.C., Pack Corps	1	-	1	-	
Clerk	-	1	-	1	All found by Divisional
Cycle Orderlies	-	4	-	4	Train.

Divisional Troops Pack Company.

	Officers	N.C.Os.	O. Ranks	Artificers	Pack Animals	Pack Saddles	
O.C. Company	1	-	-	-	-	-	T.O. of M.G. Battalion.
Sergeants	-	4	-	-	-	-	3 Sgts. & 6 Cpls. from M.G.Battn.
Corporals	-	8	-	-	-	-	1 Sgt. & 2 Cpls. from Pioneer Bn.
Drs. for Pack Animals	-	-	91	-	91	91	80 to be provided by M.G. Battn.
" " Spare "	-	-	9	-	9	-	20 " " " " Pioneer "
Farriers	-	-	-	2	-	-	1 from M.G. Bn. 1 from Train.
Saddlers	-	-	-	2	-	-	=do= =do=

Infantry Brigade Pack Company.

	Officers	N.C.Os.	O. Ranks	Artificers	Pack Animals	Pack Saddles	
O.C. Company	1	-	-	-	-	-	Brigade Transport Officer.
Section Commdrs.	4	-	-	-	-	-	Battn. Transport Officers.
Sergeants	-	4	-	-	-	-	(To be provided from 1st Line
Corporals	-	5	-	-	-	-	(Transport.
Drs. for Pack Horses	-	-	107	-	107	107	(To be provided from 1st Line
" " Spare "	-	-	15	-	15	-	(Drivers & Brakesmen.
Farriers	-	-	-	4	-	-	(From 1st Line Transport.
							1 from Bde. Coy. A.S.C. & 4 from 1st Line Transport.

P.T.O.

Infantry Brigade Pack Company. (continued.)

	Animals		Drivers	
Each Battalion will mobilize	25	3 spare.	25	3 for Spare animals.
Bde. H.Q. forself & T.M.B. will mobilize	7	3 "	7	3 "

52nd (Lowland) DIVISION.

ADMINISTRATIVE CIRCULAR MEMORANDUM No. 14.

Protection against enemy bombing.

1. Immediate steps are to be taken by all units provided with animals to protect them against enemy bombing.

2. Standings will be protected by revetted traverses of earth three to six feet high, built as close round the standing as circumstances permit. The standings themselves will be sub-divided by traverses between every 6 or 8 horses, each end of the standing being similarly protected.

3. Similarly all huts, which have not already been protected with splinter proof earth walls 3 feet high round their outsides, will be provided with this protection forthwith.

13th June, 1918.

(Sd). C.G.MAUDE, Lieut. Colonel.
A.A. & Q.M.G., 52nd (Lowland) DIVISION.

appx I A Branch
52 Division

52nd (Lowland) DIVISION.

ADMINISTRATIVE CIRCULAR MEMORANDUM No. 15.

DIVISIONAL RECEPTION CAMP.

1. A Divisional Reception Camp commanded by Major J.G. COATES, 9th Battn. attached 1/9th Battn. Highland Light Infantry has been formed.

2. The Camp for the present will be located at Villers Camp and Rispin Camp, VILLERS AU BOIS.

3. The objects of the Camp are :-
    (a) To accommodate, equip and distribute to units all reinforcements.
    (b) To accommodate nucleus personnel left out of action under the provisions of Section XXX of S.S. 138.

4. (A) Villers Camp will be reserved so far as possible for reinforcements and any Schools which may be assembled there by Divisional order.
    (B) Rispin Camp will be set aside for the nucleus personnel.

5. O.C., Reception Camp may call upon S.A.A. Section, D.A.C., (Headquarters, F.9.c.9.8. Mont St Eloi) for transport to the extent of 2 G.S. Wagons per day. Any transport required in excess of this will be applied for to Divisional Headquarters.

6. All reinforcements for the Division will be directed to the Camp at Villers Au Bois, and will be distributed from there.
    Casuals returning from leave, Schools, etc., will report to their Units direct. Those for Brigades in the line will report to their Battalion Details at Rispin Camp.

7. O.C., Reception Camp, will be responsible for,
    (a) The sanitation and cleanliness of both Camps.
    (b) The discipline, except for that of the nucleus personnel who will be under their own officers for discipline.
    (c) The fitting and testing of box respirators of all reinforcements.
        This will not in any way absolve unit Commanders from the responsibility of seeing that all ranks under their Command are provided with box respirators which have been fitted and tested.
    (d) The affixing to tunics of units' distinguishing badges, a supply of which will be obtained periodically from D.A.D.O.S.
    (e) The checking of the equipment. Any deficiencies found will be reported direct to the Quartermaster of the Unit concerned, and men will be sent to their Quartermaster Stores to have their deficiencies made up before joining their Units.
    (f) The bathing of all as soon as possible after arrival.
    (g) He is not responsible for the training of nucleus personnel or of those at Divisional or other Classes.
    (h) Ranges and Assault Courses will be allotted to him and he will sub-allot them amongst those under training.

8. Reinforcements will be passed as quickly as possible from Viller Camp to Rispin Camp or to join their Units as the case may be.

9. The following returns will be made by O.C., Reception Camp :-
    (a) Reinforcements: By 1400 daily to Divisional Headquarters, the numbers by Units, of reinforcements received up to 1200, names of officers being stated.

P.T.O.

(Reinforcements - continued)
Divisional Headquarters will wire this information to units, who will immediately take those reinforcements on to strength.
Tho' reinforcements to 1200 Thursdays will be included in the weekly strength return ("A" Return No. 8.) due at Divisional Headquarters on Saturdays.
O.C., Reception Camp will forward nominal rolls of reinforcements to Units direct, and will advise them of any casualties which occur in the Reception Camp.

(b) **Strength**: By 1400 daily to Divisional Headquarters, a statement showing by Units the numbers of nucleus personnel in Camp made up to 1200.

[signature]
Lieut. Colonel.

15th JUNE, 1913. A.A. & Q.M.G., 52nd (Lowland) DIVISION.

LEAVE:

B.L. 2/84

Headquarters.
R.A.	155th Inf.Bde.	17th North'd. Fus.	Div.Emp.Coy.
R.E.	156th Inf.Bde.	D.A.D.V.S.	Divnl.Train.
Sig.Coy.	157th Inf.Bde.	A.P.M.	D.R.D.O.
A.D.M.S.	52nd M.G.Battn.	Camp Commdt.	

1. The leave allotment issued with this Office BL 2/74 of 29/5/18 ceases with the sailing of 19th instant.

2. The new allotment for this Division is
   (a) Ordinary Leave .... 35 per day.
   (b) Re-engagement Leave .... 9 per day.

3. The new daily sub-allotments which come into force with sailing of 20th instant are attached in Schedule, Ordinary Leave (a), Re-engagement Leave (b).

4. Attention is drawn to A.G./441/P.S./1 dated 25/5/18, issued with G.R.O. No. 4110 dated 26/5/18.

5. The train timings are as follows :-
   Mont St. Eloi .... dept. 1730)
   Aubigny .... "   1740) by Empty Supply
   Tincques .... "   1800) Train.
   St. Pol .... arr. 1904)
   St. Pol .... dep. 2133)

   Party will change at St. POL into empty Supply Train from BARLIN No. R.B.L. 40.
   Parties should report to R.T.O. half an hour before train is due to depart from St. Eloi.

6. D.R.D.O. will pay men at Lancaster Camp between the hours of 1400 and 1530.

7. Officers proceeding on leave will report to the D.R.D.O.
   The senior officer proceeding will take charge of the party.
   He will march the whole party from Lancaster Camp to St. Eloi Station and will be responsible for them until embarkation.

8. The allocations of leave are made on the following basis :-
   (1) R.E. includes Signal Company and Pioneer Companies.
   (2) Divisional Headquarters includes Mobile Veterinary Section, M.M.P., D.A.D.O.S. and other ranks attached to D.H.Q. as orderlies, etc.
   (3) All other detached men come on their Unit allotment.

9. This Office BL 2/74 dated 29/5/18 should be destroyed on 18th instant.

15th JUNE, 1918.

Major.
D.A.A.G., 52nd (Lowland) DIVISION.

ORDINARY LEAVE ALLOTMENT - SCHEDULE "A"

UNIT.	Sun.	Mon.	Tues.	Wed.	Thurs.	Fri.	Sat.
155th Inf. Brigade.	8	8	7	7	7	7	7
156th Inf. Brigade.	7	7	7	8	8	7	7
157th Inf. Brigade.	7	7	7	7	7	8	8
Divnl. Artillery.	5	5	4	4	4	4	4
Divnl. Engineers.	2	2	2	2	3	3	3
Machine Gun Battn.	1	1	2	1	1	1	1
Pioneer Battalion.	1	2	2	2	1	1	1
Divisional Train.	1	-	1	1	1	1	1
A.D.M.S.	1	2	2	2	1	1	1
Employment Coy.	1	-	-	-	1	1	1
Divisional H.Q.	1	1	1	1	1	1	1

RE-ENGAGEMENT LEAVE ALLOTMENT - SCHEDULE "B"

UNIT.	Sun.	Mon.	Tues.	Wed.	Thurs.	Fri.	Sat.
155th Inf. Brigade	2	2	2	2	2	2	2
156th Inf. Brigade.	2	2	2	2	2	2	2
157th Inf. Brigade.	2	2	2	2	2	2	2
R.A.M.C.	2	2	-	-	-	-	-
Divisional Train.	1	-	-	-	-	-	-
Divisional H.Q.	-	-	1	1	-	-	-
Divisional Engineers	-	-	2	2	-	-	-
Divisional Artillery	-	-	-	-	1	1	-
Pioneer Battalion.	-	-	-	-	-	-	3
Machine Gun Battalion.	-	-	-	-	2	2	-
Divisional Employment Coy.	-	1	-	-	-	-	-

52nd (Lowland) Division. Appendix XIII

ADMINISTRATIVE CIRCULAR MEMORANDUM No. 13.

15th JUNE, 1918.

SANITATION:

1. The sick rate in the Division is at present unusually high, whilst the standard of sanitation is low.

2. The G.O.C. wishes Commanding Officers to take immediate steps to impress on all ranks the great importance of sanitation, and particularly to enforce the following points which are now frequently neglected :—

   (a) See that all latrines are fly-proof, particularly at the junction of the seat and the ground, and round the lids.
   Have all latrine seats cleaned regularly.
   Insist on all men closing lids after use.

   (b) Cover up all food from flies. A supply of butter muslin to be obtained from D.A.D.O.S.

   (c) Insist on food not being thrown on the ground, and keep grease traps in a proper condition.

   Lieut. Colonel.
   A.A. & Q.M.G., 52nd (Lowland) DIVISION.

"A" Branch
52 Division

App XIV

LEAVE: BL 2/85

Headquarters,
   R.A.   155th Bde.   D.A.D.V.S.   Camp Commdt.
   R.E.   156th Bde.   Divn. Train.   Div. Emp. Coy.
   Sig. Coy.   157th Bde.   D.A.D.O.S.   D.R.D.O.
   A.D.M.S.   52nd M.G.Battn.   D.A.D.V.S.

1. Cancel this Office BL 2/84 of 15th June, 1918.

2. The leave allotment issued with this Office BL 2/74 of 29/5/18 ceases with sailing of 20th June, 1918.
   The new allotment for this Division is,
   (a) Ordinary Leave .... 60 per day.
   (b) Re-engagement Leave .... 5 per day.

3. The new daily sub-allotment which comes into force with sailings of 21st instant are attached on Schedules, (A) Ordinary Leave, (B) Re-engagement Leave.

4. Attention is drawn to A.G./441/P.S./1 dated 25/5/18, issued with G.R.O. No. 4110 dated 28/5/18.

5. The train timings are as follows :-
  Mont St. Eloi .... dep. 1730)
  Aubigny ....   1740) by Empty Supply
  Tinques ....   1800) Train.
  St. Pol .... arr. 1904
  St. Pol .... dep. 2133
  Party will change at St. POL into empty Supply Train from BARLIN No. R.B.L. 40.
  Parties should report to R.T.O. half an hour before train is due to depart from St. Eloi.

6. D.R.D.O. will pay men at Lancaster Camp between the hours of 1400 and 1530.

7. Officers proceeding on leave will report to the D.R.D.O.
  The senior officer proceeding will take charge of the party.
  He will march the whole party from Lancaster Camp to St. Eloi Station and will be responsible for them until embarkation.

8. The allocations of leave are made on the following basis :-
  (1) R.E. includes Signal Company and Pioneer Companies.
  (2) Divisional Headquarters includes Mobile Veterinary Section, M.M.P., D.A.D.O.S. and other ranks attached to D.H.Q. as orderlies, etc.
  (3) All other detached men come on their Unit allotment.

J. Malloch
Major.
17th JUNE, 1918.
D.A.A.G., 52nd (Lowland) DIVISION.

ORDINARY LEAVE ALLOTMENT - SCHEDULE "A"

UNIT:	Sun.	Mon.	Tues.	Wed.	Thurs.	Fri.	Sat.
R.A.M.C.	2	2	2	3	3	3	3
Divnl. Train	1	1	1	1	2	2	1
Divisional H.Q.	1	1	1	1	1	1	1
155th Inf. Bde.	12	12	13	13	13	13	13
156th Inf. Bde.	13	13	12	12	13	13	13
157th Inf. Bde.	13	13	13	13	12	12	13
R.E.	4	4	5	4	4	4	4
R.A.	9	9	8	8	8	8	8
5th R.I.R. (P)	1	2	2	2	1	1	1
M.G. Battn.	3	2	2	2	2	2	2
Div. Emp. Coy.	1	1	1	1	1	1	1

RE-ENGAGEMENT LEAVE ALLOTMENT - SCHEDULE "B"

UNIT:	Sun.	Mon.	Tues.	Wed.	Thurs.	Fri.	Sat.
155th Brigade.	4	4	-	-	-	-	-
156th Brigade.	-	-	4	4	-	-	-
157th Brigade.	-	-	-	-	4	4	-
R.A.M.C.	-	-	-	-	1	1	1
Divnl. Train.	1	-	-	-	-	-	-
Divisional H.Q.) & Div. Emp. Coy.)	-	1	1	-	-	-	-
R.E.	-	-	-	-	-	-	2
R.A.	-	-	-	-	-	-	2
M.G. Battn.	-	-	-	1	-	-	-

SECRET.   Copy No. 13

52nd (Lowland) DIVISION.

ADMINISTRATIVE INSTRUCTION No. 14.

17th June 1918.

With reference to 52nd Divisional Order No.110 dated 16/6/18.

1. **REFILLING DUMPS.**

   From 20th June inclusive as follows:-

   155th Infantry Brigade.   LEADLEY SIDING. A.2.c.5.9.

   157th Infantry Brigade.   BLACKPOOL SIDING. A.7.d.4.8.

2. **LORRIES.**

   (a) 4 Lorries will report at FRASER CAMP, MONT ST.ELOY at 4 p.m. on the 19th June
   (b) 20 Lorries will report at FRASER CAMP at 9.30 a.m. on the 20th June.
   These lorries will be available for taking Troops to NEUVILLE ST.VAAST AREA, and bringing back Troops to Reserve area, until relief is completed.

3. **BILLET IMPROVEMENT.**
   157th Infantry Brigade will take over and continue the billet improvement work now being undertaken by 155th Infantry Brigade.

4. **HORSE STANDINGS, etc.**

   (a) The same sites at present occupied by the Transport will be taken over by Brigades on relief.
   (b) Manure will be taken to the Manure Dumps already in use.

5. **DISCIPLINE.**
   The same restrictions as are now in force for 155th Brigade as regards men not leaving the Divisional Area, particularly with reference to ECOIVRES and other villages in 51st Division Area (i.e. all area south of an E. and W. line through cross roads F.14.b.10.6.) will hold good for 157th Brigade. This includes finding picquets in relief of those now found by 156th Infantry Brigade.

6. **ACKNOWLEDGE.**

                                                                    Major
                                                              for
                                                                    Lieut. Colonel.
                                                  A.A. & Q.M.G. 52nd (Lowland)Division.

Issued at 7.0 am

    Copy No. 1. A.D.C. for G.O.C.   8. D.A.D.V.S.
            2. "G"   9. Divisional Train.
            3. 155th Inf. Brigade.   10. S.S.O.
            4. 157th Inf. Brigade.   11)
            5. C.R.E.   12) War Diary.
            6. 52nd M.G.Battalion.   13. File.
            7. A.D.M.S.

App XV
Appendix
52 Division

52nd (Lowland) DIVISION.

ADMINISTRATIVE CIRCULAR MEMORANDUM No. 17.

17th JUNE, 1918.

DIVISIONAL CHAFF CUTTING DEPOT.

1. In order to ensure that all Units in the Division, less R.A., A.S.C. and Machine Gun Battalion (who have chaff-cutters of their own), get a daily supply of chaff issued to them, a central Divisional Chaff-Cutting Depot is being established at BLACKPOOL Siding (A.7.d.4.8.) under the supervision of the S.S.O.

2. Five chaff-cutters will be at work daily, and issue will be made to units twice a week on a time table to be arranged by S.S.O.

3. Work will commence on June 19th, and the following personnel will be supplied on that date and daily afterwards to run the depot:-

  (a) By O.C., Train,   1 N.C.O.   ) will be permanent.
                                1 Supply Issuer)

  (b) By Infantry Brigade in Reserve, Two shifts daily of 15 men each,
      1st Shift - 7-30 a.m. to 11-30 a.m.
      2nd Shift - 2 p.m. to 6 p.m.
The men detailed will report to N.C.O. i/c Divisional Chaff-Cutting Depot five minutes before their shift is due to start.

                                            Lieut. Colonel.
         A.A. & Q.M.G., 52nd (Lowland) DIVISION.

52nd (Lowland) DIVISION.

ADMINISTRATIVE CIRCULAR MEMORANDUM No. 18.

17th June, 1918.

DIVISIONAL ARMOURERS SHOP.

1. A Divisional Armourers Shop has been started at D.A.D.O.S. Headquarters (A.7.b.2.3.), consisting of 3 out of 4 of the Armourers from each Infantry Brigade. This leaves one Armourer with each Brigade to carry out minor repairs to Lewis Guns, etc.

2. The purposes for which the Divisional Armourers Shop will be used are as follows :-

   (a) To overhaul all the Lewis Guns of the Reserve Brigade during their period in the Reserve Area, if time permits.

   (b) To assist the Machine Gun Battalion by periodically inspecting and effecting minor repairs to their guns.

   (c) To hold a small reserve of Lewis Guns and Rifles to meet immediate demands from units to replace damaged weapons.

   (d) To overhaul bicycles, rifles, revolvers and Very Pistols. Units will send D.A.D.O.S. the numbers on all the bicycles in their possession, so that in case of loss, their tracing may be facilitated.

3. One Lewis Gunner per Brigade can be received at a time in the Divisional Armourers Shop for a 10 days course, during which they will be given a thorough knowledge of the working parts of the Lewis Gun. These attachments will be arranged direct between Infantry Brigades concerned and D.A.D.O.S.

Lieut.Colonel.
A.A. & Q.M.G. 52nd (Lowland) DIVISION.

52nd (Lowland) DIVISION.

ADDENDUM to ADMINISTRATIVE CIRCULAR MEMORANDUM No.10

20th June, 1918.

Reference Administrative Circular Memorandum No.10 dated 8th June, 1918.

1. The following scale will be substituted for scale shown in para.3.

2. The new scale will come into force for consumption 24th instant.

NEW SCALE.

Article.	Normal Ration.	"A" In Trenches.	"B" Out of Trenches & Divl. Troops.
Fresh Meat or Preserved Meat.	1 lb. 9 oz.	1 lb. 8 oz.	1 lb. 8 oz.
Bread or Biscuit.	1 lb. 10 oz.	1 lb. 10 oz.	1 lb. 9 oz.
Bacon.	4 oz.	4 oz.	3 oz.
Cheese.	2 oz.	2 oz.	2 oz.
Jam.	3 oz.	3 oz.	2½ oz.
Tea.	½ oz.	⅝ oz.	⅝ oz.
Sugar.	3 oz.	3 oz.	2½ oz.

3. The necessary underdrawals will be made in bulk by the S.S.O.

Lieut.Colonel.
A.A. & Q.M.G. 52nd (Lowland) DIVISION.

Appendix XIX
A Brand
52 Division

U R G E N T.   52nd (Lowland) DIVISION.

ADMINISTRATIVE CIRCULAR MEMORANDUM No. 19.

20th June, 1918.

PRECAUTIONS AGAINST P.U.O.

1. All ranks, whether sick or not, will use, morning and evening, as a gargle and mouth wash, a permanganate solution which is being issued. This solution must <u>not</u> be swallowed.

2. Units having Medical Officers may obtain the permanganate in crystal form from the nearest Field Ambulance and the Medical Officers will issue the permanganate in solution in the strength already indicated to them.

3. Units having no Medical Officer may obtain the solution ready made from the nearest Field Ambulance on supplying bottles.

4. This gargling will take place as a parade under an officer. It is only by strictly carrying this out that we can defeat the present epidemic of influenza.

C. Brand
Lieut. Colonel.
A.A. & Q.M.G., 52nd (Lowland) Division.

A Branch
52 Division

52nd (Lowland) DIVISION.

"A" SUMMARY No. 3. – 20th JUNE, 1918.

1. ACCIDENTAL & SELF-INFLICTED INJURIES:

All cases of injury which render a soldier (officer or other rank) unfit for duty must be reported in daily casualty wire. Some doubt seems to exist still as to the procedure to be adopted in above cases.

(a) Accidental Injuries are those in which the man concerned is not considered to blame. A.F. W 3428 is filled up by his Unit and forwarded through Divisional Headquarters to the D.A.G., 3rd Echelon for record.

(b) Self-inflicted Injuries are those in which the man concerned is considered to blame. All such cases must be tried by Field General Court Martial. If the man has been evacuated to a Field Ambulance, etc., the O.C., Unit will immediately inform the O.C., Medical Unit that the man is suffering from a self-inflicted wound and he will then be sent to the Special Hospital where his trial will take place in due course under Army arrangements. A.F. W 3428 should be forwarded as before to Divisional Headquarters, whence it will be forwarded to Army Headquarters. A copy of the evidence attached to A.F. W 3428 should be sent to O.C., Medical Unit.

(3) In all cases para. 2 of A.F. W 3428 must be signed by a Medical Officer.

2. Self-Inflicted Wounds Statistics:

The table set out below shows the number of convictions by Divisions, or in the case of Corps Troops by Corps, between 14th and 31st May :-

TABLE:

Divn.	1	3	4	5	11	15	20	24	40	51	52	55	56	61	Can. 1 5 4 Cav.Troops	1st Corps XI.XVIII Can.	Total
No. of Convictions.	3	7	5	2	3	1	5	8	3	3	3	6	2	2	5 3 10	1 2 1	3 80

3. Cleaning Rifles & Revolvers. (precautions against accidents).

As there is evidence that a proportion of Self-inflicted wounds are the result of carelessness, attention is called to G.R.O. No. 2638 which is re-published for information :-

"Before any attempt is made to clean a rifle, either outside or inside, the bolt will be first removed and then the magazine.

After cleaning the bolt will always be replaced and closed, springs eased and safety catch applied, before magazine is re-attached.

Revolvers are not to be cleaned, either internally or externally, without being first unloaded."

This Order is to be read out periodically on Squadron, Battery, Company and corresponding parades of other units."

4. Charge Sheets:

Avoidable delay appears to occur in the return of Charge Sheets to the Divisional A.P.M. Charge Sheets should be returned within 7 days.

P.T.O.

- 2 -

5. Field General Courts Martial:
Sufficient attention is not being paid to S.S. 412a, and it has been necessary lately to return a number of proceedings for alterations and additions. S.S. 412a. lays down clearly what is required and must be complied with.

6. Offenders under Arrest:
The Judge Advocate General ruled in a recent case that a soldier cannot be convicted of desertion arising out of the disobedience of an order to proceed to the line, on the ground that the order given was an unlawful one under the circumstances, and that an offender under arrest, either close or open, should not be called upon to perform a duty in the line. If it is desired that an offender should proceed to the trenches he can be released from arrest without prejudice to re-arrest.

7. Offence Reports:
The following table of offences for week to 14th instant is published for information :-

Offence:	Inf. Brigade 155.	156.	157.	H.Q. Bn.	R.A.	R.E.	Other Formations	Total.
Traffic Regulations.	1	1	3	1	7	4	1	18
Estaminet Regulations.	2	2	-	-	-	-	-	4
Out of Bounds.	1	2	-	-	*	*	-	5
Drunkenness.	3	1	-	-	-	-	-	4
Absent.	-	1	-	-	-	-	-	1
Failing to Salute an Officer.	-	-	-	-	-	1	-	1
Damage to Crops.	-	-	-	-	2	-	-	2

8. LEAVE:
If a soldier fails to return from leave the Unit concerned should inform the local Police forwarding the man's address, etc.

9. Sick.
The percentage of sick for five weeks to 15/6/18, is shown below. These figures will be published weekly in future.

Week-ending:	155th Bde.	156th Bde.	157th Bde.	Average.
18/5/18	2.11	2.13	1.73	2.02
25/5/18	2.82	2.00	2.77	2.53
1/6/18	2.24	1.57	2.60	2.14
8/6/18	1.52	3.81	3.54	2.93
15/6/18	5.88	4.74	2.25	4.29

10. Appointments - Posting of Officers holding higher temporary rank.
The following War Office letter regarding the position of Officers holding temporary rank in disbanded or amalgamated battalions is published for information :-

P.T.O.

(Para. 10 - continued.)

"100/Gen. No./4930 (M.S. 4.K) War Office.
 28/5/1918.
Sir,
　　With reference to your letter of the 23rd April, 1918, No. 38045 and your telegram F. 517 of the 21st instant, I am directed to inform you that it has been decided after due consideration, that officers holding higher temporary rank (i.e. Commanding Officers and Majors, Second-in-Command), on the establishment of battalions which have been, or will be, amalgamated or disbanded owing to the re-organization now in progress, may be permitted to retain their temporary rank with pay and allowances, until absorbed into the establishment of another unit, but in no case for a period exceeding 61 days.

　　　　　　　　　　XXXXXXXXXXX
　　　　　　　　　(Sgd) B.T. CHURCHER, Major,
　　　　　　　　　　D.A.M.S. for Lt. Gen. M.S.
To, F.M., C-in-C, B.E.F.

11. **Leave - Ration Allowance:**
　　G.R.O. No. 3343 is re-published for information :-
"Ration Allowance:- When officers and other ranks are granted leave Part II Orders on this subject, which are issued so that ration allowance for the correct period may be drawn, should read as follows :-
"No. .... Rank ..... Name .... is granted leave to U.K. via HAVRE from (date)........ to .... (date) and is entitled to 15 days ration allowance only"
　　　　　　　　or
"No. .... Rank ..... Name .... is granted leave to U.K. via BOULOGNE or CALAIS from (date) .... to ...... (date) and is entitled to 14 days ration allowance only."

12. **Vacancy for a Sergeant Major:**
　　The following letter has been received from the Commandant, Royal Military School of Music,
"Owing to the promotion to Quartermaster of Sergeant Major F. NUNLEY, there is now a vacancy in this School for a Sergeant Major.
　　I fear that at present the choice is likely to be small of men suitably, willing, and able to be spared. Also, judging from previous experience it is most desirable that candidates should be seen by the Commandant before being finally appointed.
　　The essential qualifications for the position are :-
(1) Liking for, and ability to deal with boys. At present all
　　the 140 pupils are boys of at most 17.1/12 years of age, but even in normal times, boys form the majority of the pupils.
(2) Considerable tact and initiative.
(3) As the Sergeant Major has to assist in the Office it is
　　necessary that he should be able to use a typewriter.
(4) Perfect sobriety is of course necessary.
(5) It would be an advantage to have as Sergeant Major a man
　　who has himself been a Band Boy and risen to the rank of
　　R.Q.M.S. or R.S.M.: and in making a selection I should give
　　preference to such a man, other things being fairly equal.
　　　　XXXXXXXXXXXXXXXXXXXXXX
　　　　　　　　　(Sgd) T.C.P. SOMERVILLE. Colonel.
　　　　　　Commandant, Royal Military School of Music."

Recommendations should be addressed to Divisional Headquarters.

- 4 -

13. **Memorial to those fallen in PALESTINE:**
A payment to A/c of the subscription from this Division has been forwarded to the Egyptian Expeditionary Force, but a number of Units have not yet replied.
The balance collected will be forwarded on 26th instant.
Will any who intend to subscribe, and have not forwarded their subscription by that date please advise Divisional H.Q. (A).

14. **REINFORCEMENTS.**
Administrative Circular Memorandum No.15, reference Divisional Reception Camp, explains the method of reporting the arrival of reinforcements.
If however, any reinforcements reach units without passing through the Reception Camp, Divisional H.Q. must be advised, names of officers will be stated.

Lieut. Colonel.
A.A. & Q.M.G., 52nd (Lowland) DIVISION.

"A" Branch
52nd Division

CONFIDENTIAL.

52nd (Lowland) DIVISION.

ADMINISTRATIVE CIRCULAR MEMORANDUM No. 20.

22nd JUNE, 1918.

OFFENCES AGAINST INHABITANTS.

Since the Division arrived in France there have been several cases of assaults on the inhabitants by men of this Division. These have not been frequent and have mostly been committed by men under the influence of drink.

At the same time the G.O.C. wishes all ranks to realise what very serious consequences even an isolated case of this kind may have. Not only is the good name of the Division impaired but the present excellent relations of the B.E.F. with the French, which are of such vital consequence for the whole of the Allied Cause, are imperilled. It must be remembered that the only inhabitants left in the forward areas are women and old men; that this is their country and not ours; that their husbands, sons and brothers, such as are left of them, are engaged in defending another part of France against the common enemy, and that in consequence we should regard ourselves as privileged to be their protectors as well as their guests. The French have suffered very much more severely in this War than we have, and yet even in the most exposed areas these women and old men continue to "carry on" on their farms and amidst the wreckage of their homes in a manner which has excited the admiration of the whole World.

The G.O.C. is certain that, if these facts are thoroughly brought home to the men, there will be none in the Division so criminal or cowardly as to lift his hand against the person or property of a French man or woman. At the same time it is to be most clearly understood that any offence of this nature will be most ruthlessly punished. The penalty for this crime under Section 6 of the Army Act is Death, and the G.O.C. is prepared to recommend that the maximum punishment be awarded in all future convictions under this Section.

The substance of the above letter is to be most carefully made known, on parade to all ranks of the Division.

Lieut. Colonel.
A.A. & Q.M.G., 52nd (Lowland) DIVISION.

App XXV   "A" Branch
            52 Division

52nd (Lowland) DIVISION.

ADMINISTRATIVE CIRCULAR MEMORANDUM No. 21.

23rd JUNE, 1918.

LEAVE.

There are probably many men, and possibly a few officers who are wondering, why, the amount of leave allotted to this Division is not greater, in view of the length of time the majority of people have been away from England, compared with other formations in this Country.

At present this Division is getting 7 times more daily leave than any other Division in France, and it is only the tactical situation which prevents this proportion being even larger. It can be readily understood that short of sending practically the whole Division on leave at the same time, there is no alternative to the present reduced allotment, if the 52nd Division is to be regarded as a fighting formation ready for action at any time.

The G.O.C. wishes O.C., Units to explain this to their men, so that they will not think that their claims to leave have been overlooked by higher authority. The question has been represented several times to G.H.Q., and although the present allotment of leave is much smaller than he would wish for the Division after its long absence abroad, the G.O.C. is satisfied that it is as large as we are entitled to during the present crisis.

Lieut. Colonel.
A.A. & Q.M.G., 52nd (Lowland) DIVISION.

Secret

A Branch
52 Division

Copy No. 12

52nd (Lowland) Division.

ADMINISTRATIVE INSTRUCTION No. 15.

24th June, 1918.

Instructions have now been received to hold only one days' rations in Localities instead of 2, consequently Administrative Instruction No.10 dated 26/5/18, Addendum to Administrative Instruction No.10 dated 6/6/18 and wire Q.827 dated 6/6/18 are hereby cancelled and following substituted. –

1. The following quantity of rations will be maintained in the various Localities –

    WAKEFIELD.
    DURHAM.
    SUBURB.
    FOYAN.
    BARNSLEY.   } Each 28 P.M. (In sandbags).
    BEEHIVE.   } 25 Biscuit Ration.
    SHEFFIELD.
    CANADA.
    SPUR POST.
    FARBUS.
    BORDER POST.
    TARE POST.
    THELUS POST.

    NOVA SCOTIA.   } Each 288 P.M.
    BOIS DE LA CHAUDIERE. } 300 Biscuit Ration.

2. The following will be maintained in Brigade Reserve for each Brigade in the line, and also by the S.S.O.

    63 cases of P.M.   3024 P.M.
    121 tins of Biscuits.   or 3025 Biscuit Rations.

3. The 52nd Machine Gun Battalion will keep on hand –

    384 P.M.
    400 Biscuits.

4. On a relief taking place these rations will be taken over and receipts given; they will also be shown in the Monthly Reserve Ration Return by the Brigade holding the line.

5. A board will be kept at each Ration Dump shewing number of rations on hand.

6. All Reserve Rations should always be stored in cellars or dug outs.

7. All rations which become surplus by this reorganisation will be returned to O.C. Train forthwith and the return for the end of June should show on hand only those rations authorised by this Memorandum; a note shewing number of rations returned to O.C. Train should be added.

8. ACKNOWLEDGE.

Issued at.........

E.F. Matin-Barrett
Major
Lieut.Colonel.
A.A. & Q.M.G. 52nd (Lowland) DIVISION.

Copy to – No.1 155th Brigade.   4 Divl. Train.   7 A.D.M.S. 10 M.G. Batt.
              2 156th Brigade.   5 "G"   8 A.P.M.   11 File.
              3 157th Brigade.   6 C.R.E.   9 S.S.O.   12) War Diary
                                                                                                                    13)

52nd (Lowland) DIVISION.

ADMINISTRATIVE CIRCULAR MEMORANDUM No. 21.

COOK - HOUSES.

1. Immediate steps are to be taken to improve the cook-houses of all units in the Division. The standard of cleanliness in some of these cook-houses is very much below the average, and the G.O.C. wishes Brigadiers and O.C., Units to give this matter their personal attention.

2. "Orders to be hung up in every Cook-house" (copy attached) were circulated on May 15th last. In some units these are neither hung up nor obeyed. Attention is called to para. 2 (b) of Administrative Circular Memorandum No. 4 dated 18/5/18.

3. The cook-houses of officers messes are to be just as clean as the men's, and are to be frequently inspected by an officer.

4. As already ordered, tables, etc., on which meat is cut up are to be covered with tin.

26th JUNE, 1918.

Lieut. Colonel.
A.A. & Q.M.G., 52nd (Lowland) DIVISION.

ORDERS TO BE HUNG UP IN EVERY COOKHOUSE.

1. <u>Every part of, and everything in, a cookhouse should be scrupulously clean at all times.</u> Cooks should take a personal pride in this.

2. <u>The cook and his assistants</u> must always wear the canvas suits authorised by G.R.O., when in the cookhouse. They must keep themselves strictly clean and must invariably wash their hands before handling food. No person may sleep, or keep kits, blankets or spare clothing in a cookhouse. No toilet operations, except the washing of hands, are to be carried out in cookhouse or store room. Every cook-house is to be provided with a wash bowl, soap and clean towel for the use of the cooks

3. <u>Food</u> must be kept covered to protect it from dust and flies and there should be a fly-proof meat cupboard in every cookhouse.

4. <u>Refuse.</u> No scraps of food, potato peelings, etc. should ever be dropped on the floor. One or more boxes or tins should be kept for the purpose of receiving all refuse or scraps.

5. <u>The cutting up table or board.</u> This should be frequently scrubbed and must always be spotlessly clean.

6. <u>Cooking utensils.</u> these must not be placed on the floor, or ground, which are always fouled by the dirt carried on boots. Camp kettles and all cooking pots should be kept clean and bright inside and outside.

7. <u>Soak-pit and grease trap:-</u> these must be provided near each cook-house.

8. <u>Limewashing</u> of the interior of the cook-house should be carried out once a week if possible.

The object of these orders is to prevent the spread of disease through contaminated food. Neglect of any one of the above precautions may be the cause of disease and death.

....

Commanding........................

SECRET.   Copy No. 33

52nd (Lowland) DIVISION.

ADMINISTRATIVE INSTRUCTION No. 16.

26th June, 1918.

Reference G.R. 27/2/2 of 25/6/18.

1. **MOVE.**
   1/5th K.O.S.Borderers, 1/8th Scottish Rifles and 1/5th A. & S. Highlanders on transfer from 52nd Division to 30th Division will leave 52nd Divisional Area by bus on June 28th.

2. **EMBUSSING.**
   (a) <u>Embussing Point.</u> - Portion of main CAMBLAIN L'ABBE - ST. ELOI Road in square W.30 (ref.1/40000 Army Map C).

   (b) <u>Times of Embussing.</u> - "A" Battalion - 10.15 a.m.
                                   "B" Battalion - 10.20 a.m.
                                   "C" Battalion - 10.25 a.m.

   157th Infantry Brigade will detail a Staff Officer to superintend the embussing of all 3 Battalions. This officer will meet the O.C. Bus Company at the road junction in W.30.c at 9.30 a.m. to arrange distribution of busses to Battalions and will bring with him the strength of each unit. Representatives of Battalions will attend at the same place and time, in order to take over and sub-allot their busses. They will bring chalk to mark the busses allotted to them.

3. **BAGGAGE, etc.**
   One blanket a man will be taken in the busses, but no other baggage.
   3 lorries will report at the camp of each Battalion at 6 a.m. 28th instant to convey -
       (a) Rations for 29th inst.
       (b) Cooking utensils.
       (c) Officers' baggage.
       (d) Battalion Advance Party.
   to the new area.
   These lorries will proceed when loaded direct to EPERLECQUES and report to Headquarters 30th Division.

4. **TRANSPORT.**
   The 1st line transport and Train vehicles (which should join units on evening 27th inst.) of these three Battalions will proceed by road on 28th inst. as follows -

DATE.	DESTINATION.	BILLETS.
June 28th.	DIVION.	Night 28/29th from Town Major HOUDAIN.
June 29th.	CREQUES.	Night 29/30th from Area Comdt. THEROUANNE.
June 30th.	EPERLECQUES.	from 30th Division.

   No restrictions as regards route.
   The transport of the three Battalions will march together and will be under the command of the senior transport Officer.
   On June 28th the head of the transport column will pass road junction W.30.c. at 8 a.m.
   Men and animals will be rationed up to and including the 30th inst.

5. **AMMUNITION.**
   Each Battalion will move with full establishment of Ammunition.

P.T.O.

- 2 -

6. DETACHED PERSONNEL.
All officers and men extra regimentally employed, less those for whom special orders have been issued, will proceed with their units.

7. EMBUSSING ORDERS.
Attention is called to this office Circular Memo. No.8 dated 27/5/18 "Movement by Bus or Lorry".

8. ACKNOWLEDGE.

E.F. Moulton-Barrett Major
for Lieut.Colonel.

Issued at.......... A.A. & Q.M.G. 52nd (Lowland) DIVISION.

Copy to - No.1. 4.D.C. for G.O.C.
2. "Q".
3. Camp Comdt.
4. Signal Company.
5. C. R. E.
6. C. R. A.
7. 155th Inf. Brigade.
8. 156th Inf. Brigade.
9. 157th Inf. Brigade.
10. A.D.M.S.
11. D.A.D.V.S.
12. A.P.M.
13. Divl. Train.
14. S.S.O.
15. 52nd M.G. Battn.
17. 17th Northd.Fus.(P).
18. Divl. Claims Offr.
19. Divl. Gas Officer.
20. D. R. D. O.
21. 52nd M.T. Coy.
22. M. S. O.
23. Salvage Officer.
24. Burial Officer.
25. D.A.D.O.S.
26. Divl. Empmt. Coy.
27. Hoopers Pump.
28. XVIII Corps "Q".
29. First Army "Q".
30. 30th Division.
31. O.C. First Army Aux. Omnibus Park.
32. File.
33.
34. War Diary.

SECRET.　　　　　　　　　　　　　　　　　　　　　Copy No. 34

52nd (Lowland) DIVISION.

CORRIGENDUM to ADMINISTRATIVE INSTRUCTION No.16.

27th June, 1918.

1. MOVE.

The 3 Battalions concerned will be transferred to 34th Division **not** 30th Division, and will proceed by bus to BAMBECQUE.

2. ROUTE.

No restrictions as to route in First Army Area.
Route in Second Army Area as follows :-
ST OMER - SALPERWICK New Road - ST. MOMELIN - BROXEELE - ZEGGERS CAPPEL - WORMHOUDT.

3. DEBUSSING POINT.

On HERZEELE - BAMBECQUE Road under arrangements of II Corps.

4. TRANSPORT.

The march of the transport of these 3 Battalions will now be as follows -

DATE.	DESTINATION.	BILLETS.
June 28th.	DIVION.	Night 28/29 from Town Major, HOUDAIN.
June 29th.	CREQUES.	Night 29/30 from Area Comdt. THEROUANNE.
June 30th.	ST. MOMELIN.	Night June 30/July 1st from Town Major, ST. MOMELIN.
July 1st.	BAMBECQUE.	34th Division.

5. RATIONS.

The 3 Battalions will proceed rationed up to the 29th instant inclusive.
The men and animals of the transport will march with rations up to July 2nd inclusive.

6. EMBUSSING.

Embussing orders remain as at present.

7. ACKNOWLEDGE.

E.L. Mullin-Barrett Major
for
Lieut.Colonel.
A.A. & Q.M.G. 52nd (Lowland) Division.

Issued at 10.30 am

Copy to -
- No.1 A.D.C. for G.O.C.
- 2 "G".
- 3 Camp Comdt.
- 4 Signal Company.
- 5 C.R.E.
- 6 C.R.A.
- 7 155th Brigade.
- 8 156th Brigade.
- 9 157th Brigade.
- 10 A.D.M.S.
- 11 D.A.D.V.S.
- 12 A.P.M.
- 13 Divl. Train.
- 14 S.S.O.
- 15 52nd M.G. Battn.
- 16 O.C. 52nd Push Tramways.
- 17 17th Northd Fus. (P).
- 18 Divl. Claims Offr.
- 19 Divl. Gas Officer.
- 20 D.R.D.O.
- 21 52nd M.T. Company.
- 22 W.S.O.
- 23 Salvage Officer.
- 24 Burial Officer.
- 25 D.A.D.O.S.
- 26 Divl. Empmt. Coy.
- 27 Hoopers Dump.
- 28 XVIII Corps "Q".
- 29 First Army "Q".
- 30 30th Division.
- 31 O.C. First Army Aux. Omnibus Park.
- 32 34th Division.
- 33 File.
- 34
- 35 War Diary.

SECRET.   Copy No. 11

52nd (Lowland) DIVISION.
ADMINISTRATIVE INSTRUCTION No. 17.

27th June, 1918.

With reference to 52nd Divisional Order No.111 dated 25/6/18.

---

1. **REFILLING POINTS.**

    From 29th June inclusive as follows –

    157th Infantry Brigade. LEADLEY SIDING. A.2.c.5.9.

    156th Infantry Brigade. BLACKPOOL SIDING. A.7.d.4.8.

2. **CAMPS.**

    The camps to be occupied will be –

    FRASER.   LANCASTER.
    OTTAWA.   DURHAM.
    HILLS.   HANSON.

    The 157th L.T.M. Battery should be accommodated in HANSON.

3. **LORRIES.**

    (a) 3 Lorries will report at FRASER Camp, MONT ST. ELOY at 2 p.m. 28th inst.
    (b) 15 lorries will report at FRASER Camp at 8.45 a.m. on the 29th inst.

    These lorries will be available for taking Troops to NEUVILLE ST VAAST Area, and bringing back troops to Reserve Area, until relief is completed.

4. **BILLET IMPROVEMENT.**

    156th Infantry Brigade will take over and continue the billet improvement work now being undertaken by 157th Infantry Brigade.

5. **HORSE STANDINGS. etc.**

    (a) The same sites at present occupied by the Transport will be taken over by Brigades on relief.
    (b) Manure will be taken to the Manure Dumps already in use.

6. **DISCIPLINE.**

    The same restrictions as are now in force for 157th Infantry Brigade as regards men not leaving the Divisional Area, particularly with reference to ECOIVRES and other villages in 51st Division Area (i.e. all area South of an E. and W. line through cross roads F.14.b.10.6.) will hold good for 156th Infantry Brigade. This includes finding picquets in relief of those now found by 157th Infantry Brigade.

7. **ACKNOWLEDGE.**

                                          E.L. Rolli-Barrett Major
                                          for Lieut.Colonel.
Issued at T.O.M.   A.A. & Q.M.G. 52nd (Lowland)DIVN.

    Copy No. 1. A.D.C. for G.O.C.   5. C.R.E.   9. Divl. Train.
            2. "G".   6. 52nd M.G.Bn. 10. S.S.O.
            3. 156th Inf. Bde.   7. A.D.M.S.   11.)
            4. 157th Inf. Bde.   8. D.A.D.V.S.   12.) War Diary.
                                                     13. File.

Army Form C. 2118.

WAR DIARY
or
INTELLIGENCE SUMMARY.
(Erase heading not required.) A Branch 52 (Lowland) DIVISION P. I.

Vol XXXVII

Place	Date 1918 July	Hour	Summary of Events and Information	Remarks and references to Appendices
A.C.Q.	1st		Location and distribution of Division is shown on Appendix I.	APP I
	2		Authority was granted for the issue of two Bocheé stretchers per R. F.A. Brigade owing to the scattered distribution.	
	3		Administrative Instruction No. A.F. 18 attached (re supply of rations in preparation for the Gas Beam attack ordered for the night of 5/6 July	APP II
	4		On issue of 40 suits Dungarees to D.T.M.S. for use of personnel in Trench Mortar pits was recommended.	
	5		Administrative Instruction No. A.F. 19 attached (re refilling points, lorries etc. in connection with relief of 155 Inf Bde by 156 Inf Bde on night of 8th/9th.)	
			An officer was ordered to proceed to America as Gas Instructor to H.Q United States Army.	
			Capt C.S. STIRLING-COOKSON, M.C., K.O.S.B. assumed duties as B.M. 157 Bde authority APP III/35/14	APP III
	6		Administrative Instruction No. No. 22 attached (re supply evidences	
			of the military Police in cases where commanding officers has demanded without calling in the Police witnesses to give evidence in person).	

WAR DIARY
or
INTELLIGENCE SUMMARY.

(Erase heading not required.) "A" Branch 52nd (Lowland) Division

Army Form C. 2118.

VOL XXXVII
P. II.

Place	Date 1918 July	Hour	Summary of Events and Information	Remarks and references to Appendices
A.C.Q.	6		Sanction received for one Vickers Machine Gun to be issued to each Machine Gun Battalion for instruction of Personnel. Left out of action.	
	7		Authority given for issue of Additional Lewis or Hotchkiss guns for each Field Coy R.E.	
	8		156 Inf Brigade relieved 155 Inf Bde in Right Section of the Line. The Division's voluntary withdrawal of rations for week ending 6" July was 6 tons 13 cwt - 404 Bevet.	
	10		Report sent to Corps stating that the trial carried with a Trench Oven was found very satisfactory. Recommended an issue of 50 per division, and that they should be constructed at Base Workshops - Notification received from Corps that S.A.A. A.P. is ineffective against Hostile Tanks, and orders it to be returned to Dump. Captain H. SAYER M.C. assumed duties as Brigade Major 156 Inf B.de on 6th inst. Authority First Army N° 1270/83. A. 2.7.18	

Army Form C. 2118.

WAR DIARY
or
INTELLIGENCE SUMMARY.

(Erase heading not required.) "A" Branch 52 (Lowland) Division

VOL XXXVII

P. III

Instructions regarding War Diaries and Intelligence Summaries are contained in F. S. Regs., Part II. and the Staff Manual respectively. Title pages will be prepared in manuscript.

Place	Date 1918 July	Hour	Summary of Events and Information	Remarks and references to Appendices
A.C.Q	11		91 Pennants were issued for the Division. Monkey Puzzle mountings. Two were issued, one each to 155 Inf Bde and 157 Bde. Authority was requested from Corps for the issue of his Stationery Box to each Brigade, 4 Intelligence Officer – for the custody of Maps and Secret papers – GOLF BAGS L.G. Carriers & Racks. 24 Golf Bags L.G. Carriers & 12 Racks were received and issued equally to the 3 Bdes viz 8 & 4 each.	
	12		Authority was requested from Corps for issue of 12 S.A.A. Carriers for each L.T.M. Battery similar to those already in use by Carriers for 18 pdr Batts. for carrying ammunition. These are reserved for carrying T.M. ammunition to & from the line on Pack Animals. Voluntary Undrawal of Rations for week ending 12-6-18. II 6 108% II 6 108%	
	13		Administrative Instructions Nº A.F. 20 attached. (re Supply Arra Stores etc.) Monkey Puzzle L.G. Mountings 4 more were allotted to Div. and issued as follows:- 2 to 155 Inf Bde 1 each to 156 & 157 Inf Bdes.	APP. IV
E.H.

WAR DIARY or INTELLIGENCE SUMMARY

(Erase heading not required.) "A" Branch 52nd (Lowland) Division

VOL XXXVII
P. IV

Army Form C. 2118.

Place	Date 1918 July	Hour	Summary of Events and Information	Remarks and references to Appendices
ALQ	13		SOCKS. Corps ask what percentage come back from Laundry in a Shrunken condition & unfit for wear. Replied 10%	
	14		Administrative Instructions No. AF21 attached (re: relieving Points 2A on relief of 157 Inf Bde by 155 on 17th)	App V
			Canvas Carriers for STOKES MORTAR BOMBS. Corps reply that the issue cannot be sanctioned. Suggest it goes up on Pack animals in the boxes in which it is packed.	
			Underdrawers for week ending 14.7.18	I. 5. A H. 6. 109
	16		One Bde of 4th Canadian Division relieved two Batt. of 156 Bde in portion of Line MERSEY LINE to OLD RIGHT BOUNDARY.	
			Band Instruments for M.Gun Batt. Issue has been approved	
	17		Monkey Puzzle A.A. Mountings. A further allotment of 12 has been made to the Division and issued four to each Brigade.	8/4

Army Form C. 2118.

WAR DIARY
or
INTELLIGENCE SUMMARY.

(Erase heading not required.) "A" Branch 52nd Lowland Division

Vol XXXVII

Place	Date	Hour	Summary of Events and Information	Remarks and references to Appendices
ACQ	1918 July 18		Relief. 155 Inf Bde relieved 157 Inf Bde in left sector. Authority for the issue of Lewis Guns to Batteries R.H. and R.F.A. to complete to scale of 4 per battery. Warning order received from VIII Corps for the Division to move into G.H.Q. Reserve.	
	19.		Administrative Instruction No. A.F. 22 attached (re move of Brigade Group to G.H.Q. Reserve). All formations warned that all preparations must be made for open fighting & transport be overhauled. Voluntary underdrawal of Rations for week ending 19-7-18.	App VI. In Cwt # 4-14-13½ In Cwt # 4-14-13½
	20.		Move. 154 Inf Bde (Reserve) was relieved by 23rd Inf Bde 8th Div. and moved by Tactical trains to the following areas:— AUCHEL Brigade Headquarters 1/7 H.L.I. 1/2nd Lowland Field Ambulance RAIMBERT 1/6 H.L.I. 157 L.T.M.B. 1574 Coy A.S.C. LOZINGHEM 1/5 H.L.I.	G.H.

Army Form C. 2118.

WAR DIARY
or
INTELLIGENCE SUMMARY.

(Erase heading not required.) "A" Branch 52nd Division

VOL XXXVII

Instructions regarding War Diaries and Intelligence Summaries are contained in F. S. Regs., Part II. and the Staff Manual respectively. Title pages will be prepared in manuscript.

Place	Date 1918	Hour	Summary of Events and Information	Remarks and references to Appendices
ACQ	20		Administrative Instructions No A.F. 23 attached (re move of 156 Inf Bde Group to G.H.Q. Reserve)	App VII
			Administrative Instructions No A.F. 24 attached (re moving of 52nd Divl Artillery on the 21st inst)	App VIII
			Administrative Instruction No A.F. 25 attached (re move of 155 Inf Bde Group to G.H.Q. Reserve on 23rd inst)	App IX
	21st		Divisional Artillery moved by inward march to area lately occupied by 8th Divl Artillery ie HERMIN – BOIS DU HAZOIS. R.A. H.Q. to CUVIGNY. 156 Inf Bde was relieved by 8th Division in the Right Section of the line. on relief 156 Bde moved to MONT ST ELOI. Two Coys 52nd Divl M Gun Batt relieved by two coys 8th M Gun Batt.	
			Administrative Instruction No A.F. 26 attached (re move of D.H.Q. and Divisional Troops to G.H.Q. Reserve)	App X

Army Form C. 2118.

WAR DIARY
or
INTELLIGENCE SUMMARY.

(Erase heading not required.) "A" Branch 53rd (Welsh) Division

VOLXXXVII

Place	Date	Hour	Summary of Events and Information	Remarks and references to Appendices
ACG	1918 July 21		Location of 5²ⁿᵈ Divisional Artillery Headquarters. — Nature of Billets	PW@
			CUVIGNY RA Headquarters. — Billets	
			HERMIN 9ᵗʰ Bde. R.F.A. — do	
			BARAFFLE 19ᵗʰ Battery — do	
			GAUCHIN LEGAL 20ᴅ do — do	
			HERMIN 28ᵗʰ Battery — do	
			D/69 — do	
			BOIS DE HAZOIS 56ᵗʰ Bde R.F.A. — Tents & Shelters	
			BURTON D.A.C. —	A few billets
			D.T.M.O. —	mainly Tents & Shelters
			X/52 T.M. B.y	originally a large
			4/52 T.M. B.y	number of these troops were in the open.

J.H.

WAR DIARY
or
INTELLIGENCE SUMMARY.

Army Form C. 2118.

Vol XXXVII

(Erase heading not required.) "A" Branch 52nd Division

Place	Date	Hour	Summary of Events and Information	Remarks and references to Appendices
A.Q.	1918 July 22		156 Inf Bde moved by march route to the following locations:-	
			BARLIN Brigade Headquarters B Coy 52 M. Gun B 412 Field Coy R.E. 219 Coy A.S.C.	
			BOIS D'OLHAIN 1/4 R. Scots 1/7 R. Scots 1/7 Sco. Rifles 156 L.T.M.B. (Tents)	
			CITÉ JEANNE D'ARC 1/1st Low. Field Ambulance	
			155 Inf Bde was relieved in left section (MÉRICOURT) by 26 Inf Bde 8 D.W. and moved by motor Bus to G.H.Q. Reserve at the following locations	
			VERDREL Bde. Headquarters 1/4 R.S. Fus.	
			FRESNICOURT 155-T.M.B. 1/3 Low. Field Amb.	
			OLHAIN 218 Coy A.S.C. 410 Field Coy R.E.	
			CAMBLAIN L'ABBÉ 1/5 R.S. Fus 1/4 K.O.S.B.	
			GOUY-SERVINS "A" Coy 52 M.M. Gun Coy	A.H.

HQ AEF 62D / Vol 4 / July 1918

On His Majesty's Service.

Secret

Officer in Charge
A.G.3's Office
A Box

CONFIDENTIAL

War Diary
"A" Branch. 52ⁿᵈ (Lowland) Division
1ˢᵗ to 31ˢᵗ July 1918

VOLUME XXXVII

Army Form C. 2118.

WAR DIARY
or
INTELLIGENCE SUMMARY.

(Erase heading not required.) "A" Branch 52', (Lowl) Division.   Vol XXXVII

Place	Date 1918 July	Hour	Summary of Events and Information	Remarks and references to Appendices
ACQ	23		Divisional Headquarters moved to PERNES.	
			The Division stands at six hours notice to move from 12 noon -	
			Relief of Division by 8th Division complete -	
PERNES	23		Lieut-Colonel MAUDE relieved D.S.O.M.C. A.A. & Q.M.G. returned from leave having been recalled by wire on 19th inst -	
	24.		G.O.C. was recalled from leave by wire.	
			Administrative Instructions No. A.F. 27 attached issued on 22nd inst (2)	App XI
			Supply System in New Area -).	
	25.		A Dump for Surplus Kit was formed at CINEMA HOUSE 52 Bw Reception Camp, and formations were ordered to send all kit in at once in case of a move -	App XII

Q.H

Army Form C. 2118.

WAR DIARY
or
INTELLIGENCE SUMMARY.

VOL XXXVII

(Erase heading not required.) "A" Branch 52nd Division

Place	Date 1918	Hour	Summary of Events and Information	Remarks and references to Appendices
PERNES	July 27		56th Brigade R.F.A. and D.A.C. moved from OURTON into billets at DIVIDN. Corps ask for opinion as to whether "Last's" memo "Flash" funnel to mask a general issue to formations to whom shoemakers tools are authorized.	
	28		Two new Pattern Carriers for 6" Trench Mortar Bombs went for use with pack saddles were issued to D.T.M.O. for trial report.	
	29		Warning order received for Division to move into line. Administrative Instructions No. A.F. 28 (re move of 156 IY Bde & APP XIII MAROEUIL Area and 157 Bde to BARLIN. 88 Remounts arrived for the Division Substitution of maize meal for Oatmeal when latter not available - Corps advised this was not recommended - but that a substitution of 3oz Bread or 2oz Flour was -	APP XIII G.H.

WAR DIARY
or
INTELLIGENCE SUMMARY.

"A" Branch 52" Division

VOL XXXVII   Army Form C. 2118.

Place	Date	Hour	Summary of Events and Information	Remarks and references to Appendices
PERNES	1918 July 30		Administrative Instruction No A.F. 29 attacked (re move of H.Q. 3 Inf Bdes into line).	App XIV
			Administrative Instruction No A.F 30 attached. (re move of divisional Troops VD.H.Q. to MAROEUIL Area.	App XV.
	31		Corps advised that it is recommended that Ignitor Sets, in connection with Stokes Mortars for A A firing, be issued with detonators crimped to fuzes of lengths of 4 secs, 5 secs, & secs.	
			Petrol Lighters. Corps asked for opinion as to whether these in place of matches in order to save freights.	

G.H.

WAR DIARY
or
INTELLIGENCE-SUMMARY.

(Erase heading not required.)

VOLUME XXXVII.

1/31st JULY, 1918. Army Form C. 2118.

"A" BRANCH, 52nd (Lowland) DIVISION.

page 1

STRENGTH OF DIVISION. WEEK ENDING - 27/7/18.

	Offrs.	Other Ranks.
Divisional Troops.	16	119
Divisional Artillery.	103	2151
Divisional Engineers.	37	711
155th Infantry Brigade.	149	2986
156th --do--	145	2972
157th --do--	140	3143
Divisional Train.	21	670
17th Bn. Northumberland Fus.(P)	34	886
52nd Battalion, Machine Gun Corps	46	919
984th Divnl. Employment Coy.	2	296
R.A.M.C.	20	700
TOTAL.	713	15553

INFANTRY BRIGADES - REINFORCEMENTS RECEIVED FOR MONTH OF JULY.

Week ending.	Offrs.	O.R.
6/7/18.	4	174
13/7/18.	5	314
20/7/18.	-	335
27/7/18.	10	623
TOTAL.	19	1482

CASUALTIES - INFANTRY BRIGADES.

Week ending.	Killed Offrs.	O.R.	Wounded Offrs.	O.R.	Missing Offrs.	O.R.	Sick Offrs.	O.R.
6/7/18.	1	3	1	14	-	-	-	178
13/7/18.	-	5	1	23	-	-	5	188
20/7/18.	-	-	-	8	-	-	12	173
27/7/18.	-	-	-	6	-	-	5	172
TOTAL.	1	8	2	51	-	-	22	711

First Army Pro Forma No. 3.

52nd (Lowland) DIVISION.

Strength Return made up to 12 noon Saturday, 27th JULY, 1918.

UNIT.	A. Strength Return excluding attached.		B. Not present with the unit and not at the disposal of C.O. (included in Column A).		A. *minus* B. Available Fighting Strength (including personnel of Battalion Transport and Quartermaster's Stores).	
	Officers.	O.R.	Officers.	O.R.	Officers.	O.R.
155th Inf. Brigade.						
1/4th Bn. R. S. F.	42	910	22	128	20	782
1/5th Bn. -do-	42	991	14	129	28	862
1/4th Bn. K.O.S.B.	51	992	15	120	36	872
TOTAL.	135	2893	51	377	84	2516
156th Inf. Brigade.						
1/4th Bn. Royal Scots	46	984	14	123	32	861
1/7th Bn. -do-	45	940	18	122	24	881
1/7th Bn. S. Rifles.	44	979	16	129	28	850
TOTAL.	135	2903	48	374	87	2529
157th Inf. Brigade.						
1/5th Bn. H. L. I.	42	1018	9	113	33	905
1/6th Bn. -do-	40	1017	16	136	24	881
1/7th Bn. -do-	42	1023	17	147	25	876
TOTAL.	124	3058	42	396	82	2662
17th Bn. Northumberland Fus. (N.E.R.P.)	33	886	3	37	30	849
GRAND TOTAL.	427	9740	144	1184	283	8556
52nd Battalion, Machine Gun Corps.	45	913	6	70	39	843
TOTALS ...						

First Army Pro Forma No. 3—continued.

DETAILS OF OFFICERS "TAKEN ON" OR "STRUCK OFF" STRENGTH.

UNIT.	Rank.	Name.	Initials.	Remarks.

"A" BRANCH, WAR DIARY.
52nd (Lowland) DIVISION.
VOLUME XXXVII.

52nd (Lowland) DIVISION - INFANTRY BRIGADES.

ABSTRACT OF STRENGTH - COLUMN 'B'. WEEK ENDING 27/7/1918.

UNIT.	Courses. O.	Courses. O.R.	Sick. O.	Sick. O.R.	Leave. O.	Leave. O.R.	Brigade Employ. O.	Brigade Employ. O.R.	Divnl. Employ. O.	Divnl. Employ. O.R.	Extra Regt. Employ. O.	Extra Regt. Employ. O.R.	Total. O.	Total. O.R.
1/4th Bn. R.S.F.	1	14	7	15	6	73	1	15	1	25	-	-	16	142
1/5th Bn. R.S.F.	3	9	2	5	5	77	1	17	-	4	1	13	12	125
1/4th Bn. K.O.S.B.	3	11	2	5	5	67	1	14	2	20	-	-	13	117
	7	34	11	25	16	217	3	46	3	49	1	13	41	384
1/4th Bn. R. Scots	3	11	5	24	6	56	-	20	1	14	-	1	15	126
1/7th Bn. R. Scots	3	11	2	18	9	58	2	23	3	16	-	-	19	126
1/7th Bn. S. Rifles	3	11	3	20	5	68	3	23	1	11	-	-	15	133
	9	33	10	62	20	182	5	66	5	41	-	1	49	385
1/5th Bn. H.L.I.	2	12	2	21	2	75	2	18	-	11	-	-	8	137
1/6th Bn. H.L.I.	4	13	1	20	3	58	2	17	3	25	-	-	13	133
1/7th Bn. H.L.I.	2	13	1	23	6	63	2	18	5	16	-	-	16	133
	8	38	4	64	11	196	6	53	8	52	-	-	37	403
GRAND TOTAL.	24	105	25	151	47	595	14	165	16	142	1	14	127	1172

SECRET.   G.R. 6/1/9.

DAILY LOCATION REPORT No. 20, as for 6 a.m. Sunday 30th June.
Reference Maps :-
  1/20000 MAROEUIL.
  1/40000 ARMY MAP B.
  1/10000 LENS Sheet 11.

Appendix I.
A Branch 52 Division

Serial No.	UNIT.	Location H.Q.	Remarks.
1.	Divisional Headquarters	W.30.b.2.4.	CHATEAU D'ACQ.
2.	**155th Infantry Brigade.**	Line: RIGHT SECTION.	
3.	Brigade Headquarters.	A.6.c.6.5.	THELUS CAVES.
4.	1/4th R.S.F.	T.27.d.3.4.	Line, Left.
5.	1/5th R.S.F.	B.9.a. central.	Line, Right.
6.	1/4th K.O.S.B.	T.26.d.6.4.	Line, Centre.
	155th L.T.M. Battery.	A.5.d.3.5.	Line.
	156th Infantry Brigade.	RESERVE BRIGADE.	
7.	Brigade Headquarters.	F.8.d.3.1.	WHITE HOUSE, MONT ST. ELOY.
8.	1/4th Royal Scots.	A.2.d.9.6.	Hills Camp, NEUVILLE ST. VAAST.
9.	1/7th -do-	F.8.a.7.0.	Fraser Camp, MONT ST. ELOY.
10.	1/7th Scottish Rifles	F.8.a.2.7.	Ottawa Camp, MONT ST. ELOY.
11.	156th L.T.M. Battery.	A.8.b.3.4.	Hanson Camp, ST. VAAST.
	157th Infantry Brigade.	Line: LEFT SECTION.	
12.	Brigade Headquarters.	S.27.b.0.5.	
13.	1/5th H.L.I.	S.24.a.2.0.	Support.
14.	1/6th -do-	T.13.b.5.2.	Line, Left.
15.	1/7th -do-	T.20.c.2.1.	Line, Right.
16.	157th L.T.M. Battery.	T.13.b.5.1.	Line.
	Divnl. Artillery.		
17.	Headquarters.	W.30.a.3.6.	700 yards W. of CHATEAU D'ACQ
18.	D.T.M.O.	A.2.d.3.5.	
19.	Right Group (52nd A.F.A. Brigade & A/56 & C/56 Btys. 9th Bde. R.F.A. 122 Bty. 19, 20, 28, & D/69 Btys)	A.6.c.6.7.	THELUS CAVES.
20.	9th Bde. R.F.A.	A.6.c.6.7.	
21.	52nd A.F.A. Brigade.	A.8.c.5.7.	
22.	Left Group (242nd A.F.A. Bde. & 527/56 & B/56 Btys.)	S.27.b.00.00.	
23.	H.Q. 56th A.F.A. Bde.	S.26.c.1.8.	
24.	52nd D.A.C. (less S.A.A. Section.	F.8.b.50.50.	
25.	S.A.A. Sect. D.A.C.	F.9.c.9.8.	MONT ST. ELOY.
26.	X/52 T.M. Battery.	T.28.a.40.15.	
27.	Y/52 -do-	T.20.d.65.25.	

/Divnl. Engineers.

Serial No.	UNIT.	Location H.Q.	Remarks.
	Divnl. Engineers.		
28.	Headquarters.	W.30.a.3.5.	700 yards W. of CHATEAU D'ACQ.
29.	410th Field Coy.	A.8.c.5.6.	AUX REITZ.
30.	412th -do-	A.1. central.	
31.	413th -do-	F.4.a.3.4.	BERTHONVAL.
	52nd Bn. M.G.C.		
32.	H.Q.	A.9.a.25.25.	Cubitt Camp, NEUVILLE ST. VAAST.
32a.	1 Company.	X.19.d.20.80.	VILLERS AU BOIS.
33.	1½ Company.	Line, Right Section.	
34.	1½ Company.	Line, Left Section.	
35.	17th Bn. North'd Fus (B)	A.9.a.	Cellar Camp, NEUVILLE ST. VAAST.
36.	52nd Div. Train. H.Q. & 217, 218, 219 & 220 Coys.	A.2.c.3.5.	LAR TARGETTE.
37.	1/1st Low. Field Amb.	X.19.a.	VILLERS AU BOIS.
38.	1/2nd -do-	A.8.c.5.7.	AUX REITZ.
39.	1/3rd -do-		MONT ST. ELOY.
40.	Detraining Centre.	V.29.a.75.85.	Near MINGOVAL.
41.	1/1st Low. Mob. Vet. Section.	A.15.central.	

(Sd) W.H.G. JENKINS, Capt.
for Lieut. Colonel.
G.S.
52nd Division.

Appendix II
"A" Branch 52nd Division

SECRET.   COPY NO. 14

52nd (Lowland) DIVISION.

ADMINISTRATIVE INSTRUCTION No. AF. 18.

3rd July, 1918.

With reference to 52nd Divisional Order 113 dated 2/7/18.

1. Two days rations will be sent up to Brigades in front line on the night 4/5th July, in preparation for the Gas beam attack on the night 5/6th July.

2. The extra days rations thus sent up will accordingly be consumed during the 24 hours following the Gas attack.

3. Should the attack be postponed, however, rations will be sent up nightly from transport lines as usual, until the night of attack, and the extra days rations will be kept for the day following the attack.

4. The S.S.O. will arrange to issue rations daily after the arrival of the Pack Train, so that in the event of any postponement, rations will be available to be sent up at short notice.

5. ACKNOWLEDGE.

                                        for Lieut. Colonel,
Issued at 10 a.m.   A.A. & Q.M.G. 52nd (Lowland) Division.

Copy to -   1 A.D.C. for G.O.C.
            2 "G"
            3 155th Inf. Brigade.
            4 156th Inf. Brigade.
            5 157th Inf. Brigade.
            6 C. R. A.
            7 C. R. E.
            8 52nd Division M.G. Battn.
            9 S. S. O.
           10 A.D.M.S.
           11 17th Northd. Fus. (P).
           12 File.
           13)
           14) War Diary.

Appendix III
"A" Branch 52nd Division

SECRET.   COPY NO. 11

52nd (LOWLAND) DIVISION.

ADMINISTRATIVE INSTRUCTION NO A.F. 19.

5th July, 1918.

With reference to 52nd Divisional Order No.114 dated 4/7/18.

1. **REFILLING POINTS.**

   From 8th July inclusive as follows -

   156th Infantry Brigade. LEADLEY SIDING. A.2.c.5.9.

   155th Infantry Brigade. SIDING AT F.9.c.

2. **CAMPS.**

   The camps to be occupied will be -

   FRASER.   LANCASTER.
   OTTAWA.   DURHAM.
   HILLS.   HANSON.

   The 155th L.T.M. Battery should be accommodated in HANSON.

3. **LORRIES.**

   (a) 3 Lorries will report at FRASER Camp, MONT ST ELOY at 8.45 a.m. on 7th inst.
   (b) 12 Lorries will report at FRASER Camp at 8.45 a.m. on the 8th inst.

   These Lorries will be available for taking Troops to NEUVILLE ST VAAST Area, and bringing back troops to Reserve Area, until relief is completed.

4. **BILLET IMPROVEMENT.**

   155th Infantry Brigade will take over and continue the billet improvement work now being undertaken by 156th Infantry Brigade.

5. **DISCIPLINE.**

   The same restrictions as are now in force for 156th Infantry Brigade as regards men not leaving the Divisional Area, particularly with reference to ECOIVRES and other villages in 51st Division Area (i.e. all area South of an E. and W. line through cross roads F.14.b.10.6.) will hold good for 155th Infantry Brigade. This includes finding picquets in relief of those now found by 156th Infantry Brigade.

7. **ACKNOWLEDGE.**

                                          E.L. Moulton-Barrett Major
                                          for
Issued at 7 p.m.   Lieut.Colonel.
                                          A.A. & Q.M.G. 52nd (Lowland) DIVISION.

Copy No. 1 A.D.C. for G.O.C.   7. A.D.M.S.
         2 "G"   8. D.A.D.V.S.
         3 156th Inf. Bde.   9. Divl. Train.
         4 155th Inf. Bde.   10. S.S.O.
         5 C.R.E.   11.)
         6 52nd M.G. Battn.   12.) War Diary.
                                   13. File.

Appendix III
A Branch 52nd Division

52nd (Lowland) DIVISION.

ADMINISTRATIVE CIRCULAR MEMORANDUM No. 22.

EVIDENCE OF MILITARY POLICE.

1. One or two cases have occurred lately where charges brought by the Military Police have been dismissed by Officers Commanding Units, without calling the police witnesses to give evidence in person.

2. This procedure is not only highly irregular, but is likely to weaken the authority of the Military Police.

3. It is to be clearly understood that G.R.O. No. 2473 (page 63, A.Gs. Extracts from G.R.Os.) refers only to the taking of the Summary of Evidence for a F.G.C.M. At Courts Martial themselves or prior to a Summary award by a Commanding Officer, where the accused denies the charge, the police will always attend in person.

4. In future, whenever a charge brought by the Military Police is dismissed by a Commanding Officer, the charge sheet and any attached documents, together with a short report from the unit concerned as to the manner in which the police evidence failed, will be forwarded to Divisional Headquarters, through the A.P.M.

6/7/18.

Lieut. Colonel.
A.A. & Q.M.G., 52nd (Lowland) DIVISION.

Appendix IV
'A' Branch 52nd Division

COPY NO. 18

SECRET.

52nd (LOWLAND) DIVISION.

ADMINISTRATIVE INSTRUCTION No. A.F. 20.

13th July, 1918.

With reference to 52nd Divisional Order No.115 dated 13/7/18.

1. AREA STORES etc.

    (a) The following will be retained by 156th Infantry Brigade -

        Yukon Packs.
        Soyers Stoves.
        Hot Food Containers.

    (b) The following will be handed over to the 4th Canadian Division -

        Petrol Tins.
        Rat Traps. (less Brigade Reserve)
        and Reserve Rations as are at present in the area to be vacated by 156th Infantry Brigade.

    (c) Receipts should be obtained for all stores handed over, and forwarded to this office.

2. ACCOMMODATION.

    Reference paragraph 7 of above mentioned order, accommodation will be found as follows for the Battalion of 157th Infantry Brigade to be accommodated in NEUVILLE ST VAAST. -

    (a) The troops of 155th Infantry Brigade occupying HANSON CAMP will move to CINEMA CAMP (A.8.a.6.1) on the morning of the 15th instant; move to be completed by 10 a.m. A Staff Officer will point out this camp at 3 p.m. 14th inst.

    (b) The Battalion of 157th Infantry Brigade on relief from the line will occupy HANSON CAMP.

3. ACKNOWLEDGE.

E.F. Moulton-Barrett Major
for
Lieut.Colonel.
A.A. & Q.M.G. 52nd (Lowland) Division.

Issued at 7 p.m.

```
Copy No. 1 to G.O.C.           13.   D.A.D.O.S.
        2    "G"                14.   S.S.O.
        3    155th Inf. Bde.    15.-16 4th Canadian Division.
        4    156th Inf. Bde.    17.   File.
        5    157th Inf. Bde.    18-19. War Diary.
        6    C.R.E.
        7    M.G. Battalion.
        8    A.D.M.S.
        9    D.A.D.V.S.
       10    Divl. Train.
       11    Divl. Signal Coy.
       12    A.P.M.
```

Appendix V
'A' Branch 52 Division

SECRET.　　　　　　　　　　　　　　　　　　COPY No. 11

52nd (LOWLAND) DIVISION.

ADMINISTRATIVE INSTRUCTION No. A.F. 21.

14th July, 1918.

With reference to 52nd Divisional Order No.116 dated 14/7/18.

1. **REFILLING POINTS.**

    From 17th July inclusive as follows -

    155th Infantry Brigade. LEADLEY SIDING. A.2.c.5.9.

    157th Infantry Brigade. SIDING AT F.9.c.

2. **CAMPS.**

    The camps to be occupied will be -

    FRASER.　　　　LANCASTER.
    OTTAWA.　　　　DURHAM.
    LE PENDU.　　　SURBURBAN. (2 Coys. in each).

    The 157th L.T.M. Battery should be accommodated in CUBBITT CAMP.

3. **LORRIES.**

    (a) 3 Lorries will report at FRASER CAMP, MONT ST ELOY at 9.30 a.m. on 17th inst.
    (b) 12 Lorries will report at FRASER CAMP at 9 a.m. on the 18th inst.

    These Lorries will be available for taking Troops to NEUVILLE ST VAAST Area, and bringing back Troops to Reserve Area, until relief is completed.

4. **BILLET IMPROVEMENT.**

    157th Infantry Brigade will take over and continue the billet improvement work now being undertaken by 155th Infantry Brigade.

5. **DISCIPLINE.**

    The same restrictions as are now in force for 155th Infantry Brigade as regards men not leaving the Divisional Area, particularly with reference to ECOIVRES and other villages in 4th Canadian Division Area (i.e. all area south of an E. and W. line through cross roads F.14.b.10.6) will hold good for 157th Infantry Brigade. This includes finding picquets in relief of those now found by 155th Infantry Brigade.

6. **ACKNOWLEDGE.**

Issued at 7 p.m.

for Lieut.Colonel.
A.A. & Q.M.G. 52nd (Lowland) Division.

Copy No. 1 A.D.C. for G.O.C.　　7 A.D.M.S.
　　　　2 "G"　　　　　　　　　　 8 D.A.D.V.S.
　　　　3 155th Inf. Bde.　　　　 9 Divl. Train.
　　　　4 157th Inf. Bde.　　　　10 S.S.O.
　　　　5 C.R.E.　　　　　　　　　11)
　　　　6 52nd M.G. Battn.　　　 12) War Diary.
　　　　　　　　　　　　　　　　　13 File.

SECRET.

Appendix No VI
A Branch 52 Division
Copy No...1...

52nd (LOWLAND) DIVISION.

ADMINISTRATIVE INSTRUCTION No. A.F. 22.

19th July, 1918.

With reference to 52nd Divisional Order No.117 dated 19/7/18

1. INFORMATION.

157th Infantry Brigade, 1/2nd Lowland Field Ambulance and 220th Company, A.S.C. will be transferred by tactical trains, as per attached time table, on the 20th instant from the 8th Corps to the 17th Corps and will be billetted as follows -

   AUCHEL.
   Brigade Headquarters, "A" Battalion and 1/2nd Lowland Field Ambulance.
   RAIMBERT.
   "B" Battalion, Light Trench Mortar Battery and 220th Company A.S.C.
   LOZINGHEM.
   "C" Battalion.

2. MOVE.

   The move will be carried out as follows -

   (a) Dismounted personnel by tactical trains in accordance with attached time table.

   (b) Transport will march to the Billetting Area of their respective units under the orders of O.C. 220th Company A.S.C. Head of column to pass WINNIPEG CAMP (F.7.b.9.9.) 7.30 a.m. 20th instant. The transport of 1/2nd Lowland Field Ambulance will join the column at LES 4 VENTS.

3. ENTRAINING AND DETRAINING OFFICERS.

   G.O.C. 157th Infantry Brigade will detail an entraining officer and a detraining officer to report to the R.T.O.s
   (a) of the entraining station 2 hours before the first train leaves,
   (b) of the detraining stations on arrival of the first train.

   The entraining officer will travel on the last train allotted to his Brigade Group.

   The detraining officer will remain on duty till after the arrival at the detraining station of the last train of his Group.

4. ENTRAINING AND DETRAINING.

   (a) G.O.C. 157th Infantry Brigade Group will be responsible for the order of entrainment of the units and their arrival at entrainment station.

   (b) The last unit on each train should arrive at the entraining station not less than one hour before the train is due to start.

   (c) On arrival at detraining station units will be met by guides from Billetting Parties and led to Billetting Areas.

P.T.O.

- 2 -

5. **LOADING PARTY.**

   G.O.C. 157th Infantry Brigade will arrange for loading and unloading parties for any baggage which may require to be taken by train.

6. **SUPPLIES.**

   (a) Railhead will remain at MONT ST ELOY till further orders.

   (b) M.T. Company will deliver rations for consumption on the 22nd and subsequently to a Refilling Point to be selected in 157th Brigade Area.

   (c) Rations for the 21st will be carried in the Supply Wagons of the Train.

7. **LORRIES.**

   O.C. 52nd Divisional M.T. Company will detail lorries as follows in connection with the move.-

   (a) One lorry to accompany march of transport. This lorry will be under the orders of the O.C. 220th Company A.S.C. and will deal with breakdowns, stragglers, etc. No man will, however, be allowed to ride on the lorry without written permission from an officer. This lorry will join the column at LES 4 VENTS.

   (b) 4 lorries to report Headquarters 157th Infantry Brigade MONT ST ELOY at 8 a.m. to take Q.M. Stores etc. to new area.

   (c) 1 lorry to report 1/5th H.L.I., FRASER CAMP, MONT ST ELOY at 1.30 p.m. to convey cooking utensils etc. of portion of Brigade which leaves by 2nd train to new area.

8. **AMMUNITION.**

   Full establishment of S.A.A. will be taken in Horse Transport.

9. **STATES.**

   A Movement Order showing the number of personnel proceeding by each train will be handed by units to the R.T.O. on arrival at the entraining stations.

10. **POLICE.**

    The A.P.M. will arrange for 1 Sergeant and 4 police to be attached temporarily to the 157th Infantry Brigade. They will proceed to new area with transport, and will report to 157th Infantry Brigade MONT ST. ELOY at 7 a.m.

11. **ACKNOWLEDGE.**

Issued at..9.30.p.m.

E.J. Mullin Barrett
for Lieut Colonel.
A.A. & Q.M.G. 52nd (Lowland) Division.

SECRET.   Appendix No. VI
                                                           "A" Branch 52nd Division
                    52nd (LOWLAND) DIVISION.   Copy No....20...

             ADMINISTRATIVE INSTRUCTION No. A.F. 22.

                                                    19th July, 1918.

With reference to 52nd Divisional Order No.117 dated 19/7/18

1. INFORMATION.

        157th Infantry Brigade, 1/2nd Lowland Field Ambulance and 220th Company, A.S.C. will be transferred by tactical trains, as per attached time table, on the 20th instant from the 8th Corps to the 17th Corps and will be billetted as follows -

    AUCHEL.
        Brigade Headquarters, "A" Battalion and 1/2nd Lowland Field Ambulance.
    RAIMBERT.
        "B" Battalion, Light Trench Mortar Battery and 220th Company A.S.C.
    LOZINGHEM.
        "C" Battalion.

2. MOVE.

        The move will be carried out as follows -

    (a) Dismounted personnel by tactical trains in accordance with attached time table.

    (b) Transport will march to the Billeting Area of their respective units under the orders of O.C. 220th Company A.S.C. Head of column to pass WINNIPEG CAMP (F.7.b.9.9.) 7.30 a.m. 20th instant. The transport of 1/2nd Lowland Field Ambulance will join the column at LES 4 VENTS.

3. ENTRAINING AND DETRAINING OFFICERS.

        G.O.C. 157th Infantry Brigade will detail an entraining officer and a detraining officer to report to the R.T.O.s
    (a) of the entraining station 2 hours before the first train leaves,
    (b) of the detraining stations on arrival of the first train.

        The entraining officer will travel on the last train allotted to his Brigade Group.

        The detraining officer will remain on duty till after the arrival at the detraining station of the last train of his Group.

4. ENTRAINING AND DETRAINING.

    (a) G.O.C. 157th Infantry Brigade Group will be responsible for the order of entrainment of the units and their arrival at entrainment station.

    (b) The last unit on each train should arrive at the entraining station not less than one hour before the train is due to start.

    (c) On arrival at detraining station units will be met by guides from Billetting Parties and led to Billetting Areas.

                                                              P.T.O.

- 2 -

5. **LOADING PARTY.**

    G.O.C. 157th Infantry Brigade will arrange for loading and unloading parties for any baggage which may require to be taken by train.

6. **SUPPLIES.**

    (a) Railhead will remain at MONT ST ELOY till further orders.

    (b) M.T. Company will deliver rations for consumption on the 22nd and subsequently to a Refilling Point to be selected in 157th Brigade Area.

    (c) Rations for the 21st will be carried in the Supply Wagons of the Train.

7. **LORRIES.**

    O.C. 52nd Divisional M.T. Company will detail lorries as follows in connection with the move -

    (a) One lorry to accompany march of transport. This lorry will be under the orders of the O.C. 220th Company A.S.C. and will deal with breakdowns, stragglers, etc. No man will, however, be allowed to ride on the lorry without written permission from an officer. This lorry will join the column at LES 4 VENTS.

    (b) 4 lorries to report Headquarters 157th Infantry Brigade MONT ST ELOY at 8 a.m. to take Q.M. Stores etc. to new area.

    (c) 1 lorry to report 1/5th H.L.I., FRASER CAMP, MONT ST ELOY at 1.30 p.m. to convey cooking utensils etc. of portion of Brigade which leaves by 2nd train to new area.

8. **AMMUNITION.**

    Full establishment of S.A.A. will be taken in Horse Transport.

9. **STATES.**

    A Movement Order showing the number of personnel proceeding by each train will be handed by units to the R.T.O. on arrival at the entraining stations.

10. **POLICE.**

    The A.P.M. will arrange for 1 Sergeant and 4 police to be attached temporarily to the 157th Infantry Brigade. They will proceed to new area with transport, and will report to 157th Infantry Brigade MONT ST. ELOY at 7 a.m.

11. **ACKNOWLEDGE.**

                                            E.L. Mullin-Barrett Major
                                            for
                                            Lieut Colonel.
Issued at..9.30.p.m.   A.A. & Q.M.G. 52nd (Lowland) Division.

SECRET.   COPY NO. 19

52nd (LOWLAND) DIVISION.

ADMINISTRATIVE INSTRUCTION NO. A.F. 23.

20th July, 1918.

With reference to 52nd Divisional Order No.117 dated 19/7/18.

1. **INFORMATION.**

    156th Infantry Brigade, 1/1st Lowland Field Ambulance, 412th Field Company, R.E., 219th Company, A.S.C. and "B" Company Machine Gun Battalion will be transferred by March Route from the 8th Corps to the 17th Corps on the 22nd instant.

    March will be carried out under orders to be issued by B.G.C. 156th Infantry Brigade.

2. **ACCOMMODATION.**

    Billets will be in 1st Corps Area and Advanced Parties should report 1st Divisional Reception Camp in BOIS D'OLHAIN (Q.8.c.9.9, reference sheet 44 B S.E.).

    Billets for 156th Brigade Headquarters will be allotted by Town Major BARLIN, to whom Headquarter representatives should report.

3. **BILLETTING PARTIES.**

    (a) Billetting parties will proceed direct to new area in lorries on the 21st instant, and will be responsible for meeting units on arrival

    (b) 2 lorries for conveyance of this party will start from LATTA CAMP at 7.30 a.m. on the 21st instant.

    (c) The following should be the strength of billetting parties.

(i) Brigade Headquarters.	1 officer.
(ii) Per Infantry Battalion.	1 officer 3 O.R.
(iii) Per smaller Unit.	1 officer 1 O.R.

    A bicycle a man should be taken.

4. **LORRIES.**

    O.C. M.T. Company will detail lorries as follows in connection with the move -

    (a) 1 lorry to accompany the march of the Brigade Group. This lorry will deal with breakdowns, stragglers etc. No man will, however, be allowed to ride on the lorry without written permission from an officer. O.C. M.T. Company will arrange direct with 156th Infantry Brigade as to time and position of rendezvous.

    (b) 14 lorries will be at the disposal of 156th Infantry Brigade. O.C. M.T. Company will arrange direct with B.G.C. as to hour and position of Rendezvous.

                                                                  P.T.O.

5. **SUPPLIES.**

(a) Railhead will remain at MONT ST ELOY till 22nd; from 23rd inclusive it will be at HOUDAIN.

(b) Rations for 23rd instant will be carried in the Supply Wagons of the Train.

6. **AMMUNITION.**

Full establishment of S.A.A. will be taken in Horse Transport.

7. **TRAIN WAGONS.**

Baggage and Supply Wagons of the Train will join units by 6 p.m. 21st instant.

8. **POLICE.**

The A.P.M. will arrange for 1 Sergeant and 4 police to be attached temporarily to the 156th Infantry Brigade. They will report to 156th Infantry Brigade MONT ST ELOY at 7 a.m. 22nd instant.

9. **STORES.**

(a) All Trench and Area Stores, including Reserve Rations, will be handed over to relieving units. Soyers Stoves, Hot Food Containers and S.D. Clothing for Gas Cases will also be handed over, numbers so handed over to be reported to Divisional Headquarters.

(b) Yukon Packs, anti-gas combination clothing and Meat Safes will be taken with the Brigade.

(c) The Chaffcutter in the Transport Lines will be handed over to Area Commandant, BERTHONVAL FARM.

(d) Paraffin retained for a special purpose should be handed over to relieving units or Area Commandants.

10 **ACKNOWLEDGE.**

Issued at... 6 p.m.

E.F. Moulton-Barrett Major
for Lieut.Colonel.
A.A. & Q.M.G. 52nd (Lowland) Division.

Copy to -
No.		No.	
1	A.D.C. for G.O.C.	11	D.A.D.O.S.
2	"G"	12	52nd M.T. Company.
3	156th Inf. Bde.	13	French Mission.
4	52nd Divl. Train.	14	1st Corps.
5	S.S.O.	15	17th Corps.
6	A.D.M.S.	16	8th Corps.
7	D.A.D.V.S.	17	Town Major. BARLIN.
8	C.R.E.	18	File.
9	O.C. Signal Coy.	19)	
10	A.P.M.	20)	War Diary.

SECRET.   COPY NO...17.

Appendix VIII
A Branch 52 Division

52nd (LOWLAND) DIVISION.

ADMINISTRATIVE INSTRUCTION NO. A.F. 24.

20th July, 1918.

With reference to 52nd Divisional Order No.117 dated 19/7/18 and Addendum No.1 thereto.

1. **INFORMATION.**

    52nd Divisional Artillery will move by March Route on the 22nd instant to the area lately occupied by the 8th Divisional Artillery i.e. HERMIN - BOIS DU HAZOIS.

    R.A. Headquarters will be located at CUVIGNY.

2. **MOVE.**

    The 52nd Divisional Artillery will move under the orders of the C.R.A. 52nd Division.

3. **SUPPLIES.**

    (a) Railhead will remain at MONT ST ELOY till 22nd instant; from the 23rd instant inclusive it will be at HOUDAIN.

    (b) Rations for 23rd instant will be carried in the Supply Wagons of the Train.

4. **TRAIN VEHICLES.**

    Supply and baggage wagons of the Train will report at the wagon lines at 6 p.m. 21st instant.

5. **LORRIES.**

    O.C. 52nd Division M.T. Company will detail 13 lorries for the journey; they will report as follows -

    2 R.A. H.Q.   21st at 4 p.m.
    3 Campbell Road.   22nd at 7 a.m. for 56th Bde. R.F.A.
    4 TARGETTE Cross Roads. 22nd at 7 a.m. for D.T.M.O.
    3 TARGETTE Cross Roads. 22nd at 7 a.m. for 9th Bde. R.F.A.
    1 D.A.C. H.Q. MONT ST
              ELOY.   22nd at 7 a.m.

6. **AMMUNITION.**

    Full establishment of Ammunition will be carried.

7. **POLICE.**

    The A.P.M. will arrange for 1 Sergeant and 4 police to be attached temporarily to the C.R.A. They will report to C.R.A. at 7 a.m. 22nd instant.

8. **STORES.**

    (a) All area and trench stores including reserve rations and S.D. Clothing for gas cases will be handed over to the incoming units.

    Numbers handed over should be reported to Divisional Headquarters.

    (b) Meatsafes should be taken.

P.T.O.

9. ACKNOWLEDGE.

E.L. Moulton-Barrett Major
for Lieut.Colonel.
A.A. & Q.M.G. 52nd (Lowland) Division.

Issued at 7 p.m.

Copy to - No.1 A.D.C. for G.O.C. 11 S.S.Q.
         2   "G"   12 VIII Corps.
         3   C.R.A.   13 XVII Corps.
         4   A.D.M.S.   14 I Corps.
         5   D.A.D.V.S.   15 8th Division.
         6   Divisional Train.   16 File.
         7   52nd M.T. Coy.   17)
         8   O.C. Signal Coy.   18) War Diary.
         9   A.P.M.   19 French Mission
        10   D.A.D.O.S.

Appendix IX
A Branch 52nd Division

SECRET.   COPY NO. 22

52nd (LOWLAND) DIVISION.

ADMINISTRATIVE INSTRUCTION NO. A.F. 25.

20th July, 1918.

With reference to 52nd Divisional Order No.117 dated 19/7/18.

1. INFORMATION.

The 155th Infantry Brigade, 1/3rd Lowland Field Ambulance, 410th Field Company, R.E., 218th Company, A.S.C. and "A" Company 52nd Battalion, Machine Gun Corps will be transferred on the 23rd instant from the 8th Corps to the 17th Corps and will be billetted as follows -

UNIT.	PLACE.	COMMANDANT WHO WILL ALLOT BILLETS.
155th Inf. Bde. Hqrs.	VERDREL.	Area Comdt. VERDREL.
"A" Battalion.	VERDREL.	- do -
Trench Mortar Battery.	FRESNICOURT.	- do -
1/3rd Low. Field Ambce.	FRESNICOURT.	- do -
218th Company, A.S.C.	OLHAIN.	Town Major OLHAIN.
410th Field Company.R.E.	OLHAIN.	- do -
"B" Battalion.	CAMBLAIN L'ABBE.	Area Comdt. CAMBLAIN L'ABBE.
"C" Battalion.	CAMBLAIN L'ABBE.	- do -
"A" Company, 52nd Battn. Machine Gun Corps.	GOUY - SERVINS.	Area Comdt. GOUY - SERVINS.

2. MOVE.

The Brigade Group as detailed above will proceed to the new billetting areas of the respective units by route march under orders to be issued by G.O.C. 155th Infantry Brigade.

3. BILLETTING PARTIES.

(a) Billetting Parties will proceed direct to new area in motor lorries on 21st instant and will be responsible for meeting units on arrival.

(b) The following should be the strength of billetting parties -

	Officers.	O.R.
Brigade Headquarters.	1	-
Per Infantry Battalion.	1	3
Per Smaller Units.	1	1

1 Bicycle per man should be taken.

(c) 2 lorries for conveyance of this party will start from BERTHONVAL at 2 p.m. on 21st instant.

4. SUPPLIES.

(a) Railhead will be at MONT ST. ELOY till 22nd and at HOUDAIN from 23rd (inclusive).

(b) Rations for the 23rd will be carried in the Supply Wagons of the Train.

P.T.O.

5. **LORRIES.**

O.C. 52nd Divisional M.T. Company will detail lorries as follows in connection with the move. -

(a) One lorry to accompany march of Brigade Group. This lorry will be under the orders of O.C. 218th Company, A.S.C. and will deal with breakdowns, stragglers, etc. No man will, however, be allowed to ride on the lorry without written permission from an officer. O.C. M.T. Company will arrange direct with 155th Infantry Brigade as to hour and position of rendezvous.

(b) 14 lorries will be at disposal of 155th Infantry Brigade to take Q.M. Stores etc. to new area. O.C. M.T. Company will arrange direct with 155th Infantry Brigade as to hour and position of rendezvous.

6. **AMMUNITION.**

Full establishment of S.A.A. will be taken in Horse Transport.

7. **STORES.**

(a) All Trench and Area stores (including Reserve Rations) will be handed over to relieving units. Any Soyers Stoves, Hot Food Containers, S.D. clothing for gas cases will also be handed over, and numbers notified to Divisional Headquarters.

(b) Yukon Packs, Anti-gas Combination Clothing and Meat-Safes will be taken with the Brigade.

(c) Paraffin retained in various camps for a certain purpose should be handed over to the incoming unit or the Area Commandant.

(d) Chaff Cutters in the Transport Lines will be handed over to Area Commandant BERTHONVAL FARM.

8. **POLICE.**

The A.P.M. will arrange for 1 Sergeant and 4 police to be attached temporarily to the 155th Infantry Brigade. Time and place of reporting should be arranged direct with B.G.C. 155th Infantry Brigade.

9. **TRAIN WAGONS.**

Baggage wagons of the Train will join units at Transport Lines at 8 a.m. Supply Wagons at 3 p.m. on 22nd.

10. **ACKNOWLEDGE.**

Issued at... 8.30 p.m.

E.F. Moulki-Barrett Major
for Lieut.Colonel.
A.A. & Q.M.G. 52nd (Lowland) Division.

Copy to -
No. 1 A.D.C. for G.O.C.
2 "G"
3 155th Inf. Bde.
4 52nd Divl. Train.
5 S.S.O.
6 A.D.M.S.
7 D.A.D.V.S.
8 C.R.E.
9 O.C. Signal Coy.
10 A.P.M.
11 D.A.D.O.S.
12 52nd M.T. Company.
13 French Mission.
14 1st Corps.
15 17th Corps.
16 8th Corps.
17 Area Comdt. VERDREL.
18 Town Major OLHAIN.
19 Area Comdt. CAMBLAIN L'ABBE.
20 Area Comdt. GOUY-SERVINS.
21 File.
22)
23) War Diary.

"A" Form.
MESSAGES AND SIGNALS.

Army Form C. 2121.
(In pads of 100.)

TO: War Diary

Sender's Number.	Day of Month.	In reply to Number.	AAA
Q. 242	22		

Reference Admin. Instruction A.F.26
dated 21/7/18 AAA No. 3
train ZERO hour 9.50 a.m.
AAA No.4 train ZERO
hour 3 p.m. AAA
Entraining Station MONT ST ELOY AAA
Acknowledge

Time: SEFO

J. L. Moulton

SECRET.	COPY NO. 23

52nd (LOWLAND) DIVISION.

ADMINISTRATIVE INSTRUCTION NO. A.F. 26.

21st July, 1918.

With reference to 52nd Divisional Order No. 117 dated 19/7/18

1. **INFORMATION.**

    52nd Divisional Headquarters, Headquarters and 413th Field Company R.E., 52nd Divisional Signal Company, Headquarters Divisional Train, Reception Camp Personnel, Divisional Employment Company, Mobile Veterinary Section, 17th Northumberland Fusiliers (Pioneers), 52nd Battalion Machine Gun Corps (Headquarters and 1 Company) will be transferred by tactical trains, as per attached time table, on the 23rd instant, from the 8th Corps to the 17th Corps and will be billetted as follows -

UNIT.	PLACE.
52nd Divisional Headquarters.	PERNES.
Divisional Train Headquarters.	PERNES.
Mobile Veterinary Section.	PERNES.
17th Northumberland Fusiliers (Pioneers).	TANGRY.
413th Field Company, R.E.	LOZINGHEM.
Reception Camp.	HOUDAIN.
Divisional Employment Company.	PERNES.
52nd Battalion Machine Gun Corps (Headquarters and 1 Company).	PERNES.
52nd Divisional Signal Company.	PERNES.
Royal Engineer Headquarters.	PERNES.

    Further details will be issued later.

2. **MOVE.**

    The move will be carried out as follows -

    (a) Dismounted personnel by tactical trains in accordance with attached table.

    (b) Transport will march to the billetting area of their respective units under the orders of O.C. Divisional Train. Head of column to pass junction of main MONT ST ELOY - CAMBLAIN L'ABBE road and road leading to CHATEAU D'ACQ at 8 a.m. on 23rd instant.

3. **BILLETTING PARTIES.**

    (a) Billetting Parties will proceed direct to new area in motor wagons on 22nd instant and will be responsible for meeting units on arrival.

    (b) The following should be the strength of billetting parties -

	Officers.	O.R.
52nd Divisional Headquarters.	1	2
Divisional Train Headquarters.	1	1
Mobile Veterinary Section.	1	
52nd Divisional Signal Company.	1	
17th Northumberland Fusiliers (Pioneers).	1	3
413th Field Company, R.E.	1	1
Divisional Employment Company.	1	1
Reception Camp.	1	2
52nd Battalion, Machine Gun Corps.	1	1
R.E. Headquarters.	1	2

    Where possible bicycles should be taken.

P.T.O.

3. BILLETING PARTIES contd.

(c) 2 lorries for conveyance of this party will start from TARGETTE Corner, NEUVILLE ST VAAST, at 8 a.m. on 22nd. Parties from Divisional Headquarters, Divisional Employment Company and Reception Camp will join the lorry at junction of MONT ST ELOY - CAMBLAIN L'ABBE Road and Road leading to VILLERS AU BOIS at 8.15 a.m.

(d) 1 Cable Section, Divisional Signal Company, will proceed to new area on the 22nd instant under arrangements to be made by O.C. Signal Company.

4. ENTRAINING AND DETRAINING OFFICERS.

O.C. 17th Northumberland Fusiliers will detail an Entraining and Detraining Officer for the 1st train and O.C. 52nd Battalion, Machine Gun Corps an Entraining and Detraining Officer for the 2nd train. Entraining officers will report to R.T.O. 2 hours before their train leaves and Detraining officers immediately on arrival at railway destination.

5. ENTRAINING AND DETRAINING.

(a) The order of entrainment of the units and arrival at entrainment stations are as shown in attached table.

(b) The last unit on each train should arrive at the entraining station not less than one hour before the train is due to start.

(c) On arrival at detraining station units will be met by guides from Billetting Parties and led to Billetting Areas.

6. SUPPLIES.

(a) Railhead will remain at MONT ST ELOY till 22nd instant. From 23rd (inclusive) Railhead will be at HOUDAIN.

(b) Rations for the 24th will be carried in the Supply Wagons of the Train.

7. LORRIES.

O.C. 52nd Divisional M.T. Company will detail lorries as follows in connection with the move on the 23rd instant.

(a) One lorry to accompany march of transport. This lorry will be under the orders of the O.C. 52nd Divisional Train and will deal with breakdowns, stragglers, etc. No man will, however, be allowed to ride on the lorry without written permission from an officer. This lorry will join the column at the junction of main MONT ST ELOY - CAMBLAIN L'ABBE Road and road leading to CHATEAU D'ACQ.

				Time.	Place.
(b) 5	lorries	report	to Div.Hqrs.	7 a.m.	CHATEAU D'ACQ.
2	"	"	" W.S.O.	7 a.m.	BERTHONVAL.
2	"	"	" Hoopers Dump.	7 a.m.	Hoopers Dump.
1	"	"	" (Divl.Employ-ment Coy.) (Divl.Reception Camp.)	7 a.m.	Reception Camp, VILLERS AU BOIS.
1	"	"	" 17th Northd. Fusiliers.	7 a.m.	Cellar Camp, A.3.c.2.2.
1	"	"	" Coy. 52nd Bn. M.G. Corps.	7 a.m.	AUXREZIZ
1	"	"	" Div. Canteen & Cookery School	7 a.m.	Fraser Camp MONT ST ELOY.
4	"	"	" D.A.D.O.S.	7 a.m.	Blackpool Siding.

Appendix X
A Branch 52 Division

8. **AMMUNITION.**

Full establishment of S.A.A. will be taken in Horse Transport.

9. **STATES.**

A Movement Order showing the number of personnel proceeding by each train will be handed by units to the R.T.O. on arrival at the entraining stations.

10. **TRAIN WAGONS.**

Baggage and Supply Wagons will rejoin units at 6 p.m. on 22nd instant.

11. **ACKNOWLEDGE.**

E.F. Moullin-Barrett Captⁿ
for
Lieut.Colonel.
A.A. & Q.M.G. 52nd (Lowland) Division.

Issued at 12.30 p.m.

Copy to –
- No. 1 A.D.C. for G.O.C.
- 2 Camp Commandant D.H.Q.
- 3 C.R.E.
- 4 A.D.M.S.
- 5 O.C. Divl. Train.
- 6 O.C. Signal Coy.
- 7 52nd M.G. Battn.
- 8 O.C. Reception Camp.
- 9 O.C. Employment Coy.
- 10 O.C. Hoopers Dump.
- 11 "G".
- 12 "A".
- 13 D.A.D.V.S.
- 14 A.P.M.
- 15 D.A.D.O.S.
- 16 French Mission.
- 17 17th Corps.
- 18 8th Corps.
- 19 C.R.A.
- 20 17th Northd. Fus. (P).
- 21 52nd M.T. Company.
- 22 S.S.O.
- 23 8th Division.
- 24 File.
- 25)
- 26) War Diary.
- 27 Canteen Offr
- 28 Baths Offr

P.T.O

Train Number.	Date.	Time of departure.	Unit.	Hour to arrive at entraining station. (MONT ST ELOY)	Detraining Station.	Order of entrainment.
3.	23/7/18	ZERO Hour.	52nd Divisional Headquarters. 52nd Divisional R.E. Hqrs. 52nd Divisional Train Hqrs. Mobile Veterinary Section. 52nd Divl. Signal Company. 17th Northumberland Fusiliers.	ZERO – 85 " – 80 " – 75 " – 70 " – 65 " – 60	PERNES.	1 2 3 4 5 6
4.	23/7/18	ZERO Hour.	413th Field Company R.E. Divl. Employment Company. Reception Camp. Hqrs. 52nd Bn. M.G. Corps. C.Coy. 52nd Bn. M.G. Corps.	Zero – 80 " – 75 " – 70 " – 65 " – 60	PERNES.	1 2 3 4 5

SECRET.   COPY NO. 23.

Appendix XI
A Branch 52 Div.

52nd (Lowland) DIVISION.

ADMINISTRATIVE INSTRUCTION NO. A.F. 27.

22nd July, 1918.

Reference Map 1/40,000 44B old 36 B.

SYSTEM OF SUPPLY IN NEW AREA.

RAILHEAD - HOUDAIN Commencing 23rd instant.

UNIT.	REFILLING POINT.	TRANSPORT TO R.P.	TRANSPORT TO UNIT.
155th Inf. Brigade.	ESTREE CAUCHIE. Q.31.d.9.1.	M. T.	2nd Line Transport.
156th Inf. Brigade.	CITE' No. 9. Q.2.d. central.	"	"
157th Inf. Brigade.	CROSS ROADS. C.21.b. central.	"	"
Royal Artillery.	ROAD. O.11.a.4.8.	"	"
Divisional Troops.	ROAD. H.16.c.8.8.	"	"

At the Refilling Points, Train wagons will be loaded in detail and will carry rations to unit's Transport Lines.

ACKNOWLEDGE.

Issued at 4 p.m.

E. F. Mallin-Barrett Major
for Lieut.Colonel.
A.A. & Q.M.G. 52nd (Lowland) Division.

Copy to - No. 1 G.O.C.
2 "G".
3 Camp Comdt.
4 O.C. Signal Coy.
5 C.R.E.
6 C.R.A.
7 155th Inf. Bde.
8 156th Inf. Bde.
9 157th Inf. Bde.
10 A.D.M.S.
11 D.A.D.V.S.
12 A.P.M.
13 Divl. Train.
14 S.S.O.
15 52nd M.G. Battn.
16 17th Northd. Fusiliers (P).
17 Divl. Employment Coy.
18 Divl. Reception Camp.
19 52nd M.T. Company.
20 D.A.D.O.S.
21 W.S.O.
22 File.
23)
24) War Diary.

Appendix XII.
"A" Branch 52 Division

Q. 205/3.

Camp Comdt.   O.C. Reception Camp.   O.C. Signal Coy.
C.R.E.   O.C. Employment Coy.
O.C. Divl. Train.   D.A.D.O.S.
O.C. 52nd M.G.Battn. D.A.D.V.S.

1.   In view of a possible early move all units will arrange to collect surplus kits, stores etc. and take to a Divisional Dump which has been formed at CINEMA HOUSE, Reception Camp, PERNES, under charge of Major L.D. MURRAY (this to be done by 12 midday on 26th instant).

2.   A guard will be supplied by the Divisional Employment Company.

3.   Units should send representatives to hand over kits, stores etc. to the guard at the Reception Camp.

4.   Arrangements have already been made for the collection of kit of Brigade Groups.

25/7/18.

Patrick Spens Capt
                /r Major.
D.A.Q.M.G. 52nd (Lowland) Division.

Appendix XIII
'A' Branch 52 Division

SECRET.   COPY NO. 19

52nd (LOWLAND) DIVISION.

ADMINISTRATIVE INSTRUCTION No. A.F. 28.

29th July, 1918.

With reference to 52nd Division wire No. G.A.411 dated 29/7/18.

1. **INFORMATION.**

    (a) 156th Infantry Brigade Group will move by march route from their present area to the MAROEUIL area on the 30th instant.

    (b) 157th Infantry Brigade Group will move by march route from their present area to the area now occupied by 156th Infantry Brigade Group on the 30th instant.

2. **ACCOMMODATION.**

    156th Infantry Brigade Group will obtain billets from 4th Canadian Division.

3. **BILLETTING PARTIES.**

    (a) Billetting Parties will proceed direct to new areas in lorries to-day, the 29th instant, and will be responsible for meeting units on arrival.

    (b) 2 lorries for conveyance of each party will report at each Brigade Headquarters to-day at 1 p.m.

    (c) The following should be the strength of billetting parties.

    (i) Brigade Headquarters.   1 officer.
    (ii) Per Infantry Battalion.   1 officer 3 O.R.
    (iii) Per smaller Unit.   1 officer 1 O.R.

    A bicycle a man should be taken.

4. **LORRIES.**

    O.C. M.T. Company will detail lorries as follows in connection with the move, in addition to those detailed in para.3 -

    (a) 1 lorry to accompany the march of the transport of each Brigade Group. This lorry will deal with breakdowns, stragglers, etc. No man will, however, be allowed to ride on the lorry without written permission from an officer. O.C. M.T. Company will arrange direct with B.G.C's Infantry Brigades as to time and position of rendezvous.

    (b) 7 lorries will be at the disposal of each of 156th and 157th Infantry Brigades. These lorries will be available to make 2 runs. O.C. M.T. Company will arrange direct with B.G.C's as to hour and position of rendezvous.

P.T.O.

5. **SUPPLIES.**

   (a) Rations for 156th Infantry Brigade Group for the 31st will be carried in the Supply Wagons of the Train.

   (b) Rations for 157th Infantry Brigade Group for the 31st will be delivered direct to units in their new area by Train Wagons.

   (c) Further instructions will be issued regarding change of Railhead and Refilling Points in the new area.

6. **AMMUNITION.**

   Full establishment of S.A.A. will be taken in Horse Transport.

7. **TRAIN WAGONS.**

   Baggage and Supply Wagons of the 156th Infantry Brigade Group and Baggage Wagons only of 157th Infantry Brigade Group will join units at 6 p.m. to-night, the 29th instant.

8. **POLICE.**

   A.P.M. will arrange for 1 Sergeant and 4 police to be attached temporarily to each of 156th and 157th Infantry Brigades.

9. **ACKNOWLEDGE.**

E. F. Moulton-Barrett Major
for
Lieut. Colonel.
A.A. & Q.M.G. 52nd (Lowland) Division.

Issued at 11.30 a.m.

Copy to – No. 1 A.D.C. for G.O.C.　　11 A.P.M.
        2   "G"　　　　　　　　　　12 D.A.D.O.S.
        3   156th Inf. Brigade.　13 52nd M.T. Company.
        4   157th Inf. Brigade.　14 French Mission.
        5   52nd Divl. Train.　　15 17th Corps.
        6   S.S.O.　　　　　　　　16 Town Major, BARLIN.
        7   A.D.M.S.　　　　　　　17 4th Canadian Division.
        8   D.A.D.V.S.　　　　　　18 File.
        9   C.R.E.　　　　　　　　19)
       10 O.C. Signal Coy.　　 20) War Diary.
        　　　　　　　　　　　　 21 52nd M.G. Battn.

SECRET.

Appendix XIV
"A" Branch 52' Division
Copy No. 20

52nd (LOWLAND) DIVISION.

ADMINISTRATIVE INSTRUCTION NO. A.F. 29.

30th July, 1918.

With reference to 52nd Division Order No. 118 dated 29/7/18.

1. **INFORMATION.**
    The following moves take place on the 31st instant:—
    (a) 155th Brigade Group by Train from CAMBLAIN L'ABBE to ZIVVY DUMP and thence to line,— entraining at 6 a.m. Further details will be issued.
    Transport will march under orders of B.G.C. 155th Inf. Bde.
    (b) 156th Brigade Group to line.
    (c) 157th Brigade Group to MADAGASCAR Area by route march.

2. **ACCOMMODATION.**
    157th Brigade Group will be allotted billets by Divl. Staff Officer who will meet the advance party in the MARCEUIL Area.

3. **BILLETING PARTIES.**
    (a) Billetting parties of 155th and 157th Brigades will proceed direct to new area in lorries today, 30th instant, and will be responsible for meeting units on arrival.
    (b) Two lorries for conveyance of each party will report at each Inf. Brigade Hd. Qrs. at 9 a.m. on 30th instant.
    (c) The following should be the strength of billetting parties:—
     (i) Brigade Hd. Qrs.   1 Officer.
     (ii) Per Inf. Battn.   1 Officer, 3 Other Ranks.
     (iii) Per Smaller Unit,   1 Officer, 1 Other Rank.
    A bicycle a man should be taken.

4. **LORRIES.**
    O.C., M.T. Company, will detail lorries as follows in connection with the moves in addition to those detailed in para 3:—
    (a) 1 lorry to accompany the march of the transport of each Brigade Group. This lorry will deal with breakdowns, stragglers, etc. No man will, however, be allowed to ride on the lorry without written permission from an Officer. O.C., M.T. Company will arrange direct with B.Gs.C. Inf. Brigades as to time and position of the rendezvous.
    (b) 7 lorries will be at disposal of each of 155th and 157th Inf. Brigades. These lorries will be available to make two runs. O.C., M.T. Company will arrange direct with B.Gs.C. as to hour and position of rendezvous.
    (c) 6 lorries for 'C' Company, M.G. Battalion at BARLIN at 6 a.m., 31st instant.

5. **SUPPLIES.**
    (a) Railhead on the 31st will be MONT ST. ELOY
    (b) Rations for 1st August for 155th and 157th Brigades will be carried in Train wagons.

6. **AMMUNITION.**
    Full establishment of S.A.A. will be taken in Horse Transport.

— 2 —

7. **TRAIN WAGONS.**
    (a) Baggage and Supply wagons of 155th Brigade Group will join units at 6 p.m. on the evening of the 30th.
    (b) The baggage wagons of 157th Brigade are already with the units, while the Supply wagons should join units by 6 p.m. 30th instant also.

8. **POLICE.**
    A.P.M. will arrange for 1 Sergeant and 4 Police to be attached temporarily to 155th Inf. Brigade.

9. **TENTS.**
    All tents should be handed over to the Area Commandants or Town Majors concerned.

10. **TRENCH & AREA STORES.**
    List of Stores taken over should be forwarded to D.H.Q. 96 hours after having taken over the line.

11. **ACKNOWLEDGE.**

Issued at 1.30 a.m.

E. F. Malthus-Barrett Major
for
Lieut. Colonel,
A.A. & Q.M.G. 52nd (Lowland) Division.

Copy to — No. 1 A.D.C. for G.O.C.　　12 A.P.M.
　　　　　　2 'G'　　　　　　　　　　13 B.A.D.O.S.
　　　　　　3 155th Inf. Bde.　　　　14 52nd M.T. Company.
　　　　　　4 156th Inf. Bde.　　　　15 French Mission.
　　　　　　5 157th Inf. Bde.　　　　16 17th Corps.
　　　　　　6 52nd Divl. Train.　　　17 Town Major, BARLIN.
　　　　　　7 S.S.O.　　　　　　　　　18 4th Canadian Divn.
　　　　　　8 A.D.M.S.　　　　　　　　19 File.
　　　　　　9 D.A.D.V.S.　　　　　　　20) War Diary.
　　　　　 10 C.R.E.　　　　　　　　　21)
　　　　　 11 O.C., Signal Company.　 22 52nd M.G. Battalion.

SECRET.   COPY NO. 22

52nd (LOWLAND) DIVISION.

ADMINISTRATIVE INSTRUCTION NO. A.F. 30.
                                              30th July, 1918.

With reference to 52nd Division Order No.118 dated 29/7/18.

1. **INFORMATION.**

    The following moves will take place on dates specified.

    (a) 984th Employment Company and Divisional Reception Camp by rail on the 31st instant.

    (b) Headquarters and "C" Company, 52nd Battalion Machine Gun Corps and billetting party 17th Northumberland Fusiliers (P) on the 1st August by rail.

    (c) Divisional Headquarters by lorry on the 2nd August.

    (d) 1/1st Lowland Mobile Veterinary Section by road on 2nd August.

    (e) M.T. Company (less 16 vehicles) on the 2nd August.

    (f) 17th Northumberland Fusiliers (P) ½ by rail and ½ by lorry on the 3rd August.

2. **ENTRAINING AND DETRAINING OFFICERS.**

    An officer should be detailed to supervise the entraining and detraining of each train. This officer will report to the R.T.O. one and a half hours before the train is due to start.
    Troops for entrainment should arrive at the station at least 1 hour before the train is due to start.

3. **ENTRAINING STATION.**

    The entraining station in each case will be PERNES, and the train in each case is timed to start at 10.34 a.m.

4. **LORRIES.**

    O.C. M.T. Company will detail lorries as under -

    (1) 3 to report O.C. 984th Employment Company at 8 a.m. 31st instant at Billet No.10 PERNES.

    (2) 1 to Headquarters 52nd Battalion Machine Gun Corps, PERNES, at 8 a.m. 1st August.

    (3) 13 to report Divisional Headquarters at 6.30 a.m. 2nd August.

    (4) 16 to report O.C. 17th Northumberland Fusiliers (P) at TANGRY at 8 a.m. on the 3rd August.

5. **SUPPLIES.**

    Rations for the day following the move will be drawn from new Refilling Points on arrival at destination.

                                                        P.T.O.

6. **TRANSPORT.**

   All Transport will proceed by road under orders of the O.C. Units concerned.

7. **AMMUNITION.**

   Full establishment of S.A.A. will be taken in Horse Transport.

8. **TRAIN WAGONS.**

   Baggage Wagons of the Train will report to Units at 6 p.m. on the day previous to the day each unit moves.

9. **TENTS.**

   All tents should be handed over to the Area Commandants or Town Majors concerned.

10. **ACKNOWLEDGE.**

Issued at 6.45 p.m.

E.F. Mallé-Sarrett Major
for
Lieut. Colonel.
A.A. & Q.M.G. 52nd (Lowland) Division.

```
Copy to -   No.1  A.D.C. for G.O.C.           15.  52nd Bn. M.G. Corps.
              2   "G"                         16.  Camp Commandant.
              3   Divl. Train.                17.  17th Northd. Fus (P).
              4   S.S.O.                      18.  D.A.D.V.S.
              5   A.D.M.S.                    19.  Reception Camp.
              6   C.R.E.                      20.  Employment Company.
              7   O.C. Signal Coy.            21.  File.
              8   A.P.M.                      22.)
              9   D.A.D.O.S.                  23.) War Diary.
             10   52nd M.T. Company.
             11   French Mission.
             12   17th Corps.
             13   4th Canadian Division.
             14   D.A.A.G. 52nd Division.
```

1/4

CONFIDENTIAL.

ORIGINAL.

52nd (Lowland) Division

— WAR DIARY —

for.
August.

VOLUME XXXIX

HQ aro 52D
956

Signal

WAR DIARY
INTELLIGENCE SUMMARY

(Erase heading not required.) 'A' Branch 59 (2nd Lowland) Division. P.I

Army Form C. 2118.
1/31 Aug 1918
VOL XXXIX

Place	Date 1918 August	Hour	Summary of Events and Information	Remarks and references to Appendices
PERNES	1			
MARŒUIL	2		Divisional Headquarters move to Headquarters of 4th Canadian Division at MARŒUIL.	
			XVII Corps ask for suggestions as to improvement of situation in the Area.	
	3.		Corps advised, with regard to replacement of Pistol Lights for metals, that 5% Reserve of Lights should be kept to replace unserviceable, that a supply of petrol should always be available, that ample supply of matches be issued for Orderlies and Office use.	
			Corps advised all 15 pr. Guns at present unfit for Anti-Tank defence and to be replaced by 18-pdrs.	
			Corps advised that the use of general issue of "Laces, menders, Hooks" would be fully compensated for by the utility of these articles for sewing officers as well as "Huggers", allowing of boots of smaller fit other men sized 7 and 9.	

Army Form C. 2118.

WAR DIARY
or
INTELLIGENCE SUMMARY.

(Erase heading not required.) A' Branch 52: (Rutland) Division   VOL XXXIX   P. II

Place	Date	Hour	Summary of Events and Information	Remarks and references to Appendices
MAROEUIL	1918 August 4		Corps ask for recommendation on use of wooden soled trench boots - Proposed to issue a proportion in lieu of Gum boots thigh about winter.	
	6		Suggested improvements in Light Railway system put forward to Corps. First Course of Instruction in repair of Lewis guns at Divisional Armourers Shop started - Two Battery Artificers. Corps asks if supply of Hand Tobacco could be discontinued owing to difficulty of supply at home. Replied recommended it should be continued -	
	7		Corps advised that it is recommended that 50 armbands per Division be supplied for water patrols -	
	9		Corps advised that goggles for night firing are satisfactory as issued	App I
	10		Administrative Instruction No. A F 31 attached (re Straggler Post(s)) issued to Division. Further 24 Hankey Puzzle roundings.	94.

Army Form C. 2118.

WAR DIARY
or
INTELLIGENCE SUMMARY.
(Erase heading not required.)

A Branch 52nd (Lowland) Division VOL XXXIX P.11

Place	Date 1916 August	Hour	Summary of Events and Information	Remarks and references to Appendices
MARŒUIL	11		No 23 <u>Administrative Circ. memorandum</u> attached (re Divisional Reception Camps and Nuclei) Corps advised of suggested method of carrying R.E. Lewis Guns	App II
	13		<u>Administrative Circ. memorandum</u> No 24 attacked (re loading & maintenance of vehicles) Expendable Belts for Vickers Guns. 2500 were issued for trial report of these now recommended.	App III
	14		<u>Climbing Irons</u>. Corps advised issue of these not recommended.	
	15		<u>Administrative Instruction</u> No A.I. 32 attached (Re relief of Division by 51st Division) Golf Bag Carriers for Lewis Guns. Corps advised these are serviceable though quality of material & workmanship is inferior Carriers for 6" T.M. Bombs for use with new Pack Saddlery found satisfactory. Suggest Bando Supporting to Strong Band & Carry chus and 8 phr. Swivers widened	App IV

DWW

Army Form C. 2118.

VOL XXXIX

A Branch 52 Division

P IV

WAR DIARY
or
INTELLIGENCE SUMMARY.

(Erase heading not required.)

Place	Date 1918 August	Hour	Summary of Events and Information	Remarks and references to Appendices
MAROEUIL	15		Administrative Circ. Memo No 25 attached (re Canteen Stores 2/c)	App V
			155 Inf Bde in relief by 23rd Inf Bde moved to CAUCOURT Area	
	16		Relief of 156 Inf Bde by 154 Inf Bde. 156 Bde moved to Villedou BERLES area	
			Divisional Headquarters closed at MAROEUIL & opened at VILLERS CHATEL	
			Relief of 157 Inf Bde by 24 Inf Bde. 157 moved to MONT ST ELOY area	App VI
VILLERS CHATEL	17		Administrative Instruction No 2 A.F. 33 attacked (Showing location of Division)	
			Wooden Soled boots in lieu of Gum thgt - Corps advised would be given an opinion owing to having been such a short time in France	
			Administrative Circ. Memo No 26 attacked (re Scale of an Inf Bde Pack Transport)	App VII
	19		Issue of Paraffestyptic to R.A. Corps advised considered unnecessary	

Army Form C. 2118.

WAR DIARY
or
INTELLIGENCE SUMMARY.

(Erase heading not required.) "A" Branch 53rd (Welsh) Division

VOL XXXIX

Instructions regarding War Diaries and Intelligence Summaries are contained in F. S. Regs., Part II. and the Staff Manual respectively. Title pages will be prepared in manuscript.

Place	Date August 1916	Hour	Summary of Events and Information	Remarks and references to Appendices
VILLERS CHATEL	20	4 pm	Warning Order received by Corps. Division to be prepared to move by march route tonight	P.V
		10.15 pm	Division commenced moving	
	21		Divisional Headquarters closed at VILLERS CHATEL and opened at HERMAVILLE CHATEAU	
	22		Administrative Arrangements Nº A.F. 34 attached (Arrangements in connection with Current Operations)	App VIII
	"	1 pm	Division Headquarters closed at HERMAVILLE and opened at CHATEAU BRETENCOURT	
BRETENCOURT			MOVES	
		9.56 pm	155 Infy Bde moved to SOMBRIN, BARLY, GOUY-ARSE	
			157 " " " BELLACOURT, GROSVILLE, BRETENCOURT AREA	
	23		Corps asked for air service, but reply received not available meant next two journeys	

Army Form C. 2118.

Vol XXXIX

WAR DIARY
or
INTELLIGENCE SUMMARY.
(Erase heading not required.)

A Branch 52 (Lowland Division) HQ

Place	Date	Hour	Summary of Events and Information	Remarks and references to Appendices
BLAIREVILLE	August 1918 24		Divisional HQ moved to BLAIREVILLE at 8 AM this morning. Railhead changed to BOUY. Remounts. Marched for train. Water Tanks. Two 500 gall & two 200 gall mobile water tanks were issued to Div. Two with GS were returned to No 3 Sect HQ Train. Divisional train concentrated at GRETENCOURT. SOLIDIFIED ALCOHOL 5000 D were drawn	
	25		Mobile Vet Sect moved to BRETENCOURT. Reserved Tanks to be carried in turn of the baggage wagons of each Bde. War Cutters. A special issue was made to 155 Inf. Bde.	
	26		Rum Issue. Corps ordered an issue to be held by the train, & that it will not be issued without Corps Sanction. Corps issues daily rations cannot be sanctioned. Serious shortage & twice weekly issue of D.D.R. shortages due. Animals. 6 Casualties	

Army Form C. 2118.

WAR DIARY
or
INTELLIGENCE SUMMARY.

(Erase heading not required.)

"A" Squadron 52 (Lowland) Division P VII

Vol XXXIX

Place	Date 1918 August	Hour	Summary of Events and Information	Remarks and references to Appendices
BLAIREVILLE	26		Rum Issue sanctioned	
			Authorisation given to draw further 227 galls.	
			Solicited Alcohol. Auth: given to draw 5 oro B.	
			Booth's Stores wanted to be handed over to relieving division. If not returned to Base.	
	27		Railhead changed to BEAUMETZ RIVIÈRE	
			Watering arrangements for horses and drinking opened.	
			Changes owing to scarcity. Charges only to be issued on demand by Remount Officer with Army or Corps. Corps advise situation as regards Horse fleet is serious.	
			Bdes. movements. The three Bdes relieved + received in MERCATEL area. 50 stellers were issued.	
			Issue of Cucumber. Corps ask if this would be appreciated.	
			Captures. 2 TMs and 1 M.g captured returned to Ordnance	
			Rum Issue sanctioned	

Army Form C. 2118.

WAR DIARY
or
INTELLIGENCE SUMMARY.
(Erase heading not required.)

VOL XXXIX

"A" Branch 52nd (Lowland) Division P.M.

Instructions regarding War Diaries and Intelligence Summaries are contained in F. S. Regs., Part II. and the Staff Manual respectively. Title pages will be prepared in manuscript.

Place	Date 1918	Hour	Summary of Events and Information	Remarks and references to Appendices
BLAIREVILLE	Aug 28		Issue of Clean Clothing 15000 pieces plus 15000 socks may be drawn weekly from C.L.O. SKIPTON.	
			Division reorganising	
	29		Observations in future during operations by Captain to be at Transport lines in order to keep in touch with Division H.Q.	
			Preserved meat. From 29th onwards 50% Fresh & 50% Preserved will be on Ration.	
			Corps advised that P.M. will be coming up to B.H. lines, in view of coming events asked for this to be stopped.	
			Solidified Alcohol. Unit to draw 5000 my	
			Rum. 800 galls. allowance up to & Sept	
			Div'l Commander to sanction issues	
			Reception Camp. 1 G.S. Wagon loaned to it from Amm. H. Transport Coy.	
			Clean Clothing Issued to 3 Batts.	

Army Form C. 2118.

Vol. XXXIX

WAR DIARY
INTELLIGENCE SUMMARY.
(Erase heading not required.) A Branch 52nd (Lowland) Division ̶H̶Q̶ D.K.

Instructions regarding War Diaries and Intelligence Summaries are contained in F. S. Regs., Part II. and the Staff Manual respectively. Title pages will be prepared in manuscript.

Place	Date	Hour	Summary of Events and Information	Remarks and references to Appendices
BLAIREVILLE	30		Divisional Dump to be formed at Braken Hutz T1 d 2.3	App/x
	31.		Administrative Instruction N° A.F. 35 attached (re position of forward Ammunition Dumps)	
			Railhead changed to BOISLEUX	
			Oats from today for 10 days 1 lb extra per head will be issued	
			Solicited alcohol authority to draw 5000 J.J. w.m.	
			Summers Sights to be drawn on the scale of 1 set per gun sent to R.E. Coy and R.A. B.Kys.	
			Scarcity of animals owing to scarcity & to minimize loco lines must not be established near Railheads or water points	

J. Harding Capt G.H.
for D.A.A.G.
52 D (Lowland) Division

WAR DIARY or INTELLIGENCE SUMMARY

52nd (Lowland) Division. "A" and "Q" **AUGUST 1918** Vol. XXXIX

Army Form C. 2118.

STRENGTH OF DIVISION.
(Week ending 31st Aug. 1918.)

	Officers	Other Ranks
Divisional Troops	19	133
Divisional Artillery	93	2044
Divisional Engineers	39	937
155th Infantry Bde.	133	2743
156th Infantry Bde.	137	2443
157th Infantry Bde.	103	2097
Divisional Train	22	380
17th (Bn. Northumberland Fusiliers) (P)	35	896
52nd Bn. Machine Gun Corps	43	842
98th Divisnl. Employmt. Coy.	2	292
Royal Army Medical Corps	20	684
	646	13491

INFANTRY BRIGADES – REINFORCEMENTS
(Received for month of August.)

Week ending	Officers	Other Ranks
3rd. August	2	42
10th August	3	64
17th August	1	148
24th August	4	42
31st August	–	–
	10	296

CASUALTIES – INFANTRY BRIGADES.

Week ending	KILLED Offrs	KILLED O.R.s	WOUNDED Offrs	WOUNDED O.R.s	MISSING Offrs	MISSING O.R.s	SICK Offrs	SICK O.R.s
3rd. August	–	2	6	31	–	1	4	114
10th August	–	2	1	48	1	1	6	111
17th August	1	2	2	51	–	1	2	128
24th August	1	–	1	12	–	–	6	203
31st August	12	156	52	1282	4	185	6	335
	14	160	60	1424	4	186	24	891

52nd (Lowland)

31st AUGUST.

155th Inf. Bde.						
1/4th R.S.Fus.	41	851	14	168	27	683
1/5th R.S.Fus.	32	818	10	163	22	655
1/6th K.O.S.B.	46	918	15	165	31	733
	119	2587	39	496	80	2091
156th Inf. Bde.						
1/4th R.Scots.	42	795	18	256	24	539
1/7th R.Scots.	41	760	18	441	23	319
1/7th Sco.Rif.	43	814	15	127	28	587
	126	2378	49	924	77	1454
157th Inf. Bde.						
1/5th H.L.I.	26	696	16	192	10	504
1/6th H.L.I.	32	630	18	189	14	441
1/7th H.L.I.	33	668	18	147	17	521
	91	1994	52	528	41	1466
17th North'ld Fus. (N.E.R.Pioneers)	34	896	3	47	29	849
Grand Total.	370	7855	143	1965	227	5890
52nd Bn. H.G.C.	42	836	9	103	33	733

Major General,
Commanding 52nd (Lowland) Division.

Copy to:-
Headquarters,
XVII Corps."A".

"TAKEN ON STRENGTH"

Unit	Rank	Name	Initials	Notes
1/4th R.Scots.	2/Lieut.	Hudson,	H.	3rd.R.S.attd.Reinft.
1/7th R.Scots.	"	Sharp,	T.S.	" " " "
" "	"	Hawthorn,	J.	" " " "
1/7th Sco.Rif.	Lieut.	Souter,	G.	Reinforcement.
" " "	2/Lieut.	Gilchrist,	J.	" 6th S.R.attd.
" " "	"	Herd,	F.S.	"
" " "	"	Brown,	W.A.	"
1/5th H.L.I.	"	Bryson,	A.	"
1/6th H.L.I.	"	Welsh,	W.	"
" "	"	Hartle,	G.	"
" "	"	Baird,	W.	"
1/7th H.L.I.	Lieut.	Muir,	J.McG.	"
" "	2/Lieut.	Brown,	R.	"
" "	"	Crawford,	J.	"
" "	"	McInnes,	D.	" 5th H.L.I attd

"STRUCK OFF STRENGTH"

Unit	Rank	Name	Initials	Notes
1/4th R.Scots.	Lieut.	Gardener,	G.	Wounded.
" "	2/Lieut.	Alley,	J.	"
1/7th R.Scots.	Lieut.	McLauchlan,	M.T. M.C.	"
" "	"	McNab,	J.	"
" "	"	McCulloch,	J.C.	"
" "	"	Spence,	S.J.	"
" "	2/Lieut.	Weir,	J.C.	"
" "	Capt.	MacKenzie,	K.	Missing. 9th R S attd
1/7th Sco.Rif.	Lieut.	Haugh,	J.W.N.	Int.Off.155th Bde.
" " "	2/Lieut.	Reed,	A.J.	Transferred to U.K.
" " "	"	Glass,	R.	Wounded.
" " "	"	Tosson,	P.J.	"
" " "	"	Reid,	D.McA.	Invald U.K. 5th S R attd
2/5th Bn. H.L.I.	Lieut.	MALCOLM,	A.H.	Wounded.
-do-	"	Legate.	F.	"
-do-	2/Lt.	TURNER. B.D.		"
-do-	Lt.Col.	HEITLON,	J.B.	Wounded
-do-	Capt.	Miller.	R.M.	missing
-do-	"	Watson.	L.H.	wounded
-do-	"	Fyfe.	T.A.	"
-do-	Lieut.	Parr.	J.W.	missing
-do-	"	BAIN.	G.D.	Wounded
-do-	"	Girvan.	J.	"
-do-	2/Lt.	McKie.	J.	missing
-do-	"	Williamson.	E.T.	Wounded
-do-	"	Brodie.	G.F.	"
-do-	"	Sanderson.	C.H.	"
-do-	"	Robertson.	J.R.	"
	Capt. & QM.	Clark.	T.	To U.K.

STRUCK OFF STRENGTH. (continued).

1/6th Bn. H.L.I.	2/Lieut.	MacIntosh.	K.A.	Killed.
-do-	"	Smith.	F.G.	"
-do-	Lieut.	Cummings.	R.J.A.	"
-do-	Lt.Col.	Anderson. (Cmdg D.S.O.)	J.	Wounded.
-do-	Capt.	TIDD.	K.G.	"
-do-	Lieut.	FINDLAND.	J.W.	"
-do-	Lieut.	Wilson.	J.P.	"
-do-	"	Thomson.	W.D.	"
-do-	"	Bruce,	C.	"
-do-	2/Lt.	West.	E.G.C.	"
-do-	"	Johnston.	D.	"
-do-	"	Hogg.	D.	"
-do-	"	Fraser.	D.McH.	"
1/7th Bn. H.L.I.	Capt.	Youden.	S.E.	Killed.
-do-	2/Lt.	McCallum.	W.H.	"
-do-	"	Pullar.	T.H.	"
-do-	Lieut.	Strachan.	J.F.	Wounded.
-do-	"	Muir.	R.E.R.	"
-do-	"	Miller.	A.E.H.	"
-do-	Capt.	Mullen.	E	"
-do-	Lieut.	Woodburn.	L.H.	"
-do-	2/Lieut.	Ross	M.	"
-do-	"	Petrie.	J.A.	"
-do-	"	Campbell.	A.	"
-do-	"	Barbour.	A.S.	"
52nd Bn. M.G.C.	Lieut.	Dunand.	A.M.	Missing.
-do-	Lieut.	Kerr.	H.G.	Wounded.
-do-	Lieut.	THIMBLEBY	A.L.L.	Wounded

SECRET.

Appendix I.
"A" Branch 52" Division

COPY NO. 66

52nd (Lowland) DIVISION.

ADMINISTRATIVE INSTRUCTION No. AF. 31.

Reference Map -
MAROEUIL 1.20,000

10th August, 1918.

STRAGGLERS POSTS.

1. The following Tables "A" and "B" give the organisation of STRAGGLERS POSTS for the Divisional Sector.

2. Personnel referred to in Table "B" must know the way to their Posts by day and night but will only man them on issue by A.P.M. Division of the order "MAN STRAGGLERS".

3. 2/Lieut. R.Y. CARNEGIE, The Black Watch (Royal Highlanders) attached 5th Bn. Royal Irish Regt (P) will be in permanent charge of the 1st Line Battle Stragglers Posts.
    Lieut. A.C.M. MUIRHEAD, K.O.S.B., Divisional Burial Officer will on order "MAN STRAGGLERS" take charge of Prisoners of War Cage.
    Lieut. W.S. MILLER, 984th Divnl. Emp. Coy., Divisional Salvage Officer, will similarly take charge of Forward Battle Stragglers Collecting Station on receiving the order 'MAN STRAGGLERS'.

4. ACKNOWLEDGE.

[signature] Major
Lieut. Colonel.
A.A. & Q.M.G., 52nd (Lowland) DIVISION.

Issued at 5.30 p.m.

Copy No.		Copy No.	
1	A.D.C. for G.O.C.	40 to 44	A.D.M.S.
2	"G".	45	D.A.D.V.S.
3	"Q".	46	Divnl. Train.
4 to 9	155th Brigade.	47	S.S.O.
10 to 15	156th Brigade.	48	Camp Comdt.
16 to 21	157th Brigade.	49 to 60	A.P.M.
22 to 27	C.R.A.	61	2/Lieut. R.Y. CARNEGIE.
28 to 31	C.R.E.	62	Divnl. Burial Officer.
32	O.C., Signal Coy.	63	Divnl. Salvage Officer.
33 to 37	O.C., M.G. Battn.	64	XVIIth Corps.
38	17th Bn. North'ld Fus. (P)	65 to 66	War Diary.
39	D.A.D.O.S.	67	File.

TABLE "A".   POSTS PERMANENTLY MANNED (by personnel from Infantry Battalions.)

Map co-ordinate	No. of post	Description.	Off.	Sgts.	Cpls.	L/Cpls.	Ptes.	Remarks.
A.12.d.8.9.	1	⎫				1	3	
A.17.d.7.5.	2	⎪				1	3	
A.23.b.5.1.	3	⎬ 1st Line Battle Stragglers Post.	1	1		1	3	
A.24.c.3.4.	4	⎪				1	3	
E.5.b.6.6.	5	⎪			1	1	3	
G.5.d.1.4.	6	⎭					3	
A.28.a.9.2.		Forward Battle Stragglers Collecting Station.	1	1			3	⎫ Remainder of personnel given under TABLE 'B'
A.28.a.9.2.		Prisoners of War Cage.		1			3	⎭
		TOTAL.	1	3	1	5	24	

TABLE "B".

POSTS MANNED ONLY ON WARNING ORDER 'MAN STRAGGLERS'.

Map co-ordinate.	No. of Post.	Description.	Off.	Sgt.	Cpl.	L/Cpl.	Pte.	Remarks.
A.14.a.9.5.	1)	2nd Line Battle Stragglers Posts.			1	1	3	Manned by Divnl. Salvage Personnel.
A.14.d.0.4.	2)			1	1	1	3	
A.20.b.3.2.	3)				1	1	3	
A.26.d.7.2.	4ø)							
A.20.b.3.2.		2nd Line Battle Stragglers Collecting Station.				1	1	Manned as alternative position by personnel of Forward Battle Stragglers Collecting Station.
F.15.d.6.0. to)	1)	3rd Line Battle Stragglers Posts.				1	1	Half permanently manned; half Divnl. Salvage personnel.
F.22.a.5.1.	2ø)					1	1	
F.22.d.5.1.	3ø)					1	1	
F.28.c.3.5.					1	1	3	M.M.P. Patrol.
F.28.c.2.0.	4)							Manned by Divnl. Salvage personnel.
L.4.a.8.5.		Rear Prisoners of War cage.				1	1	Manned as alternative position by personnel of Forward Prisoners of War cage and Battle Stragglers Collecting Station.
F.27.b.8.5.		3rd Line Battle Stragglers Collecting Station.				1	1	
A.28.a.9.2.		Forward Battle Stragglers Collecting Station.	1	1	1		5	Manned by Divnl. Salvage personnel.
A.28.a.9.2.		Prisoners of War cage.	1	1	1	1	12	N.C.O. and 6 privates from each of Divnl. Burial and Divnl. Salvage personnel.
		TOTAL.	2	1	2	5	30	

ø Traffic Control Post permanently manned.

Appendix I
A. Branch 52 Division

52nd (Lowland) DIVISION.

ADMINISTRATIVE CIRCULAR MEMORANDUM No. 23.

DIVISIONAL RECEPTION CAMP AND NUCLEI.

1. The Divisional Reception Camp is at present organised to deal with Reinforcements joining the Division and casuals passing to and from it. The establishment has been fixed to meet these requirements.

2. The present Divisional arrangements by which the nuclei (left in reserve when battalions are in the trenches) are located in the Divisional Reception Camp, while having many advantages has the disadvantage that the Reception Camp Staff cannot cope with the work (cooking, sanitary, pioneer) involved.

3. Up to now the nuclei have made their own cooking arrangements. This means dual control, sharing cook-houses, etc., and has not been satisfactory.

4. It is now proposed to establish a permanent nuclei staff of 3 N.C.Os. and 9 O.R. These men will be attached to the Reception Camp Staff and with these under his command O.C., Reception Camp, will be responsible for all feeding and sanitary arrangements in the camp. Nuclei will still be called upon to keep their huts and their portion of the camp in order.

5. No restriction will be placed on units changing the men referred to in paragraph 4 should they wish to do so, but it is hoped that this will be done as seldom as possible. The advantages of supplying responsible men and keeping the same at the work are self-evident.

6. The men will be supplied as follows, and should report to O.C., Reception Camp, by 1800 on 12th instant.

155th Brigade.	... N.C.O.	cook.
156th Brigade.	... N.C.O.	sanitary.
C.R.E.	... N.C.O.	pioneer.

each Brigade.	...(1 O.R.	cook.
	(1 O.R.	sanitary.
	(1 O.R.	pioneer.

The 157th Brigade will supply a Sergeant (Sergt. J. BROWN, 1/6th Bn. H.L.I.) to act as Sergeant Major.

7. If necessary N.C.Os. with acting unpaid rank may be sent but as the feeding and comfort of the nuclei will largely depend on these N.C.Os. this should be kept in view when the men are chosen.

8. Complete instructions regarding the Reception Camp, superseding those issued for VILLERS AU BOIS (Administrative Circular Memorandum No. 15) will be issued with the Notes for the Administration of the Area.

11th August, 1918.

J. Mulloch Major
for
Lieut. Colonel.
A.A. & Q.M.G., 52nd (Lowland) DIVISION.

Appendix III
A Branch 52 Division

52nd (LOWLAND) DIVISION.

ADMINISTRATIVE CIRCULAR MEMORANDUM No. 24.

CARE OF VEHICLES.

1. The following points are forwarded for information, inattention to which indicates that the vehicles are not properly looked after :-

    (1) Overloading of vehicles.

    (2) Tightening up of all bolts and nuts.

    (3) Keeping wood-work in repair.

    (4) Fitting of brakes.

    (5) Periodical examination and greasing of springs.

    (6) Washering up the wheels and greasing of pipe boxes.

2. Particular attention should be paid to the washering up of wheels. If the play of a wheel exceeds 1/16 inches it shows neglect in the wheel not having been washered up as play developed.

3. Excessive play causes the pipe box and the axle tree arm to wear very quickly, and this eventually leads to condemnation of both.

4. Arrangements should therefore be made for a frequent inspection of all vehicles, at which in addition to the above, it should be ascertained that all accessories and spare parts are complete and in good order.

5. An Inventory of these pasted on a board should be kept in the locker of each vehicle.

6. Copies of this Inventory can be obtained from the Stationary Office, stating description of vehicle for which required.

E. F. Mullie-Barrett Major
for
Lieut. Colonel.

A.A. & Q.M.G. 52nd (Lowland) Division.

13/8/18.

Appendix IV

A Branch 52" Division

SECRET.   COPY NO. 26

52nd (Lowland) DIVISION.

ADMINISTRATIVE INSTRUCTION No. AF. 32.

Reference Map :
    LENS - 1/100,000   15th August, 1918.

With reference to 52nd Divisional Order No. 123 of 14/8/18.

1.   On relief units of 52nd Division will eventually be located as shown in attached location list i.e. in the area now occupied by the corresponding units of 51st Division.

2.   Details with regard to moves by light railway will be wired direct to units concerned as soon as the necessary arrangements have been made.

3.   All baggage should be taken to the new area, where if necessary a dump will be formed.   Lorries in the usual proportion will be allotted to units for the move.

4.   Acknowledge.

                                                    Lieut. Colonel.
                        A.A. & Q.M.G., 52nd (Lowland) DIVISION.

Issued at 1000

Copy No. 1 A.D.C. for G.O.C.   14. Divnl. Signal Coy.
          2 "G"   15 A.P.M.
          3 155th Infantry Brigade.   16 D.A.D.O.S.
          4 156th   -do-   17 Camp Commandant.
          5 157th   -do-   18 Divnl. Gas Officer.
          6 C.R.A.   19 Divnl. Claims Officer.
          7 C.R.E.   20 Divnl. M.T. Coy.
          8 M.G. Battalion.   21 XVIIth Corps. "Q"
          9 17th North'ld Fus. (P)   22 Divnl. Reception Camp.
         10 A.D.M.S.   23 Divnl. Emp. Coy.
         11 D.A.D.V.S.   24 51st (Highland) Division.
         12 Divnl. Train.   25 File.
         13 S.S.O.   26 to 27 War Diary.
                                            28 French Mission.

Appendix IV
"A" Branch 52 Division

LOCATION LIST.

	UNIT.	Location.
1.	52nd Divnl. H.Qrs.	VILLERS CHATEL.
2.	155th Inf. Bde. H.Qrs.	CAUCOURT (Billet No. 3)
3.	"A" Bn. 155th Inf. Brigade.	GAUCHIN LEGAL.
4.	"B" Bn. -do-	HERMIN.
5.	"C" Bn. -do-	CAUCOURT.
6.	L.T.M. Batty -do-	GAUCHIN LEGAL.
7.	156th Inf. Bde. H.Qrs.	CHATEAU BERLES.
8.	"A" Bn. 156th Inf. Brigade.	VILLERS BRULIN - BETHONSART.
9.	"B" Bn. -do-	BERLES - VANDELICOURT.
10.	"C" Bn. -do-	SAVY - BERLETTE.
11.	L.T.M. Batty -do-	BERLES.
12.	157th Inf. Bde. H.Qrs.	CHATEAU de la HAIE.
13.	"A" Bn. 157th Inf. Brigade.	CHATEAU de la HAIE AREA.
14.	"B" Bn. -do-	MARQUEFFLES HUTS
15.	"C" Bn. -do-	CHATEAU de la HAIE AREA.
16.	L.T.M. Batty -do-	-do- -do-
17.	17th Bn. North'ld Fus. (P)	ESTREE CAUCHIE.
18.	52nd Divnl. M.G. Bn.	CAMBLIGNEUL.
19.	52nd Divn. R.E. H.Q.	MINGOVAL (Billet No. 4).
20.	"A" Field Coy. R.E.	BOUVIGNY.
21.	"B" -do-	AUBIGNY.
22.	"C" -do-	CAUCOURT.
23.	A.D.M.S.	VILLERS CHATEL.
24.	"A" Field Ambulance.	CAMBLIGNEUL.
25.	"B" -do-	GOUY SERVINS.
26.	"C" -do-	AUBIGNY.
27.	52nd Divnl. R.A. H.Qrs.	AUBIGNY (chateau).
28.	"A" Brigade, R.F.A.	ACQ.
29.	"B" -do-	ACQ.
30.	52nd D.A.C.	FREVIN CAPELLE.
31.	51 (Medium) T.M.Bs.	FREVIN CAPELLE. (if relieved)
32.	Divnl. Train H.Qrs.	MINGOVAL.
33.	"A" Coy. Divnl. Train.	CAPELLE FERMONT.
34.	"B" Coy. -do-	AUBIGNY.
35.	"C" Coy. -do-	ESTREE CAUCHIE.
36.	"D" Coy. -do-	HERIPRE - CAUCOURT.
37.	D.A.D.O.S.	MINGOVAL.
38.	D.A.D.V.S.	VILLERS CHATEL.
39.	Mobile Veterinary Section.	AGNIERES.
40.	Divnl. M.T. Coy.	SAVY.
41.	Divnl. Gas Officer.	VILLERS CHATEL.
42.	Divnl. Claims Officer.	-do-
43.	Divnl. Employment Coy.	-do-
44.	Divnl. Reception Camp.	AUBIGNY.

Appendix V
A Branch 52 Division

52nd (Lowland) DIVISION.

ADMINISTRATIVE CIRCULAR MEMORANDUM No. 25.

DIVISIONAL DRY CANTEEN.

1. Commencing on 15th August a new scheme for dealing with Canteen Stores will come into force.

2. By this scheme the Expeditionary Force Canteen becomes practically a wholesale establishment dealing with the various Corps, who in turn issue the stores to Divisions and Corps Troops according to ration strength. Retail sale will be confined to a minimum figure.

3. Division will deal with all troops who are rationed by them.

4. To meet the new conditions the following arrangements have been made :-

   (a) A Divisional Wholesale Canteen has been established.

   (b) Units will be advised of the arrival of stores and also of the articles and quantities available for them. Distribution will be on ration strength.

   (c) A date will be given by which all stores must be removed, any not removed by the time named will be treated as not required by unit to which they are allotted.

   (d) Certain stores of which small quantities only are likely to be required (such as notepaper pads, shaving soap, etc.,) will be sold retail as available, all other sales will be wholesale.

   (e) 3% discount will be allowed off schedule prices on wholesale transactions. No discount will be allowed on articles sold retail.

   (f) A proportion of the stores allotted for the Division will be reserved for Reception Camp according to the strength there, and for any retail canteens established in the forward areas.

5. All stores must be paid for CASH ON DELIVERY.

15th August, 1918.

Lieut. Colonel.
A.A. & Q.M.G., 52nd (Lowland) DIVISION.

SECRET. Copy No...31....

52nd (Lowland) DIVISION.

ADMINISTRATIVE INSTRUCTION No. AF. 33.

17th August, 1918.

With reference to Administrative Instruction No. AF. 32 of 15th instant, Formations and Units will be concentrated into areas shown in the Location List issued with above Instruction by the following dates :-

Unit or Formation	Move to	Completed by
Divnl. H.Qrs.	VILLERS CHATEL.	16/8/18
155th Inf. Brigade.	CAUCOURT AREA.	midnight 18/19/8/18
156th -do-	SAVY AREA.	16/8/18
157th -do-	CHATEAU de la HAIE AREA.	midnight 17/18/8/18.
17th Bn. North'ld Fus. (P).	ESTREE CAUCHIE.	mid-day 17/8/18.
M.G. Bn. H.Qrs.)		16/8/18
A, B, C Coys,)	CAMBLIGNEUL.	-do-
D. Coy.)		17/8/18
R.E. H.Qrs.	MINGOVAL.	16/8/18.
410th Field Coy. R.E.	CAUCOURT.	midnight 18/19/8/18.
412th -do-	BOUVIGNY.	-do-
413th -do-	AUBIGNY.	16/8/18.
A.D.M.S.	VILLERS CHATEL.	-do-
1/1st Low.Fld.Amb.	CAMBLIGNEUL.	midnight 18/19/8/18.
1/2nd -do-	GOUY SERVINS.	mid-day 17/8/18.
1/3rd -do-	AUBIGNY.	16/8/18.
H.Q., R.A.	AUBIGNY.	-do-
9th Brigade, R.F.A.	ACQ.	midnight 17/18/8/18.
56th -do-	ACQ.	16/8/18.
D.A.C.	FREVIN CAPELLE.	-do-
T.M. Battery.	NOT RELIEVED	STILL IN THE LINE.
H.Q., Divnl. Train.	MINGOVAL.	17/8/18.
217th Coy. A.S.C.	CAPELLE FERMONT.	18/8/18.
218th -do-	CAUCOURT.	midnight 18/19/8/18.
219th -do-	AUBIGNY.	16/8/18.
220th -do-	ESTREE CAUCHIE.	midnight 17/18/8/18.
D.A.D.O.S.	MINGOVAL.	17/8/18.
D.A.D.V.S.	VILLERS CHATEL.	16/8/18.
1/1st Mob.Vet.Sect.	AGNIERES	mid-day 18/8/18.
Divnl. M.T. Coy.	SAVY.	18/8/18.
Divnl. Gas. Officer.	VILLERS CHATEL.	16/8/18.
Divnl. Claims Offr.	-do-	-do-
Divnl. Emp. Coy.	AUBIGNY.	19/8/18.
Divnl. Reception Camp	AUBIGNY.	-do-

2. Acknowledge

Lieut. Colonel.
A.A. & Q.M.G., 52nd (Lowland) DIVISION.

P.T.O.

- 2 -

Issued at 1030

Copy No.			
1	A.D.C. for G.O.C.	17	Camp Commandant.
2	"Q"	18	D.G.O.
3	155th Infantry Brigade.	19	Divnl. Claims Offr.
4	156th –do–	20	Divnl. M.T. Coy.
5	158th –do–	21	XVIIth Corps. "Q"
6	C.R.A.	22	Divnl. Reception Camp.
7	C.R.E.	23	Divnl. Emp. Coy.
8	M.G. Battalion.	24	French Mission.
9	17th Bn. North'ld Fus (P)	25	W.S.O.
10	A.D.M.S.	26	Divnl. Burial Officer.
11	D.A.D.V.S.	27	Divnl. Salvage Offr.
12	Divnl. Train.	28	D.R.D.O.
13	S.S.O.	29	51st (Highland) Division.
14	Divnl. Signal Coy.	30	File.
15	A.P.M.	31 to 32	War Diary.
16	D.A.D.O.S.		

SECRET.

Copy No... 31

52nd (Lowland) DIVISION.

AMENDMENT TO ADMINISTRATIVE INSTRUCTION No. AF. 33.

18th August, 1918.

Location of 412th and 413th Field Coys. R.E. is respectively AUBIGNY and BOUVIGNY, not as stated in Administrative Instruction No. AF. 33.

[signature]
Lieut. Colonel.
A.A. & Q.M.G., 52nd (Lowland) DIVISION.

Addressed to all recipients of Administrative Instruction No. AF. 33.

Appendix VII
"A" Branch 52 Division

52nd (LOWLAND) DIVISION.

ADMINISTRATIVE CIRCULAR MEMORANDUM No.26.

PACK TRANSPORT.

1. In consequence of the reduction of Infantry Brigades by one Battalion, the following amendments will be made to Administrative Circular Memorandum No.13 (PACK TRANSPORT).

Each Infantry Brigade Pack Company.

	Officers.	N.C.O's.	O. Ranks.	Artificers.	Pack Animals.	Pack Saddles.	
O.C. Company.	1	-	-	-	-	-	Brigade Transport Officer.
Section Commdrs.	3	-	-	-	-	-	Battn. Transport Officers.
Sergeants.	-	3	-	-	-	-	) To be provided from 1st Line
Corporals.	-	4	-	-	-	-	) Transport.
Drs.for Pack Horses.	-	-	82	-	82	82	(To be provided from 1st Line
Drs.for Spare Horses.	-	-	12	-	12	-	(Transport.
Farriers.	-	-	-	3	-	-	To be provided from 1st Line Transport.
Saddlers.	-	-	-	4	-	-	1 from Bde. Coy. A.S.C. & 3 from 1st Line Transport.

19/8/18.

E.L. Mullin-Barrett Major
for Lieut.Colonel.
A.A. & Q.M.G. 52nd (Lowland) Division.

SECRET.

LOCATION OF DUMPS.

DIVISIONAL DUMPS.

BRIGADE DUMPS.

M.G. BATTN. DUMPS.

	BLAINVILLE. R.34.c.4.2.	AVONDALE. R.13.b.9.8.	R.13.b.9.8.; R.15.a.1.2; R.19.b.2.4.; R.19.a.0.2. Q.29.c.4.4.; Q.29.b.1.8. Q.24.c.4.8. EACH.	R.34.d.6.4.	M.15.b.3.4. Pioneers. M.27.c.1.7. R.Mails.	Plchem. M.14.a.2.8.	B.4.d.4.3.	R.36.a.3.2.	R.34.d.6.4.	R.29.d.3.1.	M.19.d.8.7.	S.4.c.8.2.
S.A.A.	500000	500000	25000.	70000	54000	123000	94000	25000	124000	100000	99000	80000	140000
S.A.A., A.P.	1850	5000											
Tracer.	17000	2000			2000								
Blank.	6000	8000											
Pistol Webley.	6000	6000		580				580					
" Colt.	8000	4000											
T.M.C. Otgs. Green.	2400	2000		115									
" M.C.T. Rings.	2000	2400		100									
" "	2000	2500		100									
Grenades No.5.	2500	5000		240	122			3895					
" 23.	2500	1000	320.	600	400	330.	210	60					
" 27.	1000			120									
" 32 R/R/T.	108	72											
" 32 G/G/G.	155	1000		240	144			594					
" 34	322	5000		400				30					
" 36	2000	2000		420				45					
" 36 R/R Hand.	1700												
" " " Hand.	260				48								
Very Lights 1"	2000	1800		1644	200			600	336				
D.I.	500	300		30									
Red.	300	150		45									
Green.	2500	1500											
Ground Flares. White.	2500	2500											
Red.	2500	1000											
Green.													
Rockets Ast.													
White.	24	24											
Red.	24												
Green.	500			120	60			1260					
Rods 11"	558												
" 6" for 27 R.G.s.	1800												

Appendix VIII
A Branch 52 Division

Copy No. 35

SECRET.   52nd (Lowland) DIVISION ADMINISTRATIVE
ARRANGEMENTS IN CONNECTION WITH CURRENT
OPERATIONS No. A.F. 34.

22nd August, 1918.

Reference 1/20,000 Map.
Sheet 51c.

1. S.A.A., GRENADE, ETC. STORES.
   (a) Main Divisional Dump — BLAIREVILLE (R.34.c.4.4.)
   (b) Main Brigade Dump — BLAIREVILLE QUARRY (R.34.d.4.4.)
   (c) Forward Brigade Dump — M.34.d.8.3.

   A list of other S.A.A., etc., Dumps in present 59th Divisional Area is attached for information, marked "A".

2. RESERVE RATIONS.
   One day's reserve rations for a Brigade Group will be dumped at 156th Infantry Brigade Headquarters BLAIREVILLE QUARRY.
   A certain quantity of Solidified Alcohol will also be in Brigade Reserve.

3. WATER.
   (a) Two 500 gallon and five 100 gallon Mobile Water Tanks will be in reserve at Divisional Headquarters. Application for water from this source should be made to 52nd Division "Q".
   (b) 1000 filled 2 gallon petrol tins will be dumped in the Main and Forward Brigade Ammunition Dumps (see 1 (b) and (c) above).
   (c) 1200 filled water bottles are also in Brigade Dumps.
   (d) A list of Water points in the back area is attached, marked "B".

4. R.E. DUMPS.
   Main Divisional R.E. Dump — GROSVILLE. R.26.a.6.0.
   Advanced R.E. Dumps. — S.5.d.8.4.
                          M.35.d.6.7.

5. MEDICAL ARRANGEMENTS.
   Regimental Aid Posts — Front Line Right R.A.P. S.4.c.9.0.) Ref.
                          Front Line Left R.A.P. M.35.a.2.9.) Sheet
                          Support Right   R.A.P. S.2.b.5.0.) 51b.
                          Support Left   R.A.P. M.27.c.1.9.) 1/
                          Advanced Dressing Station M.31.b.1.6)40000

   Corps Main Dressing Station. Q.31.d.5.6.) Sheet 51c
) 1/40,000.

6. PRISONERS OF WAR.
   (a) Advanced Prisoners of War Collecting Station BLAIREVILLE QUARRY.
   (b) Divisional Prisoner of War Cage R.27.c.1.1.

   Prisoners will be brought back to (a) under Brigade arrangements. From (a) to (b) by an escort supplied by 59th Division.

7. TRAFFIC CONTROL AND STRAGGLERS.
   Existing Traffic Control and Straggler Posts and Stragglers Collecting Stations will be manned by 59th Division.
   A.P.M., 52nd Division, has particulars of these Posts.
   A list showing position of Battle Straggler Posts and Straggler Collecting Station etc., is attached, marked "C".

P.T.O.

8. **VETERINARY.**

The Veterinary arrangements will be as follows :-

(a) Collecting Post at Divisional Headquarters, BRETENCOURT.
(b) The evacuation will be carried out through
   (1) 1/1st North Midland M.V.S. at BRASSEUX.
   (2) VIth Corps V.E.S. at GOUY en ARTOIS.

9. **BURIAL.**

Bodies will be sent to Forward Collecting Post at R.22.b.4.7. If this cannot be done under Brigade arrangements application is to be made to Division "Q" for extra labour.

From the Forward Collecting Post the Divisional Burial Officer (located at Divisional Headquarters) will arrange to collect bodies and convey to BELLACOURT CEMETERY (R.25.c.3.3.).

10. **ACKNOWLEDGE.**

[signature]

Lieut. Colonel.
A.A. & Q.M.G., 52nd (Lowland) Division.

Issued at 9.15 p.m.

Copy to No.			
1	A.D.C. for G.O.C.	17 to 18	155th Brigade.
2	"G"	19 to 28	156th Brigade.
3	C.R.A.	29 to 30	157th Brigade.
4	C.R.E.	31	59th Division "Q"
5	O.C., Signals.	32	56th Division "Q"
6	A.D.M.S.	33	VIth Corps. "Q".
7	D.A.D.V.S.	34	File.
8 to 9	D.A.P.M.	35 to 36	War Diary.
10	Divnl. Burial Officer.		
11	W.S.O.		
12	S.S.O.		
13	Divnl. Train.		
14	North'ld Fus. (P)		
15	M.G. Battalion.		
16	D.A.D.O.S.		

ADMINISTRATIVE ARRANGEMENTS.

A.P.M. ARRANGEMENTS.

(a) Battle Straggler Posts.
   No. 1.   R.33.a.9.4.
   No. 2.   R.27.d.2.2.
   No. 3.   R.22.c.2.0.

(b) BATTLE Straggler Collecting Station.

Same as A.P.M's Advanced Headquarters at GROSVILLE, 1 N.C.O. and 6 men are also required to handle the Stragglers here, to be furnished by the Brigade in Reserve.

(c) Prisoners of War Camp.

This is located at R.27.d.2.3.
The Corps Cage is at GOUY-EN-ARTOIS. Q.19.a.

WATER SUPPLY.

LOCATION.		Horse Trough.	Water Cart R.Ps.	Pumping Station.	Hand Pumps.	Reservoirs.	REMARKS.
BARLY.	P.15.a.7.1.	1	1	-	-	-	84' 30 Horses.
	P.15.a.8.0.	-	-	1	-	-	
	P.15.a.8.1.	-	-	-	-	1	3100 gal.
	P.15.a.2.0.	1	-	-	-	-	224' 75 Horses.
	P.15.b.5.5.	-	-	1	-	-	2 - 600 gal tanks
GOUY.	P.18.b.7.2.	1	-	-	-	-	308', 105 Horses.
	P.18.b.8.6.	-	1	-	-	-	
	P.18.c.6.5.	-	-	1	-	-	
	P.18.c.9.6.	-	-	1	-	-	
	Q.13.a.0.8.	-	-	-	2	1	8250 gal.Res.
	P.24.b.0.9.	1	-	-	-	-	245', 82 Horses.
	P.24.b.1.8.	-	1	-	-	-	
	P.24.c.1.7.	-	-	-	-	1	1600 gal. tank. 8 stand pipes.
MONCHIET.	Q.21.c.0.4.	1	-	-	-	-	140' 50 Horses.
	Q.21.c.2.7.	1	-	-	-	-	84' 30 Horses.
	Q.21.c.3.5.	1	-	-	-	-	84' 30 Horses.
	Q.21.d.1.5.	-	-	1	-	1	2000 gal.
	Q.21.d.7.4.	-	-	-	-	1	375 gal.
	Q.21.d.7.5.	-	-	-	1	-	
BEAUMETZ.	Q.23.d.7.8.	-	-	1	-	1	2300 gal.
	Q.23.d.7.7.	1	-	-	-	-	192' 64 Horses.
	Q.23.d.7.6.	-	2	-	-	-	
	Q.36.a.8.4.	1	-	-	2	-	65'
	Q.32.a.7.0.	-	-	-	-	2	2 - 1600 gal.tanks
BASSEUX.	Q.34.d.6.5.	1	-	-	-	-	100' 35 Horses.
	Q.35.d.7.7.	1	-	-	-	-	
RIVIERE.	R.26.a.5.3.	-	1	-	-	-	
BRETENCOURT & GROSVILLE.	R.27.a.3.4.	-	-	1	-	-	
	R.27.a.4.5.	1	-	-	-	-	70' 20 Horses.
	R.27.a.4.7.	-	-	-	1	-	
	R.26.c.4.5.	1	-	-	-	-	96' 32 Horses.
	R.26.c.6.6.	-	-	-	1	-	
	R.26.d.8.8.	-	-	-	-	5	5 - 1600 gal.
	R.26.d.8.9.	-	-	1	-	-	
	R.26.b.3.2.	1	-	-	-	2	97'
FERMONT.	R.21.d.2.2.	1	-	-	-	6	58'
BELLACOURT.	R.31.a.2.8.	1	-	-	-	-	120' 40 Horses.
	R.31.a.3.9.	-	-	-	1	-	
	R.31.b.3.9.	1	-	-	-	-	60' 20 Horses.
	R.31.b.5.9.	-	-	-	1	-	
	R.33.a.9.5.	1	-	-	-	-	180' 50 Horses.
BAILLEULVAL.	W.3.b.6.3.	1	-	-	-	-	45' 15 Horses.
	W.3.b.7.3.	-	-	-	1	-	
	W.4.a.4.6.	1	-	-	-	-	50' 15 Horses.
	W.4.a.5.8.	-	1	-	-	-	
	W.4.a.6.7.	-	-	-	1	-	
WAILLY WOOD CAMP.	R.10.d.45.30.						2 - 400 gal.tanks

Appendix IX
A Branch 52 (Low) Divn

SECRET. COPY NO. 25

52nd (Lowland) DIVISION.

ADDENDUM to ADMINISTRATIVE INSTRUCTION No. AF.35.

31st August, 1918.

In continuation of Administrative Instruction No. AF. 35 dated 31st August.

1. The following forward Ammunition Dumps are in existence –

U.20.d.8.4.	S.A.A.	100,000.
	T.M.C.	500.
	No.23 Grenades.	2,000.
	No.35 Grenades.	500.
	S.O.S. No.32.	30.
U.19.d.8.7.	S.A.A.	50,000.
	No.23 Grenades.	2,000.
	T.M.C.	175.
U.19.c.2.2.	S.A.A.	100,000.
	No.23 Grenades.	2,600.
	T.M.C.	600.
	Red Flares.	750.
	V.P.A. 1" White.	600.
	Webley.	2,000.
	S.O.S. No.32 Grenades.	6.

U.7.central. – Brigade Re-equipping Dump.

S.A.A.	100,000.
No.23 Grenades.	2,000.
V.P.A. 1" White.	2,000.
Red Flares.	2,500.
Webley.	400.
T.M.C.	201.

2. ACKNOWLEDGE.

E.F. Noble-Barrett Major
for Lieut.Colonel.
A.A. & Q.M.G. 52nd (Lowland) Division.

Issued at 12.15.

Copy to No. 1 A.D.C. for G.O.C.
2 "G".
3 155th Brigade.
4 156th Brigade.
5 157th Brigade.
6 Divl. Train.
7 S.S.O.
8 C.R.A.
9 C.R.E.
10 A.D.M.S.
11 O.C. Signal Coy.
12 D.A.P.M.
13 D.A.D.O.S.
14 M.G. Battalion.
15 17th Northd. Fus (P).
16. D.A.D.V.S.
17. Camp Comdt.
18. Divl. Reception Camp.
19. Divl. Employment Coy.
20. 52nd M.T. Coy.
21. Div. Salvage Officer.
22. Divl. Burial Offr.
23. File.
24.)
25.) War Diary.
26. W.S.O.

Army Form C. 2118.

WAR DIARY
or
INTELLIGENCE SUMMARY.
(Erase heading not required.)

Instructions regarding War Diaries and Intelligence Summaries are contained in F. S. Regs., Part II. and the Staff Manual respectively. Title pages will be prepared in manuscript.

Place	Date	Hour	Summary of Events and Information	Remarks and references to Appendices

CONFIDENTIAL.

52nd (Lowland) DIVISION.

"A" & "Q" Branch.

WAR DIARY.

From 1st September 1918 to 30th September 1918.

VOLUME. XL.

Army Form C. 2118.

VOL XI

WAR DIARY
or
INTELLIGENCE SUMMARY.

(Erase heading not required.) A Branch 52' (Lowland Division) P-1

Instructions regarding War Diaries and Intelligence Summaries are contained in F. S. Regs., Part II. and the Staff Manual respectively. Title pages will be prepared in manuscript.

Place	Date 1918 Sept	Hour	Summary of Events and Information	Remarks and references to Appendices
ST LEGER	1.		Pack Saddles. 50 were issued to Each Brigade for use of T.M.S.	
			Water Cart refilling point established at Sugar Factory BOYELLES.	
			Pumps & troughs constructed and working E. of CROISILLES.	
			Cocoa & milk - Authority given to draw 40003 -	
	2		Ammunition Dump. Dump at T.9.b.5.b. was taken over from 57 D.W.	
			Armstrong Huts 4 allotted to Each Divisional HQ qrs.	
	3		Supply Lorries. Corp placed Divisional Supply lorries at disposal of Division from today.	
			Solidified Alcohol. Authority given to draw 50000	
			Anti-Tank Rifles. Corps advise. Specimen urgently required at Corps	
			Guns captured to be sent Corps Salvage Dump -	
			Animals 19.2 Arrived for Division	
	4.		Administrative Instruction No 37 attached (Re relief by 56 Division)	App I.
			Fresh Meat. Troops instructed to draw as large a proportion as possible.	G.H.

Army Form C. 2118.

WAR DIARY
or
INTELLIGENCE SUMMARY.

(Erase heading not required.) Abranch 5? (Lowland) Division P II

VOL XL

Instructions regarding War Diaries and Intelligence Summaries are contained in F. S. Regs., Part II. and the Staff Manual respectively. Title pages will be prepared in manuscript.

Place	Date	Hour	Summary of Events and Information	Remarks and references to Appendices
LEGER	1916 Sept 5		Issues of Ammunition. Field Ambulances & Div¹ Train to be issued with V.B. (Ammunition defective for age pack or eye sight but fit for slow work). Proportion 5% not blind (2 L.D. & 2 H.D. per Coy). Train 5% blind (2 L.D. & 10 H.D. per train). Slipping of Tangent Sights. Only a few cases experienced in every 2 or 6z. Suggested remedy proved effective.	
	6		Administrative Instruction Nº A.F.86 attacked (Ref. locations, distribution of bivouacs etc).	App II.
			Guns Captured. 1 - 5.9" How., 3, 4.2 guns, 15 - 1.77 mm guns, 140 m. guns, 14 T.m⁵ 24 minenwerfers.	
			NOYOEUIL Dump & Dest in charge of division in Dec¹; all serviceable BULLECOURT ammunition salved to be sent there.	
			Water supply. Corps advised of difficulty during advance, and recommendations made that each division be supplied with appliances.	end

D. D. & L., London, E.C.
(A8004) Wt. W1771/M231 739,000 5/17 Sch: 52 Forms/C2118/14

WAR DIARY
INTELLIGENCE SUMMARY
(Erase heading not required.) A Branch 53 Division

Army Form C. 2118.

VOL XL

Place	Date	Hour	Summary of Events and Information	Remarks and references to Appendices
ST LEGER	1918 Sept 7		Bicarbonate of Soda. As supplies are limited all indents must be countersigned by D.D.M.S. Corps.	
	8		War Paper Articles used by Germans are wanted by G.H.Q. Corps to be notified of any found.	
	9		Winter Articles. In view of conditions under which troops are living it is recommended that these should be now issued.	
	10		Water Tank Lorries. Ordered to be returned.	
			Bealls Stores ordered to be returned to A.D.O.S.	
			S.O.S. Grenades. 400 allotted to Div in lieu of 400 handed over in relief.	
			Leather Equipment. Complaint received that this is to forward until oil at the Base, that it leaves the clothing.	

Army Form C. 2118.

WAR DIARY
or
INTELLIGENCE SUMMARY.
(Erase heading not required.)

Vol XL

A "B" Coy No 52 (Lowland) Division ? D

Instructions regarding War Diaries and Intelligence Summaries are contained in F. S. Regs., Part II. and the Staff Manual respectively. Title pages will be prepared in manuscript.

Place	Date 1918 Sept	Hour	Summary of Events and Information	Remarks and references to Appendices
ST. LEGER	11		Gunners Corps inform that owing to the abnormal prices, it is not now proposed to issue them. Captain H.C.C. Tippett. Royal Dublin Fus. (S.R.) appointed to H.Q. from 15th Inf Bde. Vice Captain. WILL M.C. to 16 Division.	
	12.		V.B. House. Corps state there will not now be established to Train of Ambulances.	
	13.		Administrative Instructions No. A.F. 39 attached (re Supply arrangements during operations) Divisional Headquarters moved to QUEANT D.7.A.5.7. Graham U. Leflo. Y Sulord & forwarded to Corps Amm Dump	App III
QUEANT	14		Administrative Instruction No. A.F. 40 (re Locations, supplies etc) attached.	App IV

WAR DIARY
or
INTELLIGENCE SUMMARY.

Army Form C. 2118.

Vol XL

A Boyant 52 (Cleveland) Division R.E.

Place	Date	Hour	Summary of Events and Information	Remarks and references to Appendices
QUEANT	1918 Sept 15		**Leather Jerkins** Recommended that these now be issued	
			Blankets The issue of one blanket per man is approved	
	17		**T. Bases for Vickers Guns.** Decided to have also a hand store, on the basis of 16 per ride of front held, 4 lbs to be pooled in case of emergency.	
	18		**Incendiable Bells for Vickers Guns.** A test was made with these & they were found to satisfactory as the ordinary kets.	
	19		**Rum** Auth. granted to draw 250 gals.	
			Solidified Alcohol Auth. granted to draw 10,000 ℔	
			Advanced S.A.A. Dumps formed at D.T.C. from which units will draw by 1st line transport.	

Army Form C. 2118.

WAR DIARY
or
INTELLIGENCE SUMMARY.

(Erase heading not required.) A Branch 52" (Lowland) Division

Vol XI

Instructions regarding War Diaries and Intelligence Summaries are contained in F. S. Regs., Part II. and the Staff Manual respectively. Title pages will be prepared in manuscript.

Place	Date 1918 Sept	Hour	Summary of Events and Information	Remarks and references to Appendices
QUEANT	20		Clothing. Corps advise 30,000 pieces can be changed weekly.	
	22		Solidified Alcohol. Auth. granted to draw 10,000 @ 225 pulls.	
			Rum	
	23		Major (Temp. Brig-General) G. H. HARRISON D.S.O. Border Regt and M.G. Corps. assumed command 155 Inf. Bde vice Brig. General T. FORBES ROBERTSON V.C. D.S.O. M.C. BORDER Regt	
			Bt Lieut-Col (Temp Major General) F.T. MARSHALL C.M.G. D.S.O Seaforth Highlanders assumed command of the Division vice Major-General J. HILL C.B. D.S.O. TO England.	
			Mackintosh Capes. Recommended that these be issued to mounted men, cyclists, sentries, Traffic Control Orderlies. 3600 x gloves in the Division - Ground Sheet MK.VII could then be dispensed with, subject to MK.V being issued in lieu.	A.H.

Army Form C. 2118.

p.v.11

Vol XL

WAR DIARY
or
INTELLIGENCE SUMMARY.
(Erase heading not required.) "A" Poranch 52 (Lowland) Division

Place	Date 1916 Sept	Hour	Summary of Events and Information	Remarks and references to Appendices
QUEANT	24		Administrative Instruction No. A.F. 41 attached (re Supplies etc during operations)	App I
	25		Addendum to Administrative Instructions No. A.F.41 (re traffic, greatcoats etc) attached	App II
	26		Appendix A to Administrative Instructions No. A.F. 41 attached (re water)	App III
			163 Remounts arrived for Divison	
			6 L.D. horses captured from enemy	
	27		Corps show A.R.P's will be formed J10a2.3 & J9d8.9. as soon as tactical situation permits. Corps advised Divn. strongly recommend moving of 2 hughes to M.G. Bn.	

Reid

Army Form C. 2118.

WAR DIARY
or
INTELLIGENCE SUMMARY.
(Erase heading not required.)

Instructions regarding War Diaries and Intelligence Summaries are contained in F. S. Regs., Part II. and the Staff Manual respectively. Title pages will be prepared in manuscript.

Place	Date	Hour	Summary of Events and Information	Remarks and references to Appendices
QUEANT	1916 Sept 28		Authority given to draw 100 gms. rum	
	29		Remounts 32 riding arrived for Drummers	
	30		Four 100 Gallon water tanks transferred to 63rd Divn. from 52"Divn.	

Maude Hyslop
R.F.A.

52nd (Lowland) Division.   **WAR DIARY** or **INTELLIGENCE SUMMARY.**   "A" and "Q"   SEPTEMBER 1918.   Vol. XL

Army Form C. 2118.

Instructions regarding War Diaries and Intelligence Summaries are contained in F.S. Regs., Part II. and the Staff Manual respectively. Title pages will be prepared in manuscript.

(Erase heading not required.)

Place	Date	Hour	Summary of Events and Information	Remarks and references to Appendices

STRENGTH OF DIVISION.
(Week ending 28th Sept. 1918)

	Officers	Other Ranks
Divisional Troops	18	135
Divisional Artillery	90	2103
Divisional Engineers	36	922
155th Infantry Bde.	115	2302
156th Infantry Bde.	120	2191
157th Infantry Bde.	117	2199
Divisional Train	22	374
17th Bn. Northumberland Fusiliers (P.)	35	890
52nd Bn. Machine Gun Corps	46	840
984th Divisnl. Employment Coy	2	310
Royal Army Medical Corps	20	693
	621	12959

INFANTRY BRIGADES - REINFORCEMENTS
RECEIVED FOR MONTH OF SEPTEMBER.

Week ending	Officers	Other Ranks
7th September	18	117
14th September	6	188
21st September	27	303
28th September	15	448
	66	1056

CASUALTIES - INFANTRY BRIGADES.

Week ending.	KILLED		WOUNDED		MISSING		SICK.	
	Offs.	O.Rs	Offs.	O.Rs	Offs.	O.Rs	Offs.	O.Rs
7th September	5	54	24	265	–	32	3	311
14th September	–	1	3	13	–	–	3	84
21st September	7	46	14	241	–	39	6	263
28th September	7	98	34	801	1	103	3	317
	19	199	75	1320	1	174	15	975

52nd (Lowland) Division.

Abstract Column "B" ---- Week-ending 28/9/18.

UNIT.	Courses. O.	Courses. O.R.	Sick. O.	Sick. O.R.	Leave. O.	Leave. O.R.	Pioneers. O.	Pioneers. O.R.	Bde.Employ. O.	Bde.Employ. O.R.	Div.Employ. O.	Div.Employ. O.R.	Extra Regtl.Employ. O.	Extra Regtl.Employ. O.R.	Total. O.	Total. O.R.
155th Inf. Bde.																
1/4th R.S.Fus.	1	17	6	29	1	81	–	–	2	41	1	21	–	–	11	189
1/5th R.S.Fus.	2	14	4	34	1	128	–	–	1	25	3	10	–	24	11	235
1/4th K.O.S.B.	3	17	2	22	2	82	–	–	2	22	2	8	–	25	11	176
	6	48	12	85	4	291	–	–	5	88	6	39	–	49	33	600
156th Inf. Bde.																
1/4th R.Scots.	1	21	3	36	4	76	–	–	–	18	2	37	–	2	10	190
1/7th R.Scots.	1	19	3	28	4	95	–	–	1	23	4	54	1	14	14	233
1/7th Sco.Rif.	1	15	2	18	3	96	–	–	4	26	3	34	–	–	13	189
	3	55	8	82	11	267	–	–	5	67	9	125	1	16	37	612
157th Inf. Bde.																
1/5th H.L.I.	3	26	3	17	2	100	–	–	1	11	–	19	1	1	10	174
1/6th H.L.I.	3	21	1	19	2	94	–	32	4	39	3	54	–	–	13	227
1/7th H.L.I.	3	22	3	32	3	116	–	–	1	35	5	21	1	1	16	226
	9	69	7	68	7	310	–	32	6	85	8	94	2	1	39	627
Grand Total.	18	172	27	235	22	868	–	–	16	240	23	258	3	66	109	1839

52nd (Lowland) Division.

Strength Return made up to 12 noon Saturday, 28th Sept. 1918.

UNIT.	"A" Strength Return excl. attd.		"B" Not present with the unit & not at disposal of C.O. (incl. in col. 'A')		"C" Available Ft. Str. (incl. persnl of Battn. transport and Q.M. Stores.)	
	Officers.	O.R.	Officers.	O.R.	Officers.	O.R.
155th Inf. Bde.						
1/4th R.S.Fus.	27	654	11	189	16	465
1/5th R.S.Fus.	36	736	11	235	25	301
1/4th K.O.S.B.	35	793	11	176	24	617
	98	2183	33	600	65	1503
156th Inf. Bde.						
1/4th R.Scots.	26	615	10	190	16	425
1/7th R.Scots.	33	656	14	233	19	423
1/7th Sco.Rif.	35	687	13	189	22	498
	94	1958	37	612	57	1346
157th Inf. Bde.						
1/5th H.L.I.	33	680	10	174	23	506
1/6th H.L.I.	31	618	13	227	18	391
1/7th H.L.I.	32	653	16	226	16	427
	96	1951	39	627	57	1324
17th N.F.(P)	33	890	7	52	26	838
Grand Total.	321	6982	116	1891	205	5091
52nd Bn. M.G.C.	45	834	5	90	40	744

Appendix I
"A" Branch 52 Division

COPY NO. 28

SECRET.   52nd (LOWLAND) DIVISION.

ADMINISTRATIVE INSTRUCTION NO. A.F. 37.

4th SEPTEMBER, 1918.

Reference 1/20,000 map sheet 51B. S.W.

In connection with 52nd Division wire G.A.445 dated 4/9/18.

1. MOVES.
   (a) The following moves will take place to be completed by 12 noon 6th inst.

   52nd Divisional Train to S.6.d.
   Mobile Veterinary Section to S.6.d.
   D.A.D.O.S. to S.9.a.

   (b) The S.A.A. Section, D.A.C., will remain in its present place.

2. SHELTERS.
   Shelters will be taken over from the corresponding units of 56th Division in the new bivouac areas.

3. GREATCOATS ETC.
   (a) The greatcoats etc. of units which were dumped near BOIRY-BECQUERELLE (T.1.d.3.2.) should be drawn under Brigade arrangements before the arrival of Brigades in the new areas.

   (b) Three lorries (1 for each Brigade) will be at the present dump by 1200 noon 5th instant, and may be used for carrying the coats etc. to the new areas.

   (c) An officer from each Brigade will be sent to the Greatcoat Dump by 1200 noon 5th instant to superintend this work.

4. SUPPLY ARRANGEMENTS.
   (a) Divisional Train will deliver rations (less R.A.) for the 6th to new Brigade Refilling Points (new Brigade Transport Lines) at 6 p.m. on the 5th instant.

   (b) R.A. Supply arrangements will remain as at present till further orders.

5. BATTLE EQUIPMENT.
   The following will be handed over by units to corresponding units of 56th Division on relief :-

   Waterbottles.)
   Petrol Tins.   ) Surplus to establishment.
   Wirecutters.   )
   50 Packsaddles per Infantry Brigade.
   24 Packsaddles from D.A.D.O.S. 52nd Division to D.A.D.O.S. 56th Division.

6. MEDICAL.
   A.D.M.S. will take over medical arrangements of 56th Division.

/7.

-2-

7. PROVOST.
D.A.P.M. will take over Traffic Control and Provost Duties from 56th Division.

8. ACKNOWLEDGE.

[signature]

Lieut. Colonel.
A.A. & Q.M.G. 52nd (Lowland) Division.

Issued at 11.30 p.m.

Copy to No.1 A.D.C. for G.O.C.
2 "G".
~~3 155th Inf. Brigade.~~
~~4 156th Inf. Brigade.~~
~~5 157th Inf. Brigade.~~
6 Camp Comdt.
~~7 O.O. Signal Coy.~~
~~8 C.R.E.~~ ?
~~9 C.R.A.~~
10 A.D.M.S.
11 D.A.D.V.S.
~~12 D.A.P.M.~~
13 Divl. Train.
~~14 52nd M.G. Battn.~~
15. ~~17th Northd. Fus.~~
16. D.A.D.O.S.
17. ~~W.S.O.~~
18. S.S.O.
19. 52nd M.T. Company.
~~20. Reception Camp.~~
~~21. Employment Company.~~
22. Burial Officer.
23. 56th Division.
24. File.
25.)
26.) War Diary.
27. French Mission
28. SaSection Cal.
29. Salvage Off.

Appendix II
A Branch 52 (Division)

SECRET.   COPY NO. 28

52nd (Lowland) DIVISION.

ADMINISTRATIVE INSTRUCTION NO. A.F. 38.

6th September, 1918.

With reference to 52nd Division wire No. G.H.486 dated 6/9/18.

1. **LOCATIONS.**

   Field Ambulances - 1st Lowland Field Ambulance to 156th
                      Infantry Brigade Area, approx. B.3.a.
                      2nd Lowland Field Ambulance to 157th
                      Infantry Brigade Area, approx. U.25.a.

   Divisional Train, to area about T.21.central. Move from
                     present area to be complete by 6 p.m.
                     7th instant.

   S.A.A. Section,   T.13. (BOYELLES).
     D.A.C.
   Mobile Veterinary   T.21.central.
     Section.
   Divisional   MONCHIET.
     Reception Camp.
   D.A.D.O.S.   Sugar Factory, BOYELLES.

2. **TENTS AND BIVOUAC SHELTERS.**
   These will be distributed to formations and units as soon as received from Corps in accordance with attached distribution list (Appendix "A"). Separate instructions as to drawing these tents and shelters will be sent out later.

3. **WATER.**
   There are Horse watering points at -
                     CROISILLES.
                     ST. LEGER.

   Water Carts can be refilled at -
                     CROISILLES.
                     ST LEGER.

4. **BATHS.**
   (a) Baths, capacity 100 men an hour, have been erected at -
                     S.10.d.0.5.
                     T.1.d.2.1.
   Clean underclothes will be available at these places.

   (b) These baths will be allotted to units as follows -

	S.10.d.0.5.	T.1.d.2.1.
Sept. 8th.	156th Infantry Brigade.	157th Infantry Brigade.
Sept. 9th.	M.G. Battn. in morning. Pioneer Bn. in afternoon.	155th Infantry Brigade.
Sept.10th.	A.D.M.S. in morning. Divl. Train in afternoon.	C.R.E. in morning. S.A.A. Section, D.A.C. in afternoon.

5. **GREATCOATS AND KITS.**
   Six lorries (two for each Infantry Brigade) will be at the Greatcoat Dump at 9 a.m. on the 7th instant.
   These may be used for bringing greatcoats, kits, etc. to new areas.
   The lorries allotted to 156th Infantry Brigade will also bring up the coats, etc. of the Machine Gun Battalion.

-2-

6. **SALVAGE.**
Brigades etc. will collect all salvage in their areas and place it in one heap near a convenient road.
The contents, positions and approximate weight of these heaps will be reported to Divisional Headquarters. Arrangements will then be made to remove the salvage to a Corps Dump.

7. **SANITATION, ETC.**
Units will erect latrines, incinerators, refuse pits and field ovens as soon as possible in their new areas.

8. **ACKNOWLEDGE.**

E.F. Knollis-Barrett Major
for
Lieut.Colonel.
A.A. & Q.M.G. 52nd (Lowland) Division.

Issued at 10.45 p.m.

Copy No. 1 to A.D.C. for G.O.C.
2 to "G".
3   Camp Comdt.
4   Signal Coy.
5   C.R.E.
6   C.R.A.
7   155th Inf. Brigade.
8   156th Inf. Brigade.
9   157th Inf. Brigade.
10   A.D.M.S.
11   D.A.D.V.S.
12   D.A.P.M.
13   Divl. Train.
14   52nd M.G. Bn.
15   17th Northd. Fus. (P).
16   D.A.D.O.S.
17   W.S.O.
18   S.S.O.
19   Reception Camp.
20   Employment Coy.
21   Burial Officer.
22   Salvage Officer.
23   French Mission.
24   Canteen Officer.
25   S.A. Section D.A.C.
26   52nd M.T. Company.
27   File.
28 } War Diary.
29 }

APPENDIX "A".

(A) Distribution of Bivouac Shelters.

UNIT.	IN POSSESSION.	TO COME.	TOTAL.
Divisional Headquarters.	20.	-	20.
155th Infantry Brigade.	50.	250.	300.
156th Infantry Brigade.	50.	250.	300.
157th Infantry Brigade.	50.	250.	300.
17th Northd. Fus. (P).	40.	60.	100.
Machine Gun Battalion.	40.	60.	100.
R.A.	60.	120.	180.
R.E.	-	~~80~~ 70	~~80~~ 70
A.D.M.S.	-	~~40~~ 30	~~40~~ 30
Divl. Train.	-	20.	20.
Signal Company.	-	20.	20.
W.S.O.	-	10.	10.
Mobile Vety. Section.	-	5.	5.
Salvage Company.	-	10.	10.

(B) Distribution of Tents.

155th Infantry Brigade.	8.	52nd M.G. Bn.	2.
156th Infantry Brigade.	8.	Divl. Train.	2.
157th Infantry Brigade.	8.		
R.A.	2.		
17th Northd. Fus. (P).	2.		

Appendix III
"A" Branch 52nd Division No 14

SECRET.

52nd (Lowland) DIVISION.

ADMINISTRATIVE INSTRUCTION No. AF. 39.

SUPPLY ARRANGEMENTS DURING ACTIVE OPERATIONS.

1. The following principles with regard to the supply within the Division of rations, ammunition, ordnance stores, and water during active operations were found to work well during the late fighting, and will be adhered to in future.

2. INFANTRY BRIGADES.

   (a) The 1st Line Transport of each Infantry Brigade (less any vehicles actually with units) will be brigaded, and will be located at a point to be selected from time to time by the Brigadier General Commanding.

   (b) The Staff Captain or Assistant Staff Captain will be with the Brigade Transport, and will be responsible for the following :-

   (i) Sending up rations, ordnance stores, water and ammunition to the units of the Brigade.
   (ii) Keeping in close touch with his Brigade Headquarters and with Divisional Headquarters. Informing the latter whenever he moves his transport lines, giving new locations and time of arrival there.
   (iii) Demanding refills of ammunition and water direct from Divisional Headquarters "Q".
   (iv) Informing Divisional Train, repeating to Divisional Headquarters, when and where he wishes rations for the next day delivered. Should the supply vehicles of the Train arrive at Brigade Transport lines just before the latter move, they will accompany the Brigade transport to their new halting place, and will then, having delivered their supplies, concentrate as ordered by O.C., Divisional Train.

3. ORDNANCE.

   As regards Ordnance Stores, D.A.D.O.S. during a battle will be located at Headquarters, Divisional Train, and will be prepared to send forward stores as requested by units. An Ordnance representative will live with each Brigade Transport lines.

4. ROYAL ARTILLERY AND OTHER DIVISIONAL UNITS.

   The above principles apply equally to the R.A., and such units as the M.G. and Pioneer Battalions and the Field Companies. R.E.
   In the case of the R.A. the D.A.C. (less S.A.A. Section) will be directly under the orders of the C.R.A. who will arrange for the supply of ammunition forward of the A.R.P.
   Normally units such as the M.G. Battalion, Pioneer Battalion, etc. will be administered direct by Divisional Headquarters, but in the event of any of their sub-units being attached to an Infantry Brigade for any considerable time or at any considerable distance (e.g. in the case of an advance guard), a proportion of their 1st Line Transport will be added to the Brigade transport concerned and they will be administered for the time being through the Staff Captain of the Brigade.

5. ACKNOWLEDGE.

13th September, 1918.

Lieut. Colonel.
A.A. & Q.M.G., 52nd (Lowland) Divn.

- 2 -

Copy No. 1 155th Brigade.
2 156th Brigade.
3 157th Brigade.
4 C.R.A.
5 C.R.E.
6 A.D.M.S.
7 Divisional Train.
8 S.S.O.
9 Signal Coy. R.E.
10 M.G. Battalion.
11 North'ld Fus. (P).
12 D.A.P.M.
13 File.
14) War Diary.
15)
16 D.A.D.O.S.
17 Camp Comdt.
18 52nd M.T. Coy.
19 W.S.O.

"A" Form.
MESSAGES AND SIGNALS.

TO	Army	

Sender's Number.	Day of Month.	In reply to Number.	AAA
*G.421.	14		

Ref. A.I. A.F. 40 dated 14/9/18
Location 157th Brigade AAA For U read V.

From
Place: 52nd Division.
Time

SECRET. COPY NO. 29

Appendix IV
A Branch 52 Division

52nd (Lowland) Division.

ADMINISTRATIVE INSTRUCTION No. A.F. 40.

14th September, 1918.

With reference to 52nd Division Order No. 131.

1. **LOCATIONS.**
The attached Location List shows the position of units etc. after relief of 57th Division.

2. **SUPPLIES.**
O.C. Divisional Train will deliver rations to 1st Line Transport of units on completion of their moves.
After doing so Train Companies will return to their new locations, and will be refilled by M.T.

3. **RATIONS.**
The party mentioned in para. 10 of 52nd Division Order No.131 will be rationed by the Left Brigade.

4. **MOVE.**
   (a) The Baggage Wagons of the Train will rejoin their units by 6 a.m. on the morning of the move.

   (b) The following lorries will be detailed by Divisional M.T. Company to assist the moves of formations -

Date.	No. of Lorries.	For what unit.	To report at, Time.	Place.
Sept. 15th.	2	155th Infantry Brigade.	9 a.m.	Brigade H.Q. B.5. central.
Sept. 16th.	2	156th Infantry Brigade.	9 a.m.	Brigade H.Q. B.2.d.
Sept. 16th.	2	157th Infantry Brigade.	9 a.m.	Brigade H.Q. B.6.a.
Sept. 17th.	5	Divisional Headquarters.	8 a.m.	Divl. Hqrs. T.21.d.

5. **ACKNOWLEDGE.**

Issued at 8.p.m.

E.F. Moulton-Barrett Major
for Lieut. Colonel.
A.A. & Q.M.G. 52nd (Lowland) Division.

Copy to No.1 A.D.C. for G.O.C.
2 "G".
3 Camp Comdt.
4 Signal Coy.
5 C.R.E.
6 C.R.A.
7 155th Inf. Bde.
8 156th Inf. Bde.
9 157th Inf. Bde.
10 A.D.M.S.
11 D.A.D.V.S.
12 D.A.P.M.
13 Divl. Train.
14 52nd M.G. Battn.
15 17th Northd. Fus. (P).
17 D.A.D.O.S.
18 S.S.O.
19 52nd M.T. Company.
20 W.S.O.
21 Burial Officer.
22 Salvage Officer.
23 Reception Camp.
24 Employment Coy.
25 French Mission.
26 Canteen Officer.
27 O.C. S.A.A. Section, D.A.C.
28 File.
29
30 War Diary.

SECRET.   52nd (Lowland) Division.

LOCATION LIST.

Map Reference 51.B. Sheet 57.C.

UNIT.	LOCATION.	TRANSPORT LINES.
DIVISIONAL HEADQUARTERS.	D.7.a.5.7.	
DIVISIONAL ARTILLERY.		
Headquarters.	D.7.a.5.7.	
9th Brigade R.F.A.	D.4.d.1.8.	U.29.c.
56th Brigade R.F.A.	D.16.a.2.7.	C.9.central.
D.A.C. (less S.A.A. Section).	U.19.d.	
S.A.A. Section.	C.4.d.2.3.	C.4.d.2.3.
DIVISIONAL ENGINEERS.		
Headquarters.	D.7.a.5.7.	
410th Field Company.	D.8.c.2.9.	V.19.c.9.5.
412th Field Company.	D.7.b.6.9.	V.25.a.3.0.
413th Field Company.	C.5.b.8.8.	C.5.b.8.8.
155th INFANTRY BRIGADE.	D.15.b.5.6.	C.4.a.
156th INFANTRY BRIGADE.	C.6.b.4.8.	U.28.central.
157th INFANTRY BRIGADE.	U.28.d.0.0.	C.6.d.
17th NORTHD. FUS. (P).	D.7.c. & d.	D.7.c.4.4.
52nd BATTN. M.G. CORPS.	V.28.c.	V.26.a.
DIVISIONAL TRAIN.		
Headquarters.	C.1.d.8.3.	
No.1 Company.	C.3.b.3.8.	
No.2 Company.)		
No.3 Company.)	C.1.d.8.3.	
No.4 Company.)		
Refilling Point.	R.A. Group - C.3.b.3.8. Remainder of Division - C.1.d.8.3.	
R.A.M.C.		
A.D.M.S.	D.7.a.5.7.	
1st Low. Field Ambce.	D.1.d.5.9.	D.1.d.5.9.
2nd Low. Field Ambce.	C.11.c.7.6.	
3rd Low. Field Ambce. (Corps M.D.S.).	U.25 central.	
Division A.D.S.	D.1.d.5.9.	
D.A.P.M.	D.7.a.5.7.	
D.A.D.O.S.	C.7.a. central.	
Divl. Salvage Officer.	C.16.b.0.9.	
Divl. Burial Officer. (with Div.Pioneer Bn.).	D.7.c.	

P.T.O.

-2-

UNIT.	LOCATION.	REMARKS.
DIVL. RECEPTION CAMP.	BOISLEUX AU MONT.	From 15th inst.
DIVL. BULK CANTEEN.	ECOUST.	
DIVL. BATHS OFFICER.	ECOUST.	
Adv. Clothing Exchange.	C.7.a. central.	
DIVL. S.A.A. & GRENADE DUMP.	C.3.a.	
52nd M.T. COMPANY.	S.14.b.2.8.	
52nd MOBILE VET. SECTION.	U.16.d.9.5.	
DIVL. EMPLOYMENT COY. H.Q.	BOISLEUX AU MONT.	
REINFORCEMENT RAILHEAD.	BOISLEUX AU MONT.	From 15th inst.
SUPPLY RAILHEAD.	BOISLEUX AU MONT.	
MOBILE WORKSHOPS.	ST. LEGER. T.28.d.2.1.	
ADV. GUN PARK.	BIHUCOURT.	

TRAFFIC CONTROL POSTS.

U.27.b.2.8.   D.2.d.2.2.
C.2.a.8.2.   D.2.a.2.6.
D.1.d.5.5.   V.28.c.4.8.
D.2.c.0.0.   V.28.b.4.9.
D.2.c.8.0.

Traffic Posts in NOREUIL by Guards Division.

Proposed Prisoner of War Cage. - D.2.a.7.1.

WATER POINTS.

LOCATION.	REMARKS.
BOISLEUX AU MONT. S.9.d.7.4.	Water Cart Refilling Point. 2 Standpipes. Troughs.
BOYELLES. S.18.b.5.0.	Water Cart Refilling Point. 1 Standpipe. Troughs.
CROISILLES. T.24.a.5.5.	(a) Water Cart Refilling Point. 1 Standpipe. Troughs. (b) 3 wells.
BULLECOURT. U.20.d.8.4.	Troughs.
(Factory). U.22.b.0.6.	Water Cart Refilling Point. 2 Standpipes. Troughs.
ST. LEGER. T.28.c.7.5.	Water Cart Refilling Point. 1 Standpipe. Troughs.
QUEANT. D.1.d.7.5. D.8.a.2.9.	Troughs. Troughs.

WATER POINTS contd.

LOCATION.	REMARKS.
ECOUST.	3 wells with Troughs. Water Cart Refilling Point.
LONGATTE. C.9.b.2.7.	Troughs.
NOREUIL.	2 wells with Troughs. Water Cart Refilling Point.

SECRET.   Copy No..........

52nd (Lowland) DIVISION.

ADDENDUM TO ADMINISTRATIVE INSTRUCTIONS No. AF. 41.

25th SEPTEMBER, 1918.

1. **TRAFFIC.**

    (a) The GUARDS DIVISION will have Traffic Control posts at the following points on the main CAMBRAI Road :-

    (i)   CROSS ROADS...   J.9.b.6.2.
    (ii) BOURSIES......   J.5.d.3.3.
    (iii) CROSS ROADS...   K.1.a.9.3.

    (b) No traffic will move EAST of a line NORTH and SOUTH through road junction J.9.b.6.2. until the crossing over the CANAL DU NORD (E.27.d.1.3.) is reported available.

    (c) The signal that this crossing is ready for traffic will be given by the R.E. Officer in charge of the work who will hoist a RED FLAG. This signal will then be repeated by the control posts shown in (a) above.

    (d) As soon as the crossing over the Canal (E.27.d.1.3.) is ready, D.A.P.M., 52nd DIVISION, will take over the traffic control there.

    (e) In consequence of above, 157th Infantry Brigade and other Troops, to which the CAMBRAI Road has been eventually allotted, will use cross country tracks for any transport they require to send forward before the crossing at E.27.d.1.3. is finished.

2. **GREATCOATS, ETC.**

    Brigades will arrange to dump, under cover of a proportion of the shelters in their possession, greatcoats and other articles of equipment not required on Z day.
    One man per unit will remain to guard these dumps. These men will be rationed under Brigade arrangements.
    These dumps will be located in positions whence their contents can be brought forward by H.T. The locations of these dumps will be reported as soon as possible to Divisional Headquarters.

3. **ACKNOWLEDGE.**

                                                    Lieut. Colonel.
                               A.A. & Q.M.G., 52nd (Lowland) DIVISION.

Issued at 6.15 p.m.

Copy No.					
1	A.D.C. for G.O.C.	12	D.A.P.M.	23	S.A.A. Sect.
2	"G"	13	Divnl. Train.	24	Senior Chaplain.
3	Camp Comdt.	14	52nd M.G. Bn.	25	52nd M.T. Coy.
4	Signal Coy.	15	17th North'ld Fus	26	Senior Chaplain Non C. of E.
5	C.R.A.	16	S.S.O.		
6	C.R.E.	17	D.A.D.O.S.	27	French Mission.
7	155th Brigade.	18	W.S.O.	28	D.G.O.
8	156th Brigade.	19	Burial Officer.	29	XVIIth Corps "Q"
9	157th Brigade.	20	Salvage Officer.	30	57th Divn. "Q"
10	A.D.M.S.	21	Receptn. Camp.	31	63rd Divn. "Q"
11	D.A.D.V.S.	22	Divnl. Emp. Coy.	32	Guards Divn. "Q"
				33	4th Cndn Divn.
				34	Advd. Divnl. S.A.A. Dump.

35 to 36 War Diary.
37 File.

SECRET.   COPY NO. 34

52nd (LOWLAND) DIVISION.

APPENDIX "A" to ADMINISTRATIVE INSTRUCTION NO. A.F.41.

26th September, 1918.

WATER. Within XVII Corps Area :-

(1) 52nd Division will be responsible for the area West of and including the Canal du NORD (and MOEUVRES) for the purpose of developing new water sources.

(2) 155th Infantry Brigade will supply water picquets of 1 N.C.O. and 3 men for Traffic Control at each new water point developed by C.R.E., on application from the latter.

(3) The following additional information regarding water is published for information :-

"A" WATER POINTS (with pumps and troughs) in hand.

    PRONVILLE - D.9.a.2.9.
    LOUVERVAL - J.10.a.9.5.
    VALLEY S.W. of MOEUVRES - D.30.b.2.6.

"B" WATER POINTS to be developed as soon as circumstances permit.

    SUGAR FACTORY - E.29.a.8.8.
    FONTAINE NOTRE DAME - F.15.
    QUARRY POND, South edge of BOURLON WOOD, about F.20.a.2.9.
    MOEUVRES.

E.F. Mallin Sawett Major
for Lieut.Colonel.

Issued at 10 a.m.   A.A. & Q.M.G. 52nd (Lowland) Division.

Copy No. 1 A.D.C. for G.O.C.   19. Burial Officer.
2 "G".   20. Salvage Officer.
3 Camp Comdt.   21. Reception Camp.
4 Signal Coy.   22. Employment Coy.
5 C.R.A.   23. S.A.A. Section D.A.C.
6 C.R.E.   24. 52nd M.T. Company.
7 155th Inf. Bde.   25. D.G.O.
8 156th Inf. Bde.   26. XVII Corps "Q".
9 157th Inf. Bde.   27. 57th Division "Q".
10 A.D.M.S.   28. 63rd Division "Q".
11 D.A.D.V.S.   30. Guards Division "Q".
12 D.A.P.M.   31. 4th Canadian Division.
13 Divl. Train.   32. Adv. Divl. S.A.A. Dump.
14 52nd M.G. Bn.   33. File.
15 17th Northd. Fus.   34.)
16 S.S.O.   35. War Diary.
17 D.A.D.O.S.
18 W.S.O.

Appendix V
A Branch 52 Division

SECRET.   COPY NO. 34

52nd (LOWLAND) DIVISION.

ADMINISTRATIVE INSTRUCTIONS NO. AF 41.

24th September, 1918.

Reference 52nd Divisional Order No. 136 of 24th September, 1918.

1. **SUPPLIES.**

   Railhead. - BOISLEUX AU MONT.

   Refilling Point (less R.A.). - ECOUST. (C.1.d.9.9.).

   R.A.   - C.3.b.

   (a) Preserved Meat will be issued to Infantry Brigades, R.E. Companies, Pioneer Battalion and Machine Gun Battalion (less a proportion of Fresh Meat for Transport Details) for consumption on Z day.

   (b) Separate instructions will be given to O.C. Divisional Train regarding issues of Rum and Solidified Alcohol during operations.

   (c) Supply Situation on morning of Z Day.

   (i) On the man. - Iron Ration and rations for Z day. Commanding Officers of Units moving forward will ensure that the latter have been distributed to and are carried by individuals prior to the advance.

   (ii) In Train Vehicles ready to deliver to units. - 1 days rations.

   (iii) In M.T. Company Lorries. - 1 days rations.

2. **AMMUNITION.**

   A. S.A.A. & GRENADE DUMPS.

   (a) Forward Brigade etc. dumps. -

   155th Inf. Brigade. - TADPOLE DUMP. - D.18.d.5.3.
   156th Inf. Brigade. - D.30.c.9.9.
   157th Inf. Brigade. - D.30.c.9.7.
   Machine Gun Battn. - (E.25.b.5.7.
   (2 dumps).   (E.19.c.3.2.

   Brigades etc. will be responsible for finding the personnel for their dumps, and for sending forward ammunition etc. from these to the fighting troops. If required, these dumps will be refilled by Brigade 1st Line Transport, which will in turn refill from the Divisional Dump.

   Brigades etc. will clearly mark their dumps, and the approaches leading to them, with Notice Boards.

   (b) Rear Brigade Dumps. -

   Brigade Headquarters - D.15.b.0.7.
                          D.27.b.3.8.

   These two dumps will be in charge of 155th Infantry Brigade, but will be available as emergency dumps to issue to any formation on demand.

P.T.O.

(c) Divisional Dump D.7.central (just W. of QUEANT-
    LAGNICOURT Road.
        Until such time as Brigade Transport Lines move
    East of the QUEANT - LAGNICOURT Road, 1st Line
    Limbers will refil from this Dump.

(d) Corps S.A.A. Dumps. -
                    BULLECOURT. (C.3.a.)
                    NOREUIL.   (C.11.d.)
                    LAGNICOURT. (C.18.b.)

"B" GUN & HOWITZER AMMUNITION.
(a) A.R.Points. - BULLECOURT (C.3.a.)
                  NOREUIL   (C.11.d.) Being fed by
                                        Broad Guage.
                  LAGNICOURT (C.18.b.) Not to be drawn
                                        upon until Z Day.

(b) Corps Dumps.- T.9.b. (All natures of ammunition)
                  ECOUST. (C.2.a.) Heavy.
                  MEIN.   (C.2.c.) Field.

(c) Army Dump. - MERCATEL (2,000 tons all natures).

(d) Railheads. - BOISLEUX AU MONT.
                 BOYELLES.
                 VAUX VRAUCOURT (under construction).
        When the tactical situation admits an A.R.P.
    will be opened near LOUVERVAL.
        All ammunition must be collected from vacated
    gun positions before fresh supply are drawn from
    A.R.P's.

"C" MOBILE RESERVES.
(a) S.A.A. Section D.A.C. will be under the direct
    orders of "Q". This Section will remain in its
    present location C.4.d., ready to either refil
    1st Line Transport or to move forward to a new
    position as ordered.
        An officer from the S.A.A. Section will report
    to Divisional Headquarters "Q" at 6 p.m. on Z-1
    day, and will remain there during operations.

(b) Nos. 1 & 2 Sections D.A.C. will work under the
    direct orders of the C.R.A..

3. WATER. "A" Men.
(a) Brigades will establish advanced dumps of drinking
    water in the vicinity of their Advanced Grenade Dumps,
    and will be responsible for forwarding water to the
    fighting troops. As large a reserve as possible
    should be retained in Brigade charge and only the
    minimum sent forward with attacking troops.

(b) In addition to petrol tins etc. already in
    possession of units the following may be drawn at
    once for this purpose. -

	Petrol Tins.	Waterbottles.
156th Inf. Brigade.	150.	250.
157th Inf. Brigade.	150.	250.
Machine Gun Battn.	50.	-

    Petrol Tins from Divisional S.A.A. Dump (D.7.
                                            central).
    Waterbottles from D.A.D.O.S.

/(c)

-3-

(c) A mobile reserve of water lorries (total 2,100 gallons) is situated at ECOUST under the Divisional Water Officer. Water lorries can be sent up to refil water carts as required on direct application to Divisional Water Officer.

In an emergency the lorries can be sent direct up to units, but application for this must be made to Division "Q".

"B" ANIMALS.
  (a) Available water points -
    PRONVILLE (D.9.a.2.8).
    QUEANT. (D.1.d.central).
    NOREUIL. (C.10.c.) Small supply.
    LONGATTE. (C.9.b.)
    MORCHIES. (I.6.c.) A large supply
        N.B. Only troughs N. of the village. Those in the village belong to VI Corps.

In addition water is being brought up by train to NOREUIL and emptied into tarpaulins for watering horses. The position of this water point is C.15.b.central.

It is hoped to open up a water point at LOUVERVAL as early as possible.

  (b) C.R.E. will arrange to develop as much water as possible in and South of MOEUVRES as soon as the tactical situation admits.

4. TRAFFIC.
  (a) The main lorry routes are shown on Third Army Forward Area Traffic Map (already issued).
As operations proceed the main line of supply for the Division will become CROISILLES - LAGNICOURT - LOUVERVAL road. The LAGNICOURT - LOUVERVAL road will be made into a double wat road as early as possible.

  (b) D.A.P.M. will arrange for Traffic Control on all roads and tracks SOUTH of MOEUVRES (exclusive). MOEUVRES will be controlled by 63rd Division.

  (c) Troops and empty H.T. must use crosscountry tracks as far as possible.

  (d) Animals proceeding to and from water must on no account use Lorry Routes. All O.C. Wagon and Transport Lines must be prepared to reconnoitre new routes to water and if necessary will cut wire or fill in old trenches to accomplish this end.

  (e) Vehicles must not halt on main Lorry Routes. They must pull clear of the road or down a side road.

  (f) Special attention is called to S.S. 724 - March Discipline and Traffic Control.

  (g) The QUEANT - PRONVILLE - MOEUVRES road will be used as little as possible by transport of this Division.

  (h) The following tracks and roads are allotted to Formations for supply purposes from Z day inclusive. -

P.T.O.

Track "M" to 155th Infantry Brigade and attached Troops.
Track "Q" to 156th Infantry Brigade and attached Troops.
LAGNICOURT - LOUVERVAL - CAMBRAI road to 157th Infantry Brigade, attached troops and M.G. Battn.

Reference Map "A" issued with 52nd Divisional Order No.136.

(j) D.A.P.M. will be ready to take over control of the Crossings over the Canal du NORD at -
    E.20.d.7.6.
    E.27.c.
    E.26.b.
as soon as the tactical situation admits.

(k) In addition to existing Traffic Posts D.A.P.M. will arrange to control the following -
Water Point at MORCHIES (I.6.c.) - 1 N.C.O. & 6 men.
Water Point at NOREUIL (C.15.b.) - 1 N.C.O. & 3 men.

(m) Traffic control at BULLECOURT, QUEANT and PRONVILLE Water Points will be found by the Canadian Corps.

PROVOST.
"A" STRAGGLERS.
(i) Brigades will arrange to block the exits from their areas with advanced Straggler Posts. Any stragglers stopped by these posts will be sent back direct to their units.
(ii) Behind those Brigade Posts, a line of Straggler Posts, and a Straggler Collecting Station will be established under Divisional Control.
Separate orders on this subject are being issued to D.A.P.M.

"B" PRISONERS OF WAR.
Corps Cage - NOREUIL.
Divisional Cage. - D.1.c.3.1. (near D.H.Q.)
Brigades will detail escort as laid down in this office A.135/1 of 12/9/18. These escorts must know the nearest route to the Divisional Cage.
Prisoners will not be sent back by the PRONVILLE - QUEANT road. They will use crosscountry tracks as far as possible.

6. MEDICAL.
Locations.- A.D.M.S. D.7.a.5.7.
1/2nd Lowland Field Ambulance. - C.9.central.
1/3rd Lowland Field Ambulance. - U.25.central.
(Corps Main Dressing Station).
1/1st Lowland Field Ambulance. - D.1.d.5.9.
(Divisional Advanced Dressing Station).

Relay Posts.	Regtl. Aid Posts.
D.17.d.3.8.	E.13.d.0.8.
D.18.c.5.8.	D.18.d.2.6.
D.18.d.2.6.	E.19.a.8.3.
E.19.a.0.9.	E.19.a.1.0.
E.19.a.8.3.	
Trolley Post.	Horsed Ambulance Post.
D.17.a.5.9.	D.17.b.1.3.
	Motor Car Post.
	D.15.d.5.5.

17.

7. **VETERINARY.**
   Advanced Collecting Station. - D.7.a.5.8. (Near D.H.Q.)
   Mobile Veterinary Section. - ECOUST.
   Veterinary Evac. Station. - BOISLEUX AU MONT.

8. **BURIAL.**

   (a) The Burial Parties detailed in this office A.135/1 of 12/9/18 will concentrate under the Divisional Burial Officer at Headquarters 17th Northumberland Fusiliers (P) (D.7.a.) at 6 p.m. Z-1 day. They will be rationed to Z day inclusive, after which day they will be attached for rations to the 17th Northumberland Fusiliers (P).

   (b) The Divisional Burial Officer will reconnoitre a site for a new Divisional Cemetery in the vicinity of MOEUVRES, to be taken unto use as soon as the tactical situation admits This site will be notified to D.A.A.G., D.H.Q.

   (c) Senior Chaplains will detail a Chaplain of each demonination to be attached to the Divisional Burial Officer from Z day inclusive.

9. **SALVAGE.**
   Divisional Salvage Dump. - Near Divisional Grenade Dump
                                 (D.7.central.)
   Forward Corps Salvage Dump. - ECOUST.

   (a) The Divisional Salvage Officer will be located at the Divisional Salvage Dump, and messages for him can be sent either direct there or through D.H.Q.

   (b) As soon as the tactical situation permits, Brigades will at once start salvage operations in their immediate vicinity. "Salvage Areas" are allotted to Brigades as follows -
   - 156th Infantry Brigade - All ground in Divisional Area East of Canal du NORD. (exclusive).
   - 157th Infantry Brigade - HINDENBURG Front Line and both banks of the Canal in E.26, K.2.b., K.3.a.
   - 155th Infantry Brigade - All ground North of main CAMBRAI road and West of grid line between E.25 and E.26

   (c) Salvage collected will be gathered in suitable dumps near a road or track, but not so near as to necessitate vehicles collecting it having to remain on the road.

   (d) D.H.Q. and the Divisional Salvage Officer will be notified of the position of these Brigade Salvage Dumps.
   In the event of a further advance taking place the "Caretakers", in accordance with this office A.135/1 of 12/9/18, will remain in charge of the dumps till collected by the Divisional Salvage Company.

   (e) Every effort must be made to salve British rifles in serviceable condition. If left exposed to weather for any length of time, they deteriorate rapidly. These rifles must, therefore, when collected be placed under exemporized cover at once, and should be conditioned as early as possible by an armourer.

P.T.O.

- 6 -

(f) Returning vehicles of 1st line transport must be systematically used to evacuate salvage to Divisional Salvage Dump. British Rifles and equipment must be evacuated first. If circumstances admit vehicles from the S.A.A. Section D.A.C. will be provided in addition.

(g) All roads and tracks must be cleared of loose boxes or rounds of ammunition.

(h) Every effort is to be made to re-issue salved material to make good deficiencies.

(j) All empty Train or S.A.A. vehicles passing the Divisional Salvage Dump will take back a load to the Corps Salvage Dump.

10. BATTLE STORES.
(a) In addition to the petrol tins and waterbottles mentioned in para.3 the following are available and may be drawn at once. -
    156th Infantry Brigade) 150 wirecutters and
    157th Infantry Brigade) 25 pairs hedging
) gloves each.

(b) Each Brigade will retain the 50 Pack Saddles already issued. A reserve of 24 Pack Saddles is with the S.A.A. Section D.A.C.

11. TENTAGE.
(a) For the purposes of these operations the following number of tents and shelters may be retained by units (less R.A.) for transport lines etc. -

	Tents.	Shelters.
Divisional Headquarters.	20.	20.
Each Infantry Brigade.	8.	50.
Divisional Train.	8.	20.
Machine Gun Battalion.	3.	35.
Pioneer Battalion.	3.	50.
C. R. E.	3.	20.
Mobile Veterinary Section.	2.	5.

(b) Every precaution is to be taken to prevent loss of this tentage during operations as it cannot be replaced at present. Units will be held responsible for any losses.

(c) Divisional R.A. retains the tentage now in possession.

(d) All tentage in excess of the scale laid down in para. (a) will be returned to D.A.D.O.S. by noon Z-1 day. Units etc. will report when this has been done and the amount returned.

12. RECEPTION CAMP.
(a) From Z day inclusive reinforcements and personnel returning from leave will remain at the Divisional Reception Camp pending orders to join their units.

(b) In addition to the parties found from the nucleus as detailed in this office A.135/1 of 12/9/18, the following will be sent to report D.A.P.M., D.H.Q. by noon Z-1 day -
    1 officer, 5 N.C.O's and 20 men.

/They

They will be used for the Divisional Stragglers Posts and Collecting Station, and will arrive at D.H.Q., rationed up to Z day inclusive.

13. **MISCELLANEOUS.**
Brigades etc. will send to this office a copy of their Administrative Instructions issued in connection with these operations.

14. **ACKNOWLEDGE.**

C.Maude
Lieut.Colonel.

Issued at 11 p.m.   A.A. & Q.M.G. 52nd (Lowland) Division.

Copy No.1 to	A.D.C. for G.O.C.	21	Reception Camp.
2	"G"	22	Employment Company.
3	Camp Comdt.	23	S.A.A. Section D.A.C.
4	Signal Company.	24	Senior Chaplain.
5	C.R.E.	25	52nd M.T. Company.
6	C.R.A.	26	Senior Chaplain non C. of E.
7	155th Inf. Bde.	27	French Mission.
8	156th Inf. Bde.	28	D.C.O.
9	157th Inf. Bde.	29	XVII Corps "Q".
10	A.D.M.S.	30	57th Division "Q".
11	D.A.D.V.S.	31	63rd Division "Q".
12	D.A.P.M.	32	File.
13	Divl. Train.	33)	
14	52nd M.G.Bn.	34)	War Diary.
15	17th Northd.Fus.		
16	S.S.O.		
17	D.A.D.O.S.		
18	V.S.O.		
19	Burial Officer.		
20	Salvage Officer.		

Army Form C. 2118.

WAR DIARY
or
INTELLIGENCE SUMMARY.
(Erase heading not required.)

CONFIDENTIAL.

Original

52nd. (Lowland) Division.

"A" and "Q" Branch.

WAR DIARY

for

OCTOBER 1918

Volume XLI

Army Form C. 2118.

52nd (Lowland) Division WAR DIARY or "A and Q" INTELLIGENCE SUMMARY.

OCTOBER 1918 Vol XLI

(Erase heading not required.)

Instructions regarding War Diaries and Intelligence Summaries are contained in F.S. Regs., Part II. and the Staff Manual respectively. Title pages will be prepared in manuscript.

PAGE ONE

Place	Date 1918	Hour	Summary of Events and Information Ref/Maps 1/40000 51c, 57c, 44, 44a.	Remarks and references to Appendices
GRAINCOURT	1		Advanced Headqrs moved to CANTAING MILL F.27.c. (44a)	
"	3		Rear Headqrs moved to GRAINCOURT. K.5.6.24. (44a)	
"	"		Admins. Instructions No 42 issued	Appendix I a
"	"		Admins. Instructions No 43 issued	Appendix I b
"	4		Scale of Monkey Rugs & Mountings for Lewis guns reduced to 61 per Division	
"	5		Circular Memo. No 27 issued ref Regulations for Watering Parties.	
"	6		Admins. Instructions 44 and 45 issued	Appendices I c and II
VAULX-VRAUCOURT	"		Div. Hdqrs moved to VAULX VRAUCOURT.	
"	7		Personnel of Division and proportion of transport entrained at VAULX VRAUCOURT, detraining at TINCQUES.	
LE CAUROY	"		Div. Hdqrs opened at LE CAUROY	
"	"		D.A.D.o.S. instructed to issue Blankets, at scale of 1 per man	
"	11		52nd Divl. M.G. Battalion rejoined Division, and moved into Billets at HOUVIN.	

Army Form C. 2118.

52nd (Lowland) Division WAR DIARY or INTELLIGENCE SUMMARY.

"A and "Q"

OCTOBER 1918.

Vol. XLI

Instructions regarding War Diaries and Intelligence Summaries are contained in F.S. Regs., Part II. and the Staff Manual respectively. Title pages will be prepared in manuscript.

(Erase heading not required.)

Summary of Events and Information
— PAGE TWO —

Place	Date	Hour	Summary of Events and Information	Remarks and references to Appendices
LE CAUROY	11		50 new pattern Soft Bag Carriers for Lewis Guns received, old pattern to be returned.	
"	12 to 16		Training carried out during forenoons. Recreation in afternoon. Bathing and Re-equipping. Games, material issued to units. Divisional Concert Party and Band entertained troops.	
"	17		Four heavy and four light Machine guns issued for instructional purposes, to be returned when leaving VIII Corps area. Circular memorandum No 28 issued (re Dress).	
"	18		Suggestion by VIII Corps that the grocery portion of Iron Ration be dispensed with as it is seldom fit for use owing to impossibility of keeping it in sound condition during active operations. S.4b. 52nd Div. Admin. Instructions issued for move from LE CAUROY area. (Appendix III)	
"	19		52nd Division moved from LE CAUROY. Div. Hdqrs to CHATEAU D'ACQ. 155 Bde group to BULLY GRENAY. 156th Bde group to CHATEAU DE LA HAIE. 157 Bde group to MONT ST. ELOY. 52nd Div. Admin. Instructions No 47 issued for move. (Appendix IV)	
"	20		52nd Division moved from CHATEAU D'ACQ area. Div. Hdqrs to CITÉ ARMAND VOISIN. HENIN LIETARD. 155 Bde group to FOURIERS. 156 Bde group to BILLY MONTIGNY. 157 Bde group to HENIN LIETARD. Corps advise supply of Anti-Tank Rifle Grenades now available for instructional purposes only, and not to be taken into the line without orders from G.H.Q.	

Army Form C. 2118.

52nd (Lowland) Division WAR DIARY or INTELLIGENCE SUMMARY.

"A and Q" F.S. Regs., Part II.

OCTOBER 1918.
Vol. XLI

— PAGE THREE —

Place	Date	Hour	Summary of Events and Information	Remarks and references to Appendices
HENIN LIETARD	21		Memo to VIII Corps agreeing to proposed abolition of grocery portion of Iron Ration. Bde groups and other units moved in accordance with 52nd Div. Administ: Instruction No. 48 (issued 20/10)	(Appendix V)
			155 Bde group to COURCELLES, 156 Bde group to AUBY, 157 Bde group FLERS-in-Divis. Hdqrs remains at HENIN LIETARD.	
CH. MAISON BLANCHE (Q.20.c.)	22		52nd Division Hdqrs move to Chateau MAISON BLANCHE. Units informed that after move on 24th, no lorries will be supplied to help move. Blankets, extra kits etc will therefore require to be dumped.	
—"—	23		Corps advise that in the event of necessity lorries at disposal for moving Div. Hdqrs. and R.E. which are taken from Amm Section must be returned to same later fast in chain of supply.	
			Circular memo No. 29 issued ref Divisional Canteen & No. 30 ref Reinforcements and 52nd Division Hdqrs move to FLINES. Leave Personnel Circular issued giving instructions for making improvised "Tommy Cookers". (No 31)	
FLINES	24 25 27		52nd Division moved into Corps Quarters.	
			Administrative Instruction No. 50 (No. 49 omitted) issued for move of Div. Hdqrs from FLINES to SAMEON.	(Appendix VI)
—"—			Circular memo. No. 32 issued informing units that a man under suspended sentence is not precluded from going on Leave.	
—"—	27		Remounts — 39 arrived. Circular Memorandum No 33 issued ref. Precautions against Chilled Feet.	

Army Form C. 2118.

WAR DIARY
or
INTELLIGENCE SUMMARY

52nd (LOWLAND) DIVISION. "A" and "Q" Part II.

OCTOBER 1918.
Vol. XLI

PAGE FOUR

Place	Date	Hour	Summary of Events and Information	Remarks and references to Appendices
FLINES	28		52nd Division takes over left sector of VIII Corps front at CHATEAU L'ABBAYE - 15h15. Inf Bde in the line.	
SAMEON	29		52nd Div. Hdqrs move to SAMEON. 32 Remounts arrived.	
—	30		Circular memo. No 34 re Distinguishing Marks issued to all concerned.	
—	31		Effective Strength Return attached.	(Appendix VII)
			Casualty Return attached.	(Appendix VIII)

Capt.
for DAAG.

War Diary. October. Appendix I a.

SECRET. COPY No. ....

52nd (Lowland) DIVISION.

ADMINISTRATIVE INSTRUCTIONS NO. AF 42.

1st OCTOBER, 1918.

Reference – 52nd Divisional Order No. 137 of 30/9/18.

1. **MOVES;**
    Following moves will take place to be completed by midnight October 1st/2nd.

    S.A.A. Section, D.A.C.   to Sugar Factory, E.29.a.
    Mobile Vet. Section   to neighbourhood of Divisional Train, E.25.d.
    D.A.D.O.S. and Divisional Canteen.   to neighbourhood of Divisional Train, E.25.d.
    Water Lorries.   to Sugar Factory, E.29.a.
    Advanced Divisional H.Q.   to CANTAING MILL, F.27.c.
    Rear Divisional H.Q.   to E.28.b.

2. **AMMUNITION:**
    Divisional S.A.A. etc. Dump   L.2.a. central
    A.R.Ps.   E.27.c. (being pushed forward by Light Rly.)
          E.23.d.
          E.20.a.2.6.

3. **WATER.**

    Sugar Factory, E.29.a.)
    FONTAINE   )   Waterpoints.

    GRAINCOURT   )
    ANNEUX   )   Wells only.
    CANTAING   )

4. **MEDICAL:**
    Advanced Dressing Station   ANNEUX.

5. **PROVOST:**
    Prisoner of War cage   L.1.d.6.8.

    D.A.P.M. will be prepared to take over traffic control from 63rd Division, but will not actually do so till further orders.

6. **SHELTERS, etc.**
    Brigades and Units may either take forward tents and shelters, or dump them under Brigade arrangements.
    In the latter case steps will be taken to safeguard these dumps, as missing shelters cannot be replaced.

7. **ORDNANCE:**
    D.A.D.O.S. will make every effort to issue leather jerkins to the Division as soon as possible. The order of priority in which units will draw has already been sent out.
    Blankets will not at present be issued.

8. **SALVAGE;**
    Salvage will continue to be sent to Divisional Salvage Dump, E.27.c.1.2.

    P.T.O.

2.

9. R.E. Stores.   F.20.a.9.9.

10.
10. ACKNOWLEDGE.

[signature]
Lieut. Colonel.
A.A. & Q.M.G., 52nd (Lowland) DIVISION.

Issued at 1100

Copy No. 1   to A.D.V. for G.O.C.
       2   "Q".
       3   Camp Comdt.
       4   Signal Coy.
       5   C.R.A.
       6   C.R.E.
       7   155th Inf. Brigade.
       8   156th Inf. Brigade.
       9   157th Inf. Brigade.
     10   A.D.M.S.
     11   D.A.D.V.S.
     12   D.A.P.M.
     13   Divnl. Train.
     14   52nd Battn. M.G.C.
     15   17th North'd. Fus.
     16   S.S.O.
     17   D.A.D.O.S.
     18   W.S.O.
     19   Burial Officer.
     20   Salvage Officer
     21   Reception Camp.
     22   S.A.A. Section, D.A.C.
     23   52nd M.T. Coy.
     28   French Mission.
     25   D.G.O.
     26   XVIIth Corps "Q"
     27   57th Division "Q"
     28   63rd Division "Q"
     29) Rear D.H.Q.
     30)
     31   File.
     32) War Diary.
     33)

War Diary. October. Appendix I.G

SECRET.   Copy No.......

52nd (LOWLAND) DIVISION.

ADMINISTRATIVE INSTRUCTION NO. AF 43.

3rd October, 1918.

1. The following Administrative Area is allotted to the Division (reference 1/20,000 Map).

   Northern Boundary... A straight line from LA FOLIE (inclusive) to GRAINCOURT (inclusive).
   Western Boundary ... A North and South line through K.5.a.cent.
   Southern Boundary... Along grid line dividing K.5, K.6, L.1, L.2 from K.11, K.12, L.7 and L.8. respectively, thence (from L.3.c.0.0.) a straight line to F.30.c.0.0.

2. D.A.P.M. will arrange for traffic control and water point control within this area, relieving any posts of 57th or 63rd Division therein by 1800, 4th instant.

3. The following sub-areas are allotted for Salvage and Burial -

   (a) East of Scheldt Canal .... Infantry Brigade in front line.
   (b) Between Scheldt Canal and a North and South line through F.28.central .... Infantry Brigade in Support.
   (c) From the latter boundary to a North and South line through LA JUSTICE L.1.d.. Infantry Brigade in Reserve.
   (d) From latter boundary to Divisional Western boundary. .... Divisional Burial and Salvage Officers working under directions of D.A.A.G.

4. All dead men and any dead animals within these areas will be buried forthwith by the above. In future all units, including Wagon and Transport Lines, will be held responsible for burying all dead animals within 300 yards of their bivouacs and within 12 hours of arriving thereat. D.A.P.M. will be responsible for bringing to notice any neglect to obey this order.

5. Salvage will be sent by Brigades, etc., to the new Divisional Salvage Dump at GRAINCOURT. D.A.A.G. will choose a site for this Dump and notify its exact location by wire to units. Salvage Officer will send a party forthwith to take over this Dump.

6. C.R.A. will be responsible for salving all field gun ammunition from rear gun positions.

7. All personnel employed on Water Duties West of LOUVERVAL will be withdrawn under arrangements to be made by the W.S.O.

8. ACKNOWLEDGE.

Issued at 2000.

E.F. Mullin-Barrett Major
for
Lieut-Colonel,
A.A. & Q.M.G., 52nd (Lowland) Divn.

Copy No. 1 A.D.C. for G.O.C.
        2 'G'
        3) Rear H.Q.
        4)
        5 155th Inf. Bde.
        6 156th Inf. Bde.
        7 157th Inf. Bde.
        8 C.R.A.
        9 C.R.E.
       10 Div. Signal Co.
       11 52nd Bn. M.G.C.
       12 17th North'd Fus. (P)
       13 A.D.M.S.
       14 D.A.D.V.S.
       15 D.A.P.M.
       16 Div. Burial Officer.
       17 Div. Salvage Officer.
       18 U.S.O.
       19 Divl. Train.
       20 S.S.O.
       21 Div. Reception Camp.
       22 XVII Corps 'Q'
       23 57th Division Q.
       24 63rd Division Q.
       25 Camp Commandant.
       26 52nd M.T. Company.
       27 File.
       28) War Diary.
       29)

Appendix I

SECRET.   COPY NO......

52nd (LOWLAND) DIVISION.

ADMINISTRATIVE INSTRUCTION No. A.F. 44.

6th October, 1918.

With reference to 52nd Division wire G.A. 263 of Oct. 5th 1918.

1. CONCENTRATION.
    The Division (less R.A. and Machine Gun Battalion) will concentrate in the area WEST of the NORD CANAL, as already laid down, on the 6th instant, prior to entrainment in tactical trains at VAUX VRAUCOURT (personnel) and FREMICOURT (transport) on the 7th instant.
    Details of this entrainment will be issued later.

2. MOVES.
    (a) The following moves, additional to those ordered by "G" will take place on 6th instant -
        Divisional Headquarters,) to VAUX VRAUCOURT, exact
          (Advanced and Rear)   ) site notified later.
        C.R.E.   )
        S.A.A. Section, D.A.C.   to LOUVERVAL.

    Moves to be completed by 1600.

    (b) Camp Commandant will arrange to send on early a sufficient party to pitch Divisional Headquarters Camp at the site selected. The tents etc. required will be drawn as shown in para.3.

3. STORES.
    (a) All tents, shelters, Pack Saddles and other Battle Stores now in possession of formations and units will be sent to D.A.D.O.S. (E.25.b.) by 1500 6th instant. These will be placed in a special dump which will be taken over by 24th Division as soon as possible.

    (b) For accommodation night 6/7th October the following tents and shelters may be drawn from XVII Corps Headquarters "Q" (J.3.&.) at noon 6th instant -

	Tents.	Shelters.
Divisional Headquarters.	17	25
Each Infantry Brigade.	13	220
A.D.M.S.	3	75
C.R.E.	6	150 x

x For Field Coys. & Pioneer Battalion.

    The above will be found loaded on lorries, which will take the tents and shelters to units bivouac areas, if guides are sent for them at the above hour and place.
    Captain HARDING, "Q" learner, will superintend this distribution to units.

    (c) These tents and shelters will have to be stacked ready for collection by XVII Corps on the 7th instant. Further orders in the entrainment instructions.

4. TRANSPORT.
    For purposes of this concentration and the entrainment on 7th instant units may move with S.A.A. Echelons filled in accordance with their actual fighting strength and NOT in accordance with their establishment. Any transport thus saved may be used for conveyance of Light Trench Mortars, extra kits, stores etc.

P.T.O.

-2-

5. BILLETTING PARTIES.

Billetting parties (reckoned on scale of 1 officer and 3 Other Ranks per Battalion, and 1 officer and 1 Other Rank per smaller unit all with bicycles) will leave LOUVERVAL Cross Roads J.9.b. by lorry at 1300 on 6th instant for new area.

O.C. Divisional M.T. Company will detail 4 lorries to convey these parties who will proceed to TINCQUES Railway Station and report to D.A.Q.M.G. on arrival.

They will be rationed up to 8th instant inclusive.

Each party will take a copy of the LENS 1/100,000 Map.

6. DETACHED PARTIES.

(a) The Burial Party will rejoin their units and the Burial Officer the Pioneer Battalion by 1800 on 6th inst.

(b) The following will be sent to Divisional Reception Camp by 1800 on 6th instant under arrangements to be made by D.A.A.G.

(i) The Divisional Salvage Company (less 1 cyclist, who will be left to hand over to 24th Division and will then rejoin the Company not later than 0800 7th inst.)

(ii) Men at the Baths ECOUST.

(iii) Officer and men in charge Divisional S.A.A. Dump (L.2.a.) less 1 N.C.O. left to hand over to 24th Division.

(iv) One man in charge S.A.A. Dump QUEANT (D.7.b.)

Two lorries, additional to those already detailed to move Rear Divisional Headquarters, will report to D.A.A.G. at 1100 at GRAINCOURT for the conveyance of the above parties to the Divisional Reception Camp.

(c) Separate orders will be issued to D.A.P.M. with reference to relief of Traffic Control men.

7. ACKNOWLEDGE.

C.G.Maude
Lieut.Colonel,
A.A. & Q.M.G. 52nd (Lowland) Division

Issued at 0230.

Copy No.			
1	A.D.C. for G.O.C.	18	Camp Comdt.
2	"G".	19	Div. Reception Camp.
3	155th Inf. Bde.	20	Div. Employment Coy.
4	156th Inf. Bde.	21	S.A.A. Section D.A.C.
5	157th Inf. Bde.	22	W.S.O.
6	C.R.E.	23	Burial Officer.
7	Pioneer Battn.	24	Salvage Officer.
8	A.D.M.S.	25	O. i/c S.A.A. Dump (L.2.a.)
9	D.A.D.V.S.	26	XVII Corps "Q".
10	Divl. Train.	27	24th Division "Q".
11	S.S.O.	28	French Mission.
12	Div. M.T. Company.	29	Canteen Officer.
13	Signal Coy.	30	D.G.O.
14	Rear D.H.Q.	31	File.
15	)	32	War Diary.
16	D.A.P.M.	33	)
17	D.A.D.O.S.		

Appendix II

SECRET.　　　　　　　　　　　　　　　　　　　　　　　COPY NO...

52nd (LOWLAND) DIVISION.

ADMINISTRATIVE INSTRUCTION NO. A.F. 45.

6th October, 1918.

1. **MOVES.**
    52nd Division, less R.A. and Machine Gun Battalion, will move from XVII Corps to VIII Corps.
    (a) Personnel and proportion of transport by tactical trains on 7th instant.
    (b) Remainder of transport by road on 7th instant and subsequent days.
    Entrainment and march tables attached.
    (c) D.A.D.O.S., Motor Ambulances and M.T. Company by road to new area: no restriction as regards route.

2. **ENTRAINING.**
    (a) D.A.A.G. will superintend entrainment of Division at VAUX VRAUCOURT and FREMICOURT. His Headquarters will be at VAUX VRAUCOURT. He will be responsible for notifying Q.M.G., G.H.Q., Third and First Armies of progress of entrainment in accordance with G.R.O. No.4743.
    (b) Entraining officers will be detailed as follows :-
    　　At VAUX VRAUCOURT, one officer from 155th Inf. Brigade.
    　　At FREMICOURT, one officer from 156th Inf. Brigade.
    　　These officers will report to the R.T.O's of their respective entraining stations 2 hours before the first train leaves. They will be responsible for the entrainment of all troops of the Division leaving their respective stations, and will travel on the last train leaving these stations.
    (c) All transport and animals will arrive at FREMICOURT 3 hours before their train leaves.
    　　All personnel will arrive at VAUX VRAUCOURT 1 hour before their train leaves.
    (d) 157th Infantry Brigade will detail 2 loading parties, each of 1 officer and 30 Other Ranks, to report to R.T.O's VAUX VRAUCOURT and FREMICOURT respectively, 2 hours before the first trains are due to leave these stations. These parties will load on trains all baggage and stores brought to entraining station by lorries and will help to entrain horses and vehicles. The lorry loads should be put on the trains before any personnel starts entraining. These loading parties will travel on the last trains leaving their respective stations. (N.B. If numbers permit these 2 loading parties may be found from men at Reception Camp).
    (e) G.O.C.'s Infantry Brigade will be responsible for the order of entrainment of their own and attached units, and their arrival at entrainment stations.
    (f) A movement order showing the number of personnel proceeding by each train will be handed by units to the R.T.O. on arrival at entraining stations.

3. **DETRAINING.**
    (a) D.A.Q.M.G. will superintend detrainment at TINCQUES, LIGNY St. FLOCHEL and PETIT HOUVIN. His Headquarters will be at TINCQUES. He will be responsible for notifying Q.M.G., G.H.Q. and FIRST Army of progress of detrainment in accordance with G.R.O. No. 4743.
    (b) G.O.C's 155th, 156th and 157th Infantry Brigades will each detail a detraining officer to report to the R.T.O. of their respective detraining station on arrival of the first train. This officer will remain on duty until the last troops of the Division have arrived at the detraining station.

P.T.O.

3. DETRAINING. contd.
(c) Each Brigade will also detail an unloading party from the troops on the first train, which will remain on duty at the detraining station till the arrival of the last train.

4. BILLETTING PARTIES.
Billetting parties leave by lorry to-day (in accordance with Administrative Instructions No. A.F.44 of 6/10/18, para.5) for new area.
They will meet trains at detraining stations on 7th and 8th instants and guide units to new billetting areas.

5. LORRIES.
(I) O.C. 52nd M.T. Company will detail the following lorries in connection with the moves on the 7th instant:-
(a) 8 lorries to report to Camp Commandant, Divisional Headquarters, VAUX VRAUCOURT at 1000, 7th instant, to convey portion of Divisional Headquarters to new area.
(b) 2 lorries to report to each Infantry Brigade H.Q. at 0800, 7th instant, to help convey extra stores to entraining station. Infantry Brigade will wire O.C. M.T. Company as soon as possible exact location of their new Headquarters.
On completion of duty these lorries will rejoin M.T. Company.
(c) 1 lorry to report to C.R.E. same time and date and under same conditions as (b) above.
(d) 3 lorries to report to Divisional Reception Camp at MORCHIES at 0800, 7th instant to carry heavy baggage to entrainment station.
(e) 13 lorries to report to D.A.D.O.S. 0800, 7th instant, to convey blankets to FREMICOURT.
(f) In addition Canteen Officer and Baths Officer will each have their usual 2 lorries to convey Canteen Stores and dirty clothing to new area.

(II) On arrival in new area O.C. M.T. Company will detail lorries as in (b), (c) and (d) to report to detraining stations to assist units to new billetting areas. If these lorries have not arrived by the time units detrain, kits etc. will be dumped at the station and a guard left until the lorries appear.

6. SUPPLIES.
Railhead on the 7th .... VAUX VRAUCOURT.
Railhead on the 8th .... TINCQUES.
Destination of M.T. Company in new area .... TINCQUES.

(a) Troops will entrain and march rationed up to 8th instant inclusive; O.C. Divisional Train will arrange to deliver rations for the 8th instant to units as soon as possible.
(b) Rations for the 9th will be delivered on 8th instant.
(i) For troops moving by train, to Brigade Dumps in the new area, to be arranged and notified to units by the S.S.O.
(ii) For troops marching by road, to a Refilling Point to be arranged between O.C. Divisional Train and O.C. Divisional M.T. Company.
(c) On arrival in new area until the transport marching by road joins the Division, supplies will be drawn from Railhead by M.T. and sent to Brigade Refilling Points as in (b)(i) above.

/7.

7. **R.A. and MACHINE GUN BATTALION.**
   (a) Headquarter Company, Train, together with Supply and Baggage Wagons of Machine Gun Battalion, will remain in present area.
   (b) M.T. Company will also leave 2 Sections for the use of the above formations.
   (c) D.A.D.O.S. will leave a Warrant Officer and 1 lorry who will be attached to Headquarter Company Train and will administer R.A. and Machine Gun Battalion from an Ordnance point of view.

8. **WATER.**
   All Water Carts will entrain full.

9. **ORDNANCE.**
   D.A.D.O.S. will arrange to convey blankets now on his charge by lorries shown in 5 (e) above to FREMICOURT on 7th instant where they will be loaded on to the first transport train (dep. 1415).
   G.O.C. 156th Infantry Brigade will allot trucks on this train to D.A.D.O.S. for the conveyance of these blankets.

10. **RECEPTION CAMP.**
    The tents and shelters and any area stores at the Reception Camp will be stacked ready to be handed over to 24th Division. If not taken over before the Reception Camp entrains, one N.C.O. will be left in charge of the Dump.

11. **TENTS.**
    All tents and shelters issued for accommodation of troops on night October 6/7th (para.3 (b) of Administrative Instructions A.F.44 of 6/10/18) will be stacked in Brigade or Unit Dumps by 0900 7th instant ready for collection by XVII Corps.
    All formations and units, who have drawn these tents, will wire Divisional Headquarters by 2000 6th instant the intended location of these Dumps so that arrangements may be made with XVII Corps for their collection.
    Each Brigade or Unit will leave one man in charge of their Dump till it is collected. These men will subsequently proceed to VAUX VRAUCOURT and entrain by the first available train for the new area.

12. **ACKNOWLEDGE.**

Issued at 1600.

Lieut. Colonel,
A.A. & Q.M.G. 52nd (Lowland) Division.

Copy No. 1 A.D.C. for G.O.C.
2 "G".
3 Camp Comdt.
4 Signal Coy.
5 C.R.E.
6 C.R.A.
7 155th Inf. Bde.
8 156th Inf. Bde.
9 157th Inf. Bde.
10 A.D.M.S.
11 D.A.D.V.S.
12 D.A.P.M.
13 Divl. Train.
14 S.S.O.
15 17th North. Fus.
16 M.G. Battn.
17 52nd M.T. Coy.
18 D.A.D.O.S.
19. S.A.A. Section, D.A.C.
20. W.S.O.
21. Divl. Reception Camp.
22. Divl. Employment Coy.
23. Canteen Officer.
24. French Mission.
25. D.A.A.G.
26. D.A.Q.M.G.
27. D.G.O.
28. XVII Corps "Q".
29. 24th Division "Q".
30. R.T.O. VAUX VRAUCOURT.
31. R.T.O. FREMICOURT.
32. File.
33.)
34.) War Diary.

ENTRAINING TABLE.

"A". ENTRAINING STATION - VAUX VRAUCOURT.

No. of Train.	Type.	Unit.	Dep.	Detraining Station.	Time arr.
1.	Personnel.	Portion D.H.Q. (with Signal Coy.) 156th Inf. Brigade.	1315.	TINCQUES.	1550.
3.	Personnel.	17th N.F. Pioneers 412th Field Company, R.E. Dismt. personnel 1st L.F.A. Divl. Reception Camp.	1515.	TINCQUES.	1750.
4.	Personnel.	155th Inf. Brigade.	1615.	LIGNY.	1805.
6.	Personnel.	410th Field Company, R.E. 413th Field Company, R.E. Dismt. personnel 2nd L.F.A. Dismt. personnel 3rd L.F.A.	1815.	LIGNY. PETIT HOUVIN.	2105. 2210.
7.	Personnel.	157th Inf. Brigade.	1915.	PETIT HOUVIN.	2310.

"B" ENTRAINING STATION - FREMICOURT.

Train No.	Type.	Unit.	Der.	Detraining Station.	Arr.
2	Transport.	156th Inf. Brigade Group Transport. e.g. 4 L.G. Limbers per Bn. 3 Cookers per Bn. 2 Water Carts per Bn. Bde. Sig. Section Limber. 1 S.A.A. Limber per Bn. 1 Limber, 412th Fd. Coy. R.E. 1 Limber, 1st Low. Fd. Ambce. 17th Northd.Fus. - 3 Cookers. 2 Water Carts. All chargers and Pack Animals. Blankets of Division.	1415.	TINCQUES.	1650.
5.	Transport.	155th & part 157th Inf. Brigade Group Transport. e.g. 4 L.G. Limbers per Bn. 3 Cookers per Bn. 2 Water Carts per Bn. Bde. Sig. Section Limber. 1 S.A.A. Limber per Bn. 1 limber for each 410th) Fd.Coys. 413th) 1 limber for each 2nd) Low.Fd.Amb. 3rd) All chargers and Pack Animals.	1715.	LIGNY.	2005.

P.T.O.

"B" ENTRAINING STATION - FREMICOURT contd.

Train No.	Type.	Unit. and	Dep.	Detraining Station.	Arr.
8.	Transport.	157th Inf. Brigade/mixed Transport. e.g. 4 L.G. Limbers per Bn. 3 Cookers per Bn. 2 Water Carts per Bn. Bde. Sig. Section Limber. 1 S.A.A. Limber per Bn. All Officers Mess Carts of Inf. Bns. of 3 Inf. Brigades. 1 Maltese Cart per Inf. Brigade.	2015.	PETIT HOUVIN.	0010

TRANSPORT AND MOUNTED PERSONNEL MARCH TABLE.

Date.	Units.	From.	To.	Route.	Under orders.	Remarks.
Oct. 7th.	155th) 156th) Inf. Brigade Transport. @ 157th) Divl. H.Q.(with C.R.E.) Tpt. Divl. Signal Coy. Transport. @ 17th Northd. Fus. Transport. @ 3 Fd. Companies R.E. Transport @ 3 Fd. Ambulances Transport. @ Mobile Veterinary Section. Divisional Train. S.A.A. Section, D.A.C.	LOUVERVAL AREA.	RIVIERE. GROSVILLE.	VAUX VRAUCOURT-ST. LEGER-BOYELLES.	Lt.Col. MATTHEW, C.M.G.,D.S.O. O.C. Divisional Train.	Billets from Area Comdt. BRETENCOURT.
Oct. 8th.	-- ditto --	RIVIERE-GROSVILLE AREA.	LE CAUROY AREA.	Via BEAUMETZ-LEZ-LOGES.	--ditto--	Under orders FIRST Army. Not to enter GOUY en ARTOIS.

NOTE 1. Exact starting point to be fixed by O.C. Train, who will issue detailed orders to above units.
NOTE 2. Column not to enter ST. LEGER before 1200. 7th inst.
NOTE 3. On arrival in RIVIERE-GROSVILLE Area. O.C. Divisional Train will wire direct to FIRST Army the position of his Headquarters for the night October 7th/8th in accordance with G.R.O. 5050. He will sign the wire "O.C. 52nd Division Transport".
NOTE 4. Each Infantry Brigade will detail an officer to command the Transport of all its units. C.R.E. will detail the senior officer to command Transport of 3 Field Companies and Pioneers. Camp Commandant will arrange for Divisional Signal Company and Divisional Headquarter Transport to march under command of one officer.

@ Less vehicles and animals by tactical trains.

War Diary. October. Appendix III

52nd (Lowland) DIVISION.

ADMINISTRATIVE INSTRUCTIONS No. AF 46.

18th OCTOBER, 1918.

With reference to 52nd Division wire GH 409 of 18/10/18.

1. **MOVES:**
   The Division will move tomorrow, 19th instant, from Le CAUROY area as follows :-

   (A) **155 Inf. Brigade Group:**
   (i) Personnel and proportion of transport by tactical trains (TINCQUES and LIGNY St. FLOCHEL to BULLY GRENAY) in accordance with entraining Table to be sent later.
   (ii) Remaining Transport by road in accordance with march Table attached.

   (B) **156 and 157 Inf. Brigade Groups:** by road to CHATEAU de La HAIE and MONT St. ELOI areas respectively as already ordered.

   (C)(i) **Divisional H.Q.** by road and lorry to CHATEAU D'ACQ.

   (ii) Mobile Vety. Section.) by road to MONT ST ELOI. Billets to
        S.A.A. Sect. D.A.C.   ) be allotted by 157th Infantry Brigade.

   (D) (i) The following will remain in their present locations pending further orders :-
        Divisional M.T. Company.
        D. A. D. O. S.
        Divisional Reception Camp.
        Divisional Canteen.

   (ii) Divisional Baths Officer and "THISTLETOPS" will join Reception Camp.

2. **ENTRAINING AND DETRAINING.**
   (a) D.A.A.G. will superintend entrainment of 155th Brigade Group at LIGNY ST FLOCHEL and TINCQUES.
   G.S.O.3 will superintend detrainment at BULLY GRENAY.

   (b) 155th Infantry Brigade will detail Entraining and Detraining Officers and loading parties at the above stations, and will comply with the various points laid down in 45/1 Q.A.1 of September, 1918 (General Instructions regarding moves by rail and road of Divisions and Divisional R.A.).

P.T.O.

3. **LORRIES.**
For the purposes of this move lorries will be allotted :-
(a) For Advance Parties.
(b) For Blankets, extra kit, etc.
as follows :-

Unit.	No. of lorries.	Rendezvous.	Time & Date.
155th Inf.Bde.Group.	3≠	155th Inf.Bde.H.Q. MAIZIERES.	0700 19th. inst.
156th Inf.Bde.Group.	3ø	156th Inf.Bde.H.Q. IZEL LEZ HAMEAU.	0700 19th. inst.
157th Inf.Bde.Group.	3ø	157th Inf.Bde.H.Q. GRAND RULLECOURT.	0700 19th. inst.
Divisional Hqrs.	4ø	D.H.Q., LE CAUROY.	0900 19th. inst.

≠ After assisting Entrainment will proceed to BULLY GRENAY and assist with Detrainment.
ø Will do two journeys if required.

4. **SUPPLIES.**
(a) <u>RAILHEADS.</u> TINCQUES .... 19th instant.
THELUS .... 20th instant.

(b) <u>Supply Situation on 19th instant.</u>
Supplies for 19th instant with units.
Supplies for 20th instant on Train vehicles.
Supplies for 21st instant drawn from Railhead (TINCQUES) by M.T. and convoyed to following Refilling Points in new areas -
(i) For 155th Infantry Brigade Group ... The Square BULLY GRENAY (R.5.c.7.4.)
(ii) For 156th Infantry Brigade Group ... W.5.central (Near CHATEAU DE LA HAIE).
(iii) For 157th Infantry Brigade Group and Divisional Units (ECOIVRES) F.13.central.

5. **ACKNOWLEDGE.**

(signature)
Lieut.Colonel,
A.A. & Q.M.G. 52nd (Lowland) Division.

Issued at 2130.

War Diary - October
Appendix IV

SECRET.   COPY NO......

52nd (LOWLAND) DIVISION.

ADMINISTRATIVE INSTRUCTIONS NO. A.F. 47.

19th October, 1918.

Reference 1/40,000 Map Sheet 44A.

With reference to G.H. 430 of 19th instant.

1. **MOVES AND LOCATIONS.**
    Units will move to-morrow 20th instant to the billetting areas shown on attached list.
    On completion of moves reports as to exact locations of units will be sent to Divisional Headquarters.

2. **SUPPLIES.**
    Railhead from 20th instant inclusive - THELUS.
    Supplies will be drawn as follows to-morrow -
    (a) Supplies (for 22nd inst.) arriving at Railhead by Pack Train on 20th inst. will be sent by Light Railway to LA COULOTTE (N.31 central).
    (b) Supplies for 21st inst. will be delivered to units by Train wagons before to-morrow's march. These Supplies can be taken to new area in lorries allotted for extra kit etc.
    (c) Train Companies will march empty to LA COULOTTE, where they will pick up Supplies for 22nd instant and proceed to the billetting areas of their Brigade Groups.
    Orders for the concentration of the Train (to take place probably on 21st instant) will be issued later.

3. **LORRIES.**
    To carry Advance parties, blankets, greatcoats and extra kits, the following lorries will be detailed to-morrow, 20th inst.

UNIT.	NO. OF LORRIES.	RENDEZVOUS.	TIME.
155th Inf.Bde.Group.	6	Bde. H.Q. LIEVIN.	0700
156th Inf.Bde.Group.	6	Bde. H.Q. CHATEAU DE LA HAIE.	0700
157th Inf.Bde.Group.	6	Bde. H.Q. MONT ST ELOI.	0700
M.G. Battn.	2	MARQUEFFLES Huts.	0700
Divl. Reception Camp.	5	MAIZIERES.	0700
Divisional Headquarters	6	CHATEAU D'ACQ.	0900

4. ROYAL ARTILLERY.

The Divisional Artillery is moving by rail to-morrow to rejoin the Division.

It will be accommodated for the night October 20/21st in the ST ELOI and LA TARGETTE Area.

First Railhead with Division - THELUS on October 21st.

5. WATER.

The following are water points in new area -
Canal de la Haute Deule.
   O.26.a.7.5.
   O.27.a.5.4.
   O.21.b.
Numerous pumps in houses.

6. ROADS.

All lorries will use the road LIEVIN - LENS - HENIN LIETARD.

7. ACKNOWLEDGE.

Issued at 2000.

C. Mander
Lieut. Colonel.
A.A. & Q.M.G. 52nd (Lowland) Division.

Copy No.		Copy No.	
1	A.D.C. for G.O.C.	20	Div. Employment Coy.
2	"G"	21	S.A.A. Section D.A.C.
3	155th Inf. Bde.	22	W.S.O.
4	156th Inf. Bde.	23	Burial Officer.
5	157th Inf. Bde.	24	Salvage Officer.
6	C.R.E.	25	Canteen Officer.
7	17th N.F.	26	O.C. Concert Party.
8	A.D.M.S.	27	French Mission.
9	D.A.D.V.S.	28	D.G.O.
10	Divl. Train.	29	VIII Corps "Q".
11	S.S.O.	30	File
12	M.G. Battn.	31	)
13	C.R.A.	32	) War Diary.
14	Div. M.T. Coy.	33	Town Major, HENIN LIETARD.
15	O.C. Signal Coy.	34	Town Major, ST ELOI.
16	D.A.P.M.	35	Town Major, NEUVILLE ST. VAAST.
17	D.A.D.O.S.		
18	Camp Comdt.		
19	Div. Reception Camp.		

LOCATION LIST FOR NIGHT OCTOBER 20/21st.

DIVISIONAL HEADQUARTERS.	O.35.b.3.0. (CITE ARMAND VOISIN) HENIN LIETARD.
C. R. E.	-do-
A.D.M.S.	-do-
D.A.P.M.	-do-
DIVL. SIGNAL COMPANY.	-do-
D.A.D.V.S.	-do-
FRENCH MISSION.	-do-
155th INF. BRIGADE GROUP.	FOUQIERES (and all accommodation in squares O.20, O.21 and O.26 & 27 North of Main Road).
	MONTIGNY. (O.22.)
156th INF. BRIGADE GROUP.	BILLY MONTIGNY (less M.G. Battn. Area).
157th INF. BRIGADE GROUPE.	HENIN LIETARD.
52nd M.G. BATTALION.	BILLY MONTIGNY (sq. O.26).
52nd DIVL. TRAIN H.Q.	HENIN LIETARD.
MOBILE VETERINARY SECTION.	FOUQIERES (O.21)) by same road as that
S.A.A. SECTION D.A.C.	FOUQUIERES (O.21)) allotted to 157th Inf. Brigade.
D.A.D.O.S.	THELUS.
DIVL. M.T. COMPANY.	BILLY MONTIGNY.
DIVL. RECEPTION CAMP. (including Employment Coy. etc.).	HILL CAMP, NEUVILLE ST VAAST.

All Advance Parties should report to Town Major HENIN LIETARD (O.29.central).

War Diary October. Appendix V

52nd (LOWLAND) DIVISION.

ADMINISTRATIVE INSTRUCTIONS No. A.F. 48.

20th October, 1918.

Reference G.H. 442 of 20th instant.

1. **ACCOMMODATION.**

   On arrival in new areas the following accommodation is at disposal of Brigade Groups -

   155th Brigade - COURCELLES.
   CITE BASSE NOYELLES.
   MARAIS DELABY.

   156th Brigade - AUBY.
   PT. d'AUOY. } less Machine Gun Battn. Area.

   157th Brigade - FLERS.
   PLANQUE.
   WAGNONVILLE.

   Exact locations of units to be reported as soon as possible to Divisional Headquarters.
   There are no Town Majors in the above areas.

2. **MOVES.**

   (a) 410th Field Company, R.E. to RACHES.) All move on
   412th Field Company, R.E. to AUBY.   ) 21st inst.
   413th Field Company, R.E. to COURCELLES.)

   (b) S.A.A. Section, D.A.C. remains at FOUQIERES.

   (c) Mobile Veterinary Section to HENIN LIETARD to-morrow.

   (c) Divisional Train concentrate at HENIN LIETARD after delivering rations to units to-morrow.

   (d) Divisional Headquarters remains at HENIN LIETARD 21st instant, moves to CHATEAU, MAISON BLANCHE (Q.20.c) on 22nd instant.

   (e) 1/1st Lowland Field Ambulance - 4 VENTS to LIEVIN on 21st instant.

3. **SUPPLIES.**

   (a) Divisional R.A. will draw rations from Railhead (THELUS) by Horse Transport to-morrow, and on all subsequent days that it remains in ST. ELOI Area.

P.T.O.

-2-

3. SUPPLIES contd.

(b) Supplies for remainder of Division drawn to-morrow from Railhead by M.T. and delivered at a Refilling Point in HENIN LIETARD to be chosen by Divisional Train.

(c) 218th, 219th and 220th Companies A.S.C. march to new areas with Brigade Groups to-morrow, deliver rations for 22nd inst. at end of days march, and then concentrate at HENIN LIETARD under orders of O.C. Divisional Train.

(d) S.S.O. will arrange with Divisional M.T. Company to ration 410th Field Company direct by lorry as long as it remains at RACHES.

4. LORRIES.

Divisional M.T. Company will detail following lorries for move of Brigade Groups to-morrow -

Unit.	No. of Lorries.	Rendezvous.	Time.
155th Inf. Brigade.	6	Bde. H.Q. FOUQIERES.	0700.
156th Inf. Brigade.	7	Bde. H.Q. BILLY MONTIGNY.	0700.
157th Inf. Brigade.	6	Bde. H.Q. HENIN LIETARD.	0700.
Machine Gun Battn.	2	Battn. H.Q. BILLY MONTIGNY.	0700.

5. DIVISIONAL HEADQUARTERS.

155th Infantry Brigade will send one platoon under an officer in the extra lorry placed at their disposal to clean up the new Divisional Headquarters (Chateau, MAISON BLANCHE) as early as possible to-morrow.

This work must be completed by 1200 22nd instant.

6. ACKNOWLEDGE.

[signature]
Lieut. Colonel.
A... Q..G. 52nd (Lowland) Division.

Issued at 2115.

Copy No. 1	A.D.C. for G.O.C.	11	S.S.O.	21	S.A.A. Sect.
2	"G"	12	M.G. Battn.	22	W.S.O.
3	155th Inf. Bde.	13	C.R.A.	23	Burial Offr.
4	156th Inf. Bde.	14	Div. M.T. Co.	24	Salvage Offr.
5	157th Inf. Bde.	15	Signal Coy.	25	Canteen Offr.
6	C.R.E.	16	D.A.D.M.S.	26	Concert Party.
7	17th M.F.	17	D.A.D.O.S.	27	French Mission.
8	A.D.M.S.	18	Camp Comdt.	28	D.G.C.
9	D.A.D.V.S.	19	Div. Reception Camp.	29	VIII Corps "Q"
10	Divl. Train.	20	Div. Employment Co.	30	T.H. HENIN LIE- TARD.
		31	File.		
		32) 33)	War Diary.		

War Diary October Appendix No. VI

SECRET.   COPY N......

52nd (LOWLAND) DIVISION.

ADMINISTRATIVE INSTRUCTIONS No. A.F. 50.
27th October, 1918.

With reference to 52nd Division Orders 140 & 141 of 26th/27th October, 1918.

1. MOVES.
October 28th.

UNIT.	FROM.	TO.	ROUTE.
H.Q. Divisional Train & 218th Company, A.S.C.	ROOST WARENDIN.	BEUVRY-LES-ORCHIES.	FLINES - COUTICHES - ORCHIES.
219th & 220th Companies, A.S.C.	LES ARCINS.	BEUVRY-LES-ORCHIES.	No restrictions.
D.A.D.O.S.	ROOST WARENDIN.	BEUVRY-LES-ORCHIES.	FLINES - COUTICHES - ORCHIES.
Divisional Canteen.	ROOST WARENDIN.	BEUVRY-LES-ORCHIES.	FLINES - COUTICHES - ORCHIES.
Div. Baths Officer.	Reception Camp.	COUTICHES.	No restrictions.
S.A.A. SECTION, D.A.C.	ROOST WARENDIN.	O.3.b. LE PLUVINAGE.	FLINES - ORCHIES. (not to pass thro' COUTICHES before 1400).
Mobile Vety. Section.	ROOST WARENDIN.	BEUVRY-LES-ORCHIES.	No restrictions.
Div. Reception Camp (part)	VITRY-EN-ARTOIS.	DOUAI (Barracks).	No restrictions.

October 29th.

Divisional Headquarters.)		
C.R.E.)		
A.D.M.S.) FLINES.	SAMEON.	
D.A.P.M.)		
D.A.D.V.S.)		
Divisional Sig. Coy.)		

2. SUPPLIES.

(a) Supplies for 155th Infantry Brigade Group and Divisional Troops will be loaded at 1000 to-morrow, and will be taken to new area as above (except those for D.H.Q. which will be delivered at FLINES) by 218th Company, A.S.C. Later unit will not pass through COUTICHES before 1300.

After delivering to units 218th Company, A.S.C. will concentrate at BEUVRY.

Meeting point for 218th Company and guides from units in new area.-

LANDAS Church.

P.T.O.

2. SUPPLIES. contd.
(b) Refilling Points for 28th instant -

UNITS.	REFILLING POINTS.
Whole Division (less R.A.)	BEUVRY.
Royal Artillery.	WAZIERES.

3. **LORRIES.**
In connection with above moves O.C. Divisional M.T. Company will detail lorries as follows :-

DATE.	TIME.	NO. OF LORRIES.	RENDEZVOUS.	PURPOSE.
Oct.29th.	0830	4	FLINES.	To move D.H.Q. to SAMEON.

4. **BLANKETS.**
155th Infantry Brigade and 2 Companies Machine Gun Battalion will dump blankets and stores, which cannot be carried on mobile scale of transport, at Divisional Blanket Dump FLINES before to-morrows move.
A guard of one man per unit will be left in charge, to be rationed from 29th instant inclusive by Area Commandant FLINES.
Nominal roll of men left to be sent to Divisional Headquarters in duplicate.

5. **PROVOST.**
D.A.P.M. will arrange to take over Traffic Control in new area from 29th instant.
Divisional Prisoners of War Cage will be at I.36.c.6.4, a guard of 1 N.C.O. and 6 men being provided by D.A.P.M.
All prisoners captured will be sent to this point under Brigade arrangements.

6. **AMMUNITION.**
S.A.A., Grenades, etc. will be supplied on demand to units Transport Lines by S.A.A. Section D.A.C., which will send a Mounted Orderly by 1200 29th instant to remain at 156th Infantry Brigade Headquarters.
All demands for ammunition etc. must be repeated to Division "Q".
Units are forbidden to dump any ammunition which, in case of a forward move, could not be carried by their first line transport.

7. **TOWN MAJORS.**
Captain G.D. SEMPILL, 4th K.O.S.B., will move on 28th inst. from FLINES and take over duties of Town Major, SAMEON Area from 12th Division.
157th Infantry Brigade will detail an officer on 28th inst. to take over duties of Town Major, LANDAS, from 12th Division.

8. **VETERINARY.**
Troops in LANDAS will not occupy stables in that place, as they are infected with mange.

9. **TRAFFIC OFFICERS.**
155th Infantry Brigade will detail 3 Traffic Officers to take over duties from the 3 Officers 12th Division at the bridges over the DECOURS and SCARPE rivers in squares J.34.a. and J.29.b.
The above officers will report at 1200 28th instant and will be attached for 24 hours to the corresponding 12th Division Officers, before themselves taking over the actual duties at noon 29th instant.
The orders, as regards Traffic Control over these bridges will for the present be those issued by 12th Division.
The 3 officers of 52nd Division will be under control of D.A.P.M. from 1200 29th instant.

10. **ACKNOWLEDGE.**

(signature)
Lieut. Colonel.
A.A. & Q.M.G. 52nd (Lowland) Division.

Issued at 1930.

Copy No.				
1	A.D.C. for G.O.C.		21	S.A.A. Section D.A.C.
2	"G"		22	W.S.C.
3	155th Inf. Bde.		23	Burial Officer.
4	156th Inf. Bde.		24	Salvage Officer.
5	157th Inf. Bde.		25	Canteen Officer.
6	C.R.E.		26	French Mission.
7	17th M.F.		27	D.G.O.
8	A.D.M.S.		28	Capt. SEMPILL, T.M.FLINES.
9	D.A.D.V.S.		29	VIII Corps "Q".
10	Divl. Train.		30	12th Division "Q".
11	S.S.O.		31	File.
12	M.G. Battn.		32)	War Diary.
13	C.R.A.		33)	
14	Div. M.T. Coy.			
15	Signal Coy.			
16	D.A.P.M.			
17	D.A.D.O.S.			
18	Camp Comdt.			
19	Div. Reception Camp.			
20	Div. Employment Coy.			

Appendix VII

52nd (Lowland) Division.

STRENGTH RETURN MADE UP TO 12 NOON SATURDAY, 26th October, 1918.

UNIT	(i) Strength for previous wk. in accord. with AG's Instr.		(ii) Increase dur-ing wk. drafts etc. taken on str. of unit.		(iii) Totals fr. (i) & (ii)		(iv) Decrease dur-ing wk. cas-etc. deducted fr. str. of unit.		'A' Strength excl. uding arrd.		'B' Not present with unit & not at dispos-al of C.O. Incl. in Col'A'		'A' minus 'B' Available Ft. str., including Personnel of Bn.Transport & G.M. Stores.	
	O.	O.R.	O.	O.R.	O.	O.R.	O.	O.R.	O.	O.R.	O.	O.R.	O.	O.R.
155th Inf. Bde.														
1/4th R.S.Fus.	31	627	1	22	32	649	-	21	32	628	12	242	20	386
1/5th R.S.Fus.	26	650	3	13	29	663	-	6	29	657	9	190	20	467
1/4th K.O.S.B.	33	645	3	15	36	660	2	12	34	648	9	178	25	470
	90	1922	7	50	97	1972	2	39	95	1933	30	610	65	1323
156th Inf. Bde.														
1/4th R. Scots	35	694	1	11	36	705	2	20	34	685	10	194	24	491
1/7th R. Scots	40	776	1	25	41	801	-	22	41	779	14	232	27	547
1/7th Sco. Rif.	36	678	-	19	36	697	-	13	36	684	15	209	21	475
	111	2148	2	55	113	2203	2	55	111	2148	39	635	72	1513
157th Inf. Bde.														
1/5th H.L.I.	40	662	1	12	41	674	-	12	41	662	17	205	24	457
1/6th H.L.I.	39	620	1	18	40	638	1	11	39	627	14	216	25	411
1/7th H.L.I.	47	662	1	13	48	675	-	15	48	660	11	217	37	443
	126	1944	3	43	129	1987	1	38	128	1949	42	638	86	1311
17th N.Fus.(P).	33	841	-	4	33	845	-	8	33	837	13	247	20	590
	360	6855	12	152	372	7007	5	140	367	6867	124	2130	243	4737
52nd Bn. M.G.C.	48	878	-	28	48	906	5	18	43	888	9	189	34	699

52nd (Lowland) Division.

Abstract Column "B" — week-ending 26/10/18.

UNIT	Courses B.	Courses O.R.	Sick O.	Sick O.R.	Leave O.	Leave O.R.	Bde.Employ O.	Bde.Employ O.R.	Div.Employ O.	Div.Employ O.R.	Extra Regt.Employ O.	Extra Regt.Employ O.R.	Total O.	Total O.R.
155th Inf. Bde.														
1/4th R.S.Fus.	3	32	4	14	3	148	1	27	1	21	–	–	12	242
1/5th R.S.Fus.	1	20	3	17	3	129	–	15	2	9	–	–	9	190
1/4th K.O.S.B.	2	20	2	14	2	115	2	14	1	15	–	–	9	178
	6	72	9	45	8	392	3	56	4	45	–	–	30	610
156th Inf. Bde.														
1/4th R.Scots.	3	51	4	16	2	115	–	21	1	8	3	3	10	194
1/7th R.Scots.	2	38	2	21	3	128	4	23	3	21	–	1	14	232
1/7th Sco.Rif.	2	30	4	11	3	123	5	24	1	21	–	–	15	209
	7	99	10	48	8	366	9	68	5	50	3	4	39	635
157th Inf. Bde.														
1/5th H.L.I.	1	35	6	14	6	128	2	14	1	13	1	1	17	205
1/6th H.L.I.	1	32	6	18	3	124	2	19	1	21	1	2	14	216
1/7th H.L.I.	3	38	–	1	3	135	–	21	4	21	1	1	11	217
	5	105	12	33	12	387	4	54	6	55	3	4	42	638
Grand Total.	18	276	31	126	28	1145	16	178	15	150	3	8	111	1883

Appendix VIII

52nd (Lowland) Division. WAR DIARY OCTOBER 1918.
"A" and "Q" INTELLIGENCE SUMMARY. Vol. XLI

Army Form C. 2118.

Instructions regarding War Diaries and Intelligence Summaries are contained in F. S. Regs., Part II. and the Staff Manual respectively. Title pages will be prepared in manuscript.

(Erase heading not required.)

Place	Date	Hour	Summary of Events and Information	Remarks and references to Appendices

STRENGTH OF DIVISION.
(Week ending 26th Oct 1918)

	Officers	Other Ranks
Divisional Troops.	18	132
Divisional Artillery	78	1851
Divisional Engineers	36	921
155th Infantry Bde.	109	1987
156th Infantry Bde.	121	2214
157th Infantry Bde.	143	2036
Divisional Train	22	358
17th Bn. Northumberland Fusiliers (P.)	34	838
52nd Bn. Machine Gun Corps	44	868
98th Divisional Employment Co.	2	294
Royal Army Medical Corps.	20	651
	627	12150

INFANTRY BRIGADES - REINFORCEMENTS RECEIVED FOR MONTH OF OCTOBER.

Week ending	Officers	Other Ranks
5th October	19	419
12th October	38	282
19th October	17	207
26th October	9	155
	83	1063

CASUALTIES - INFANTRY BRIGADES

Week ending	KILLED		WOUNDED		MISSING		SICK	
	OFFS.	O.Rs	OFFS.	O.Rs	OFFS	O.Rs	OFFS	O.Rs
5th October	3	18	23	116	7	30	7	163
12th October	—	32	2	296	—	49	2	65
19th October	—	—	—	2	—	—	6	118
26th October	—	—	1	2	—	—	7	107
	3	50	26	416	7	79	22	453

CONFIDENTIAL

Army Form C. 2118.

WAR DIARY
or
INTELLIGENCE SUMMARY.
(Erase heading not required.)

52nd (LOWLAND) DIVISION

"A" and "Q"

WAR DIARY

November. 1918.

Vol. XLII

52nd (Lowland) DIVISION   WAR DIARY   NOVEMBER 1918

INTELLIGENCE SUMMARY.   VOL. XLII

"A" and "Q"

Army Form C. 2118.

PAGE ONE

Ref Maps (1/40000) Sheets 44 45 38.

Place	Date	Hour	Summary of Events and Information	Remarks and references to Appendices
SAMEON	1		Three officers and 20 other ranks attended Corps Sports in Horse management today.	
— " —	2		1375 litres of Beer issued for sale to troops. "A and Q" Summary No 1 issued to units. Baths (capacity one Battalion per diem) opened at MONT du PRAY (J.27.d.5.6.) Admins. Eric. Memo. No 35 re Personnel retained, pay, employment, issued. Divisional M.T. Coy moved from RACHES to BOUVIGNIES.	(Appendix I) (Appendix II)
— " —	3		Routine order issued re soldiers in possession of deceased soldiers kits. Orders received ref forthcoming relief of 8th Div. by 52nd Division.	(Appendix III)
— " —	4		"A and Q" Summary No 2 issued to units. Units instructed to forward no more names as candidates for Commissions.	(Appendix IV)
— " —	5		Provisional Traffic Map moved to all concerned. 157th Inf. Bde ordered to detail 1 officer to act as town major of ST. AMAND, also one company for work in the town under his orders. Div. Reception Camp moved from DOUAI to BEUVRY LEZ ORCHIES.	(Appendix V)
— " —	6		The town of ST. AMAND placed out of bounds to troops not on duty. "A and Q" Summary No 3. issued to units. Div. Prisoner of War Cage opened at P.2.d.8.8.	(Appendix VI)

52nd (Lowland) DIVISION.

WAR DIARY

"A" and "Q" INTELLIGENCE SUMMARY.

NOVEMBER 1918.

Vol. XLII.

Army Form C. 2118.

Summary of Events and Information
PAGE TWO

Place	Date	Hour	Summary of Events and Information	Remarks and references to Appendices
SAMEON	6		Warning issued to all units re danger of poisoning by fumes from Charcoal Braziers.	
— " —	7		"A and Q" Summary No 4 issued to all units. Corps Boundary extended to the south, 157th Bde moving up on right of 155th Bde.	(Appendix VII)
— " —	8		New cemetery opened at J.27.d.1.1. Patrols of 157th Bde report no enemy resistance encountered.	
MONT DE PERUWELZ	9		Divisional Hdqrs. closed at SAMEON and opened at MONT de PERUWELZ. ~~Was troops up of forces with enemy~~ Divisional Hdqrs moved to SIRAULT.	
SIRAULT	10			
— " —	11		Hostilities ceased at 1100 today in accordance with terms of Armistice.	
— " —	12		Division remained on line occupied yesterday between NIMY and JURBISE.	

WAR DIARY or INTELLIGENCE SUMMARY

52nd (Lowland) Division

NOVEMBER, 1918

VOL. XLII

Army Form C. 2118.

PAGE THREE

Place	Date	Hour	Summary of Events and Information (Ref.map. Sheet 45 1/40,000 Sheet 44)	Remarks and references to Appendices
SIRAULT	13		Information received that 52nd Division will shortly join XXII Corps, Second Army forming part of the force to proceed to GERMANY.	
"	14		A and Q Summary No 5 issued to units. Admin. Instructions AF 51 issued to units re parade at MONS on 15th Nov.	(Appendix VIII) (Appendix IX)
"	15		52nd Division transferred to XXII Corps. Division does not move at present, and continues to be administered by 16 VIII Corps re closing down of AUSTRALIAN Divisions.	(Appendix X) (Appendix XI)
"	16		Memo issued re closing down of A and Q' Summary No 6 issued to units.	
"	17		Divisional Reception Camp moves to BRUAY. A and Q' Summary No 7 issued to units. Lt. Col. Thomson D.S.O. 5th Bn. Vaughan Rifles took over duties of G.S.O.1.	(Appendix XII)
Chateau de la Bruyere. NIMY	18		Div. Headqrs moved to Chateau de la Bruyere, NIMY.	
"	19		Br.genl. Price, Commdg. 157th Inf. Bde took over temporary command of Div. on Maj. Genl. Marshall proceeding on leave to England.	

Army Form C. 2118.

52nd (Lowland) DIVISION   WAR DIARY   NOVEMBER 1918

or

"A" and "Q" INTELLIGENCE SUMMARY.   Vol. XLII

(Erase heading not required.)

Instructions regarding War Diaries and Intelligence Summaries are contained in F. S. Regs., Part II. and the Staff Manual respectively. Title pages will be prepared in manuscript.

PAGE FOUR.

Place	Date	Hour	Summary of Events and Information	Remarks and references to Appendices
Ch. de la Bruyère. NIMY	20		"A and Q" Summary No 8 issued to all units concerned. Refilling Point now at BAUDOUR.	(Appendix XIII)
"	21		Revised list of Bridges, west of ESCAUT and HAISNE rivers inclusive, issued with Summary No 8 yesterday.	
"	22		52nd M.G. Battalion concentrated in BAUDOUR. Baths opened in GHLIN J 25 b. (sheet 45) capacity 800 per day.	
"	23		Letter of Appreciation from Corps Commander VIII Corps distributed to all ranks of Division.	
"	24		XXII Corps Headqrs. moved from SEBOURG to MONS. "A and Q" Summary No 9 issued to units.	(Appendix XIV)
"	25		A 147/1 issued to all units ref. Divisional Ceremonial Parade to be held at MONS on 30th Nov. "A and Q" Summary No 10 issued to units.	(Appendix XV)
"	26		Arrangements made for 3 lorries to be attached from today to Div. Artillery for 3 days to enable parties of NCOs and men to visit WATERLOO. "A + Q" Summary No 11 issued to all units	(Appendix XVI)

WAR DIARY or **INTELLIGENCE SUMMARY**

Army Form C. 2118.

52nd (Lowland) DIVISION "A" and "Q"

NOVEMBER 1918

VOL XLII

Summary of Events and Information

PAGE FIVE

Place	Date	Hour	Summary of Events and Information	Remarks and references to Appendices
Ch. de la Bruyere NIMY	27		Divisional Ceremonial Parade ordered for 30th, postponed till further notice. "A" + "Q" Summary No 12 issued to units.	Appendix No XVI
—"—	28		Divisional Rest Station opened at LENS for accommodation of cases likely to recover within 10 days, except Scabies and Influenza.	
—"—	29		1st L.F.A. moved to NEUFVILLES. 52nd Machine Gun Battalion moved to CAMBRON ST VINCENT. "A" + "Q" Summary No 13 issued to units.	Appendix No XVII
—"—	30		Railhead opened today at VALENCIENNES.	

Army Form C. 2118.

52nd (Lowland) Division.
"A" & "Q" Branch.

WAR DIARY
NOVEMBER, 1918.
Vol. XLII
INTELLIGENCE SUMMARY.

(Erase heading not required.)

Instructions regarding War Diaries and Intelligence Summaries are contained in F.S. Regs., Part II and the Staff Manual respectively. Title pages will be prepared in manuscript.

Place	Date	Hour	Summary of Events and Information	Remarks and references to Appendices
			Strength of Division. (Week-ending 29/12/18.)	
				Offrs. O.R.
			Divnl. Troops.	18 126
			Divnl. Artillery.	89 2060
			Divnl. Engineers.	35 912
			155th Inf. Bde.	124 2173
			156th Inf. Bde.	132 2446
			157th Inf. Bde.	146 2123
			17th N.Fus. (P).	40 854
			52nd Bn. M.G.C.	48 879
			Divnl. Train.	21 368
			984 Div. Employ. Coy.	2 287
			Royal Army Med. Corps.	22 655
				677 12,883
			Infantry Brigades - Reinforcements received for the month of November.	
			Week-ending	Offrs. O.R.
			2nd November.	6 139
			9th November.	15 151
			16th November.	4 213
			23rd November.	9 235
			30th November.	19 541
				53 1279

Casualties Infantry Brigades.

WEEK-ENDING	Killed.		Wounded.		Missing.		Sick to Fd. Ambces.	
	O.	O.R.	O.	O.R.	O.	O.R.	O.	O.R.
2/11/18.	-	1	1	28	-	-	10	106
9/11/18.	-	-	-	9	-	-	7	91
16/11/18.	-	5	-	-	-	-	3	67
23/11/18.	-	4	-	21	-	-	5	70
30/11/18.	-	-	-	-	-	-	2	91
	-	8	1	58	-	1	27	425

52nd (Lowland) Division.

STRENGTH RETURN UP TO 12 NOON Saturday, 30th NOVEMBER 1915.

	(I) Strength as per previous wk. in accordance with A/B's. Distr.		(II) Increase during wk. due to drafts etc. taken on strength of unit.		(III) Totals (I) & (II)		(IV) Decrease during wk. due to discharges etc. struck off strength of unit.		"C" Strength on-not present with unit, with 8 O.R. at disposal of G.O.C. Incl.in Col.V.		"D" Strength Available Incl. Strength not at disposal of G.O.C. Stores.		Remarks.
U N I T .	O.	O.R.	O.	O.R.	O.	O.R.	O.	O.R.	O.	O.R.	O.	O.R.	
155th Inf. Bde.													
1/4th R.S.Fus.													
1/5th R.S.Fus.													
1/4th K.O.S.B.													
156th Inf. Bde.													
1/4th R. Scots.													
1/7th R. Scots.													
1/7th Scot. Rif.													
157th Inf. Bde.													
1/5th H.L.I.													
1/6th H.L.I.													
1/7th H.L.I.													
1/7th H.Fus.(?)													
52nd Bn. M.G.C.													

*(Incl.7 Off.at
**(Bde. L.G.Course

52nd (Lowland) Division.

Abstract Column "B" ----- Week-ending 30/11/18.

UNIT.	Courses. O.	Courses. O.R	Sick. O.	Sick. O.R.	Leave. O.	Leave. O.R.	Ede.Employ. O.	Ede.Employ. O.R.	Div.Employ. O.	Div.Employ. O.R.	Extra Regtl.Employ. O.	Extra Regtl.Employ. O.R.	TOTAL. O.	TOTAL. O.R.
155th Inf. Bde.														
1/4th R.S.Fus.	4	13	6	22	2	65	1	17	1	16	-	2	14	135
1/5th R.S.Fus.	1	9	1	32	5	54	-	15	1	6	-	1	7	88
1/4th K.O.S.B.	1	7	1	14	4	52	-	14	-	11	-	-	5	98
	6	29	8	57	11	171	1	46	1	33	-	3	26	319
156th Inf. Bde.														
1/4th R. Scots.	2	6	7	11	2	64	-	7	1	8	-	2	12	98
1/7th R. Scots.	4	11	5	22	1	77	1	9	3	19	1	1	15	139
1/7th Sco.Rif.	2	8	1	10	3	96	1	7	1	4	-	-	8	125
	8	25	13	43	6	237	2	23	5	31	1	3	35	362
157th Inf. Bde.														
1/5th H.L.I.	9*	14	2	10	2	110	2	7	1	15	-	2	16	158
1/6th H.L.I.	11**	17	3	6	3	53	-	9	1	15	-	1	17	101
1/7th H.L.I.	2	8	1	-	2	52	-	11	4	12	-	1	9	84
	22	39	6	15	7	215	2	27	6	42	-	3	42	341
Grand Total.	34	93	26	95	24	625	5	96	12	106	2	9	103	1022

*(Incl. 7 Off.at
*(Bde.L.G.Course.

November War Diary
Appendix I

SECRET.   COPY NO.......

HEADQUARTERS 52nd (LOWLAND) DIVISION.

"A" & "Q" SUMMARY No. 1.

1. "A. Q." SUMMARY.
This Summary will be issued as often as necessary, and will surplant the "A" Summary, hitherto issued occasionally from this office, and in addition will contain "Q" information of a secret nature.
This Summary will be issued on the same scale as D.R.O's, plus a copy to Corps Headquarters, and is not to be taken further forward than Battalion etc. Headquarters.

2. RAILHEAD for NOVEMBER 3rd.   REFILLING POINT FOR NOV. 3rd.
   SOMAIN.   BEUVRY.
Reception Camp remains at DOUAI for the present.

3. LIGHT RAILWAY.
Light Railway will probably be through to FLINES on 2nd instant and linked up with DOUAI Station on 3rd.
This should be of assistance in moving up personnel from Reinforcement Camps.

4. AMMUNITION DUMP & RAILHEAD.
An Army Dump is in course of establishment where all natures of ammunition will be stored.
There is good road and lorry access to this Dump.
The location of the Dump is B.19.b. Sheet 51A. N.W. and is parallel to the SOMAIN - ANICHE Road.
The Dump will be known as ST. LOUIS Dump.
PLANQUES Ammunition Dump is in process of being closed down.
SOMAIN (ST. LOUIS) will be Ammunition Railhead as soon as PLANQUES is closed.
Thereafter ammunition empties will be sent to SOMAIN.
The date of the change will be notified by wire to all concerned.

5. FIELD SUPPLY DEPOT.
A Field Supply Depot is being formed at PAVE DE VALENCIENNES, where it is intended to stock as a commencement :-
   100,000 mens' rations.
   50,000 iron rations.
   50,000 horse rations.
and a complement of medical comforts. This will be made up with the stocks at present held at ARRAS Supply Depot.
The Supply Depot at WAVRANS will be handed over to L. of C. as soon as they take over that area.
(First Army D.D.S.T. No. ST.C/440 dated 29/10/18).

P.T.O.

6. LOCATIONS.
(i) The office of D.D.S. & T. First Army is now situated at Sheet 51A/A.29.c.3.8.
(ii) No.44 Ordnance Mobile Workshop (Light) is now at PLACQUE.
(iii) No.4 Ordnance Mobile Workshop (Light) and No.19 Ordnance Mobile Workshop are now at ORCHIES.

7. BATHS.
(a) It is hoped that Baths will shortly be available in the LANDAS and LECELLES Areas.

(b) Baths (capacity a Battalion a day) are situated and are working at MONT du PROY (J.27.d.6.6.). They are controlled by G.O.C. Infantry Brigade in front line, and application should be made to him, by units outside the Brigade, for allotment of these Baths.

(c) Baths Officer and Divisional Clean Clothing Store are at BEUVRY.

Edmund

Lieut. Colonel,
A.A. & Q.M.G. 52nd (Lowland) Division

D.H.Q.
2/11/18.

November War Diary Appendix II

52nd (Lowland) DIVISION.

ADMINISTRATIVE CIRCULAR MEMORANDUM No. 35.

PERSONNEL EXTRA REGIMENTALLY EMPLOYED.

1. In order to comply with the conditions of O.B./1919 of September, 1918, (Organization of an Infantry Battalion), which lays down that not more than 30 men from each Infantry Battalion are to be extra-regimentally employed, the N.C.Os. and men shown below will rejoin their units by 1800, November 6th, rationed up to November 7th inclusive.

UNIT:	No. of men	How Employed	Remarks.
1/4th Bn R.S.Fus.	1	Clerk to A.P.M.	
	1	Loader D.H.Q.	
	2	Pioneers, Reception Camp.	
	1	Guide for Drafts Reception Camp.	
	1	Butcher. =do=	
1/5th Bn R.S. Fus.	1	Batman to Lieut. Drummond.	
	1	Butcher att. Mob. Vet. Sect.	
1/4th Bn K.O.S.B.	1	D.A.D.O.S. Storeman.	
1/4th Bn R.Scots.	1	Clerk to Mob.Vet. Sect.	temporarily attd.
	1	Guide to Drafts at Reception Camp.	
	1	Butcher attd. Mob.Vet. Sect.	
1/7th Bn R.Scots.	1	Batman to Capt. SCOTT attd. D.A.D.O.S.	
	1	Pioneer, D.H.Q.	
	5	attached D.A.D.O.S.	
	1	Pioneer, Reception Camp.	

P.T.O.

UNIT.	No. of Men.	How Employed.	Remarks.
1/7th Bn Scots Rif.	1	Batman to Lt. CARMICHAEL attd. 412th Field Coy. R.E.	
	1	Batman to Claims Officer.	
	5	attached Salvage Officer.	
	3	Water duty with Lt. O'HARA.	
	3	Reception Camp. (Pioneers & Waiter)	
1/5th Bn H.L.I.	1	Batman to Div. Burial Officer.	
	1	attached D.A.D.O.S.	
	2	Reception Camp.	
	1	Batman to Capt. MOIR.	At ARRAS.
1/6th Bn H.L.I.	5	Reception Camp........	1 Sgt. A/C.S.M. can remain.
	1	Batman to Capt. DALY.	
1/7th Bn H.L.I.	2	Batmen to Lts. BRODIE and McLEAN.	with Concert party.
	1	Batman to Major MURRAY.	with XVII Corps.
	2	Loaders at D.H.Q.	
	1	D.A.D.O.S.	
	2	Reception Camp. Pioneer & Waiter.	

2. The following, who are at present shown by units as detached from their Battalions, have been taken on to an establishment and should be struck off the strength accordingly :

1/4th Bn R.S.Fus........ 1 groom at D.H.Q.
1/4th Bn K.O.S.B........ 1 groom at D.H.Q.
                           1 batman to Gas Officer (Capt. THIN.)
1/7th Bn R.Scots ...... 1 Batman to Rev. SEMPLE.
1/7th Bn S. Rifles .... 1 Loader at D.H.Q.
                           1 batman to Vet. Officer . 56th Bde. R.F.A.

                           1 Clerk "Q" Office, D.H.Q.

(3)

3. O.C., Divisional Employment Coy., will arrange to replace the "A" men, returned to their units in accordance with para. 1, by "B" men from the Unit under his command.

[signature]

Lieut. Colonel.
2nd NOVEMBER, 1918.   A.A. & Q.M.G., 52nd (Lowland) DIVISION.

November War Diary
Appendix III

ROUTINE ORDERS

BY

Major General F.J. MARSHALL, CMG., DSO., Commanding 52nd (Lowland) Division.
2nd NOVEMBER, 1918.

394. **EFFECTS of DECEASED SOLDIERS.**

Attention is called to General Routine Order No. 5397 dated October 27th, 1918.
The warning to all ranks against being in possession of articles belonging to deceased soldiers without proper authority is to be read out on parade.

[signed]
Lieut. Colonel.
A.A. & Q.M.G., 52nd (Lowland) DIVISION.

NOTICE.

DIVINE SERVICE. A Presbyterian Service will be held on Sunday, 3rd November, 1918, at 0930, in the open space adjoining the R.E. Dump, SAMEON.

November War Diary
Appendix IV

SECRET.　　　　　　　　　　　　　　　　　　　　　　COPY NO.........

HEADQUARTERS 52nd (LOWLAND) DIVISION.

"A" & "Q" SUMMARY No. 2.

1. MOVES.

	From.	To.	Date.
Divisional Reception Camp.	DOUAI	BEUVRY.	5/11/18.
Divisional M.T. Company.	RACHES.	BOUVIGNIES.	2/11/18.

2. DIVISIONAL RECEPTION CAMP.
On moving to BEUVRY, O.C. Reception Camp will arrange for guides to meet personnel trains at SOMAIN, the new Reinforcement Railhead.

Men marching from SOMAIN to rejoin the Division will proceed direct to the Reception Camp, and will not stage via M.T. Company Headquarters.

3. ST. AMAND.
157th Infantry Brigade will relieve Town Major ST AMAND and one Company INFANTRY at present found in that place by 8th Division. Relief to be completed by 1200, 5th instant.

4. FORAGE IN CAPTURED AREAS.
(a) Hay in ricks or stored in barns which has been grown obviously on French soil will not be touched until instructions are received (VIII Corps Q.M.46 of 29/10/18).
(b) Any German rye straw found will be reported to O.C. Divisional Train, who has received orders as to its disposal.

5. ORDNANCE MOBILE WORKSHOPS.
No.4 Ordnance Mobile Workshop (Light) - ORCHIES.
(I.O.M. Lt. WIGGINS).

Vehicles which clearly cannot be repaired regimentally may be sent to the above Workshop.

6. COMMISSIONS.
As the sending home of Candidates for Commissions has been suspended meantime, any proposals on hand should be retained by units.

D.H.Q.
4/11/18.

for Lieut. Colonel.
A.A. & Q.M.G. 52nd (Lowland) Division..

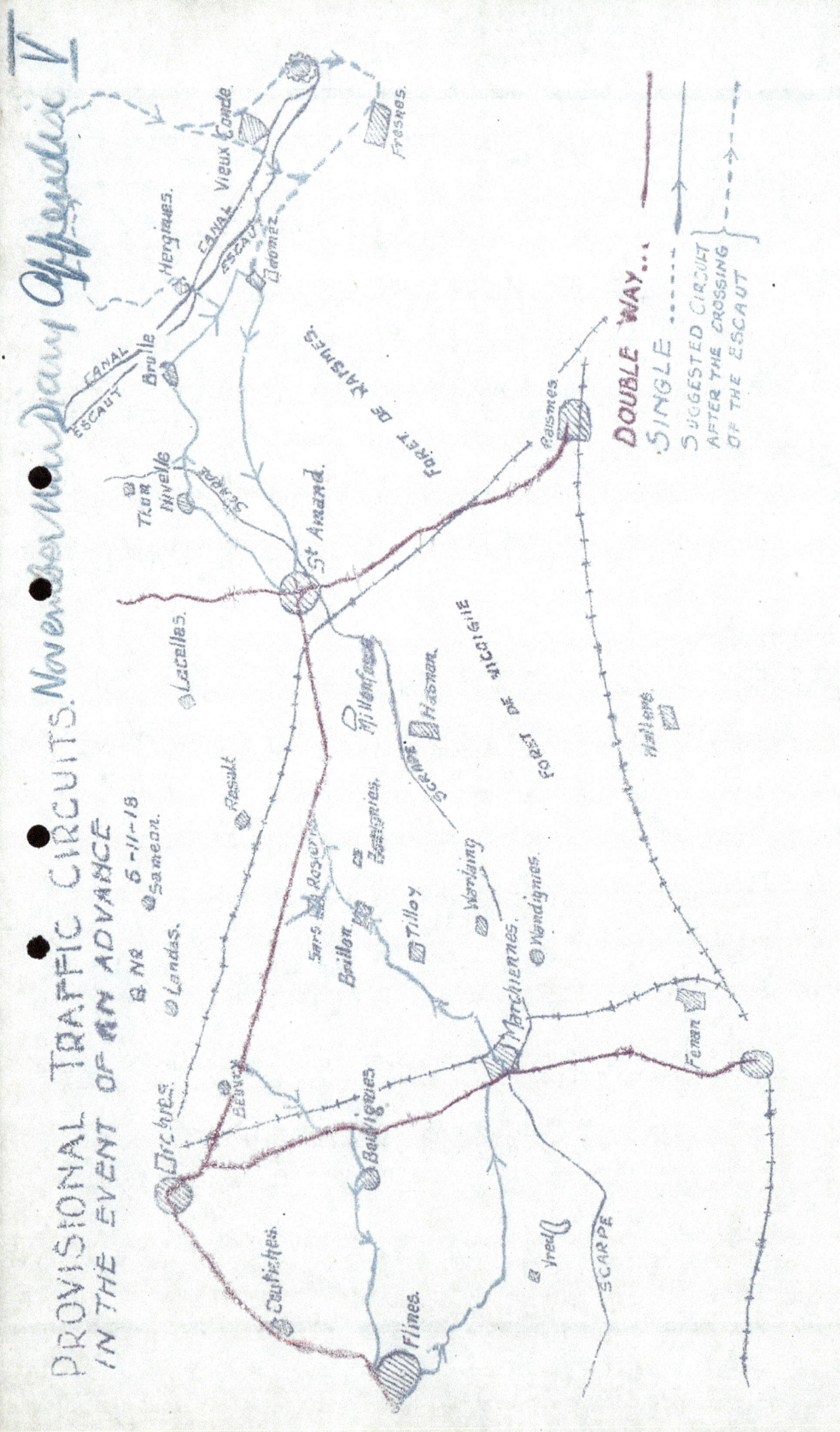

November War Diary,
Appendix VI

SECRET   HEADQUARTERS 52nd (LOWLAND) DIVISION.   COPY NO. 99

"A" & "Q" SUMMARY No. 3.

1. **MOVES.**
    (a) Ordnance Gun Park No.1 opens at SOMAIN (ST.LOUIS) B.13.d.8.2. Sheet 51A on 5th instant.

    (b) Division Prisoner of War Cage moves to P.2.d.8.8. Sheet 44 on 6th instant.

2. **SUPPLY.**
    Railhead — SOMAIN.

    Refilling Points. - 155th Infantry Brigade.)
                        156th Infantry Brigade.) BEUVRY.
                        157th Infantry Brigade.)
                        Divl.Troops & R.A. ROSULT STATION.
    from 6th instant inclusive and till further orders.

3. **ST. AMAND.**
    (a) The Town of ST. AMAND is out of bounds for all ranks not on duty.

    (b) 157th Infantry Brigade will arrange to ration the Town Majors party, ST. AMAND, from 6th instant inclusive.

4. **TRAFFIC CIRCUIT.**
    A sketch map showing the provisional Traffic circuits in the event of an Advance is issued with this Summary on the following scale -

Each Infantry Brigade.	1.
C. R. A.	4.
Divisional Train.	1.
D. A. P. M.	2.
S.A.A. Section, D.A.C.	1.

5. **ORDNANCE.**
    Attention is drawn to G.R.O. 5336 of 20/10/18.
    Authority for issue of stores over and above the scales laid down in para.3 of G.R.O. 4773 will only be granted under very exceptional circumstances.

6. **FOOT-AND-MOUTH DISEASE.** /115
    Billet No.18, SAMEON, has been placed out of bounds owing to an outbreak of Foot-and-Mouth Disease.
    Attention is drawn to G.R.O. 4890.

                                                              P.T.O.

7. **FIELD GENERAL COURTS-MARTIAL.**
   Attention is drawn to G.R.O. 5193 of 4/10/18 which reads :-
   "Charges of desertion or absence without leave brought before a Field General Court-Martial will always state the commencement and the termination of the period during which the accused is alleged to have been absent. If in any case this has inadvertently not been done, the Court must specify the period in its finding."
   Attention is also drawn to S.S. 412 b, Ch.3, para.29.

   Lieut. Colonel.

5/11/18.   A.A. & Q.M.G. 52nd (Lowland) Division.

November War Diary Appendix VII

SECRET.   COPY NO. 97

HEADQUARTERS 52nd (LOWLAND) DIVISION.

"A" & "Q" SUMMARY No. 4.

1. **RESERVE SUPPLIES.**
    100,000 mens' rations and 20,000 horse rations are being stocked at SOMAIN Railhead - large stocks will also be maintained at ANICHE and DOUAI Railheads. (D.D.S.T. No.ST.C/440 dated 4/11/18.)

2. **LIGHT RAILWAYS.**
    The 60 centimetre system is now connected with DOUAI Broad Gauge Station.
    The line is open to FLINES where a siding on the edge of the road in R.24.a. & c. is available for loading and off-loading.
    The line is being extended to COUTICHES and on to ORCHIES.
    All applications for trucks to be made to Divisional Headquarters by 1200 daily for following day's requirements.
    It is suggested that personnel could be moved to and from DOUAI by light railway.

3. **INFORMATION.**
    The following Code letters have been allotted Ammunition Railheads.
    SOMAIN (ST. LOUIS) ... ... XY.
    The office of Traffic PERNES closed at SACHIN on the 3rd November and re-opened at 00.01 hours 4th November 1918 at 95 Boulevard VAUBAN, LILLE.
    Telegraphic, D.R.L.S. and Postal Address - Traffic LILLE.

4. **CEMETERY.**
    A cemetery has been opened at J.27.d.1.1.

5. **CHARCOAL POISONING.**
    A case of death has been reported in which the cause is believed to have been carbon monoxide poisoning, the result of using a charcoal brazier where ventilation was defective.
    Officers Commanding Units will take steps to warn all ranks of the danger of using braziers in small rooms or dugouts where there is not sufficient ventilation to carry off the fumes.

6. **BILLETING CERTIFICATES IN NEWLY OCCUPIED TERRITORY.**
    In all cases where units are billeted in a town or village where no Maire or Town Major is resident, a consolidated Billeting Certificate should be compiled showing the total sums due for accommodation used for officers, O.Rs, and animals.

                                                                P.T.O.

One copy should be forwarded as usual to 1st Army Branch Requisition Office and the other copy to French Mission, 52nd Division who will forward it to the proper authority.

7. **CONSIGNMENTS FROM UNITS TO DIVISIONAL TRAIN.**
Any stores, empties etc., sent by units to Divisional Train Headquarters must be accompanied by a note as to their disposal.

8. **FROST BITE - PREVENTION OF.**
Ref D.R.O. 295 of 7/11/1918.
All men in trenches or who have to stand for any length of time in water or mud should have whale oil or anti frost grease well rubbed into the feet, before going on duty.

E.F. Moulton-Barrett Major
for
Lieut Colonel,
A.A.&Q.M.G., 52nd (Lowland) DIVISION.

7-11-18.

November War Diary
Appendix VIII

SECRET.   COPY NO......

HEADQUARTERS 52nd (LOWLAND) DIVISION.

"A" & "Q" SUMMARY No.5.

1. **SUPPLIES.**
   Railhead - BRUAY.

   Refilling Point. - N.8.

2. **LOCATIONS.**
   - Divisional Train - BAUDOUR (porcelain factory).
   - D.A.D.O.S.   -   "   "   "
   - Div. Baths Offr. -   "   "   "
   - Mob. Vety. Sect. -   "   "   "
   - S.A. Section.   - HAUTRAGE.
   - M.T. Company.   - BRUAY.
   - Workshops.   - R.19.d. Sheet 44.

3. **SUPPLY DUMPS.**
   Small emergency Supply Dumps are situated at SOMAIN, ANICHE, CANTIMPRE and DOUAI.

4. **CIVILIAN RATIONS.**
   The Ration Dump for Civilians from the 12th instant is situated at BLATON, 44/G.8.b.

5. **MEDICAL ARRANGEMENTS.**
   (i) No.4 Cdn. C.C.S. is now open at the college des Filles VALENCIENNES, and will, for the present receive all seriously wounded, as well as serious medical cases, and medical cases with high temperature.

   (ii) Slightly wounded cases, and slight medical cases will be disposed of as follows :-
   In convoys up to 100 of each :-
   (a) VIII Corps to be sent to No. 6 C.C.S. at MONTIGNY and No.42 C.C.S. at DOUAI.
   (b) Local sick will be sent to the nearest C.C.S. that is open.

   (iii) Nos. 2 and 57 C.C.Ss at BOIS de BOUCHE are closed, 23 C.C.S. at D.17.central (N. of BREBIERES) closing.

6. **VETERINARY.**
   18 V.E.S. open at MARCHIENNES (Sheet 44. T.3.a.) on the 12th instant.

7. **SALVED AMMUNITION.**
   No.4 Ordnance Ammunition Section (VIII Corps Salvage Ammunition Dump) is now located at T.3.a.6.8. Sheet 44.

8. **CENTRAL PURCHASE BOARD.**
   H.Q. Central Purchase Board has now opened at HESDIN (Rue de Jerusalem).

P.T.O.

9. **LEAVE.**

Attention is drawn to G.R.O. 4700, which is republished for information -

"4700 - LEAVE - The Confidential Circular regarding Leave A.G./441/F.S./1, dated 25th May, 1918, issued with G.R.Os dated 26th May, 1918, as amended by G.R.Os 4533 and 4496, will be amended as follows :-

(a) Cancel the first sub-paragraph of paragraph 3 and substitute-
"Under no circumstances will an officer or Other Rank be granted ordinary leave until five months have elapsed since the date of return from his last ordinary leave, or since the date of last leaving the United Kingdom.
"Preference is to be given to those who have been longest without leave. It is essential that those who have been on Service out of the United Kingdom for over one year without leave should be granted leave at the earliest opportunity."

(b) Cancel paragraph 5 and substitute -
"All applications for officers and Other Ranks to proceed on leave before their turn on the leave rosters of their units must be regarded as applications for special leave, and the Authority of the Adjutant-General, G.O.C. Army, Corps, L. of C. or R.A.F. must be obtained and quoted on the warrant. If such leave is granted, it will come out of the allotment of special leave vacancies given to the unit or formation submitting the application."

Attention is also drawn to the fact that passes for Special Leave must be marked with an "S" and the Authority quoted.

10. **CENSORSHIP.**

Under authority First Army telegram No. N.252 dated 12th instant, the regulations as to use of Cameras are cancelled.

Regulations as to censorship are relaxed. Men will now be allowed to describe where they are and the nature of their surroundings.

13/11/18.

Lieut.Colonel.
A.A. & Q.M.G. 52nd (Lowland) Division.

November War Diary
Appendix IX

SECRET.   COPY NO.......

52nd (Lowland) DIVISION.

ADMINISTRATIVE INSTRUCTIONS NO. A.F. 51.

14th November, 1918.

PARADE TO BE HELD AT MONS ON FRIDAY, NOVEMBER 15th, 1918.

1.   The First Army Commander will make an official entry into the Town of MONS on Friday, 15th instant.
   52nd Division will provide a mixed detachment of 1,000 men and two Batteries, R.F.A. to take part in the parade.

2.   The parade will consist of two parts :-
   (a) Lining the streets, whilst the Army Commander rides past, accompanied by H.R.H. the Prince of Wales and a special escort.
   (b) Marching past the Army Commander in the GRANDE PLACE.

   (a) LINING THE STREETS.

(i) C.R.A. will detail one Battery 18 pounders (one gun and wagon per sub-section) to form part of the special escort mentioned in 2 (a) above.
   This Battery will report to a representative of VIII Corps at 1000 on 15th instant at the Cross Roads in P.12.a. (on JEMAPPES - MONS Road), where detailed orders will be given it.

(ii) C.R.A. will detail one Battery R.F.A. (one gun and wagon per sub-section) to be formed up in the PLACE de FLANARE (Q.8.b.3.6.) by 1000, in a formation suitable for lining this square.

(iii) The following mixed detachments will line the BOULEVARD BADOUIN de JERUSALEM from the PLACE de FLANDRE (Q.8.b.3.6.) to the RUE VALENCIENNOIRE (Cross Roads Q.2.d.3.7.) -

155th Infantry Brigade.	250.	)
156th Infantry Brigade.	250.	)
157th Infantry Brigade.	250.	)
Machine Gun Battalion.	75.	) With a proportion of
17th Northumberland Fus.	75.	) officers.
Royal Engineers.	30.	) 156th Infantry Brigade will
R.A.M.C.	30.	) detail an officer of the
Divisional Headquarters.)		) rank of Lieut.Colonel to
Divl. Signal Company.	20.	) command parade.
Divisional Train.	20.	)

   All the above detachments will be in position by 1000.
   No restrictions as to route, except that detachments will march to the above BOULEVARD via the PLACE REGNIER au long Col (Q.2.a.7.2.), which place they will not enter till 0945.

(iv) Brigade and unit representatives (who should be mounted and need not be officers taking part in the parade) will meet a Divisional representative in the PLACE REGNIER au long Col (Q.2.a.7.2.) at 0915 on 15th instant, in order to be shown the positions in the BOULEVARD BADOUIN de JERUSALEM allotted to their units, and to guide the latter to these positions.

(v) The above detachments will line the appointed routes in single rank facing inwards. On the approach of the Army Commander they will Present Arms.

P.T.O.

(vi) Only officers of mounted units will be mounted.

DRESS.- Battle order with steel helmets.

(vii) Each Infantry Brigade will detail one pipe band to accompany its detachment. These bands will probably be massed and special instructions as to playing will be given to the senior pipe major on arrival.

(b) MARCHING PAST.

(a) After the Army Commander has ridden through the town, he will proceed to the GRANDE PLACE, where the troops lining the streets will march past in fours.

(b) The following route will be followed by the detachments from 52nd Division -
- AVENUE de NIMY.
- RUE de NIMY.
- GRANDE PLACE.
- RUE de la CHAUSSEE.
- GRAND RUE.
- RUE de CAPUCINES.
- BOULEVARD CHARLES QUINT.
- BOULEVARD BAUDEVIN le BATISSEUR.

and thence back to billets independently.

(c) An interval of 50 yards will be kept between the head of the leading 52nd Division detachment and the rear of the preceding Division detachment.

(d) The Army Commander hopes that any officers, who are not on duty with troops and can be spared to attend, will be present. They should arrive by 1030.

Places will be reserved for them for the march past either on the platform in front of the Hotel de VILLE (GRANDE PLACE) or on the pavement on the right of this stand.

One lorry will report to each Infantry Brigade Headquarters at 0830 tomorrow morning to take spectators to MONS and back. Similarly one lorry will leave Divisional Headquarters ("C" Office) at 0900 with officers from Divisional Troops.

(e) A.D.M.S. will arrange for a Motor Ambulance to be at the PLACE de FLANDRES by 1000 to deal with any casualties that occur.

3. ACKNOWLEDGE.

Lieut.Colonel.
A.A. & Q.M.G. 52nd (Lowland) Division.

Issued at 2100.

Copies to No.1 G.O.C.
2. "G"
3. 15th Inf.Bde.
4. 156th Inf.Bde.
5. 157th Inf.Bde.
6. C.R.A.
7. C.R.E.
8. 17th N.F.
9. M.G.Bn.
10. A.D.M.S.
11. D.A.D.V.S.
12. Divl.Train.
13. M.T.Coy.
14. Signal Coy.
15. D.A.P.M.
16. D.A.D.O.S.
17. Camp Comdt.
18. Reception Camp.
19. Employment Coy.
20. S.A. Section D.C.
21. Div.Baths Offr.
22. French Mission.
23. Belgian Mission.
24. D.G.O.
25. VIII Corps.
26. File.
27.)
28.) War Diary.

November War Diary
Appendix X

Q.205/8

Camp Comdt.	155th Brigade.	D.A.D.V.S.	17th Northd. Fus.
Signal Coy.	156th Brigade.	D.A.P.M.	Capt. Scott c/o D.A.D.O.S.
C.R.E.	157th Brigade.	Divl. Train.	O.i/c 52nd Div. Dump.
C.R.A.	A.D.M.S.	M.G. Bn.	AUBIGNY.
			O.C.M.T.Coy.

1. It is proposed to close down the AUBIGNY Dump.

2. In order to do this the stores in the dump will be sub-divided into the following sub-groups :-
   (a) Government Stores for return to Base.
   (b) Stores and Kits required by Units.
   (c) Stores no longer required, which can either be left at AUBIGNY unguarded, or returned to United Kingdom.

3. Four lorries will leave Divisional Headquarters where all representatives should rendezvous at 0800 on the 16th instant and will take following personnel to make the proposed arrangements -
   1 officer per Brigade.
   1 O.R. per Battalion.
   1 officer R.F.A.
   1 O.R. per Brigade R.F.A.
   1 officer M.G. Battalion.
   1 officer 17th Northd. Fusiliers.
   1 O.R. Signal Company.
   1 officer R.A.M.C.
   1 officer R.E.

4. Lorries will return loaded on 18th instant, if possible, and will be allotted as follows :-
   1 per Infantry Brigade.
   1 for Divisional Troops and R.A.

5. They will be loaded as follows :-
   (a) Personnel sent down in accordance with para.3.
   (b) Stores and Kits required by units as per para. 2 sub-para.(b)
   All stores over and above those in the lorries referred to above must be disposed of under para. 2 sub-groups either (a) or (c).

6. The Stores for return to Base or United Kingdom will be taken to the Station by lorries on the afternoon of the 17th instant.

7. O.C. Dump and units representatives at present at AUBIGNY will remain at the Station till truckage has been arranged for and after despatch of stores will rejoin Division by train.

8. Captain SCOTT, attached D.A.D.O.S., will be the Divisional representative and will co-ordinate the arrangements; in case of doubt he will decide what stores should come under each sub-group. Captain SCOTT will also arrange with Camp Commandant about Divisional Headquarters stores at the Dump.

9. 96 hours rations will be taken by all ranks proceeding.

10. O.C. M.T. Company will arrange to detail the lorries mentioned in para. 3 above.

11. ACKNOWLEDGE.

15/11/18.

Major.
D.A.Q.M.G. 52nd (Lowland) Division.

November War Diary
Appendix XI

SECRET.　　　　HEADQUARTERS, 52nd (LOWLAND) DIVISION.　　　COPY NO......

"A" & "Q" SUMMARY No.6.

1. SUPPLIES.
   Refilling Point - TERTRE.

2. INFORMATION.
   Divisional Reception Camp moves to BRUAY 17th instant.
   Staging Camp is situated at BAUDOUR, under the command of Captain J. FYFE, M.C., 1/7th Scottish Rifles.

3. COMMISSIONS.
   No officers or other ranks for transfer to R.A.F. may now proceed to ENGLAND. All orders for interviews should be considered cancelled and all units so informed. No further applications of officers and other ranks for transfer to R.A.F. to be submitted.

4. ROADS & BRIDGES.
   (i) Bridge at N.8.b. open for traffic up to 8 ton axle load at noon 14th.
   (ii) Road open for lorry traffic, POMMEREUL - TERTRE - GHLIN - NIMY - CASTEAU.
   (iii) Chief Engineer, VIII Corps, assumes responsibility as from noon to-day for all roads up to N.2.cent. - H.14.d. cent. - H.26.d.5.0. - to N.8.b.
   The road H.14.b.cent. to N.8.b. will be inclusive to Chief Engineer.
   (iv) Owing to the failure of one of the parts of the INGLIS Bridge it will be probably 3 days before it is possible to complete the North Bridge out of CONDE.
   (v) Reference "Q" Summary No.454, para.2. the following amendments and additions are made :-

No.	Location.	Map ref.	River or canal.	Safe load.	Remarks.
7.	CONDE	R.8.d.8.0.	HAISNE.	All loads except tanks.	Completed 12th
8.	"	R.8.d.9.2.	"	do.	Now open for lorry traffic.
9.	"	R.9.a.0.7.	JARD.	do.	Will not be open for lorries till night 14/11/18 owing to broken axle in erecting trolley.
11.	STAMBRUGES.	H.1.d.4.4.	ATH-BLATON.	5 ton.	Correction from 8 tons.
14.		N.8.b.	MONS-CONDE Canal.	5 ton axle.	Complete.
17.	STAMBRUGES.	H.2.c.9.7.	ATH-BLATON.	5 ton.	
18.	PERUWELZ.	F.28.c.	Small stream.	do.	Completed. Being strengthened for 8 ton.

16/11/18.

E.S. Moultrie Barrett Major
for Lieut.Colonel.
A.A. & Q.M.G. 52nd (Lowland) Divn.

War Diary. November.
Appendix XII

SECRET.   Copy No....

Headquarters, 52nd (Lowland) DIVISION.

"A" & "Q" SUMMARY, No. 7.

1. **MINERS: RELEASE OF.**

   1. A letter has been received from Adjutant General, General Headquarters, saying that an urgent return of Coalminers ("face workers" only) is required by D.A.G. by November, 24th.

   2. This return will be made out in accordance with the attached proforma and instructions. It should be noted that this proforma is to be sent direct by units to D.A.G. A certificate that this has been done, will be sent through usual channels to reach Divisional H.Q. by 25th instant.

   3. An expert is being sent to the Division to interview these men with a view to the immediate return to United Kingdom of a selected number. Further instructions as to this will be issued.

   4. A further supply of these proformas will be sent to units as soon as received from Base.

   5. Units should keep records of the men included in this return so as to assist the interviewing officer on arrival.

2. **VENEREAL DISEASE.**
   Reference to prevalence of Venereal disease. Calomel Cream is now available at the Ambulances and Medical Officers have been advised to secure a supply.
   The fact that this cream can be obtained on application should be made known to all ranks, who should be encouraged to use it.

3. **RELEASED, PRISONERS of WAR.**
   A depot for the accommodation of released Prisoners of War British and French, has been opened at ORCHIES. Belgian prisoners of war will be accommodated at BON SECOURS. Application for relief there to be made to the Maire of BON SECOURS.

                                                    [signature]
                                                    Lieut. Colonel.
17th November, 1918.
                                        A.A. & Q.M.G., 52nd (Lowland) DIVISION.

War Diary November Appendix XIII

SECRET.   HEADQUARTERS 52nd (LOWLAND) DIVISION.   COPY NO......

"A" & "Q" SUMMARY NO. 8.

1. **SUPPLIES.**
   Refilling Point. BAUDOUR from 20th.

2. **BRIDGES.**
   Bridge at ST. GUISLAIN completed and open for traffic to carry 5 ton axle load.
   The following is a revised list of bridges West of ESCAUT and HAISNE Rivers inclusive, constructed or in course of construction to 18.00 hours 16-11-18. This list cancels all previous information.

No.	Location.	Map Ref.	River or Canal.	Safe load.	Remarks.
1.	HERGNIES.		ESCAUT.	5 ton axle.	
2.	"		JARD.	8 " "	
3.	"		"	8 " "	
4.	"		ESCAUT.	17 " "	
4a.	"		JARD.	17 " "	In course of construction.
5&6	CONDE	Dismantled			
7.	"	R.8.d.80.	HAISNE.	8 " "	
8.	"	R.8.d.92.	"	17 " "	
9.	"	R.9.a.0.7.	JARD.	Special loads As laid down in Inglis Booklet for 120 ft. span.	
10.	BLATON.	G.9.a.96.	ANTOING-POMMEROEUIL.	8 ton axle.	
10a.	"	G.15.c.88	"	17 " "	
10b.	"	G.15.c.88	"	8 " "	
10c.	"	G.22.c.80.	"	8 " "	
11.	STAMBRUGES.	H.1.d.44.	ATH-BLATON.	6 " "	
11a.	"	H.1.d.44.		17 " "	In course of Construction. Probably complete.
12.	GRANDGLISE.	G.12.a.97.	"	17 " "	In course of construction. Probably complete on 18-11-
17.	STAMBRUGES.	H.2.c.97.	"	5 " "	
13.		N.8.b.	MONS-CONDE		Coverted to No.14.
14.		N.8.b.	"	5 " "	
15.		N.8.b.	"	8 " "	
16.		O.9.a.	"	5 " "	In course of construction.
16a.		O.9.a.	"	8 " "	Being built by Army.
18.	PERUWELZ	K.28.c.	Small stream	8 " "	
19.		K.25.b.	Canal.	H.T.only.	

3. OWNERSHIP OF CAPTURED STORES.

The following is the basis which has been provisionally established concerning the ownership of captured stores.

A. A question has arisen as to how the property captured from the enemy should be treated.

B. The general principles governing this question are as follows :-

(i) Property captured from the enemy will belong to the Force by which the capture is made.

(ii) An exception is made in the case of property which can be clearly identified as having originally belonged, prior to capture by the enemy to a particular Allied Force. Such property will be treated as belonging to the force to which it belonged prior to capture, subject, in the case of railway stores or material, to the right of user by the Force re-establishing or working the railway line.

(iii) Salved property. This will be credited to or placed at the disposal of the Army to which it belongs, free of any charge for salvage.

C. The general question of salvage of railway material is dealt with by G.R.O., 2321.

D. The principles enumerated in para B will of course, not apply to property of Allied civilians, which, in case of re-capture from the enemy must be treated as still belonging to the civilians in question and must where used, be accounted for by the issue of a requisition note, payment under the requisition note being made by way of hire or purchase. In the case of railway trucks, stores or material the manner of payment will be regulated in accordance with the agreements covering railway arrangements.

4. BATHS.

Baths for officers and other ranks have been established at the coal-mine in GHLIN J.35.b. Sheet 45. Capacity 800 men a day.

Application for use should be made to the Divisional Baths Officer at Train Headquarters.

20-11-18.

Lieut.Colonel,
A.A.&.Q.M.G., 52nd (Lowland) DIVISION.

War Diary November Appendix XIV

SECRET.
HEADQUARTERS, 52nd (LOWLAND) DIVISION.
COPY NO. ......

"A" & "Q" SUMMARY NO. 9.

1. SPECIAL LEAVE.

A large number of applications for special leave are being received in this office. Vacancies for this class of leave are comparatively few.

Brigadiers and O.C., Units will carefully scrutinize all such applications before forwarding them to D.H.Q., so as to ensure that only really urgent cases are put forward.

The number of vacancies are not sufficient to allow all cases, which rest on sentimental grounds only, to be considered. Only when it is obvious that an individual is urgently required at home for business reasons or can do good by going there, should applications for special leave be forwarded.

The reasons for which special leave is granted have been tabulated and the order of priority if fairly obvious. All armies have agreed as to the following being the usual reasons :-

(a) Dangerous illness of parent, wife or child.
(b) Urgent private affairs which necessitate the individuals presence and which do not admit of delay.
(c) Death of parent, wife or child.
(d) Misconduct of wife; other circumstances which make it desirable that the custody of children should be arranged for.
(e) Marriage in case of urgent necessity.

E. F. Moulton-Barrett, Major
for Lieut.Colonel,

23rd November, 1918.   A.A.&.Q.M.G., 52nd (Lowland) DIVISION.

NOTICE.

STEAMER SERVICES TO ISLANDS ON WEST COAST OF SCOTLAND.

A revised time-table has been received and may be consulted on application to this office.

War Diary. November
Appendix XV

SECRET. COPY NO..........

HEADQUARTERS, 52nd (LOWLAND) DIVISION.

"A" & "Q" SUMMARY. NO. 10.

1. All personnel of the Canadian Corps Labour Reinforcement Pool who may be employed in Divisional area, should proceed to the Headquarters, Advanced Canadian Corps Reinforcement Camp, ANZIN.

2. Repatriated P. of W., of all nationalities are to be directed first on the Corps centres, or on the Cavalry Barracks, MONS. If they have passed behind these places they must be directed on to the LYCEE VALENCIENNES.

On no account are they to be allowed beyond those places, and lorry drivers are to be forbidden to take them further.

All traffic control and police personnel should be in possession of these orders and must see that they are carried out.

Notices to this effect must be posted on all main roads.

for Lieut.Colonel,
A.A.&.Q.M.G., 52nd (Lowland) DIVISION.

25-11-18.

War Diary November Appendix XVI

SECRET.   HEADQUARTERS, 52nd (LOWLAND) DIVISION.

"A" & "Q" SUMMARY NO. 11.

1. STAFF COURSES.
   (A) With reference to G.H.Q., letters O.B./1329 of 6/7/18 and O.B./1911/3 of 19/8/18 and 30/9/18.
   At the close of the present probationary and staff courses and in the case of Artillery Staff Learners, preliminary and advanced courses, all courses will be suspended.
   (B) In the case of each staff learner who completes a probationary or preliminary course now current and would have been recommended to go through the staff course, or advanced course, the officer who would have recommended him will sign an entry in his A.B. 439 to the effect that he has completed a probationary or preliminary course and is fit to go through a staff or advanced course.

   (C) By the present probationary and staff courses, and, in the case of Artillery staff learners preliminary and advanced courses is meant.
   (1) The probationary courses which commenced on 8/11/18.
   (2) The staff course which commenced on 15/10/18.
   (3) Similarly any preliminary and advanced Artillery course now running.

   (D) Officers now undergoing probationary and preliminary courses will not take the staff and advanced course afterwards. The instructions contained in para B above will be followed instead.
   AUTHORITY - G.H.Q. OB/1329 dated 20/11/18.

2. BREACHES OF INTERNATIONAL LAW.
   A committee has been constituted by the War Cabinet to enquire into breaches of the laws of war by the enemy.
   Will you kindly forward as early as possible to this office, for transmission to this committee any correspondence or other particulars relating to such breaches committed by the enemy against British Subjects which may have come into your possession through any branch of your staff. Reports should be forwarded as early as possible.
   AUTHORITY - First Army 9640.A. dated 21/11/18.

3. TRANSFER TO MACHINE GUN CORPS.
   Instructions have been received from the War Office that no more officers are to be transferred or seconded to the Machine Gun Corps for the present.
   Further applications will not, therefore, be forwarded.
   AUTHORITY - First Army 2224/292.A. dated 21/11/18.

4. EXCHANGE OF N.C.O's.
   The sending home of selected N.C.O's from Infantry Battalions to assist in the training of recruits is cancelled.
   AUTHORITY - War Office letter 121/FRANCE/2249 (A.G.2.A.) dated 25/11/18.

5. CASUALTY REPORTS.
   All casualties caused by enemy mines or by the explosion of enemy ammunition dumps will be reported in the daily wires as "British Cas "Battle Casualties" and not as "Injuries"
   Nil casualty reports will not be rendered in future.
   AUTHORITY - First Army 1115/887 dated 22/11/18.

P.T.O.

6. BILLETING AND REQUISITIONS IN RECONQUERED TERRITORY IN FRANCE AND BELGIUM.

As there seems to be some uncertainty as to the procedure to be adopted, the following notes are given for information :-

Billeting

BILLETING. Where the usual accommodation and facilities are obtainable, billeting areas rates applicable in the country are payable, and the usual billeting certificates must be issued - even where the inhabitant is absent.

Where there is no Maire or Municipal Authority available, the billeting certificates and distribution lists (both original and duplicate) will be completed and forwarded to the Central Requisition Office, Base, with a note to that effect.

Where the name of the owner of the house is not available, the street or billet number should be given for purposes of identification.

Wherever possible preference should be given to billetting in public buildings, such as in barracks, schools Etc. In these cases no billeting certificates will be issued without first communicating with the Central Requisition Office.

MESSES.

It is notified for guidance that the normal French rates payable for messes is Frs 1.00 for the mess room and 50 cts for kitchen.

Payment for messes is not a public expense and must be made in accordance with G.R.O. 2000.

CROPS.

According to article 555 of the French Code Civil, crops, such as beet, left in the ground are the property of the owner of ground, and, if taken, should be purchased or requisitioned in the usual way. When the owners name is not known, exact map or other references and particulars should be given on the requisition note.

SUPPLIES.

When requisitioning or purchasing supplies, careful investigation should be first made as to the ownership. Should it be discovered that the supplies were the property of the enemy, no payment need be made, but, in the case of civilian ownership the usual rules as to purchasing and requisitioning will apply.

26-11-18.

for

Lieut. Colonel,
A.A.&.Q.M.G., 52nd (Lowland) DIVISION.

War Diary November Appendix XVII

SECRET.   HEADQUARTERS, 52nd (LOWLAND) DIVISION.   COPY NO......

"A". & "Q" SUMMARY NO. 12.

1. **BRIDGES.**
   Reference "A"&"Q" Summary No. 8, the following additions and amendments to list of bridges are made.

No.	Location.	Map Ref.	River or Canal.	Safe load.	Remarks.
4a.	HERGNIES.		JARD.	17 tons axle	Completed
11a.	STAMBRUGES	H.1.d.44.	ATH-BLATON.	17 " "	Completed
16.		O.9.a.	MONS-CONDE.	5 " "	Completed
16a.		O.9.a.	-do-	8 " "	Held up for material.
16b.		O.9.d.	CARAMAN.	8 " "	Completed
18.	PERUWELZ	F.28.c.	Small Stream	12 " "	Correction from 8 ton axle.
12.	GRANDGLISE	G.12.a.9.7	ATH-BLATON.	17 " "	Completed.

Safe load for No. 10 Bridge should read 6 ton axle
"   "   " No. 17 "   "   " 8 "   "

2. **MOVES.**
   No. 4. Ordnance Workshop (Light) to QUIEVRAIN on 25th instant.

3. **RETENTION OF UNDERAGE MEN.**
   Underage men may be retained by units during present situation. (A.Gs C.R.5544/25378/A dated 18-11-18. First Army No. 1305/127A dated 21-11-18.

4. **MILITARY BANDS.**
   It has been arranged that as many bands as possible which are now in ENGLAND shall join their units.
   Application has already been made to the War Office for bands of Units in the 52nd Division, and you will be informed as to date of arrival in due course.
   (Authority G.H.Q., A.G./493/PS dated 22-11-18).

27-11-18.

E. L. Mullin. Barrett Kain
for Lieut.Colonel,
A.A.&.Q.M.G., 52nd (Lowland) DIVISION.

War Diary November
Appendix XVIII

SECRET.   HEADQUARTERS, 52nd (LOWLAND) DIVISION.

COPY NO........

"A" & "Q" SUMMARY NO. 13.

1. **RAILHEAD** - VALENCIENNES, from 30th instant.

2. **LOCATIONS.**
   XXIInd Corps Anti-Gas Store is situated at No 5 Rue de la Terre de Prince - MONS.

3. **SOAP.**
   Owing to the present difficulties in obtaining soap Etc., the utmost care should be exercised in its use.

4. **6 MONTHS TOUR OF DUTY IN U.K.**
   No more applications for 6 months tour of duty under M.S., No 28252 for Seconds-in-Command and Junior Officers should be submitted. Further Communications will follow regarding Commanding Officers. (Authority XXIInd Corps A224 dated 27-11-18).

C.F. Moulton-Barrett. Major.
for Lieut.Colonel,
A.A.&.Q.M.G., 52nd (Lowland) DIVISION.

29-11-18.

Army Form C. 2118.

WAR DIARY
or
INTELLIGENCE SUMMARY.
(Erase heading not required.)

CONFIDENTIAL.

52ND (LOWLAND) DIVISION.

"A" & "Q" BRANCH.

FOR

DECEMBER 1918.

Volume XLIII

52nd (Lowland) DIVISION WAR DIARY   DECEMBER 1918   Army Form C. 2118.

or

"A" and "Q" INTELLIGENCE SUMMARY.   VOL. XLIII

Place	Date	Hour	Summary of Events and Information	Remarks and references to Appendices
Chateau de la Bruyere. NIMY.	1918 Dec.	Ref. Maps- Sheets 38 and 45 - (1:40,000)		
	1		Units informed that Corps Court Martial officer is available every Wednesday until further notice.	
	2		'A' and 'Q' Summary No 14 issued to units	Appendix I
			Main Divisional Salvage Dump opened at I.16.b.6.8 Military Medal awarded to eight other ranks. (D.R.O. 313)	
	3		'A' and 'Q' Summary No 15 issued to units	Appendix II
			Leave Details now detrain at VALENCIENNES, reinforcements at RAISMES. Rate of exchange temporarily fixed between marks and francs at the rate of one mark to seventy centimes	
	4		Military Medal awarded to one other rank. (D.R.O. 317)	
			D.R.O. 318 forbids the indiscriminate firing of Very Lights in view of fires already caused.	
			D.R.O. 321 directs that horses are on no account to be tied to trees.	

WAR DIARY or INTELLIGENCE SUMMARY

Army Form C. 2118.

52nd (Lowland) Division   "A and Q"   **DECEMBER 1918**   Vol. XLIII

Place	Date 1918	Hour	Summary of Events and Information PAGE TWO Ref. Map Sheets 38 + 45 (1/40,000)	Remarks and references to Appendices
Ch. de la Bruyère NIMY	Dec 5		H.M. The King drove through part of area occupied by 52nd Division. Divisional Commander met His Majesty.	
—"—	6		Major General F.J. MARSHALL, CMG, DSO, resumed command of the Division on return from leave in U.K. The following officers were appointed A.D.C. to G.O.C. (D.R.O. 323):- Lieut. R. Maxwell, 8th Royal Scots. 3/11/18 2/Lt. G.W. Cosgrove, Seaford Highlanders 4/12/18	Appx I Appx II
—"—	7		"A and Q" Summary No 16 issued to units	Appendix III
—"—	8		D.R.O. mem No. 325 calls attention to the prevailing disregard of orders regarding dress of troops outside hutting areas, and orders notice boards to be erected at area limits stating "Beyond this point belts will be worn".	Appx III
			Administrative Instruction No A.F.52 ref Demobilization of Civilians re giving details of Concentration Camp to be established at VALENCIENNES.	Appendix IV
—"—	9		"A and Q" Summary No 17 issued to all units.	Appendix V

Army Form C. 2118.

52nd (Lowland) DIVISION WAR DIARY or "A" and "Q" INTELLIGENCE SUMMARY.

DECEMBER, 1918. VOL. XLIII

Instructions regarding War Diaries and Intelligence Summaries are contained in F. S. Regs., Part II. and the Staff Manual respectively. Title pages will be prepared in manuscript.

(Erase heading not required.)

Place	Date	Hour	Summary of Events and Information	Remarks and references to Appendices
Chateau Bruges NIMY	9		Area Commandants and Town Majors appointed within Divisional area (see A&Q Summary No "17")	
"	11		Units warned re maintenance of communications between formations on line of future march.	
"	12		Reports called for from all units regarding circumstances under which officers and other ranks have become missing and are enquiry has been held without a report having been forwarded up to now.	
"	13		Attention called to GRO 3596 reference return of empty supply sacks re. Every 2/1851 is to be made to ensure return of at least 70% (DRO 321)	
"	13		"A" and "Q" Summary No 18 issued to units	(Appendix VII)
"	14		Commencing today four leave trains for British soldiers daily will run from ETAPLES - CALAIS and BOULOGNE.	
"	15		Bulkhead changed to MONS up till today and Railhead	

52nd (Low) Div A+Q   Dec 1918

WAR DIARY
or
INTELLIGENCE SUMMARY.
(Erase heading not required.)

Army Form C. 2118.

Place	Date	Hour	Summary of Events and Information	Remarks and references to Appendices
Army	16		A+Q Summary No 19 issued	App to VII
	17			
	18		A+Q Summary No 20 issued	App to VIII
	19		Leave allotment to come into operation 22 received. Slight increase in officer + decrease in O.R. vacancies	
	20		Advice received of the award of 12 military medals to men of the division	
	21			
	22		Copy of Demob. Circ. No 3 received. A+Q Summary No 21 issued	
	23		Procedure to be adopted by men on leave + men proceeding on leave, advised by wire	App to IX
	24		Demob. Circ. No 4 received.	

Army Form C. 2118.

WAR DIARY
or
INTELLIGENCE SUMMARY.

S.2 (Inf) Divn   Dec 1918   Vol XLIII   App A

Instructions regarding War Diaries and Intelligence Summaries are contained in F. S. Regs., Part II. and the Staff Manual respectively. Title pages will be prepared in manuscript.

(Erase heading not required.)

Place	Date	Hour	Summary of Events and Information	Remarks and references to Appendices
MURY	26		At Q. Summary h.022 issued	App X
	29		A.F.Z. 508 furnished. The two men originally ordered not to be definitely any more adopted — philosophy meantime to ascent from philosophy in an irregular manner. Summer fully completely formed and the regiment to men content intently — meanwhile so noting intently —	
	31			

Army Form C. 2118.

52nd (Lowland) Division.

WAR DIARY December, 1918.
or
INTELLIGENCE SUMMARY. Volume XLIII.

(Erase heading not required.)

Instructions regarding War Diaries and Intelligence Summaries are contained in F. S. Regs. Part II. "A" & "Q". and the Staff Manual respectively. Title pages will be prepared in manuscript.

Place	Date	Hour	Summary of Events and Information	Remarks and references to Appendices

			STRENGTH OF DIVISION.
			 ********************
			 (Week-ending 28/12/18.)
			
			          Offrs. Other Ranks.
			 Divnl. Troops. 17 124
			 Divnl. Artillery. 89 2106
			 Divnl. Engineers. 36 924
			 155th Inf. Bde. 143 2310
			 156th Inf. Bde. 130 2541
			 157th Inf. Bde. 145 2565
			 17th N.Fus.(P). 40 855
			 52nd Bn. M.G.C. 48 889
			 Divnl. Train. 20 363
			 984 Div. Employ. Coy. 2 326
			 Royal Army Med. Corps. 21 648
			           ═════ ═════
			 Grand Total. 691 13,651
			
			 Infantry Brigades - Reinforcements.
			 ***********************************
			 Received for Month of December.
			
			  Week-ending. Offrs. Other Ranks.
			
			  7th Decr. 22 440
			  14th Decr. 7 75
			  21st Decr. 1 31
			  28th Decr. - 44
			        ═════ ═════
			        30 590
			
			 Infantry Brigades.- Sick to Fd. Ambces.
			 **************************************
			 during month of December.
			
			  Week-ending. Offrs. Other Ranks.
			
			  7th Decr. - 99
			  14th Decr. 3 102
			  21st Decr. 3 106
			  28th Decr. 2 56
			        ═════ ═════
			        8 363	

52nd (Lowland) Division.

Strength Return made up to 12 noon Saturday, 28th December, 1918.

UNIT.	(i) Strength for Previous wk. in accord. with AG's Instr.		(ii) Increase during wk. Drafts. etc. taken on strength of unit.		(iii) Totals fr: (i) & (ii)		(iv) Decrease during Cas. etc.deducted fr.str. of unit.		"A" Strength excl uding attd.		"B" Not present with unit & not at disposal of C.O. incl. in col.A.		"A"minus"B" Available fr. strength incl. personnel of Bn Transport. & Q.M.Stores.		Remarks.
&&&&	O.	O.R.	O.	O.R.	O.	O.R.	O.	O.R.	O.	O.R.	O.	O.R.	O.	O.R.	
155th Inf. Bde.															
1/4th R.S.Fus.	39	749	—	19	39	768	—	10	39	758	9	88	30	670	
1/5th R.S.Fus.	50	734?	—	4	50	738	—	12	50	726	12	104	38	622	
1/4th K.O.S.B.	40	727	—	29	40	756	1	5	39	751	8	80	31	671	
	129	2210	—	52	129	2262	1	27	128	2235	29	272	99	1963	
156th Inf. Bde.															
1/4th R. Scots.	42	845	—	10	42	855	—	8	42	847	8	59	34	788	
1/7th R. Scots.	41	843	—	8	41	851	—	8	41	843	14	81	27	762	
1/7th Sco. Rif.	37	794	—	15	37	809	1	27	36	782	12	82	24	700	
	120	2482	—	33	120	2515	1	43	119	2472	34	222	85	2250	
157th Inf. Bde.															
1/5th H.L.I.	40	842	—	18	40	860	1	4	39	856	5	88	34	768	
1/6th H.L.I.	43) 851		—	22	43	873	2	15	41	858	12	75	29	783	
1/7th H.L.I.	49	817	—	28	49	845	—	3	49	840	12	60	37	780	
	132	2510	—	66	132	2576	3	22	129	2554	29	223	100	2331	
17th N.Fus.(P).	40	858	—	2	40	860	1	6	39	854	14	88	25	766	
Grand Total.	421.	8060	—	153	421	8213	6	98	415	8113	106	805	309	7310	
52nd Bn. M.G.C.	46	879	1	15	47	894	—	10	47	884	7	56	40	828	

52nd (Lowland) Division.

Abstract Column "B" ---- Week-ending 28/12/18.

UNIT.	Courses. O.	Courses. O.R.	Sick. O.	Sick. O.R.	Leave. O.	Leave. O.R.	Bde. Employ. O.	Bde. Employ. O.R.	Div. Employ. O.	Div. Employ. O.R.	Extra Regtl. Employ. O.	Extra Regtl. Employ. O.R.	Total. O.	Total. O.R.
155th Inf. Bde.														
1/4th R.S.Fus.	-	21	2	8	4	21	-	17	3	15	-	6	9	88
1/5th R.S.Fus.	2	31	2	11	5	38	1	16	1	4	1	4	12	104
1/4th K.O.S.B.	1	26	1	6	2	16	2	15	2	12	1	5	8	80
	3	78	5	25	11	75	3	48	6	31	1	15	29	272
156th Inf. Bde.														
1/4th R. Scots.	2	9	1	4	3	21	-	8	2	9	-	8	8	59
1/7th R. Scots.	2	13	1	6	5	24	1	11	5"	20	-	7	14	81
1/7th Sco. Rif.	2	12	1	20	4	31	3	8 "	1	5	1	6	12	82
	6	34	3	30	12	76	4	27	8	34	1	21	34	222
157th Inf. Bde.														
1/5th H.L.I.	-	15	1	12	3	31	1	6	-	13	2	11	5	88
1/6th H.L.I.	4	11	1	12	3	21	1	9	2	10	1	12	12	75
1/7th H.L.I.	2	6	-	-	5	28	-	12	4	9	1	5	12	60
	6	32	1	24	11	80	1	27	6	32	4	28	29	223
Grand Total.	15	144	9	79	34	231	8	102	20	97	6	64	92	717

War Diary December Appendix I

SECRET. COPY NO. ......

HEADQUARTERS, 52nd (LOWLAND) DIVISION.

"A" & "Q" SUMMARY, NO. 14.

1. CAPTURED MATERIAL.
   Any captured guns, machine guns etc., still in possession should be forwarded to D.A.D.O.S., at once for evacuation to the Base. (Authority XXll Corps Q32/2/317 dated 28.11.18.

2. LOCATIONS.
   No. 8 Sanitary Section - MONS.
   Ordnance Officer, Corps Troops - 270 Rue de Conde, ANZIN.
   Main Divisional Salvage Dump - I.16.b.6.8.

3. CHEQUES.
   In future all cheques for the 52nd Divisional Canteen should be made payable to "G.O.C., a/c 52nd Division".

4. ARMS IN POSSESSION OF INHABITANTS.
   Instructions have been issued to the Belgian Mission by XXll Corps Headquarters to collect all arms etc., in the possession of inhabitants. These will be collected by the local gendarmes and must be taken over by the nearest British Unit on application.

5. ENTERTAINMENTS.
   (a) The programme for the "Thistletops" and the "Divisional Military Band" will be as follows :- (Both days inclusive).

Date.	"Thistletops"	Divisional Military Band.
December 5th - 9th	156th Bde.	157th Bde.
" 10th - 14th.	R.A.	155th Bde.
" 15th - 19th.	157th Bde.	156th Bde.
" 20th - 24th.	155th Bde.	R.A.

   (b) The formation to which the "Thistletops" (26 all ranks) and band (38 all ranks) are attached will ration them from the day after arrival to the day of departure inclusive.
   (c) The "Thistletops" will move by its own transport, the formation to which the Band is going will arrange the necessary transport (1 G.S. Wagon).

2-12-18.

Lieut Colonel,
A.A.&Q.M.G., 52nd (Lowland) DIVISION.

December War Diary Appendix II

SECRET.   COPY NO..........

HEADQUARTERS, 52nd (LOWLAND) DIVISION.

"A" & "Q" SUMMARY No. 15.

1. SANITATION.
    As the newly captured areas have been left by the enemy in a grossly insanitary condition, it is very necessary that all troops should do everything in their power to improve the surroundings of any area occupied by them.

    (a) Manure should be burned as far as possible; if in large quantities it is to be close packed.

    (b) Masses of kitchen refuse, rubbish, etc., should be similarly treated in improvised incinerators and not added to as is being done in many cases.

    (c) In some areas dead horses and dead Germans have been left unburied. Units occupying areas should tell off parties to bury all dead bodies. Horses being first eviscerated, or the stomach opened up, before burial.

    (d) In many places open pit latrines have been left by the enemy. These should be filled in and beaten down with spades. Civilian latrines should not be used.

    (e) Where pail latrines are found, the contents should be burned in an incinerator or buried in a spot chosen by the Medical Officer.

    (f) It is important that the large number of flies found in kitchens, billets, etc., should be killed. This is best done by spraying the flies with 5 per cent solution of cresol, or by vaporizing equal parts of cresol and water in a room, by boiling it over a Primus Stove.

    (g) It is very important that the area round walls, for 100 feet or more, should be freed from manure, refuse, etc., and that no filth should be buried near them.

    (h) Only water drawn from authorised sources should be used for drinking.

2. RESTAURANT - RESERVED FOR OFFICERS.
    The restaurant RAY, Rue des Clercs, MONS, is reserved for Officers only.

3. DETRAINING STATIONS.
    Leave details detrain at VALENCIENNES
    Reinforcements detrain at RAISMES.

4. LORRIES.
    At present lorries for taking parties on tours for educational purposes are not available, but shortly it is hoped the situation will improve. Units will then be informed of the number of lorries at their disposal and when they will be available.

                                                              P.T.O.

5. CORPS TROOPS AREA.
   A. The Corps Troops Area has been divided into subareas as shown below :-

AREA.	AREA COMMANDANT.	LOCATION.
MONS TOWN.	Major J.B. Whitmore, Town Major, Capt.J.Reid, Asst Town Major,	4 Grand Place, MONS.
GHLIN.	Lieut. A. Mather, 1/5th H.L.I.	GHLIN.
OBOURG.	2/Lieut.H.J.Piper,1/6th H.L.I.	OBOURG.

   B. Town Majors and Area Commandants of Corps areas are under the direct orders of the Corps.
   They are the Corps Representatives on the spot and all troops in their areas will accept without reserve any orders they may receive from them as to the distribution of units into billets and horse standings, arrangements for water supply and disposal and treatment of government property.

   C. With the exception of individual officers and small parties requiring temporary accommodation Town Majors and Area Commandants will billet no troops in their areas without sanction from Corps "Q".

6. RATE OF EXCHANGE.
   The rate of exchange which has been temporarily fixed by Allied Headquarters between marks and French francs is one mark equals seventy centimes. This rate has been temporarily sanctioned for British Armies.
   It is understood that the Belgian Government is buying marks at a higher rate in order to assist the Belgian civilians, therefore for any contracts made in BELGIUM it must be arranged for payment in French francs not in marks.

E.F.Knblin-Darnell Kain
Lieut-Colonel,
A.A.&.Q.M.G., 52nd (Lowland) DIVISION,

3-12-18.

December War Diary
Appendix III

SECRET.   COPY NO _____

HEADQUARTERS, 52nd (LOWLAND) DIVISION.

"A" & "Q" SUMMARY NO 16.

1. LOCATIONS.
  Corps Main Salvage Dump is situated at ANZIN Railhead.

2. GERMAN OFFICERS OR MEN FOUND WOUNDED OR SICK.
  Any German Officers or men found wounded or sick in the RHINISH Provinces in an unmoveable condition will not be considered as prisoners of war. They will be evacuated Eastwards to Germany as soon as their state of health permits.

3. LEAVE TRAIN SERVICE.
  The following timings will be in force until further notice:-

VIA CALAIS.

DOWN (C.X.)		Hours.	UP (Y.C.)	
VALENCIENNES	dep.	0532	CALAIS	dep. 0720
Raismes		0604	BETHUNE	arr. 1049
DOUAI	arr.	0740	BETHUNE	dep. 1129
DOUAI	dep.	0840	LIGNY	arr. 1330
ARRAS	arr.	1048	LIGNY	dep. 1334
ARRAS	dep.	1103	Aubigny	1415
Aubigny		1200	ARRAS	arr. 1510
LIGNY	arr.	1230	ARRAS	dep. 1525
LIGNY	dep.	1234	DOUAI	arr. 1730
BETHUNE	arr.	1414	DOUAI	dep. 1830
BETHUNE	dep.	1439	Raismes	arr. 2017
St Omer		1653	VALENCIENNES	arr. 2049.
CALAIS	arr.	1758		

VIA BOULOGNE.

DOWN (D.Y.)			UP (Y.D.)	
VALENCIENNES	dep	0334	BOULOGNE	dep. 0908
Raismes		0406	ST POL	arr. 1310
DOUAI	arr	0542	ST POL	dep. 1332
DOUAI	dep	0642	ARRAS	arr. 1522
ARRAS	arr	0850	Arras	dep. 1545
ARRAS	dep.	0910	DOUAI	arr. 1751
ST POL	arr	1046	DOUAI	dep. 1851
St POL	dep	1112	Raismes	arr. 2038
ETAPLES	arr	1327	VALENCIENNES	arr. 2110
ETAPLES	dep	1343		
BOULOGNE	arr	1442		

4. BISCUIT TINS.
  All biscuit tins should be saved as they are required for use as "guides" in the construction of latrines.

5./

£ 5. SUPPLIES.

Attention is drawn to the fact that units are constantly submitting A.Fs.W. 3334 for very small portions of the component parts of rations.

This practice is unnecessary and should cease.

With proper care and supervision, it is possible to make up any small deficiencies out of the ordinary daily issue.

Attention is also called to the fact that the representative of a unit drawing supplies is at liberty to make a complaint on the dump to his Supply Officer who will investigate the matter at once.

After supplies have been drawn, the responsibility lies with the unit for the condition of the rations and complaints cannot be received by Supply Officers.

6. IRON RATIONS.

A.Fs.W. 3334 are still being received for Iron Rations. Now that active operations have ceased, there should be no occasion for these rations to become unfit for consumption, and greater care must be exercised in looking after them, losses being charged against individuals concerned, where necessary.

7. RE-PURCHASE OF HORSES.

The following letter received from First Army is published for information:-

"Information has been received by the D.D.R., First Army, "that the War Office have been asked to state a policy in regard "to the following:-
" (a) Officers who sold their horses to the State, and wish to
"   re-purchase them.
" (b) Officers who have been riding horses the property of the
"   Government and who have become attached to them and wish to
"   purchase them.
" (c) Civilians whose horses were requisitioned on mobilization
"   and who can identify them and wish to recover them.
" (d) Officers and civilians who cannot identify horses taken
"   from them on mobilization but consider themselves entitled
"   to select Government horses in replacement at the original
"   price.
" (e) Other ranks coming under any headings (a), (b), (c), or (d).
"   A reply is awaited, and while sympathetic consideration "is anticipated, it is believed that the actual decision rests "with the Treasury.
"   You will be informed, and definite instructions will "be issued, as soon as possible.

8./

3.

3. VISITS TO WAR GRAVES IN FRANCE.

The following is a copy of a War Office Communique sent to the "Times" Newspaper, which outlines the policy at present in vogue as regards visits to graves:-

"WAR GRAVES IN FRANCE"

"Visits postponed at present"

"The Secretary of the War Office wishes to inform relatives "of fallen Officers and men that, owing to the very large "number of enquiries regarding the possibility of visiting "graves and Cemeteries in France and abroad, now being addressed "to him or the Director General of Graves Registration and "Enquiries, he very much regrets that it is not possible to "reply individually.

"He wishes to make it known generally, to prevent dis":appointment, that at present and probably for some months to "come, it will be impossible, owing to military reasons, to "make arrangements by which these visits could be permitted. "It is desirable that any applications on this subject, or as to "the location of individual graves, should be made in writing"

7th December 1918.

E. L. Mullin-Barrett, Major
for
Lieut. Colonel,
A.A. & Q.M.G., 52nd (LOWLAND) DIVISION.

December War Diary
Appendix IV

VERY URGENT.   Copy No.....

52nd (Lowland) DIVISION.

ADMINISTRATIVE INSTRUCTIONS NO. A.F. 52.

8th December, 1918.

Collection, Accommodation and Despatch of Demobilizers,
Pivotal Men and Coal-Miners.

This is to be read in conjunction with Demobilization Circular Memoranda 1 and 2.

1. A Concentration Camp for the XXII Corps will be formed at the LYCEE, VALENCIENNES and will be ready for occupation by noon, on the 14th instant.

2. The Staff organized as that of a Battalion will be detailed by Divisions. The proportion to be found from units of 52nd Division is shown in Appendix "A".

3. In the interests of all, the Divisional Commander wishes Brigades etc., to choose the best officers and other ranks for the Staff of the Camp. It should be thoroughly understood that this will in no way affect the demobilization of any individual officer or man.

4. Nominal rolls of officers and other ranks detailed will be sent to this Office by noon, December 11th.
   The date on which these individuals will join the Camp, and the arrangements for getting them there will be notified later.
   Any alterations in the names after the 11th instant and before the party join the Camp, will be wired to Divisional H.Q.

5. Commencing on a date to be notified later (probably December 14th), Coalminers and, if their despatch has been ordered by the War Office, pivotal men and demobilizers, will be collected into the Corps Concentration Camp, where they will be retained one night. On the following day they will be despatched to an Embarkation Camp.

6. Allotments will be made by the Division and through the chain of command to units as laid down in para. 8 of Demobilization Circular Memorandum No. 2.

7. Transport will be arranged by the Corps.

8. Conducting Officers on a scale of 2 officers to 100 Coalminers, will accompany drafts and will be drawn as far as possible from units from which the drafts come, and from those officers who have been longest in the country without leave to England.
   Their duties, in detail, are laid down in Appendix "B".

9. These officers will if they so desire, be granted 14 days' leave from the Disposal Station, and will rejoin their units by the normal leave route. This will be in addition to the leave allotments now in force by the normal routes.

P.T.O.

(2)

10. Duty Orders as in Appendix "D" will be given to Conducting Officers by their Unit Commanders, the name of the Dispersal Station being left blank to be filled in by the Embarkation Camp Commandant. Leave Warrants will be issued at Dispersal Stations.

11. Any Officers, Warrant Officers or Non-Commissioned Officers travelling as Demobilizers or Pivotal men may be attached for duty to Dispersal Drafts of Coalminers which are destined for the same Dispersal Station as themselves.

12. Each man will be disinfected and bathed before leaving his unit and will be provided with the certificate laid down under G.R.O. No. 3324 for men proceeding on leave.

13. The Concentration Camp Commandant will see that all men on arrival at, and departure from, the Camp are provided with a hot meal. Each man on departure will be supplied by the Camp with one complete day's train ration.
    Only the current days' ration will be taken to the Corps Concentration Camp.

14. The scale of clothing and equipment to be taken will be as laid down in Demobilization Circular Memorandum No. 1, para. XI.

15. Every soldier passing through the Camp will be in possession of his blankets as laid down in Demobilization Circular Memorandum No. 1.

16. ACKNOWLEDGE.

                           Lieut. Colonel.
A.A. & Q.M.G., 52nd (Lowland) DIVISION.

Issued at 1200

Copy No.				
1	G.O.C.	15	Camp Commandant.
2	"G"	16	Div. Emp. Coy.
3	155th Inf. Bde.	17	D.G.O.
4	156th Inf. Bde.	18	Div. Reception Camp.
5	157th Inf. Bde.	19	XXII Corps "A"
6	C.R.A.	20)	
7	C.R.E.	21)	War Diary.
8	Div. Signal Coy.	22	File.
9	17th N. Fus. (P)		
10	52nd Bn M.G.C.		
11	A.D.M.S.		
12	D.A.D.V.S.		
13	D.A.P.M.		
14	D.A.D.O.S.		

APPENDIX "A".

Detail of personnel for staff of Corps
Concentration Camp to be found by units of 52nd Division:-

From
155th Inf. Brigade.
1 Subaltern.
1 Orderly Room Staff Sgt.
1 Orderly Room Clerk.
1 Duty Sergeant.
2 privates for guard.
1 sanitary man.
1 water duty man.
1 batman.
1 men's dining hall.
1 men's cook.
3 men for general duties.
1 cyclist orderly with bicycle.

From.
156th Inf. Brigade.
1 Captain (to command a Coy)
1 Officer's mess Sergeant.
1 Sanitary Corporal.
1 Shoemaker Corporal.
1 private for guard.
1 sanitary man.
1 incinerator man.
2 batmen.
1 men's dining hall.
1 men's cook.
3 men for general duties.

From
157th Inf. Brigade.
1 Coy. Sergeant Major.
1 Sergeant for guard.
1 Sgt. for general duties.
2 orderly room clerks.
1 private for guard.
1 private for canteen or recreation room.
1 Officer's mess duty.
1 Sgt's mess cook.
1 men's cook.
4 men for general duties.
1 batman.

From
Pioneer Battalion.

1 Adjutant.
1 Coy. Q.M.S.
2 duty sergeants.
1 policeman.
1 carpenter or pioneer.

Appendix I.

DUTY ORDER

Rank.   Initials and Name   Unit.

1. You will proceed on the ....inst., to the Concentration Camp at ....(to be inserted by the O.C. Unit) for conducting duty with the men returning to the U.K. as Coalminers, Demobilizers, or Pivotal men, under the terms of G.H.Q. Circular Memorandum Nos. 1 and 2.

2. You will then under orders of the O.C. Concentration Camp, proceed with a party of men to the Special Embarkation Camp at ....(to be inserted by O.C. Unit) where you will immediately report to the Camp Commandant or his representative.

3. The latter will here allot you to the command of or for duty with a Dispersal Draft proceeding to .... Dispersal Station (to be inserted by O.C. Embarkation Camp).

4. On arrival at ....Dispersal Station (to be inserted by O.C. Embarkation Camp) you will report to the Dispersal Commandant.
   On completion of your duty you will be granted 14 days leave to your home and be given by the Dispersal Commandant
   (a) A Warrant to your home station.
   (b) A Warrant from your home station to ....
       (The name of the Port in England through which the officer would return if proceeding on ordinary leave will be inserted by the O.C. Unit).
   The Dispersal Commandant will stamp this order with the date on which you leave the Dispersal Station.

5. On completion of your leave, i.e. on the 14th day after the date stamped on this order by the Dispersal Commandant, you will embark on the return journey and proceed at once to your Unit in the Field.

6. This Duty Order will be retained on your person throughout your journey and on return will be handed over to the O.C. your Unit. It constitutes the sole authority for all stages of your journey excepting that to and from your destination on leave as covered by the warrant referred to in para. 4.

7. For further instructions as to your duty as a Conducting Officer see overleaf.

P.T.O.

DUTIES OF A CONDUCTING OFFICER.

1. You are responsible for and will maintain strict discipline amongst all men places under your command for each stage of the journey.

2. On arrival at the Concentration Camp you will report to the Camp Commandant. You will make out for your own use a nominal roll of all men allotted to your command for the journey to the Embarkation Camp. This will be entirely distinct from the roll on A.F. Z.9.
   You will detail definite N.C.Os. for duty within your party, acting N.C.Os. will be made if necessary.
   You will ascertain the time and place of parade for the next day's journey, and communicate it to all concerned.

3. On arrival at the Embarkation Camp you will report to the Camp Commandant; parties will then be recast into Dispersal Drafts.
   If you are appointed to the Command of a Dispersal Draft, you will take the following action:-
   (a) Under orders issued by the Camp Commandant, the following documents will be withdrawn from the men of your draft and handed into your custody:-
       (I) The original copy of the Dispersal Certificate (A.F. Z.10).
       (II) All three copies of the nominal rolls (A.F. Z.9.)
   (b) You will check these documents with the men of your party on parade, and report any discrepancies immediately to the Camp Commandant.
       You will then sort the documents as follows into envelopes which will be provided by the Camp Commandant:-
       Envelope 1: The Dispersal Certificates (A.F. Z.10).
       Envelope 2: Two copies of all the nominal rolls (A.F. Z.9).
       Envelope 3: The remaining copy of the Nominal Rolls (A.F. Z.9).
   (c) You will dispose of these documents as follows:-
       (1) Envelopes 1 and 3 will be handed over to the Commandant of the Dispersal Station in the U.K.
       (11) Envelope 2 will be handed over to the Embarkation Staff when your party embarks.

4. You will instruct all men of your party that the loss en route of any demobilization documents or of any article of their arms or equipment must be reported to you at once, and that it is absolutely to their/advantage to do so.
own

December War Diary
Appendix V

SECRET.
COPY NO. ......

HEADQUARTERS, 52nd (LOWLAND) DIVISION.

"A" & "Q" SUMMARY NO. 17.

1. **CANTEEN.**
To minimise congestion of traffic, formations of XXII Corps will draw their allotment from ANICHE on Wednesday, 11th instant.

2. **REPATRIATED PRISONERS OF WAR.**
The following letter received from First Army is published for information and action:-
"Repatriated Prisoners of War of all Nationalities on "arrival at MONS or VALENCIENNES, are to be sent to the Re-":patriation Centres at these places as follows:-
"At MONS   -   To Cavalry Barracks.
"At VALENCIENNES -   All Nationalities except French
                        to the LYCEE.
                     French - To the CASERNE ESPIEES.
"These repatriated Prisoners of War will not be allowed to "circulate in the streets without a ticket number to shew that "they have already reported at one of the Prisoners of War Centres.
"Ticket numbers are being issued to the Staging Camp at "MONS and to the French Mission for French P. of W. at VALENCIENNES.
"The Military Police and Gendarmes have orders to ask Prisoners "of War for these tickets, and if they are not in possession of "them, they are to be at once directed to one of the Prisoners of "War Centres."

3. **AERODROME.**
A portion of the Drill Ground (K.3., 4, 9 and 10) has been reserved as an Aerodrome. This portion is in K.4.a. Men and horsed transport must not cross the aerodrome which has been marked by flags.

4. **AREA COMMANDANTS.**
(I). Area Commandants and Town Majors have been appointed in Divisional Area as follows:-
CAMERON ST VINCENT AREA.
    Lieut. B.T. WILLIAMS, M.C., Chateau Hembise
LENS AREA. Major J.A. SMITH, 7th Scottish Rifles,
    6 Rue d'Herchies, LENS.
JURBISE AREA. Capt. A. LONGMUIR, at B.H.Q., Chateau JURBISE.
    Town Major, JURBISE. Lt. J. McGREGOR, 5th R.S.Fus.
        5th R.S.Fus. H.Q., JURBISE.
    Town Major, ERBAUT, BRUYERE, & RIVAGE.
        2/Lt. A. BAXTER, 4th K.O.S.B.,
        4th K.O.S.B. H.Q., JURBISE.
MASNUY AREA. Lieut. E.W. SMITH, 17th North'd Fus. (P),
    MASNUY ST JEAN.
MAISIERES AREA. 2/Lieut. A.J. PETRIE, 7th H.L.I.,
    98 GRAND RUE MAISIERES.
    Town Major, MAISIERES. 2/Lt. G.M. BERRIE, 7th H.L.I.,
        MAISIERES.
    Town Major, ERBISOEUL. 2/Lt. J.A. MARTIN, 5th H.L.I.,
        ERBISOEUL.
    Town Major, VUVIER ROLAND BRUYERE.
        2/Lt. R. PATERSON, M.C., 6th H.L.I.
        at D.28.b.7.3.

4. AREA COMMANDANTS, Continued.

    CASTEAU AREA.   Capt. G.K. STEWART, M.C.,
                        R.A.H.Q., The Mill, CASTEAU.
    Sub-Area, CASTEAU. Capt. E. BATTERSBY,
                        56 Bde. R.H.A. H.Q., CASTEAU.
    Sub-Area, THIEUSIES. Capt. H.H. WALSHE,
                        9th Bde. R.F.A. H.Q.,
                        THIEUSIES.
    Sub-Area, BRULOTTE. Capt. B.O. ELLIS,
                        D.A.C. H.Q., E.16.c.5.2.

(2).   Area Commandants and Town Majors should have offices specially detailed for their use. These Offices will be clearly marked by Notice Boards etc.
       The Units in whose Areas these Offices are located will provide the labour and material to make the Boards etc.

9th December 1918.

                                     Lieut. Colonel,
A.A. & Q.M.G., 52nd (LOWLAND) DIVISION.

War Diary Decr 1918
app VI

SECRET.   COPY NO. ....

HEADQUARTERS, 52nd (LOWLAND) DIVISION.
"A" & "Q" SUMMARY No. 18.

1. RUM ISSUE.
As far as possible rum for consumption on Wednesdays and Saturdays will be issued on Tuesdays and Fridays.

2. DISUSED AERODROMES.
Disused aerodromes are not to be used without authority from Army. Under no circumstances are the hangers to be used as stables.

3. DISBANDMENT OF YOUNG SOLDIERS' BATTALIONS.
Under authority A.G. 207 (O), dated 24-11-18, Nos 2 and 3 Young Soldiers' Battalions are in course of disbandment.
The personnel comprised in these Battalions (i.e., young soldiers under 19 years of age and "immatures") will be despatched to join Battalions of their own Regiments at present serving in the First, Third, and Fifth Armies. A few young soldiers and "Immatures" now at Bases will be despatched to units in like manner.
A certain percentage of above personnel are classified "B"; in spite of this, however, they will be retained with the Battalions to which they are sent and their training continued; they will not be returned to the Base as being of Category "B".
(Authority D.A.G., O.R. No. 90,000/511.0)

4. DEMOBILIZATION OF COALMINERS.
The following letter received from XXII Corps is published for information:-
"In reply to your wire D.16 of to-day's date, the ruling is that "no regular soldier with colour service to complete may be sent "home under the scheme for the release of Coalminers.
"A man who was a serving soldier at the outbreak of war is not "likely to be eligible for classification in Industrial Group 103, "except under very special circumstances.
"A soldier who had been transferred to the reserve before the "war, and had subsequently been employed as a Coalminer, and who is "now due for re-transfer to the reserve or discharge would be "eligible to be sent home."
(Authority XXII Corps, A.Q. A.4396/29, dated 11-12/18.)

5. CURRENCY. NOTES OF SMALL VALUE.
Various applications having been received regarding the provision of notes of less value than Five Francs, the following reply to a letter addressed to the Quartermaster-General has been received:-
"The scarcity of French silver has been considerable during the "past two years; but as a result of protracted negotiations it is "now hoped that French Government Notes of small value will shortly "be issued and made available."
(Authority First Army No. 9656.A., 9-12-18.)

6. LOCATIONS /

6. LOCATIONS.
```
    22nd Vet. Evac. Station      ...   RAISMES.
    No. 1 C.C.S.         ...     ...   Civil Hospital, MONS.
    No. 4 Can.C.C.S.     ...     ...   Convent des Ursulines, MONS.
    Scottish Church Hut          ...   ERBISOEUL.
    Rent Officer, 22nd Corps Area      District No 4, VALENCIENNES.
    Area Commdt., MASNUY ST JEAN,      Schoolhouse, E.18.d.2.5.
                                                   (Sheet 45)
    Nos. 2, 20 & 62 Ordnance Mobile Workshops  .. Silk Factory,
                                                     OBOURG.
    Railhead           ...         ...   MONS. 15th inst (probably)
```

7. INFORMATION. TIME-TABLE, DOVER-CALAIS, FOLKSTONE-BOULOGNE SERVICE.

Charing X depart.	Folkstone. Arr.	Dep.	B'logne Arrive.	B'logne Depart.	F'stone Arrive.	B'logne Depart	F'stone Arrive.
1200	1300	1415	1600	0930	1115	1430	1615

DOVER-CALAIS SERVICE.

Dover Dep.	Calais. Arr.	Dover. dep.	Calais. arr.	Calais. dep.	Dover. arr.	Calais. dep.	Dover. arr.
1045	1200	1445	1600	0945	1100	1445	1600

N.B. These times are liable to alteration at short notice.

8. XXII CORPS CONCENTRATION CAMP, is being formed at LYCEE, VALENCIENNES, today. Strength - Permanent Staff 13 Offrs. 204 O.R. Normal draft Strength, 16 Offrs. 600 O.Rs. Total 29 Offrs., 804 O.Rs.

13th December 1918.

Lieut. Col.,
A.A. & Q.M.G., 52nd (LOWLAND) DIVISION.

W. Diary Decr 1918
apx VII

COPY NO. 1......

SECRET.

HEADQUARTERS, 52nd (LOWLAND) DIVISION.
"A" & "Q" SUMMARY No. 19.

1. **SPECIAL LEAVE.**
In continuation of "A" & "Q" Summary No. 9, dated 25-11-18, so many applications are being received for Special Leave to settle affairs of deceased relatives, that it is now necessary to ask for the following additional information to accompany all such applications:-
   (a). Details of the affairs to be settled;
   (b). Whether it is essential for the applicant to go home at once.

   In cases where special leave is granted to a man for a marriage of necessity, the man on return must produce a certificate that the marriage has been performed.

2. **LOCATIONS.**
Div. Reception Camp ...	ECOLE ATHENEE, MONS.
Div. Baths Officer ...	do.
D.A.D.O.S. ...	Divisional H.Q., K.19.b.

   No. 1 Advanced Depot of Medical Stores, now administered by D.D.M.S., XXII Corps..... MONS.

   Canteens
   Divisions and XXII Corps Wholesale Canteen.....ANICHE.
   Stores to be drawn Wednesday 18-12-18.

3. **SUPPLIES.**
Commencing 16th instant, supplies will be drawn at 1000 by First Line Transport from the following Refilling Points:-

CASTEAU. E.30.d.8.2.	Royal Artillery. 52nd Div. Train.
PAVE. J.5.b.9.6.	155th Inf. Brigade. 157th Inf. Brigade. 2nd Low. Field Ambulance. Div. H.Q. Signal Company. C.R.E.
MASNUY ST PIERRE.	156th Inf. Brigade. 410th Field Coy R.E. 412th Field Coy R.E. 413th Field Coy R.E. 1st Low. Field Amb. 3rd Low. Field Amb. 17th North'd Fus. (P). 52nd Battn. M.G.C.

4. **DEMOBILIZATION.** The following is published for information:-
Men are being despatched by units direct to Base Ports for shipment to England with a view to demobilization. Issue orders that will ensure this practice ceasing forthwith. All Officers and men despatched for demobilization must be within allotment originating from Army H.Q. and must pass through Army Concentration Camps.
(Authority XXII Corps Wire, A.537 of 13th December 1918.)

TRAIN SERVICES.

MONS. Commencing 14th inst, train will leave MONS at 2000 hours daily for Railhead connecting with trains for ETAPLES - CALAIS and BOULOGNE.

TRAIN SERVICE FOR DEMOBILISERS etc.

The Code Letters and Time-tables given below of the various trains which will be used daily for conveying demobilisers, Pivotal men and Coalminers from the Concentration Camps at TOURNAI, VALENCIENNES and SOMAIN to the Staging Camps at HONDEGHEM and ST. POL, and from the Staging Camps to the Base Ports:-

Trains may be referred to in telegrams and correspondence by the Code Letters given in the Time-table.

No other men than those for whom the trains are intended may travel by them.

All trains from the Front to the Staging Areas will have a carrying capacity of 1,500, those from the Staging Camps to the Bases 1,200, except HHV, which will carry 1,300.

The trains to the Staging Camps commence on the 12th instant, and those to the Ports on the 13th instant.

Train TH will be a First Army Train, except that accommodation for 600 men entraining at ST. ANDRE will have to be reserved on it daily for Fifth Army men.

TIME TABLE.

Service No. 1. From Army Concentration Camps to Staging Camps: (To commence on 12th December 1918.)

	TH		AH		VL		SL
TOURNAI	Dep. 0900			VALENCIENNES	dep. 0900		
ST ANDRE	arr. 1100			SOMAIN	arr. 1010		
"	dep. 1130		1300	"	dep. 1040		1300
HONDEGHEM for				LIGNY (for			
HAZEBROUCK	arr. 1300		1430	ST POL)	arr. 1420		1640

Service No. 2 from Staging Camps to Base Ports and between Staging Camps, to commence on 13th December 1918.

	SD		SHV		HHV
ST POL	dep. 0900	ST POL	dep. 1000	HAZEBROUCK	dep. 0900
HAZEBROUCK	(arr. 1200			ST POL	arr. 1200
	(dep. 1230			"	dep. 1230
DUNKERQUE	arr. 1340	HAVRE	arr. 2210	HAVRE	arr. 0040

16th December 1918.

A.A. & Q.M.G., 52nd (LOWLAND) DIVISION.   Lieut. Colonel,

W. Diary Dec/18
app VIII

SECRET.   COPY NO. ......

HEADQUARTERS, 52nd (LOWLAND) DIVISION.

"A" & "Q" SUMMARY No. 20.

1. BURIALS.

Graves Registration Unit XIII is functioning in this Corps Area (2/Lieut. P.B. LEES, acting O.C.). The Office is at present at 4 Avenue de Mons, VALENCIENNES.

2. DEMOBILIZATION.

The following ruling has been received from G.H.Q.,
"1. Some applications have been received by Unit Commanders from
"Colliery Managers for the release as Coalminers of soldiers in
"whose A.B. 64 the Industrial Group entry shows them as belonging
"to some other group than Number 3.
"2. As similar cases may possibly arise in future, it is con-
":sidered desirable to lay down the procedure to be followed by
"Unit Commanders in dealing with such applications.
"3. The Unit Commander should inform the soldier that the entry in
"A.B. 64 must be adhered to from the military point of view, and
"should inform the soldier and the Colliery Manager, or other
"employer, that if the latter wishes to obtain the soldier's release
"he must apply to the Ministry of Labour in accordance with the
"conditions of the Ministry of Labour's Circular on Demobilization
"and Resettlement (Release of men serving with the Forces)."
(Authority First Army No. 9630/11.A. 15.12.18.)

3. TRANSPORT.

The following Notice which has been circulated in this area is published for information:-

NOTICE.

"From the 20th December 1918, no civilians will be conveyed in
"British Government vehicles from West to East."

4. LOCATIONS.

Ordnance Officer Corps Troops ...	Rue de Thirimont, MONS.
52nd Div. M.T. Coy., ...	GHLIN.
Workshops, ...	FRESNES.

5. SUPPLIES.

Ref. "A" & "Q" Summary No. 19, dated 16-12-18, para 3., for "PAVE, J.5.b.9.6." read "JURBISE Railway Station"
The following additions should be made:-
(a) to CASTEAU Group ... 1/1st Lowland Mob. Vet. Section.
(b) to JURBISE Railway Station Group, ... D.A.P.M.

6. CANTEEN STORES.

Canteen Stores will be drawn on Friday 20th instant from the Divisional Canteen at K.25.a.2.8., Sheet 45.

18th December 1918.

E.L. Moulton-Barrett Major
for Lieut.-Col.,
A.A. & Q.M.G., 52nd (LOWLAND) DIVISION.

Cancel all previous Time-Tables relating to re-inforcement and personnel Trains. The following timings will be in force until further notice:-

FIRST ARMY SERVICE.

Down (RN 110).			Up. (RN 109).		
Raismes	dep.	2315	Etaples	dep.	1140
Wallers	dep.	2350	Montreuil	"	1211
Somain	arr.	0030	Hesdin	"	1303
Bouchain	dep.	1930	Anvin	arr.	1349
Lourches	"	2045	Anvin	dep.	1353
Somain	arr.	2130	Wavrans	"	1409
Somain	dep.	0155	St Pol.	"	1419
Montigny	"	0255	St Pol.	dep.	1439
Douai	arr.	0325	Ligny	"	1457
Douai	dep.	0430	Tincques	"	1514
Brebieres	"	0500	Savy	"	1526
Vitry	"	0525	Aubigny	"	1535
Biache	"	0550	Mont St Eloi	"	1553
Arras	arr.	0640	Maroeuil	"	1603
Arras	dep.	0652	Dainville	"	1623
Dainville	"	0706	Arras	arr.	1637
Maroeuil	"	0723	Arras	dep.	1647
Mont St Eloi	"	0732	Biache	"	1735
Aubigny	2	0750	Vitry	"	1755
Savy	"	0802	Brebieres	"	1815
Tincques	"	0814	Douai	arr.	1835
Ligny	"	0832	Douai	dep.	2005
St Pol.	arr.	0848	Montigny	"	2050
St Pol.	dep.	0903	Somain	arr.	2118
Anvin	arr.	0925	Somain	dep.	2230
Anvin	dep.	0930	Lourches	"	2315
Auchy Les Hesdin	dep.	1000	Bouchain	arr.	0030
Hesdin	arr.	1008	Somain	dep.	2120
Hesdin	dep.	1010	Wallers	"	2155
Aubin St Vaast	dep.	1023	Raismes	arr.	2255
Montreuil	"	1100			
Etaples	arr.	1120			

Connects at Etaples with R.O.C. 8 for ABBEVILLE, ROMESCAMPS ROUEN and HAVRE, leaving ETAPLES at 1820

These trains are duty trains only, and are not to be used for leave takers.

Connecting train leaves MONS at 2000 hours daily.

W. Diary Decr '18
apt IX

SECRET.   COPY No. .....

HEADQUARTERS, 52nd (LOWLAND) DIVISION.

"A" & "Q" SUMMARY NO. 21.

1. LIGHT RAILWAY SERVICE, NIMY – BRUSSELS.

BRUSSELS	dep. 0750	NIMY	dep.	1320
La Roue	arr. 0810	Casteau		1340
"	dep. 0820	Neufvilles (Station)	arr.	1355
Vloesembeek	0835	" "	dep.	1405
Lennick	0900	" (Village)		1415
Herffelengen	0940	Ardoisier		1430
Enghein	arr. 1005	Noir Jambon		1445
"	dep. 1030	Enghien	arr.	1520
Noir Jambon	1110	"	dep.	1540
Ardoisier	1125	Herffelengen		1605
Neufvilles (Village)	1140	Lennick	arr.	1640
" Station	1150	"	dep.	1650
Casteau	1205	Vloesembeek		1710
NIMY	arr. 1225	La Roue	arr.	1730
		"	dep.	1740
		BRUSSELS	arr.	1800

2. ACCOMMODATION IN BRUSSELS.

A suitable building has been taken in BRUSSELS (Maison TIETZ) by the Y.M.C.A. as a Hostel for N.C.Os and men.
It will open probably next week, and will accommodate 2000 to 3000 O.Rs.
Cinemas, Concerts, and Tours to places of interest in the City will be arranged, and there will be ample facilities for obtaining meals at a moderate price.
The following provisional Tariff has been fixed:-

Bed .... 1 Franc.
Breakfast (with egg). 1 "
Dinner (meat, potatoes &
vegetables) 1.50 frs.
Tea .... 1 Franc.

Arrangements are also being made to open a Hostel under Y.M.C.A. supervision where Officers can obtain accommodation and meals at a moderate cost.
Further details regarding both these places will be published shortly.

3. SUPPLY OF METHYLATED SPIRITS.

The following wire is repeated for information:-
"Supply of methylated spirits at present very limited. AAA
"Stock on hand should be conserved to fullest extent possible AAA
"Please issue instructions for strict economy to be effected"

4. DENTAL APPOINTMENTS.

Officers wishing to make dental appointments should apply to the Dental Surgeon at 1/3rd Lowland Field Ambulance, Rue de l'Athenee, MONS.

5. DIVISIONAL CANTEEN – CHEQUES.

Attention is drawn to "A" & "Q" Summary No. 14, dated 2-12-18.
Under no circumstances should cheques for Divisional Canteen be made payable to any Account except "G.O.C. A/c, 52nd Division".

6. LOCATIONS.

        1/1st Lowland Mob. Vet. Section   K.11.a.9.6. (Sheet 45)
                                         from Monday, 23/12/18.

Ref. "A" & "Q" Summary No. 18, dated 13-12-18, para 6:-
    No. 2 Ordnance Mobile Workshop has been detailed to
    do the work required by 52nd Division.

22nd December 1918.   Lieut. Col.,
                  A.A. & Q.M.G., 52nd (LOWLAND) DIVISION.

SECRET.   COPY NO. ....

HEADQUARTERS, 52nd (LOWLAND) DIVISION.
"A" & "Q" SUMMARY NO. 22.

1. **PURCHASE BY PRIVATE FIRMS ETC OF GOVERNMENT STORES & PROPERTY.**
   The following letter from G.H.Q. is published for information:-
   "1.   It is understood that offers are being received by Directors "and others, both from Allied Civilian and Military Authorities, and "from Private Firms and individuals, for the purchase of Government "Stores and Property.
   "2.   The general lines on which such offers should be dealt with "are as follows:-
   "(a).   A definite offer, in writing, should be obtained from the "purchaser, shewing exactly what he is willing to purchase, the "price, and other conditions.
   "(b).   No definite acceptance should be given without previous "reference to G.H.Q..
   "(c).   Negotiations should be undertaken with a view to getting "an offer which, under the circumstances, is considered a fair one, " and the date and place where delivery is desired should, if "possible, be ascertained.
   "(d).   As soon as a final definite offer has been received, a "copy should be sent to G.H.Q. with your recommendation as to "whether the offer should be accepted or not.
   "   All offers received to date and which fulfil the conditions "contained in para. 2, should be forwarded to this Office (Q.F.2) as "soon as possible, and those received subsequently as soon as possible "after receipt.
   (Authority G.H.Q. No. 20,010/39 (Q.F.2), dated 13th December 1918).

2. **CANTEEN. SUPPLIES OF ORANGES ETC.**
   The following letter from Expeditionary Force Canteens A.S.C., (General Duties Section), First Army Area, is published for information:-
   "   I have received a letter from my H.Qrs in which it is regretted "that, owing to rough weather, the boat containing 10,000 cases of "oranges, and a quantity of figs and walnuts purchased by the E.F.C. "has not been able to put into Port.
   "   In order to help us in our difficulty, the merchant from whom "the goods were purchased has placed at our disposal 1000 cases of "oranges which he had in stock at BORDEAUX. These will be distribut-":ed between the Army Areas at the rate of two truck loads per Area.
   "   I am asked by my H.Qrs to explain to you that everything "possible was done to get our original contract delivered, but that "we were defeated by the elements.
   "   I understand that the oranges, figs and walnuts will be "delivered ultimately."

3. **LOCATIONS.**

   District Officer   Until 1st Jan. 1918.   COURTRAI
                         Afterwards   ...... NAMUR.

   Rent Officer   (Arrondisements of MONS,
                     SOIGNIES, CHARLEROI   MONS.
                     THUIN and ALOST.)

   No. 22 Sanitary Section which has been instructed
       to supervise the 52nd Divisional Area is located
       at No. 53 Rue de Binche, MONS.

4. LEAVE TRAINS.

The BOULOGNE Leave Train arriving at Valenciennes at 2110 hours now proceeds as far as HUY, arriving there at 0730 hours.

On the return journey the timings are as follows:-

```
HUY           ....  dep. 1730 hours
VALENCIENNES   "    0334
RAISMES        "    0406
```

afterwards proceeding as now to BOULOGNE.

This train is essentially a Fourth Army Train. There will be only 80 seats for First Army.

A second BOULOGNE Leave Train will also run principally for the Second Army, but there will be 285 seats for First Army.

Timings as follows:-

BOULOGNE	dep. 0705	MONS	dep. 0900
Anvin	arr. 1131	Valenciennes	" 1050
"	dep. 1303	Douai	arr. 1300
Arras	" 1537	"	dep. 1400
Douai	arr. 1700	Arras	" 1435
"	dep. 1800	Anvin	arr. 1635
Valenciennes	" 2030	"	dep. 1730
MONS	arr. 2300	BOULOGNE	arr. 2045

(First Army No. 145 Q.A. dated 18-12-18)

Officers' seats for this train are allotted by R.T.O. as necessary.

(First Army QA 846, dated 22-12-18)

Owing to congestion and shortage of locomotives, leave trains are liable to considerable delay. It should be pointed out to all concerned that everything possible is being done to improve timings.

5. REST STATION.

A Rest Station for Corps Troops and overflow sick from 52nd and 56th Divisions is being established in MONS.

26th December 1918.

[signature] Major
for Lieut. Col.
A.A. & Q.M.G., 52nd (LOWLAND) DIVISION.

W. Diary Dec 18
a/k XI

SECRET.   COPY NO. ....

HEADQUARTERS, 52nd (LOWLAND) DIVISION.
"A" & "Q" SUMMARY NO. 23.

1. **LADY WORKERS.**
   The following letter from First Army is published for information:-
   " The line up to which lady workers may now be employed by the Y.M.C.A. and similar institutions is extended to the Belgian German Frontier.
   " On no account will lady workers be allowed to enter Germany. This limit will also apply to mixed concert parties."
   (Authority First Army No. 9717.A. 22nd December 1918.)

2. **EQUIPMENT OF MEN FROM YOUNG SOLDIERS' BATTALIONS.**
   The following letter from O.C., No. 3. Young Soldiers' Battalion is published for information:-
   " Arms, kit and equipment of all men have been made up while with this Battalion. Where men are shown to have incomplete kits, the deficiencies have occurred when no further kits could be drawn to replace.
   " S.B.Rs have been re-examined, and, where necessary, re-tested. There have been no proper facilities for delousing since the inception of the Battalion, so there may be cases where men will be found to require delousing.
   " Few instruments for haircutting have been procurable."

3. **SIGNAL ARRANGEMENTS.**
   The following arrangements as to Signal Service are published for information:-
   1. Until further notice, Signal Offices in XXII Corps area will be closed from 2000 hours to 0730 hours daily except for dealing with the following traffic:-
      (i). Priority Telegrams signed by the Senior Staff Officer present of the formation which administers the signal office.
      (ii). Telegrams originating from Signal Offices outside First Army area.
      (iii). Messages for delivery by Special D.R.
   2. Telephone Exchanges will be manned continuously, but calls will not be made between 2000 hours and 0800 hours except for matters of urgent importance.
   3. D.R.L.S. Packets for despatch by the morning run will be handed into Signal Offices before 2000 hours the night before or at 0730 hours on the day of despatch.
   4. Steps will be taken to ensure that the normal working of Signal Offices can be resumed at half an hours notice.
   (Authority XXII Corps No. G. 5246)

4. **RETURN OF EMPTY PETROL TINS.**
   The following letter from G.H.Q. is published for information:-
   " There was a temporary marked improvement in the number of empty petrol tins returned to Bases, but this improvement has not been maintained, and reserves have again fallen dangerously low. an every effort be made to ensure the return of a greater number of empties."
   (Authority G.H.Q., 12003/176 (Q.D.1.), dated 15-12-18)

5. Ref. above. Every effort must be made to return all empty petrol tins.

LOCATIONS.

XXII Corps School will arrive from OFFIN about 7-1-19, and will be located at OBOURG.

30th December 1918.

E.F. North-Barrett Major
                    /for Lieut. Col.
A.A. & Q.M.G., 52nd (LOWLAND) DIVISION.

Army Form C. 2118.

WAR DIARY
or
~~INTELLIGENCE SUMMARY~~

(Erase heading not required.)

CONFIDENTIAL.

52ND. (LOWLAND) DIVISION.

"A" & "Q" BRANCH.

FOR

JANUARY 1919.

VOLUME XLIV.

WAR DIARY
or
INTELLIGENCE SUMMARY.

Army Form C. 2118.

Vol XLIV

A Branch
G (Intelligence) Division

JAN/1919

Place	Date	Hour	Summary of Events and Information	Remarks and references to Appendices
NIMY	1.		Description of Hoerck division to for army 2nd half of men for reinforcements left Divn	Aff I
	3.		Artd Summary Nº 24 issued	
	8.		Artd Summary Nº 25 issued	Aff II
	9.		Artd Summary Nº 26 issued	Aff III
			Admin Crse hours Nº 29. "Special Res" issued	Aff IV
	13.		Artd Summary Nº 27 issued	Aff V
			Lt Col Gurner Stoner and Lt Col Hercules report to IX Corps to take up appointment of ADMI (Humphry) — he then being sent to the same him	Aff VI

Army Form C. 2118.

WAR DIARY
or
INTELLIGENCE SUMMARY.

Vol XLIV
'A' 52 Divn

(Erase heading not required.)

JANY 1919

Place	Date	Hour	Summary of Events and Information	Remarks and references to Appendices
NIMY	15		Admin Order Memo No. 40 issued — appx	appx VI
			Divn Cmd'rs Parade held 15/1/19	appx VII
			A.O. Summary No. 28 issued	
	18		A.O. Summary No.29 issued	appx VIII
			Divn Cmd'r Parade which C/O Divn Ammunition Column paraded attached	appx IX
			3 cms Paraded itions	
		9.30 am		appx X
	24		A.O. Summary No. 30 issued	
			Attached is copy of Correspondence regarding the allotment of Demobilisation	appx XI
	25		New allotment demob came in — Scotland 18, Plumbers etc — 2, Miners, Ireland 43, England 98, Ireland 2 — Pivotal men &3, England 128, Ireland 6 — It was pointed out in a letter that this new allotment was not strictly [...]	

WAR DIARY

Army Form C. 2118.

Vol XLIV

INTELLIGENCE SUMMARY. A Coy Diary

(Erase heading not required.)

Title pages January 1919

Place	Date	Hour	Summary of Events and Information	Remarks and references to Appendices
Nivy	28		Major Genl. D.J. Marshall came S.S.O. received on leave prior to taking up appointment at War Office. Lt Genl C.S. Hamilton Moore, C.M.G., C.M.O, D.S.O. Comdt. 157 Bde took over command in general Marshall absence. The C in C Comdr. presentation to Kanya Column to the 17th Northumberland Fusiliers at Jurbise there day	
	27.			

WAR DIARY
INTELLIGENCE SUMMARY

Vol XLIV
"A" 52 Divn

JANY 1919

Place	Date	Hour	Summary of Events and Information	Remarks and references to Appendices
NINY	28		Our leave stopped on a/c of "Trouble" at Calais	
	31		hunth ended in bona hope "gunners" an actual hamber covered with snow. hietting otherwise gave rather to be evacuated & hutting pattern ever interfered with in consequence. Defeated by men demanding to defeater of men demanding 6 hundred ambulances taken 2805 GR [2881] 5th "demobilisable" on pelmpot to crowd french ambulances & with guaranty of transport 4178	Horse Dumpt 6 dato Great trouble through shortage of men in Auz M

Army Form C. 2118.

WAR DIARY

52nd (Lowland) Division.

January, 1919.   Volume XLIV.

INTELLIGENCE SUMMARY   "A" & "Q".

(Erase heading not required.)

Instructions regarding War Diaries and Intelligence Summaries are contained in F.S. Regs., Part II. and the Staff Manual respectively. Title pages will be prepared in manuscript.

Place	Date	Hour	Summary of Events and Information	Remarks and references to Appendices
			STRENGTH OF DIVISION. (Week-ending 31/1/19).	
				Offrs. Other Ranks.
			Divnl. Troops.	16 108
			Divnl. Artillery.	65 1494
			Divnl. Engineers.	33 789
			155th Inf. Bde.	124 1841
			156th Inf. Bde.	109 2084
			157th Inf. Bde.	120 2068
			17th N. Fus. (P).	36 643
			52nd Bn. M.G.C.	43 604
			Divnl. Train.	18 363
			984th Div.Employ.Coy.	2 234
			Royal Army Med. Corps.	18 437
			Grand Total.	584 10,665
			Infantry Brigades - Reinforcements. Received for Month of January.	
			Week-ending.	Offrs. Other Ranks.
			8th January.	- 42
			15th January.	- 45
			22nd January.	- 4
			31st January.	- 6
				- 97
			Infantry Brigades - Sick to Fd. Ambces. During Month of January.	
			Week-ending.	Offrs. Other Ranks.
			8th January.	4 46
			15th January.	- 58
			22nd January.	1 67
			31st January.	1 55
				6 226

52nd (Lowland) Division.

STRENGTH RETURN MADE UP TO 12 NOON SATURDAY, 1st FEBRUARY, 1919.

UNIT.	Strength for previous wk. as entered in record in accord. with A.O's. instrs.		Increase during wk. Recruits etc. taken in strength of unit.		Decrease during wk. inc. W.O. Cas. etc. deducted fr. strength of unit.		Totals fr. (i) & (ii)		Not present with unit & not at disposal of C.O.		Strength or incl. in col.'A' incl. is col.'A's Qu.Stores.		Available Ft. Strength incl. personnel in Transport.		Remarks.
	O.	O.R.	O.	O.R.	O.	O.R.	O.	O.R.	O.	O.R.	O.	O.R.	O.	O.R.	
155th Inf. Bde.	38	734	5	38	...	36	1	134	27	605	15	137	22	468	
1/4th R.S.Fus.	40	758	1	40	...	40	4	136	45	772	13	137	32	635	
1/5th R.S.Fus.	40	744	...	40	...	40	5	135	34	717	12	58	22	135	
1/4th K.O.S.B.	127	2214	6	118	11	380	116	2094	40	321	71	1683			
156th Inf. Bde.	42	847	3	46	...	46	10	145	37	701	7	52	30	645	
1/4th R. Scots	40	827	2	40	...	40	11	151	34	698	12	90	22	608	
1/7th R. Scots	34	791	5	34	...	34	4	150	30	695	11	83	19	545	
1/7th Sco. Rif.	116	2465	7	110	15	446	101	2097	30	251	71	1798			
157th Inf. Bde.	38	828	5	38	5	934	5	188	97	679	3	74	85	605	
1/5th H.L.I.	40	831	1	40	5	802	5	193	97	684	11	96	25	588	
1/6th H.L.I.	30	823	4	30	0	817	3	114	44	603	17	89	27	575	
1/7th H.L.I.	108	2483	10	100	14	2623	14	497	112	1901	31	259	19	1744	
17th M.Fus.(P).	35	827	2	38	2	829	3	183	30	645	15	79	25	524	
Grand Total.	407	7389	25	407	42	3014	8	1378	325	6470	114	858	94	5200	
52nd Bn. M.G.C.	45	535	1	46	...	603	0	242	43	604	7	60	35	544	

CHANGES IN NOMINAL ROLLS OF OFFICERS

(i.e. Explanation of increases and decreases).

UNIT.	Joined.	Struck off.	Cause.
4th R.S. Fus.		2/Lt. N.S.R.McGregor.	To U.K. Demobilised.
5th R.S. Fus.		Lt. W.H. Howatson.	" " "
	4th Border R. attd. 2/Lt. C.F.A.Keeble.		" " "
	Gordon Highlan. attd. 2/Lt. J.Freeland.		" " "
	4th R.S.F. attd. 2/Lt. G. Cheyne.		" " "
4th K.O.S.B.		Major P.L.P.Laing.	" " "
	Lt. G. Watson. K.O.S.B. attd.		" " "
	Lt. S.Mackie. K.O.S.B. attd.		" " "
		2/Lt. J. Clark.	" " "
		2/Lt. R.S. Russell.	" " "
	Major K.M. Chance. Border R. attd.		" " "
4th R.Scots.		2/Lt. W.F. Lownie.	" " "
		2/Lt. A.G. Murray.	" " "
		2/Lt. R.W. Dickson.	" " "
		2/Lt. R.Clydesdale.	" " "
	Lt.(A/Capt) H.J.Jones,MC. 5th R.S. attd.		" " "
7th R. Scots.			
	2/Lt. C.S.D.Morris. 4th R.S.attd.		U.K. for Medical Board.
	2/Lt. J.W.H.Stewart. 9th R.S.attd.		Invalided to U.K.
	Capt. M.Smith MC.		To U.K. Demobilised.
	2/Lt. J.L. Peggie. 4th R.S.attd.		" " "
		2/Lt. J. Stevenson.	" " "
	2/Lt. T.S.Sharp. R.S.attd.		" " "
7th Sco.Rifles.			
	Capt. W.S. Bow. 6th S.R. attd.		" " "
	Lt. W.M.D.Anderson.		" " "
		2/Lt. J.M. White.	" " "
		2/Lt. P.S. Herd.	" " "
5th H.L.I.	Major W. Foulis.		" " "
	Capt. J.Mailer. 1/1st High.Cys.attd.		" " "
	Capt. R.H.Morrison.MC.		" " "
	2/Lt.L.H.Welsh. H.L.I. attd.		" " "
	2/Lt. A. Wilson.		" " "
1/6th H.L.I.	2/Lt. W. Welsh.		" " "
	2/Lt. D.A. Graham.		" " "
	Lt. A.I. Henderson.		" " "
1/7th H.L.I.	Major. E. Watson. MC.		" " "
	Capt. J.A. Lyle.		" " "
	Capt. R.J. Dunlop.		" " "
	Lt. I.H. Henry.		" " "
	2/Lt. A.M. Bruce. 8th Bn.attd.		" " "
	2/Lt. R.W. Cumming. 9th Bn attd.		" " "
52nd Bn. M.G.C.	Capt. H.R. Whibley.		" " "
	Lt. B.T. Williams.		" " "
	Lt. H. Arkle.		" " "
	2/Lt. F. Warren.		" " "
	Lt. R.M. Stewart.		" " "
17th R.W. (P).	Capt. J. Blair.		" " "
	Lt. P.W. Cox.		" " "

Brig.General,

Commanding 52nd (Lowland) DIVISION.

52nd (Lowland) Division.

Abstract Column "B" --- Week-ending 1/2/19.

UNIT.	Courses.		Sick.		Leave.		Bde.Employ.		Div.Employ.		Extra Regtl. Employ.		Total.	
	O.	O.R.	O.	O.R.	O.	O.R.	O.	O.R.	O.	O.R.	O.	O.R.	O.	O.R.
155th Inf. Bde.														
1/4th R.S.Fuz.	—	28	2	3	9	27	—	18	3	13	—	12	15	107
1/5th R.S.Fus.	2"	42	1	5	5	33	2	17	2	6	1	4	13	107
1/4th K.O.S.B.	2	35	2	2	5	9	1	15	2	11	1	10	12	82
	4	105	5	13	19	69	3	50	7	33	2	26	40	296
156th Inf.Bde.														
1/4th R.Scots.	1	6	1	2	3	15	—	10	1	11	1	14	7	58
1/7th R.Scots.	2	15	—	7	7	20	1	10	3	22	—	10	12	90
1/7th Sco.Rif.	—	14	2	5	5	27	2	9	—	12	2	16	11	83
	3	35	3	14	15	62	3	29	4	45	3	40	30	231
157th Inf.Bde.														
1/5th H.L.I.	1	26	—	1	2	19	—	6	—	16	1	7	5	74
1/6th H.L.I.	1	17	—	4	6	30	1	13	2	12	1	22	11	98
1/7th H.L.I.	2	10	—	4	7	28	1	12	5	13	3	13	17	80
	4	53	—	4	15	77	1	31	7	41	4	42	31	252
Grand Total.	11	193	8	31	49	214	6	110	18	119	9	112	101	779

App I

SECRET.   COPY NO. ......

HEADQUARTERS, 52nd (LOWLAND) DIVISION.

"A" & "Q" SUMMARY NO. 24.

1. PROTECTION OF CANTEENS AND REST HOUSES.
The following letter from G.H.Q. is published for action:-
" It is desirable that protection should be given to Canteens and
"Rest Houses when the latter are in possession of large sums of money.
" Local Commanders should be informed that guards must be furnished from
"the nearest troops when an application is made showing the necessity
"for such provision."
(Authority G.H.Q. No. AG/538/17/PS., dated 25th Decr. 1918.)

2. PURCHASE OF GOVERNMENT STORES ETC BY CIVILIANS, ETC.
The following letters from G.H.Q., are published for information:
"1. It is understood that offers are being received by Directors and
" others both from allied civilian and military authorities, and
" individuals, for the purchase of Government Stores and Property.
"2. The general lines on which such offers should be dealt with are
" as follows:-
"(a). A definite offer, in writing, should be obtained from the
"   purchaser, shewing exactly what he is willing to purchase, the
"   price, and other conditions.
"(b). No definite acceptance should be given without previous reference
"   to G.H.Q.
"(c). Negotiations should be undertaken with a view to getting an
"   offer which, under the circumstances, is considered a fair one,
"   and the date and place where delivery is desired should, if possible,
"   be ascertained.
"(d). As soon as a final definite offer has been received, a copy
"   should be sent to G.H.Q. with your recommendation as to whether
"   the offer should be accepted or not.
"3. All offers received to date and which fulfil the conditions
" contained in para. 2 should be forwarded to this office (Q.F.2.) as
" soon as possible, and those received subsequently as soon as possible
" after receipt."
(Authority G.H.Q. No. 20,010/39 (Q.F.2), dated 13th Decr. 1918.)

"   Reference 20,010/39 (Q.F.2), dated 13-12-18, it should be made
"clear to all intending purchasers of huts or stores of any kind that
"it will be necessary for them in all cases to make their own arrange
":ments for conveyance of the stores by rail when this is necessary,
"and that the obligation of providing and loading the trucks should
"not devolve on the British Army.
"   No offers, therefore, for delivery of stores F.O.R. will be
"accepted."
(Authority G.H.Q. No. 21,001 (Q.F.2), dated 22nd Decr. 1918.)

3. LOCATIONS.
Subsections of No. 22 Sanitary Section have been posted as follows:-
        CASTEAU   ...   E.30. Sheet 45.
        JURBISE   ...   D.16. Sheet 45.
        NEUFVILLES...   W.25.   "   38.

2.

4. PERSONNEL AND REINFORCEMENT TRAIN TIMINGS.

Cancel all previous time tables relating to Personnel and Reinforcement Train.

The following timings remain in force until further notice:-

FIRST ARMY SERVICE.

Down (RN 110)			Up. (RN 109)		
MONS	dep.	1800	ETAPLES	dep.	1140
VANENCIENNES	arr.	1930	MONTREUIL	"	1211
VALENCIENNES	dep.	2030	HESDIN	"	1303
RAISMES	arr.	2200	ANVIN	arr.	1349
RAISMES	dep.	2310	ANVIN	dep.	1353
WALLERS	"	2350	WAVRANS	"	1409
SOMAIN	arr.	0030	ST. POL	arr.	1419
BOUCHAIN	dep.	1930	ST. POL	dep.	1439
LOURCHES	dep.	2045	LIGNY	"	1457
SOMAIN	arr.	2130	TINCQUES	"	1514
SOMAIN	dep.	0155	SAVY	"	1526
MONTIGNY	"	0255	AUBIGNY	"	1535
DOUAI	arr.	0325	MONT ST ELOI	"	1553
DOUAI	dep.	0430	MAROEUIL	"	1603
BREBIERES	"	0500	DAINVILLE	"	1623
VITRY	"	0525	ARRAS	arr.	1637
BIACHE	"	0550	ARRAS	dep.	1647
ARRAS	arr.	0640	BIACHE	"	1735
ARRAS	dep.	0652	VITRY	"	1755
DAINVILLE	"	0706	BREBIERES	"	1815
MAROEUIL	"	0723	DOUAI	arr.	1835
MONT ST ELOI	"	0732	DOUAI	dep.	2005
AUBIGNY	"	0750	MONTIGNY	"	2050
SAVY	"	0802	SOMAIN	arr.	2110
TINCQUES	"	0814	SOMAIN	dep.	2230
LIGNY	"	0832	LOURCHES	"	2315
ST. POL	arr.	0848	BOUCHAIN	arr.	0030
ST POL	dep.	0903	SOMAIN	dep.	2120
ANVIN	arr.	0925	WALLERS	"	2155
ANVIN	dep.	0930	RAISMES	arr.	2255
AUCHY LES HESDIN	"	1000			
HESDIN	arr.	1008			
HESDIN	dep.	1010			
AUBIN ST VAAST	"	1023			
MONTREUIL	"	1100			
ETAPLES	arr.	1120			

Change for MONS.

Connects with ETAPLES with Roc 8 for ABBEVILLE, ROMESCAMPS, ROUEN and HAVRE, leaving ETAPLES at 1820

These trains are duty trains only and are not to be used for leave takers.

3rd January 1919.

Lieut. Col.
A.A. & Q.M.G., 52nd (LOWLAND) DIVISION.

SECRET.   COPY NO. ....

HEADQUARTERS, 52nd (LOWLAND) DIVISION.
"A" & "Q" SUMMARY NO. 28.

1. **RAILWAY TRANSPORT.**
   The following letter from G.H.Q. is published for information:-
   " It is considered desirable to explain at some length the situation
   "as regards Railway Lines in FRANCE and BELGIUM and the traffic that
   "must necessarily be carried by them.
   " Although every effort has been, and is being made, to combat the
   "the present unpunctuality of trains, there is unfortunately no good
   "reason for anticipating an improvement in the immediate future. It
   "is therefore desired to make the whole situation clear to formations
   "in order that all possible steps may be taken to minimise the incon-
   ":venience and possible hardsip which, it is fully realised will now
   "arise.
   " The destruction of all railways in an area varying in width from
   "20 to 30 miles and extending the whole length of the British area in
   "FRANCE has naturally created a position of grave difficulty. Though
   "no time was lost in reconstructing as many of these lines as possible
   "and a number of military lines were rapidly laid across the gap, yet
   "these newly laid lines are not comparable with the permanent way which
   "they have replaced, but nevertheless they are called upon to bear an
   "even more intense traffic than in times of peace. Many months must
   "pass before the railway system across the gap has been restored to its
   "former efficiency.
   " In several instances it is not practicable to undertake the
   "reconstruction of destroyed lines with the result that the congestion
   "on the existing lines is increased. Moreover, the apparently undamaged
   "lines in the evacuated territory have been left in a disorganised state
   "and a considerable period must elapse before they can revert to pre-
   "war conditions. The personnel question is moreover one that will take
   "time to solve.
   " It will, however, be realised that the difficulties of operating
   "the existing railways are unprecedented. It is not possible to
   "limit the traffic sufficiently to ensure that delays do not occur.
   "A very considerable number of troops must, for various reasons, be
   "maintained East of the devastated area. In addition to supplying
   "them with their daily needs and the necessary reserve, the railways
   "must provide for a large civilian population newly freed from the
   "enemy. At the same time, the movements on these railways in the
   "rear has been enormously increased by the work of recommencing the
   "civil activities of France. It is naturally the desire of the French
   "and Belgian Governments to re-establish communication and civil life
   "in the restored territory with least delay. In addition the de-
   ":mobilization of the Allied Armies has to take place.
   " Rolling stock and locomotives have deteriorated and decreased in
   "number owing to the small attention which it has been possible to
   "afford them during the strenuous times of war.
   " It will be appreciated from the above that movements on railways
   "can now only be effected under the greatest difficulties, especially
   "in view of the fact that delay in one class of traffic tends to re-act
   "on all others. It is necessary that every possible limitation should
   "be placed on transport by rail, and that when issuing orders Commanders
   "should have in mind the uncertainty of the train services and should
   "make provision accordingly.

" It is thought that if the troops realise the difficulties of the
"situation they will bear any discomforts that may arise during
"demobilization with the same cheerfulness and fortitude that they
"displayed during the period of active operations in the field."
(Authority G.H.Q. No. 615. Q.A., dated 29th December 1918.)

2. BATTALION ETC SIGNS.

The following is published for information:-
"There is no objection to the names of Units now being stated on
"Battalion H.Q. and other signs."
(Authority G.H.Q. AG/2686/65/PS., dated 1-1-19.)

3. N.C.Os MESSES.

The following letter is published for information:-
"   Reference your No. 448 Q.A. of the 12th instant, recommending
"the provision of enamelled plates and mugs for N.C.Os messes, it is
"regretted that the state of supply is such that it is out of the
"question to provide the very large numbers that would be required
"for the purpose in question.
"   All available supplies will be fully taken up in meeting demands
"for Demobilization Camps."
(Authority H.H.Q. No. 4006/17 (Q.B.1), dated 25-12-18.)

4. SALE OF HUTS TO FRENCH INHABITANTS.

The following letters are published for information:-
"The Quartermaster General,
    General Headquarters.   First Army 17/2.Q.E.

"   Many applications have been received from the French inhabitants
"to purchase single huts.
"   Can you please say if any scheme is in existence or will be
"produced shortly to enable such to be effected.

First Army H.Q.   (Sgd) H. Davies, Major,
22-12-18.   for General,
                                       Commanding First Army.

                                         2.
"First Army.   21004/Q/F.2.

"   Reference your letter No. 17/2.Q.F., dated 22nd inst.
"   Instructions dealing with the sale to the French of Huts and
"material will be issued shortly.
"   In every case application for purchase must be made in writing
"and in the application the buyer will show exactly what he is willing
"to purchase, price and any other special conditions necessary.

G.H.Q.   (Sgd) J.M. Young, B.G.,
28-12-18.   for Quartermaster General.

5. LORRY ROADS.

The following roads will be maintained by Transportation in the
Corps Area:-
    (1). MONS - BRUSSELS Road.
    (2). MONS - BINCHE - CHARLEROI Road.
    (3). MONS - MAUBEUGE Road.
    (4). The MONS - VALENCIENNES Road as far as JEMAPPES.
    (5). MONS - GIVRY - BEAUMONT Road.
    (6). MONS - JURBISE - LENS - ATH Road.
    (7). The Boulevards round MONS.
The above will be maintained as two-way lorry roads.

6. R.A.F. PERSONNEL.

Instructions have been issued that all R.A.F. personnel serving with Army Units should be ordered to return to their original Squadrons as soon as possible.

Nominal Rolls of all R.A.F. personnel despatched, shewing destination, will be forwarded to this Office in quadruplicate. (Authority First Army A.73, dated 4-1-19 and A.102, dated 5-1-19)

7. COURSES.

The following letter received from A.A.G., First Army, (No. A.9818 A of 4-1-19) is published for information:-

" It appears that some of the students sent to the present "Course at the First Army Musketry Camp are under the impression "that they have thereby forfeited their turn for leave or are "losing their chance for early demobilization.
" Will you please have the matter investigated?
" All those who claim that their leave has been delayed owing "to their being sent to the Course, or that they are losing their "turn for early demobilization are being returned to their units. "If their claims have no justification, the necessary disciplinary "action should be taken."

Before forwarding names of men as students for Army Courses, the position of the men on the leave roster and their chances of demobilization must be taken into consideration.

The courses are intended to enable those who will not be demobilized immediately to make the most of the time spent in this Country.

[signature] Major
for Lt Colonel
A.A. & Q.M.G., 52nd (LOWLAND) DIVISION.

8th January 1919.

SECRET. COPY NO. .....

HEADQUARTERS, 52nd (LOWLAND) DIVISION.
"A" & "Q" SUMMARY NO. 26.

1. **DEMOBILIZATION.**

All Commanding Officers will take steps to ensure that the present position regarding demobilization is explained to all ranks, and that men proceeding on leave and to demobilize, are fully aware of all regulations affecting them. It should be made certain that Junior Commanders explain fully to all ranks both the military and economic reasons which make it necessary that demobilization can only proceed slowly.

2. **LEAVE TRAINS.**

Cancel all previous Time-tables relating to Leave Trains. The following timings will be in force until further notice. These are the only Leave Trains by which personnel of this Corps may travel.

Vacancies allotted to First Army on 2nd Leave Train, published in A. & Q. Summary No. 22 are cancelled.

VIA BOULOGNE.

DOWN. (Y.D.)			UP. (D.Y.)		
MONS	dep.	0052	BOULOGNE	dep.	0905.
Valenciennes		0245	Hesdin		1150
Raismes		0406	Blangy		1220
Wallers		0426	Anvin		1240
Somain		0456	St Pol.	arr.	1310
Montigny		0512	St Pol	dep.	1332
Douai	arr.	0542	Ligny		1350
Douai	dep.	0642	Tincques		1407
Corbehem		0707	Savy		1419
Brebieres		0720	Aubigny		1428
Vitry		0740	Frevin Capelle		1436
Roeux		0822	Mont St Eloi		1445
Arras	arr.	0850	Maroeuil		1455
Arras	dep.	0910	Dainville		1510
Dainville		0922	Arras	arr.	1522
Maroeuil		0933	Arras	dep.	1545
Mont St Eloi		0941	Roeux		1628
Frevin Capelle		0948	Vitry		1700
Aubigny		0955	Brebieres		1715
Savy		1003	Corbehem		1728
Tincquest		1015	Douai	arr.	1751
Ligny		1031	Douai	dep.	1851
St Pol	arr.	1046	Montigny		1926
St. Pol	dep.	1112	Somain		1950
Anvin		1135	Wallers		2020
Blangy		1151	Raismes	arr.	2038
Hesdin		1213	Valenciennes		2110
Montreuil		1300	MONS		-
Etaples	arr.	1327			
Etaples	dep.	1343			
Boulogne	arr.	1442			

For this train there are 365 vacancies for First Army.

VIA CALAIS.

DOWN (X.C.)			UP (C.X.)		
MONS	dep.	1800	CALAIS	dep.	0720
Change at Valenciennes.			Blaringhem		0937
Valenciennes	dep.	0532	Aire		0946
Raismes		0604	Berguette		1010
Wallers		0624	Lillers		1023
Somain		0654	Chocques		1036
Montigny		0710	Fouquereuil		1044
Douai	arr.	0740	Bethune	arr.	1049
Douai	dep.	0840	Bethune	dep.	1120
Corbehem		0905	Labugnoy		1150
Brebieres		0918	Calonne Ricouart		1216
Vitry		0938	Pernes		1223
Rooux		1010	Brias		1250
Arras	arr.	1046	Ligny	arr.	1330
Arras	dep.	1103	Ligny	dep.	1334
Dainville		1117	Tincques		1347
Duisans		1128	Savy		1358
Maroeuil		1134	Aubigny		1405
Mont St Eloi		1143	Frevin Capelle		1415
Frevin Capelle		1151	Mont St Eloi		1422
Aubigny		1200	Maroeuil		1440
Savy		1208	Duisans		1443
Tincques		1220	Dainville		1450
Ligny	arr.	1230	Arras	arr.	1510
Ligny	dep.	1234	Arras	dep.	1525
Brias		1313	Rooux		1605
Pernes		1333	Vitry		1633
Calonne Ricouart		1342	Brebieres		1655
Labugnoy		1356	Corbehem		1708
Fouquercuil		1409	Douai	arr.	1730
Bethune	arr.	1414	Douai	dep.	1830
Bethune	dep.	1439	Montigny		1905
Chocques		1453	Somain		1929
Lillers		1503	Wallers		1959
Berguettes		1528	Raismes	arr.	2017
Aire		1542	Valenciennes		2049
Blaringhem		1553	Change at Valenciennes		
Wardrecques		1600	MONS	arr.	-
Arques		1626			
St Omer		1653			
Calais	arr.	1758			

3. **TRAIN CONVOYS - PASSES.**

It has been reported that two soldiers were found in a truck on a supply train at ABBEVILLE, who stated that they were convoying two trucks from CANDAS to ST RIQUIER for the 61st Divisional Canteen, but were unable to produce any written authority.

They were therefore in danger of being arrested until their bona fides were established. No arrangements have been made by the Expeditionary Force Canteens for such convoys.

If in any instance a formation finds it necessary to detail a soldier for similar duty, the latter should be furnished with written orders signed by a Staff Officer of the formation, and bearing the Office Stamp.

(Authority - AG/2885/PS, dated 3rd January 1919.)

9th January 1919.

Lieut. Col.,
A.A. & Q.M.G., 52nd (LOWLAND) DIVISION.

App IV

52nd (Lowland) DIVISION.

Administrative Circular Memorandum No. 39.

SPECIAL LEAVE.

1. The number of applications from Other Ranks for Special Leave at present submitted to Divisional H.Q. is greater than can be dealt with on the present Divisional allotment for Special Leave.

2. The present allotment for the whole Division is one other rank per day, and this on the present Divisional strength works out roughly at one other rank per 1000 per fortnight.

It is permitted to convert an ordinary vacancy to a special one and if this done the allotment will work out at one special leave per 1000 per week.

These figures should be kept in mind in submitting applications which must be closely scrutinized before they are forwarded to Divisional H.Q. Once an application reaches Divisional H.Q. it is difficult to turn it down unless it evidently fails to meet the required conditions, and Formations and Units who forward applications are really responsible that special leave is not taken advantage of. Owing to the number of applications submitted the vacancies have been filled up to and including the sailings on 22nd instant, so that special leave is now no longer of use in enabling a man to proceed home quickly in case of serious illness.

The position has been put before Higher Authority but the policy to be followed has been definitely laid down and there appears to be no chance of an increased allotment being made.

3. The applications which receive first attention at this Office are those for men who wish to proceed home in view of the illness of wife or children or whose presence at home is required on account of family financial affairs, but it is not always possible to deal with these cases promptly on account of the number of applications received which refer in particular to the illness of more distant relatives.

It is not always made clear in applications to proceed home for financial reasons that the presence of the applicant is really essential. It is suggested that in cases of this nature a definite statement should be obtained to the effect that there is no male relative at home who could attend to the business.

Lieut. Colonel.
A.A. & Q.M.G., 52nd (Lowland) DIVISION.

13th JANUARY, 1919.

SECRET.   COPY NO. ....

HEADQUARTERS, 52nd (LOWLAND) DIVISION.
"A" & "Q" SUMMARY NO. 27.

1. NOTICE BOARDS.
   Instructions have been issued that all Notice Boards erected in Corps Area, and all names painted on houses should be standardised to the following dimensions:-
   Block lettering on white ground. Letters 20" high.
   Spacing between letters 2". Width of black lettering 2"
   A Black margin 2" in width will be painted all round.
   The space between lettering and margin will be 4".
   Direction arrows of same size.
   It is proposed to leave the signs which have already been erected as they are at present, but to adopt the lettering indicated above for any future signs which it may be found necessary to erect.

2. SUNDAY D.R.L.S.
   It is notified for information that the afternoon D.R. run will be discontinued on SUNDAYS.
   The above to take effect from 12th instant.
(Authority XXII Corps No. G. 5312.)

3. SUPPLY OF BOOTS.
   At the present time Size 7 Boots are not available at Base. Supplies are shortly expected from England.

4. LEAVE ARRANGEMENTS.
   The following wire from G.H.Q. is published for information:-
"Staff Boat will continue to use FOLKSTONE - BOULOGNE Route and Staff
"Leave Train will continue to run from LONDON to FOLKSTONE."

5. RAILWAY TRANSPORT. Reference "A" & "Q" Summary No. 25, paral:-
   The following letter from G.H.Q. is published for information:-
"   Owing to the acute railway congestion resulting from the causes re-
":ferred to in my letter No. 615 (Q.A.) dated 29-12-18, and particularly
"from the large number of trains now running daily in connection with
"demobilization, the number of rakes of heated leave stock is not
"sufficient to ensure a daily leave service to and from each Army.
"   About once in four or five days it will probably be necessary either
"to substitute ordinary stock for the heated stock or to cancel the train.
"   Two wagon building workshops are at present engaged in constructing
"additional rakes of heated stock to act as spares.
"   In the meantime it is necessary for Armies to decide whether on days
"when it is impossible to provide heated stock, covered trucks should be
"substituted in its place or the leave train should be cancelled.
"   It would not be possible to include a kitchen van in the improvised
"rakes.
"   The decision as to whether the Leave Train shall be cancelled, or run
"with unheated stock must depend on the weather and other local circum-
":stances. A.D.G.Ts of Armies should therefore keep in close touch with
"local Traffic Officers in order that they may be able to inform Army
"Headquarters directly it is found that no rake of heated stock will
"be available on a particular date. Army Headquarters will then decide
"whether the train shall be cancelled or run with unheated stock, and
"will inform local Traffic accordingly.
"   In/

" In order to provide **blankets** when ordinary stock is employed, an
"issue to each Army of 3000 blankets is hereby authorised. These
"blankets should be kept at the Station from which the Leave Train
"starts and when they are used an officer must be specially detailed
"to travel on the train and arrange for the blankets to be collected
"at BOULOGNE or CALAIS Station. The D.A.D.R.T., BOULOGNE or CALAIS,
"will then arrange for the provision of a truck for the blankets on
"the next leave train proceeding to the Army concerned. The Officer
"specially detailed will return with the blankets."
(Authority G.H.Q. No. 615 (Q.A.), dated 30-12-18.)

6. BICYCLES IN POSSESSION OF CIVILIANS.
The following letter is published for information:-
" Reference your No. 590.Q. dated 25th December 1918.
" W.D. bicycles found in the possession of civilians should be
"regarded as British property. The presumption is that they were
"sold by the Germans to avoid recapture by the British Army. If,
"however, the civilians can produce details showing the date of
"purchase and the amount paid to the Germans, with the circumstances
"under which the purchase was made, they should be advised to put in
"a claim against the French Government for subsequent recovery from
"the German Government. In such cases a receipt should be given when
"bicycles are taken over."
(Authority G.H.Q. No. 14030/82, (Q.D.2.), dated 6-1-19).
Information should be forwarded to D.A.P.M. of any such
bicycles known to be in possession of civilians.

7. TRAIN TIMINGS.
Timings between VALENCIENNES and MONS will be as under:-

VALENCIENNES	arr.	2200 hours.
	dep.	2230
BLANC MISSERON	arr.	2320
	dep.	2330
MONS	arr.	0100
MONS	dep.	0335 hours
BLANC MISSERON	arr.	0500
	dep.	0519
VALENCIENNES	arr.	0550
	dep.	0620

13th January 1919.

E.F. Mullin. Bartlett Major
for
Lieut. Col.,
A.A. & Q.M.G., 52nd (LOWLAND) DIVISION.

App VI

52nd (Lowland) DIVISION.

ADMINISTRATIVE CIRCULAR MEMORANDUM No. 40.

15th JANUARY, 1919.

DIVISIONAL CEREMONIAL PARADE.

1. The Ceremonial Parade mentioned in this Office A 147 of 26-12-18, will take place on the 18th instant, on the MAISIERES Drill Ground, (K. 9 and 10, Sheet 45.)

DRESS: Drill Order with Greatcoats. Steel helmets will NOT be worn.
Officers entitled to horses will be mounted.
Transport will not be on Parade.

2. The parade will be formed up by 1030 facing East in the following formation :-

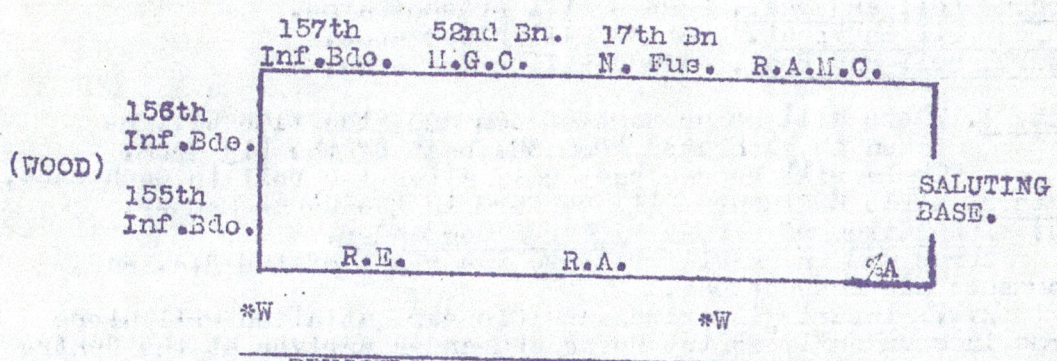

BRUSSELS ROAD

The actual formations of units will be as follows:-

R.A. Mass (D.A.C. will not parade)

R.E. Close column of companies.

Infantry Brigades. Line of battalions in close column of companies, 5 yards between battalions and Brigades.

M.G. and Pioneer Bns. Close column of companies.

(N.B. Infantry (less Rifle Battalions) will fix bayonets.

3. This parade will consist of the following phases:-

(A) Arrival of Divisional Commander - Parade will be called to attention, and will slope arms.

(B) Arrival of Corps Commander. General Salute.

(C) Inspection of parade by Corps Commander.

P.T.O.

(2).

3./continued/

(D) Presentation of M.Cs. and D.C.Ms. to Other Ranks only by Corps Commander.

(E) March past.

4. Details of the above will be as follows:-

(A) Arrival of Divisional Commander. As G.O.C. the Division reaches the Saluting Base drummers stationed in vicinity of Senior Brigadier will sound a roll of drums followed by one beat on big drum. Formations and units will come to attention and slope arms. After an interval the drums will repeat the roll and beat whereupon formations and units will order arms and stand at ease

(B) Arrival of Corps Commander. General Salute.
On arrival of the Corps Commander at the Saluting Base (see diagram in para 2) he will be received with a General Salute, the time for which will be given by the drums stationed in the vicinity of G.O.C. 52nd Division.

First roll and beat. Parade will come to attention and slope arms.
Second roll and beat. Parade will present arms.
Third roll and beat. Parade will slope arms.
Fourth roll and beat. Parade will order arms.

Note 1. There will be no word of command, the time will be taken in each case from the beat of the big drum.
There will be one beat only after the roll in each case.
Note 2. Rifle Regiments will conform in the usual manner.

(C) Inspection of parade by Corps Commander.
Corps Commander will ride to the right of the R.A. and commence his inspections.
R.E., Infantry Brigades and Pioneer Battalion will slope arms independently as the Corps Commander arrives at the centre of the formation immediately on their right, and will order arms and stand at ease after he passes the centre of the formation immediately on their left.

(D) Presentation of Medal Ribbons.
(i) Corps Commander will move to the medal table, which will be roughly about the centre of the missing side of the rectangle formed by the parade and will dismount.
(ii) By the time he has arrived there the recipients of decorations will be drawn up in two ranks facing the table and about 20 paces from it. Prior to this they will have been drawn up in rear of the interval between 155th and 156th Infantry Brigades.
(iii) As names are called out each recipient will advance to within one pace of the table. Here he will halt, salute, take one pace forward, receive his ribbon, take one pace to the rear, salute, turn to the right and fall in on a new alignment which will be pointed out on the ground.
(iv) 157th Brigade will detail an officer to be in command of recipients. He will receive separate instructions.

(E) March Past.
(i) The Corps Commander having finished distribution of medal ribbons proceeds to the Saluting Base.
(ii) Formations march past as follows:-
R.A. In line at close interval.
R.E. Close column of companies.

/continued/

(3).

4/continued/

| Inf. Battalions M.G. and Pioneer Battalions. | By close column of companies with 30 yards distance between Battalions, and 100 yards between Brigades, and other arms. Infantry will march past will fixed bayonets. |

Note 1. Each unit will be formed up in the vicinity of point "A" (see diagram para 2) ready to march past at the appropriate distance behind the preceding unit. Flags will be placed in vicinity of points "W" round which units will wheel.

Note 11. After marching past formations will clear to North-East end of the saluting base and proceed to billets independently.

The Divisional Band will play during the inspection and the massed Pipe and Drum Bands during the march past.

5. In preparation for this parade Staff Captains R.A. and Infantry Brigades and Adjutants R.E., M.G. Bn., and Pioneers will meet a Divisional Staff Officer at the entrance to the Drill Ground, K.15.b.9.9. at 1100 on 18th instant.
They will each bring with them approximate parade strength of their formations and units.

6. The following routes are allotted to formations and units for reaching and leaving the parade ground on the 18th instant.

R.A. CASTEAU - MAISIERES Main Road.

R.E. * Field Companies as for 156th Infantry Brigade.
155th Inf.Bde. JURBISE - PAVE cross roads, cross roads K.2.c.9.9.
156th Inf.Bde. MASNUY St. JEAN - GRAND CHEMIN D'EBGHIEN - K. 4 central.
157th Inf.Bde. Road junction K.25.b. - MAISIERES.
M.G. Bn.   as for 156th Infantry Brigade. *
Pioneers.   as for 156th Infantry Brigade. *
* Under orders of G.O.C. 156th Infantry Brigade.

Major,
D.A.A.G. 52nd (Lowland) DIVISION.

SECRET. COPY NO. ....

HEADQUARTERS, 52nd (LOWLAND) DIVISION.

"A" & "Q" SUMMARY NO. 28.

1. **SCHOOL BUILDINGS.**
    Orders have been received to evacuate and hand over to the Civil Authorities by the 22nd instant any School Buildings in this area that are being used by troops.
    Each Area Commandant will report to this office by 22nd instant that all School Buildings in his area have been handed over.

2. **SHORTAGE OF TIMBER.**
    The following letter is published for information:-
    " A great deal of timber is being used at the present time to make
    " up tables and forms.
    "   In view of the shortage of stocks of timber, no tables and forms
    " must be made locally unless urgently needed.
    "   Tables and forms have been demanded from the Base and are expected
    " to arrive very shortly."
    (Authority XXII Corps No. Q.82/1/2598, dated 12-1-19.)

3. **WEARING OF RIBBON OF 1914 - 15 STAR.**
    In view of Army Order XX of 1918, reference the granting of 1914-15 Star, there is no objection to Commanding Officers giving permission to those whom they know to be entitled to the medal, to wear the ribbon.
    Attention is drawn to the fact that it appears as if the final decision regarding the ribbon for the 1914-15 Medal had not yet been made.

15th January 1919.

A.A. & Q.M.G., 52nd (LOWLAND) DIVISION.
Lieut. Colonel,

SECRET.   COPY NO. .....

HEADQUARTERS, 52nd (LOWLAND) DIVISION.
"A" & "Q" SUMMARY NO. 29.

1. COAL.
   Units drawing coal from OBOURG must use Horse Transport only.

2. DEMOBILIZATION OF HORSES.
   The following instructions concerning the demobilization of horses are published for information and action:-
   " The Officer i/c of each party of animals despatched to the Base, "handed over to the Army Collecting Camp, or elsewhere, will hand over "two copies of A.F.O. 1640.A. to the consignee.
   " One original copy will be retained by the consignee as a "voucher to his A.F. A.2004, the duplicate will be receipted by him, "and will be returned to the Officer in charge of the conducting party, "and attached by the latter to his A.F. A.2004 as a voucher.
   " The latter copy will either be returned to the unit concerned "by the Officer in charge of the original conducting party, if he "is returning to his Unit direct, or, will be handed to the O.C. "Army Animal Collecting Camp, after transmission by post."
   (Authority First Army No. 582/9.Q.A.)

3. PURCHASE OF ARMY HORSES BY OFFICERS AND OTHER RANKS AT AUCTION SALES.
   With reference to G.R.O. 5959, the following advanced copies of paragraphs 2722 and 2723 of Army Demobilization Regulations are published for information.
   The forms of application referred to as Appendix H and Appendix J., will be known as Army Forms Z.81 and Z.82 respectively and will be supplied on indent from A.P. & S. Depots.
   "2722. The provisions of Para 631 Allowance Regulations are temporarily "suspended and Officers and soldiers will be allowed to purchase any "Army horses or mules offered for sale by Public Auction.
   " Any Officer or soldier who is serving, or who has served, during the "war, in FRANCE or ITALY, and is desirous of being able to ascertain "the particular sale at which his favourite horse will be disposed of "may apply in writing to the O.C. Unit, with which the horse is on "charge, to have his name scissor-clipped on the near saddle of the "animal. The application should state:-
   " (a). The name, rank, Regiment and address of the applicant.
   " (b). Full description of the horse, and
   " (c). The name and address of the person resident in ENGLAND who will "represent the applicant at the sale.
   " For form of Application see Appendix H.
   " If the O.C. Unit approves the Application and can identify the "animal and is satisfied that it is not required for retention for "further military service, he will cause the Applicant's name to be "scissor-clipped on the animal accordingly. He will, at the same time, "pass the animal, together with the application, after endorsing thereon "the marks of the animal, to the Commandant of the Animal Collecting Camp "who will forward the animal, with its documents, under the direction "of the Director of Remounts if in FRANCE, or the Deputy Director of "Remounts, if in ITALY, to the Remount Department, SWAYTHLING, near "SOUTHAMPTON for quarantine. Such special animals will be sold per-":iodically in LONDON. A week prior to the date of sale the Commandant, "Remount Depot, SWAYTHLING, will forward the application by post to the "person named therein, and inform him of the date and place of sale."

3. PURCHASE OF ARMY HORSES, (Continued).

"2. Repurchase of Army Horses at a Valuation.
"2723. (1). Any member of His Majesty's Forces in the United Kingdom,
"FRANCE or ITALY who has sold a Charger or Chargers to the Government
"during the War for allotment to him or for his own use, may repurchase
"such animals at a valuation.
" (2). Application shall be made in writing within 14 days after
"the commencement of demobilization and shall state:-
" (i). The name, rank and Regiment of the Applicant.
" (ii). Full description of the charger.
" (iii). The date and place of original sale to the Government,
" price paid, and, if known, the name of the purchasing
" Officer.
" (iv). The name and address of the person to whom the charger
" shall be sent, carriage forward, from the Port of dis-
" embarkation, if purchase completed.
" (v). The name and address of the person by whom payment will
" be made, who must be resident in the United Kingdom,
" and should be preferably the consignee mentioned in (iv)
" above.
"3. Such application shall be in the prescribed form (see Appendix J.)
"and may be forwarded through the applicants C.O. to the Director of
"Remounts, War Office, if the Applicant is in the United Kingdom,
"through the D.D.R. of the Army or Cavalry Corps, or A.D.R., L. of C.,
"if in FRANCE, or the Deputy Director of Remounts, if in ITALY, who
"shall assess the price to be paid by inspection and valuation of the
"animal, taking into consideration the group in which the horse has been
"classified and the original purchase price. After endorsing the amount
"of his valuation on the application, the D.R., D.D.R. or A.D.R. (as the
"case may be) will return it to the applicant, through his C.O. for
"his acceptance of the valuation. Such acceptance shall be endorsed
"on the application within 7 days and signed and dated by the applicant,
"whose C.O. shall then forward the Application if the applicant is in
"the United Kingdom, to the D.R., War Office, or if the applicant is
"in FRANCE or ITALY, to the Director of Remounts, or Deputy Director
"of Remounts on the Lines of Communication, who will allot a number to
"the Application and pass it to the War Office and immediately arrange
"for the transfer of the animal, after the usual period of Veterinary
"observation, to the Remount Depot at SWAYTHLING near SOUTHAMPTON,
"clearly identified by a number clipped on the near saddle corresponding
"with the number of application."

"4. After verifying the particulars of the original purchase, the
"Director of Remounts at the War Office will notify the C.O. of the
"Unit if in the United Kingdom to hand over the horse on receipt of
"the value by the Cashier of the Command.

"5. In the case of horses in FRANCE or ITALY, the Director of Remounts
"at the War Office will at once communicate with the person named in
"the application as authorised to take the animal over requesting
"him to forward a cheque to the Command Paymaster, Southern Command,
"SALISBURY, for the sum named. The applicant's cheque should be for-
":warded to the Command Paymaster within 7 days of receipt of notifi-
":cation of the amount to be paid. When the money has been received,
"the Command Paymaster will immediately notify the Commandant, SWAYTH-
":LING, who will despatch the animal, carriage forward, to the address
"named in the application, without delay. The Commandant will, at the
"same time, notify the consignee of the despatch of the animal, and
"inform the Director of Remounts at the War Office, that the transaction
"is completed
"6./

3.

3. PURCHASE OF ARMY HORSES. (Continued).

"6.   Every care will be taken to deliver horses free on rail at SWAYTH-
":LING in good condition, but the applicant shall have no claim for
"damages or compensation by reason of any loss of condition or injury
"which a horse may have suffered since the valuation.
"   In special cases of injury or other disability incurred since the
"date of the valuation, however, the Commandant of the SWAYTHLING
"Remount Depot, may submit recommendations for the reduction of the
"valuation to the Director of Remounts, War Office.
"   In the event of the death or loss of the horse prior to its delivery
"to the Railway Company the Agreement for the repurchase shall be null
"and void. Any sum paid for the horse will be returned and the applicant
"shall have no further claim against the State.
"7.   In the event of the original owner having died, or been killed on
"service, his relatives (viz. Widow, child, parent, brother or sister)
"will have the same right of re-purchase on a similar application being
"sent within 14 days, (Application received after the expiration of
"this limit will be considered if the horse is still available), after
"the first day of demobilization to the Director of Remounts, War Office,
"who will arrange for the valuation of the animal and take all necessary
"steps for carrying out the transaction."
(Authority G.H.Q., No. 2003 (Q.F.1.), dated 5th January 1919).

4. SHORTAGE OF CANDLES.

            The following letter is published for information and necessary
action:-
"   The shortage of candles on pack trains continues, and although
"endeavours have been made to meet demands from Army reserves, these
"latter are also scarcely able to make up requirements. It will be
"seen therefore, that it is essential that the strictest economy be
"practised in the use of candles, and that in all cases where hurricane
"lanterns could be supplied with M.B.O. in lieu of candles, this ought
"to be done.
"   The demand for candles has not fallen as might have been reasonably
"anticipated, now that the troops are in permanent billets.
"   It is thought that if Commanding Officers realised the difficulties
"of meeting the present demands, their requirements might be consider-
":ably curtailed. As a result of this, more candles would be available
"for issue to units stationed where there are not other means of
"illumination."
(Authority First Army, D.D.S.T., No. S. 688, dated 13-1-19.)

18th January 1919.   Lieut. Col.
                          A.A. & Q.M.G., 52nd (LOWLAND) DIVISION.

LEAVE TRAINS.

Cancel all previous Time-tables and substitute the following:-

(1). FIRST ARMY LEAVE TRAIN.

C.X.			X.C.		
Calais	dep.	0720	Mons	dep.	0245
St Omer	arr.	0835	Blanc MISSERON	"	0420
	"	0850	Valenciennes	arr	0500
Arques	dep.	0900		dep.	0532
Wardrecques	"	0932	Raismes	"	0606
Blaringhem	"	0939	Somain	"	0656
Aire	"	0948	Douai	arr.	0740) H.R.
Berguette	"	1018		dep.	0840)
Lillers	"	1031	Arras	arr.	1048
Chocques	"	1043		dep.	1103
Calonne Ricoucouart	"	1122	Marceuil	"	1134
Pernes	arr.	1134) H.R.	Aubigny	"	1200
	dep.	1227)	Ligny	"	1234
Ligny	"	1334	Pernes	arr.	1331) H.R.
Aubigny	"	1412		dep.	1432)
Marceuil	"	1440	Calonne Ricouart	"	1441
Arras	arr.	1510	Chocques	"	1504
	dep.	1525	Lillers	"	1517
Douai	arr.	1730) H.R.	Berguette	"	1538
	dep.	1830)	Aire	"	1552
Somain	"	1922	Blaringhem	"	1603
Raismes	"	2019	Wardrecques	"	1610
Valenciennes	arr.	2049	Arques	"	1636
	dep.	2120	St Omer	arr.	1650
Blanc Misseron	"	2220		dep.	1658
Mons	arr.	2350	Calais	arr.	1808

The leave allotment of the First Army is 705 (inclusive 150 miscellaneous).
These are the only trains by which Leave men for First Army may travel.

52nd (Lowland) DIVISION.

Numbers on parade at Divisional Ceremonial Parade on 18th JANUARY, 1919.

UNIT:	Officers:	Other Ranks.	Officers	Other Ranks.
Divisional Artillery:				
R.A. H.Q.	3	–		
9th Brigade R.F.A.	21	407		
56th Brigade R.F.A.	19	315		
			43	722
Divisional Engineers:				
410th Field Coy. R.E.	2	40		
412th Field Coy. R.E.	1	60		
413th Field Coy. R.E.	1	50		
			4	150
155th Inf. Brigade.				
Headquarters,	3	–		
1/4th Bn R.S.Fus.	17	418		
1/5th Bn R.S.Fus.	23	336		
1/4th Bn K.O.S.B.	20	336		
			63	1090
156th Inf. Brigade:				
Headquarters	3	–		
1/4th Bn R. Scots.	23	413		
1/7th Bn R. Scots.	11	328		
1/7th Bn Sco.Rif.	14	379		
			51	1120
157th Inf. Brigade:				
Headquarters.	3	–		
1/5th Bn H.L.I.	16	238		
1/6th Bn H.L.I.	19	412		
1/7th Bn H.L.I.	25	385		
			63	1035
52nd Battn. M.G.C.	45	883	45	883
17th North'd.Fus.(P)	22	673	22	673
R.A.M.C.	2	100	2	100
		TOTAL:	293	5773

SECRET.   COPY NO. ....

HEADQUARTERS, 52nd (LOWLAND) DIVISION
"A" & "Q" SUMMARY NO. 30.

1. **ABSENCE WITHOUT LEAVE.**
   A large number of serious cases of absence, more like desertion than absence, have been dealt with recently in a trifling manner. Commanding Officers will charge men with desertion in cases where men have been absent for some weeks, and are arrested in plain clothes. It must be remembered that a Finding of Absence without Leave may be brought in on a Charge of Desertion, if the Court so desires, but that this does not hold vice versa.

2. **RAILWAY CROSSINGS.**
   Area Commandants are responsible for the adequate guarding of Railway Crossings in their areas. They will report to the D.A.P.M., 52nd Division, any crossings they consider require to be controlled.

3. **LUXURY TAX EXEMPTION COUPONS.**
   Experience in the use of Luxury Tax Exemption Coupon Books has shown that these contain too many coupons for any one Officer or man to use whilst on leave, and in an Army Area it is not worth while for the average Officer or man to have one of these books except whilst on leave.
   In view of this, it has now been arranged that books may be transferred from one soldier to another, care being taken that the signature on the inside of the cover is cancelled by the Office stamp of the issuing authority every time a transfer takes place.

4. **REINFORCEMENT & PERSONNEL TRAIN.**
   Cancel all previous Time-tables, and substitute the following:-
   (1). First Army Service.

R.E. 109.			R.E. 110.		
Etaples	dep.	1140	Mons	dep.	1800
Montreuil	"	1211	Valenciennes	"	2015
Hesdin	"	1300	Raismes	arr.	2119
Blanchy	"	...	Raismes	dep.	2315
Anvin	arr.	1349	Somain	arr.	0030
Anvin	dep.	1353	Bouchain	dep.	1930
St Pol	arr.	1419	Lourches	"	2015
St Pol	dep.	1439	Somain	arr.	2130
Aubigny	"	1535	Somain	dep.	0155
Maroeuil	"	1603	Douai	arr.	0325
Arras	arr.	1337	Douai	dep.	0430
Arras	dep.	1347	Arras	arr.	0640
Douai	arr.	1935	Arras	dep.	0652
Douai	dep.	2005	Maroeuil	"	0725
Somain	arr.	2118	Aubigny	"	0750
Somain	dep.	2230	St Pol	arr.	0848
Lourches	"	2315	"	dep.	0903
Bouchain	arr.	0030	Anvin	arr.	0925
Somain	dep.	2120	Anvin	dep.	0930
Raismes	arr.	2255	Blangy	dep.	0942
Raismes	dep.	...	Hesdin	"	1010
Valenciennes	"	...	Montreuil	dep.	1100
Mons.	arr.	...	Etaples	arr.	1120

   1. These trains are duty trains only & are not to be used by leave takers in either direction.
   2. RE. 110 connects at ETAPLES with ROC 8 leaving ETAPLES 1820 for ABBEVILLE, LONGPRE, RO'ESCAMPS, ROUEN and HAVRE.

5. **BATHS.**

Spray Baths have been erected in the Chateau JURBISE, D.17.d.5.5.

Application for the use of these Baths should be made to H.Q., 155th Infantry Brigade.

6. **INFORMATION.**

XXII Corps Rest Station. (1/3rd Low. Field Ambulance, Maute Moyenne, MONS) closed from Sunday, 19th instant. The Corps Rest Station will be absorbed into No. 1 C.C.S.

24th January 1919.

C.F. Mulli- Barrett Major
for
Lieut. Col.,
A.A. & Q.M.G., 52nd (LOWLAND) DIVISION.

A143/1/3.

Headquarters,
    XXIInd Corps "A"
    ****

Reference your D3/20 of 18th January, 1919.

1.   The new allotment has just been received which allows for 108 men being despatched to Scottish Dispersal Stations and 98 to English ones.

2.   To-day roughly the numbers available for demobilisation (inclusive of pivotal men, etc,) is about,

        For Scotland   2284
        For England   429

3.   This gives a percentage of vacancies of about,

        Scotland   5%
        England   23%

4.   I trust that the new allotment just received is a very temporary one, and that one almost exclusively for Scotland may be issued almost at once.
    The present allotment is causing distinct heart-burnings and I hope that this may receive the fullest consideration.

Major General,
Commanding 52nd (Lowland) DIVISION.

23/1/1919.

Headquarters,
    XXIInd Corps "A"
    ****

A143/1/3.

DEMOBILISATION.
****

1. I wish to draw attention to the very small proportion of vacancies for the Scottish Dispersal Stations compared with those for English dispersal stations which are being allotted to this Division - a Scottish one.

2. The figures are as follows :-

    (a) Number of men entered on A.Form Z8 as being noew demobilised under the groups which have been passed for demobilisation,
    (i) Scottish - 3489.
    (ii) English - 1594.

    (b) The number of vacancies allotted have been for dispersal Stations,
    (i) In Scotland - 594.
    (ii) In England - 955.

    These figures include those who have proceeded to date and number who were warned to proceed yesterday and to-day but are still at the Divisional Reception Camp.

3. From above it will be seen that the number of vacancies allotted for troops coming from Scotland amount to about 17% whereas the number allotted for those coming from England amount to 60%.

4. The aboue figures can only be taken as an indication for the reasons that regular soldiers and men who receive guarantee letters are not included in the figures given in para 2 (a).

5. The reason I put this matter before you is that the men in the Division have noticed that a greater proportion of those who leave are Englishmen or at any rate are bound for England.
    One result also is that men with comparatively short service are being demobilised to proceed to England before many with much longer service who must wait for vacancies for the Scottish Dispersal Stations.

6. I hope that something can be done to increase the number of vacancies allotted for Scottish Dispersal Stations.

17/1/1919.

Major General,
Commanding 52nd (Lowland) DIVISION.

Army Form C. 2118.

WAR DIARY
or
INTELLIGENCE SUMMARY.

(Erase heading not required.)

Army of the Rhine
A'Branch
2 (British) Division

7 EB 3/1/1919

Place	Date	Hour	Summary of Events and Information	Remarks and references to Appendices
NIIN	1		Brig-General J. Marshall cmd 2 Div by order War Office/M took over duty as BGGS. Training war other Art. Gen Col Franklin have not yet returned been acting in the absence of General Marshall. Circular issued to command of 2nd Division Demobilization numbers of deaths allotment to 2nd Division (1188 England 62 Scot. 12 Ireland 2 Wales) this day Scotland allotment from this sick Demobilization 203 England 61 Irish 2 Wales 26 And Summary A.231 issued	WKS/1
	2			

WAR DIARY
INTELLIGENCE SUMMARY

Place: NIMY
Month: FEB 1919

Date	Hour	Summary of Events and Information	Remarks
3		Leave reopened to train 3% to establish 1%.	
		Demobilization. 8 Vacancies to England returned unused to fill up the returns. Demobilization claimants 6% list.	
		5 More Vacancies to England transmitted allotment received. Scotland 203 England 48 Total 2+2	2+2
4		as from 7th inst unless a guard is found no option to Demob units to Garrison who attempt hereinbefore miles to Garrison from O.C.	
		1/7 H.S.R. were advised on 7/2/19 France 10 officers 300 O.R. to "16" S.R. 19 to Bn 37 Din Rouen/Sovret headn. E. Off. 2, 163 O.R. embark 7/2/19 increasing 7/2/19. [signature]	

WAR DIARY
or
INTELLIGENCE SUMMARY

Army Form C. 2118.

Vol XLV
A" S 2 Bde

July 1919

Place	Date	Hour	Summary of Events and Information	Remarks and references to Appendices
NIW	5		Army order 14/2/1919 ref constitution of Army of Occupation received.	
	6		Orders received to send 10/A/20 OR from each Division of the Divn to other Divisions prior to the thereafter Divns to be of the Bns: there however before Conditionally relieved. Strength of Reserves been assessed to:-	

```
            Offr    OR
4 R.S.F.    10  -  260
5 R.S.F.    10  -  260
4/5 R.S.F.  10  -  260
4 R.S.      10  -  260
7 R.S.      10  -  260
7 S.R.      10  -  260
7 H.L.I.    10  -  260
6 H.L.I.    10  -  260
5 A.S.H.    10  -  3
            _____
           100 / 2360
```

WAR DIARY or INTELLIGENCE SUMMARY

Army Form C. 2118.

Vol XIV
A.S.D.[?]

July 1919

Place	Date	Hour	Summary of Events and Information	Remarks and references to Appendices
NIMY	7		By permission D.A.G. 6.7.41 new formation formed up to 9.7.41 (instead of 15.4.41) and 7.7.41 (instead of 15.4.41) (mostly). This for the forces whence to in 6th here, partes hereof are as follows: see figures now arrive at D.A.G.	

	Number of O.R.	date ready		To return to	
UNIT			UNIT	Bde	Div
4 R.S.F.	10	h	1 R.S.F.		3 Div
5 R.S.F.	10	—	2 R.S.F.		9 Div
4 K.O.S.B.	10	—	6 K.O.S.B.		9 Div
4 R.S.	10	—	2 R.S.		3 Div
7 R.S.	10	—	11 R.S.		9 Div
7 S.R.	10	—	1/6 S.R.	119 Bde	33 Div
5 H.L.I.	10	—	2 H.L.I.		2 Div
6 H.L.I.	10	—	9 H.L.I.	600 Bde	33 Div
7 H.L.I.	10	—	15 H.L.I.		32 Div
17 N.F.	10	—	36 N.F.	178 Bde	59 Div

Army Form C. 2118.

WAR DIARY
or
INTELLIGENCE SUMMARY.
(Erase heading not required.)

July 1919   Vol XIV   A 5th Bn

Place	Date	Hour	Summary of Events and Information	Remarks and references to Appendices
Nigg	8		Sevastopol Scotland 203 Soplans 61	
	9		Sevastopol Scotland 203 Soplans 61	
Nigg	10		Draft 10 Officers and 190 O.R. proceeded for trans. station 5/5th 1/4 H.L.I. 33rd Divn	
"	11		} No unusual occurrence Sevastopol continues	
"	12			
"	13			
"	14			
"	15		Draft 10 Officers 90 O.R. 17th Northumberland Fusiliers to 1/5th 36th Northumberland Fusiliers 59th Divn	
"	16		10 Officers 1/7th Scottish Rifles entrained Mons Station 5/5th 1/6 Scottish Rifles 33rd Div	

D.D. & L., London, E.C. (A8001) Wt. W17771/M2031 750,000 5/17 Sch. 52 Forms C2118/14

Army Form C. 2118.

WAR DIARY
or
INTELLIGENCE SUMMARY

Vol XLV
5th Division
A Powell

Month: February

Place	Date	Hour	Summary of Events and Information	Remarks and references to Appendices
NIMY	17th		Dunstabahn Sections 187 Captain 28	
	18th		" 187 " 29	
	19th			
	20th		Major E.P. Moreton-Barrett H.C. left the Division to take up the duties of D.A.Q.M.G. 1st Army	
	21st		Captain N.C.C. Tepper D.C. Staff Captain 1st Lt Bde took up duties of D.A.Q.M.G.	
	22nd		87 "J" Horses sent for Division to No. 4 Knee Remount Depot	
	23rd		326 "Z" Animals sent for Division for 1815c Station to Rouen for sale	
	24th		202 T horses sent from Division to No. 4 Knee Remount Depot	

WAR DIARY
or
INTELLIGENCE SUMMARY.

Army Form C. 2118.

VOL XLV

Sir Duncan
A.G. Warner

Month: February

Place	Date	Hour	Summary of Events and Information	Remarks and references to Appendices
ARMY	25th		28 Officers and 365 O.R. 14 R. Scots Fusiliers & O.R. 2th proceeded to join 9th Division 2nd Army. Training MONS Station.	
-d-	26th		22nd Corps Race Meeting held 6th Drill found at MAIZIERES	
-d-	27th		39 Y Arrivals seen for Division to view at Staging Camp MONS	
-d-	28th		16th R. Scots Fusiliers presented with Colours by deputation from AYRSHIRE County T.F. Association at VURBISE. 103 Y Arrivals sent by aviation at SOIGNIES. Personnel demobilized during February 4627	

1/5th [illegible]	[illegible]	[illegible] to 1/4th [illegible] Fusiliers.
	[illegible] attd.	
	[illegible] attd.	
	[illegible] attd.	
	[illegible] attd.	
	[illegible] attd.	
	[illegible] attd.	
	[illegible] attd.	
	[illegible] attd.	
	[illegible] attd.	
	[illegible] attd.	
	[illegible] attd.	
	[illegible] attd.	
	2nd [illegible] attd.	
	[illegible] attd.	
	4th [illegible] attd.	
	7th [illegible] attd.	
	2nd [illegible] attd.	
1/4th [illegible]	Capt. [illegible]	Transferred [illegible]
1/4th [illegible]	Lt. [illegible]	-do-
	Lt. [illegible]	[illegible]
	4th [illegible] attd.	[illegible]
1/7th [illegible]	Capt. [illegible]	Demobilised.
1/7th [illegible]	Lt. [illegible]	Transferred [illegible]
	[illegible] attd.	
1/7th [illegible]	Capt. [illegible]	Demobilised.
	[illegible] attd.	
	Lt. [illegible]	Died in [illegible]
	[illegible] attd.	
[illegible]	Major [illegible]	Demobilised.
[illegible]	[illegible]	[illegible]
		Brig-General.
[illegible]	Commanding, [illegible]	

Army Form W.3816.

STRENGTH RETURN MADE UP TO 12 NOON SATURDAY _____ 1918.

_____ {Corps
                 {Division.

UNIT.	(i.) Strength for previous week, compiled in accordance with A.G.'s instructions.		(ii.) Increase during week, due to drafts, etc., taken on strength of Unit.		(iii.) Totals from (i.) and (ii.)		(iv.) Decrease during week,—casualties, etc., deducted from strength of Unit.		"A" Strength, excluding Attached.		"B" Not present with the Unit and not at the disposal of C.O. Included in column "A."		"A minus B." Available Fighting Strength, including Personnel of Battalion Transport and Quartermaster's Stores.		REMARKS. (Brief notes regarding (ii.), (iv.), and "B," etc.)
	Officers.	O.R.	Officers.	O.R.	Officers.	O.R.	Officers.	O.R.	Officers.	O.R.	Officers.	O.R.	Officers.	O.R.	

[P.T.O.]

CHANGES IN NOMINAL ROLLS OF OFFICERS.

(*i.e.,* Explanation of Increases and Decreases.)

Unit.	Joined.	Struck Off.	Cause.

PRINTED IN FRANCE BY ARMY PRINTING AND STATIONERY SERVICES.

Army Form C. 2118.

WAR DIARY
or
INTELLIGENCE SUMMARY.
(Erase heading not required.)

Place	Date	Hour	Summary of Events and Information	Remarks and references to Appendices
			STRENGTH OF DIVISION	
			Week ending 1st March, 1919.	
			Officers. Other Ranks.	
			Divisional Troops. 5. 51.	
			Divisional Artillery. 80. 1886.	
			Divisional Engineers. 34. 698.	
			155th Infantry Bde. 28. 351.	
			156th Infantry Bde. 68. 798.	
			157th Infantry Bde. 78. 712.	
			Divisional Train. 13. 310.	
			17th Bn. Northumberland	
			Fusiliers (P). 15. 105.	
			52nd Bn. Machine Gun Corps. 32. 446.	
			Royal Army Medical Corps. 17. 405.	
			370. 5762.	
			No. of sick admitted to	
			Hospital during February. 10. 205.	

SECRET.   COPY NO. ....

HEADQUARTERS, 52nd (LOWLAND) DIVISION.
"A" & "Q" SUMMARY NO. 31.

1. SALVAGE.
The following letter from First Army is published for information and action:-
" During the present salvage operations, as many as possible of
"the wicker baskets and shell containers for German ammunition should
"be collected and stored so that they are kept in good condition.
"These baskets and containers will be urgently required when the time
"arrives for sending the German ammunition to the Base."
(Authority First Army No. Q.S. 2/2727, dated 23rd January 1919.)

2. DEMOBILIZATION OF HORSES.
The following letter from G.H.Q. is published for information and necessary action:-
" The disposal of all horses will be dealt with by the Director
"of Remounts after all remount classifications have been carried out.
" All sales on the Continent will be by auction (other than the
"transfer of horses to the Belgian Government), and individual offers
"cannot be accepted.
" No offers for horses should therefore be forwarded to the
"Quartermaster General under paragraph 2 of 21,001 (Q.F.2.) dated
"11-1-19."
(Authority G.H.Q. No. 2003/7.Q.F.1., dated 21-1-19.)

3. AMMUNITION OR EXPLOSIVES AMONGST SCRAP METAL.
When scrap metal is being despatched in trucks special care must be taken that no live ammunition or explosives are included.

4. ROYAL ARTILLERY BAND.
The Royal Artillery Band will pay a visit to the XXII Corps between 4th and 6th February 1919.
Camp Commandant, XXII Corps, is arranging for performance in MONS at 2.30 p.m. on 5th instant.

5. LOCATIONS.
XXII Corps School is now located in Cavalry Barracks, MONS.

6. INFORMATION.
The Office of Traffic, LILLE, closed at LILLE at 00.01 hours on 26th January 1919, and opened at the same hour at VALENCIENNES.

2nd February 1919.   A.A. & Q.M.G., 52nd (LOWLAND) DIVISION.

SECRET.   COPY NO. ......

HEADQUARTERS, 52nd (LOWLAND) DIVISION.
"A" & "Q" SUMMARY NO. 32.

1. **RETENTION BY UNITS OF ALL TRANSPORT EQUIPMENT.**

    The following Extract from First Army letter No. 5/96.Q.B., dated 24-1-19, is published for information and necessary action:-

    "The Q.M.G. has issued instructions that all Transport, harness "and other unit equipment must be retained on Unit charge by all "Troops.

    "The harness is to be kept in grease."

2. **LOCATIONS.**

    No. 22 Veterinary Evac. Station is now located at Cavalry Barracks, MONS.

7th February 1919.

A.A. & Q.M.G., 52nd (LOWLAND) DIVISION.

SECRET.   COPY NO. ....

HEADQUARTERS, 52nd (LOWLAND) DIVISION.
"A" & "Q" SUMMARY NO. 33.

1. LEAVE.
The following letter from First Army is published for information and necessary action:-
" When application for 30 days leave are submitted under
"Army C/1022 it should invariably be stated whether the Officer
"for whom leave is requested is likely to be demobilised or re-
":tained in the service under A.O. XIV of 29/1/1919."
(Authority First Army No. C/1022, dated 5-2-19.)

2. DEMOBILIZATION.
The following letter from XXII Corps is published for information and necessary action:-
" The personnel of Light Trench Mortar Batteries may be reduced to
"cadres (1 man) forthwith.
" Officers and Other Ranks will not be reposted, but will be
"affiliated to Battalions concerned."
(Authority XXII Corps No. G. 5403, dated 6th February 1919.)

3. DRESS. Y.M.C.A. PERSONNEL.
Permission has been given for workers of the Y.M.C.A. in the First, Third and Fifth Armies and on L. of C. to have the option of wearing mufti instead of the Y.M.C.A. uniform. If mufti is worn, the Y.M.C.A. Brassard (Khaki with Red Triangle) will be worn as a distinguishing mark by the workers of this Association.

4. LEAVE. EXTENSION.
War Office has extended leave for officers and men due normally to return via CALAIS on 5th and 6th inst till 12th and 13th respectively. This extension will not be endorsed on the Warrants.

10th February 1919.   A.A. & Q.M.G., 52nd (LOWLAND) DIVISION.

52nd (Lowland) Division.

ADMINISTRATIVE CIRCULAR MEMORANDUM. No. 41.

3rd FEBRUARY, 1919.

DIVISIONAL BAND.

1. As will be remembered the present Divisional Band was constituted in October 1915. The instruments were lent to the Division by the 1/4th Bn. Royal Scots.

2. The instruments were not at that time new, but they are now after over 3 years campaigning, very nearly done so far as use under Peace conditions is concerned. It is considered probable that nearly all of them will require to be replaced.

3. The question which has now to be faced is the best way of repaying the Battalion for the use of instruments during the period they have been used for Divisional purposes. It will be agreed that it should not be left to the Officers of the Battalion to replace the instruments.

4. The following proposal is made to meet the circumstance:-
    (a) That a Committee of three, one from each Infantry Brigade (pre-war T.F. Officers if possible) be appointed to arrange a settlement with the Battalion.
    (b) That the surplus from the Officers' Mess at No. 1 Infantry Base Depot, KANTARA, be placed at the disposal of this Committee. This fund amounting to about £140. is divisable between the Officers' Messes that then existed in the Division and works out at about 6/- per officer on the strength of the officers with the Division at the time it left Egypt.
    (c) That the instruments be handed as they stand to the Battalion. They include instruments, stands and music for which some £80 to £100 has been paid during the last 12 months or so. The old instruments are still worth some money.

5. It is believed that from the assets mentioned above a sufficient sum will be provided for the purpose required.
   Will you please reply as early as possible so that if approval is given the Committee may set to work at once with a view to an early settlement.

If ... of approving, should nominate an officer to sit on the committee

Lieut-Colonel,
A.A. & Q.M.G. 52nd (Lowland) DIVISION.

NOTICE.

1. It has been decided that on account of the weather and the exigencies of demobilisation that further Divisional Sports will not be held. In consequence the Shield will be presented to the 1/7th Bn. Royal Scots, who are leading on points :-

Result.
    1st. 1/7th Bn. Royal Scots.   40 points.
    2nd. 17th N.F. (P).   30 points.
    3rd. 1/4th Royal Scots Fusiliers. 20 points.
    4th. 2/4th Bn. K.O.S.B.   )
          1/4th Royal Scots.   ) 10 points.
          52nd Bn. M.G.C.   )

2. The Shield and Medals for all events will arrive from England on 18th February and will be issued to units for disposal.

Vol 12

Oscar Diary
March 1915

March 1919

WAR DIARY
INTELLIGENCE SUMMARY.

Place	Date	Hour	Summary of Events and Information	Remarks and references to Appendices
NIMY	1st		Feeding streng'h of Division O.R. 6074.	
-	2nd		100 Rest Z Arrivals proceeded to BASE by road via Mons Staging Camp to Sale.	
-	3rd		102 Z Arrivals sent to SOIGNIES for Sale by DADVS	
-	4th		276 Z Arrivals sent to R'Base from Mons Staging Camp by rail	
-	5th		Nothing of Interest occurred.	
-	6th		260 Rest Z Arrivals sent to BOULOGNE by rail from MONS Station.	
-	7th		Feeding streng'h of Division	
-	8th		2 officers and 141 OR proceeded to concentration Camp to demobilisation.	
-	9th		55 Z H.D and 4 Z Ydns sent to 60th Aux. H.T Coy A.S.C. MONS.	
-	10th		Draft 5 officers 150 OR K.H.L.I. proceeded to 1st ae 1/9 H.L.I. 332 Division. En training at MONS Station.	

Army Form C. 2118.

WAR DIARY
or
INTELLIGENCE SUMMARY.
(Erase heading not required.)

Instructions regarding War Diaries and Intelligence Summaries are contained in F. S. Regs., Part II. and the Staff Manual respectively. Title pages will be prepared in manuscript.

Place	Date	Hour	Summary of Events and Information	Remarks and references to Appendices
NMY	11th	-	Draft 46 O.R. & the C.O. lecturing officer & 7th Royal Scots entrained at MONS station to proceed to join 11th R Scots 9th Division. Draft 1 officer & 25 O.R. entrained MONS station to join 1/4 R.S.F. 9th Division.	
NMY	12th	-	100 Z arrivals sent to BOULOGNE from MONS station	
	13th	-	Draft 10 officers 187 O.R. 1/4 R. Scots proceeded to join 11th R. Scots 9th Division.	
	14th	-	140 X LD arrivals sent to 77 A/Bde RFA from 52 DA. 163 O.R. 52 DA sent as draft to Arty. Units of 8th Corps. 1 off. 74 O.R. 52 DA entrained at MONS to join 6 DA 2nd Army. 12 1/h. bearers sent to Base. 16 Cds sent to Base as Infficient Chauffrs. 3 officers & 91 O.R. proceeded to U.K. for demobilisation	

D. D. & L., London, E.C. (A800) Wt. W1771/M2031 750,000 3/17 Sch. 52 Forms/C2118/14

Army Form C. 2118.

WAR DIARY
or
INTELLIGENCE SUMMARY.
(Erase heading not required.)

Instructions regarding War Diaries and Intelligence Summaries are contained in F. S. Regs., Part II. and the Staff Manual respectively. Title pages will be prepared in manuscript.

Place	Date	Hour	Summary of Events and Information	Remarks and references to Appendices
MM4	15th		376 I. arrivals sent to Base by Train from Mons Staltis. 50 × LD arrivals sent to Mons Staging Camp for despatch to Base by Road	
			Draft 1 officer 19th O.R. 52 M.G. 18th proceeded by Lorry to Jai' 51 M.G. 18th	
	16th		Draft 10 officers 95 OR. 7th R Sets. Left Mons by Rail to Jai' 11 officers of R Sets to Dunster 8 officers and 153 OR proceeding to U.K. for Demobilization.	
	17th		156 Inf Bde moved to SOIGNIES. Draft 10 officers 150 OR 7H.L.I. left Mons to Jai' 15th H.L.I. 9th Divsion. 71 × L.D. Arrivals sent to Kens by Rail	
	18th		Vehicles of 157 Bde & DHQ moved to SOIGNIES	

WAR DIARY or INTELLIGENCE SUMMARY

Army Form C. 2118.

(Erase heading not required.)

Place	Date	Hour	Summary of Events and Information	Remarks and references to Appendices
NIMY	9th		52nd M.G. Bath. and 86th Bde RFA. moved to SOIGNIES. 10 officers 183 OR. proceeded to U.K. for demobilisation.	
	20th		126 T. Arrivals proceeded to ROUEN by Train for MONS.	
			17th N.F. moved to SOIGNIES. 9th Bde R.F.A. moved to SOIGNIES	
	21st		1st L/F/Bde. moved to SOIGNIES. also 13 L. Field Amb. 376 x L.D. Mules sent to 2nd Army from JURBISE station	
	22nd		155 L/F/Bde. C.R.E. & 3 Field Coys. 9 ½ L.Field Amb. moved to SOIGNIES	
	23rd		14 officers and 118 OR. proceeded to U.K. for demobilisation. 22 2 Arrivals despatches to base from MONS station	
	24th		52 Dir. Train & M.N.S. moved to SOIGNIES 95 x Arrivals sent to Base from MONS station	

Army Form C. 2118.

WAR DIARY
or
INTELLIGENCE SUMMARY.
(Erase heading not required.)

Instructions regarding War Diaries and Intelligence Summaries are contained in F. S. Regs., Part II. and the Staff Manual respectively. Title pages will be prepared in manuscript.

Place	Date	Hour	Summary of Events and Information	Remarks and references to Appendices
SOIGNIES	25th		Divisional HQ moved to SOIGNIES. Cadre Division completed concentration to Entrainment at SOIGNIES. Capt. E. S. Cookson DSO MC Bde Major 157 Infbde took over duties of DAQMG	
"	26th		All "X" Horses despatched Pars —	M/
"	27th		11 R.F. & E Horses despatched 22 Capts 425 men also 2 carts to practise — Y. animals augmented 11mm — Entrained during night	M/ M/ M/
"	28th		Y Remains Y. animals augmented 11mm — Entrained during night	M/
"	29th		On receiving Amends in lieu of food and Cart Establishment sent to Purchase Entrainment — total 19	M/
"	30th		Nothing to record	M/
"	31st		Nothing to record —	M/

Witney Lott Capt. DAA
for Lieut Gr Su:

Army Form W.3815.

STRENGTH RETURN MADE UP TO 12 NOON SATURDAY 29th March, 1918.

52nd (Corps) Division.

UNIT.	(i.) Strength for previous week, compiled in accordance with A.G.'s instructions.		(ii.) Increase during week, due to drafts, etc. taken on strength of Unit.		(iii.) Totals from (i.) and (ii.)		(iv.) Decrease during week,—casualties, etc., deducted from strength of Unit.		"A" Strength, excluding Attached.		"B" Not present with the Unit and not at the disposal of C.O. Included in column "A."		"A minus B." Available Fighting Strength, including Personnel of Battalion Transport and Quartermaster's Stores.		REMARKS. (Brief notes regarding (ii.), (iv.), and "B," etc.)
	Officers.	O.R.	Officers.	O.R.	Officers.	O.R.	Officers.	O.R.	Officers.	O.R.	Officers.	O.R.	Officers.	O.R.	
155th Brigade															
5th R.S. Fusiliers.	5	72	—	—	5	72	—	4	5	68	—	16	5	52	
4th K.O.S. Borderers.	9	90	—	—	9	90	4	18	5	72	2	23	3	49	
	14	162	—	—	14	162	4	22	10	140	2	39	8	101	
156th Brigade.															
4th Royal Scots.	14	79	—	—	14	79	7	1	7	78	2	14	5	64	
7th Royal Scots.	17	82	—	3	17	85	10	8	7	77	2	19	5	58	
8th Scottish Rifles.	8	72	—	—	8	72	1	—	7	72	4	18	3	54	
	39	233	—	3	39	236	18	9	21	227	8	51	13	176	
157th Brigade,															
5th H.L.I.	13	72	—	3	13	75	7	8	6	67	1	20	5	47	
6th H.L.I	14	88	—	1	14	89	2	16	12	73	4	27	8	46	
7th. H.L.I.	22	92	—	2	22	94	5	6	17	88	7	17	10	71	
	49	252	—	6	49	258	14	30	35	228	12	64	23	164	
17th North. Fusiliers	13	77	—	—	13	77	6	1	7	76	3	36	4	40	
	135	724	—	9	135	733	42	62	73	671	25	190	48	481	
52nd M.G. Corps.	30	151	—	—	30	151	24	4	6	147	1	30	5	117	

Commanding 52nd (Lowland) Division.

Brigadier General.

[P.T.O.

CHANGES IN NOMINAL ROLLS OF OFFICERS.

(*i.e.*, Explanation of Increases and Decreases.)

Unit.	Joined.	Struck Off.	Cause.
	52 Dm		

52nd (Lowland) DIVISION.

Instructions regarding War Diaries and Intelligence Summaries are contained in F.S. Regs., Part II. and the Staff Manual respectively. Title pages will be prepared in manuscript.

WAR DIARY
or
INTELLIGENCE SUMMARY

(Erase heading not required.)

Army Form C. 2118.

Hour, Date, Place	Summary of Events and Information	Remarks and references to Appendices

	STRENGTH OF DIVISION.
	 **********************
	 Week ending 28/3/1919
	 **********************
	                                         Officers. Other Ranks.
	 Divisional Troops. 13 45
	     " Engineers. 27 618
	     " Artillery. 62 1264
	 155th Infantry Brigade 10 140
	 156th " " 21 227
	 157th " " 35 228
	 17th Northumberland Fus. 7 76
	 52nd Machine Gun Corps. 6 147
	 R.A.M.C. 13 319
	 Divisional Train. 22 329
	     " Employment Co. - 51
	                                   ======== ========
	           Grand Total: 216 3444
	                                   ======== ========	

Army Form C. 2118.

WAR DIARY
or
INTELLIGENCE SUMMARY.
(Erase heading not required.)

52nd (Lowland) DIVISION.
****

"A and Q" BRANCH.

MAY - 1919.
****

Army Form C. 2118.

WAR DIARY
or
INTELLIGENCE SUMMARY.

52nd (Lowland) Division.   "A & Q" Branch.   MAY, 1919.

(Erase heading not required.)

Instructions regarding War Diaries and Intelligence Summaries are contained in F. S. Regs., Part II. and the Staff Manual respectively. Title pages will be prepared in manuscript.

Place	Date	Hour	Summary of Events and Information	Remarks and references to Appendices
SOIGNIES.	1/5/19 to 3/5/19		Nil.	
	4/5/19		T/Lieut-Colonel W.D.V.O. KING, DSO., Commanding 17th North'd. Fus. (P) assumed command of the Division vice A/Lieut-Colonel J.M. INGRAM, RFA. to England. Following Cadres entrained for U.K. via ANTWERP. C/56th Battery R.F.A. 527th (How) Battery R.F.A.	
	5/5/19 to 14/5/19		Nil.	
	15/5/19		1/1st Mobile Veterinary Section, R.A.V.C. broken up.	
	16/5/19 to 27/5/19		Nil.	
	28/5/19		Divisional Gymkhana held at SOIGNIES.	
	29/5/19		Divisional Aquatic Sports and Open Air Concert held in SOIGNIES.	
	30/5/19		Following Cadres entrained for U.K. via ANTWERP. H.Q., 147th Army Brigade R.F.A. A. Batt. =do= H.Q., 9th Brigade R.F.A. 19th Batt. =do= 20th Batt. =do= Part of 28th Batt. =do=	

Army Form C. 2118.

WAR DIARY
or
INTELLIGENCE SUMMARY.

(Erase heading not required.)

MAY. 1919.

Place	Date	Hour	Summary of Events and Information	Remarks and references to Appendices
	31/5/19		Following Cadres entrained for U.K. via ANTWERP. Balance of 28th Batty. 9th Brigade R.F.A. D/69th Batty. =do= 1/5th Battn. Royal Scots Fusiliers. 1/4th Battn. K.O.S. Borderers.	

W Harris

Captain.

for D.A.A.G., 52nd (Lowland) DIVISION CADRES.

Army Form C. 2118.

WAR DIARY
or
INTELLIGENCE SUMMARY.
(Erase heading not required.)

STRENGTH OF DIVISION.

Week ending 31st May 1919.

	OFFICERS.	OTHER RANKS.
Divisional Troops.	7	48
Divisional Signal Coy.	4	55
155th Inf. Bde. H.Q.	1	14
1/5th Bn. R.S.Fusiliers.	5	52
1/4th Bn. K.O.S.B.	6	37
Headquarters. R.A.	1	4
147th A/Brigade. R.F.A.	11	215
52nd D.A.C.	4	155
17th North'd Fusiliers. (P)	3	39
Divisional Train.	4	53
Divisional Engineers.	7	124
Royal Army Medical Corps.	4	173
TOTAL.	57	969

Number of sick admitted into
Hospital during May.   4   45

52nd (LOWLAND) DIVISION CADRES.

STRENGTH RETURN MADE UP TO 12 NOON SATURDAY, 31st MAY, 1919.

UNIT.	Strength for previous wk. in accord. with A.G's instr.		Increase during wk. Drafts etc., taken on strength of Unit.		Decrease during wk. Cas. ing wk. Cas. etc., deducted fr. Str. of Unit.		Totals of (i) & (ii)		Strength ex-cluding att. with unit & not at dis-posal of C.O. Incl. in Col."A"		No. present with unit & not at dis-posal of C.O. Incl. in Col."A"		Available ft. Strength incl. personnel of Bn.Transport & Q.M.Stores.		REMARKS.
	O.	O.R.	O.	O.R.	O.	O.R.	O.	O.R.	O.	O.R.	O.	O.R.	O.	O.R.	
155th Inf. Bde.															
1/4th K.O.S.B.	5	37	-	-	-	-	5	37	2	-	1	37	5	53	
1/5th R.S.Fus.	4	52	-	-	-	-	4	52	-	-	15	-	4	37	
17th North'd Fus.	9	89	-	-	-	-	9	89	2	-	16	-	7	73	
	5	40	-	-	1	-	5	39	-	-	16	-	3	23	
Grand Total.	14	129	-	-	1	-	14	128	2	-	32	-	10	96	

31st May, 1919.

Commanding 52nd (LOWLAND) Lieut-Colonel, DIVISION CADRES.

CHANGES IN NOMINAL ROLL OF OFFICERS.
(i.e. Explanation of Increases and Decreases).

UNIT.	Joined.	Struck off.	Cause.
17th North'd Fus.		Lieut. J.T. PETTY.	To U.K. for Demob.
		Lieut. A.C. HARRISON, 6th Bn.	To U.K. for Demob.

Lieut - Colonel

31st May 1919.   Commanding 52nd (LOWLAND) DIVISION CADRES

www.ingramcontent.com/pod-product-compliance
Lightning Source LLC
Chambersburg PA
CBHW081426300426
44108CB00016BA/2310